R^r   S

THE SOCIOLOGY OF POLITICAL PRAXIS

THE SOCIOLOGY OF POLITICAL PRAXIS
an introduction to Gramsci's theory

Leonardo Salamini

ROUTLEDGE & KEGAN PAUL
London, Boston and Henley

First published in 1981
by Routledge & Kegan Paul Ltd
39 Store Street,
London WC1E 7DD,
9 Park Street,
Boston, Mass. 02108, USA, and
Broadway House,
Newtown Road,
Henley-on-Thames,
Oxon RG9 1EN
Printed in Great Britain by
Ebenezer Baylis &Son, Ltd., Worcester
Copyright © L. Salamini 1981

Library of Congress Cataloging in Publication Data

Salamini, Leonardo, 1940–
The sociology of political praxis.

Bibliography: p.
Includes index.
1. Gramsci, Antonio, 1891–1937. 2. Marxian
school of sociology. I. Title.
HX288.G7S3   335.43   81–10607

ISBN 0-7100-0928-3   AACR2

To Heather, Yvonne and Alexey

CONTENTS

ACKNOWLEDGMENTS

This book is the culmination of a long effort to introduce the whole body of Gramsci's thought to the American academic community. It began in 1973 and underwent several radical modifications. Some parts in this book were read as papers at various meetings of the American Sociological Association and published later in various journals. As the years went by, the literature on Gramsci grew enormously. Interpretations and re-interpretations of his thought were developed by Gramsci's scholars, each claiming 'his' Gramsci. The focus of most studies is limited to selected aspects of Gramsci's thought. To this date, there is no full-length account in English of the structure of his theory. This book is thus the most comprehensive, informative introduction to the complex and original Marxism of Gramsci.

Numerous readers and anonymous reviewers have read and criticized the original manuscript. Many have offered valuable suggestions. I am grateful to all of them. I would like to acknowledge various grants provided by the Bradley University Board for Research which enabled me to conduct extensive research at various European Universities. I am particularly grateful to Lawrence & Wishart Publishers for granting me permission to quote extensively from their translations of Gramsci's writings: Antonio Gramsci, 'Selections from the Prison Notebooks,' 1971; Antonio Gramsci, 'Selections from Political Writings 1910-1920,' 1977 and 'Selections from Political Writings 1921-1926,' 1978. I am also grateful to the editors of the 'Sociological Quarterly,' and 'Sociological Analysis and Theory,' for permission to reprint in a modified form the following original articles: Gramsci and Marxist Sociology of Knowledge: an Analysis of Hegemony-Ideology-Knowledge, 'Sociological Quarterly,' 1974, vol.15, no.13; The Specificity of Marxist Sociology in Gramsci's Theory, 'Sociological Quarterly,' 1975, vol.16, no.1; and Towards a Sociology of Intellectuals: a Structural Analysis of Gramsci's Marxist Theory, 'Sociological Analysis and Theory,' 1976, vol.6, no.1.

INTRODUCTION

Antonio Gramsci has been called the most original Marxist thinker of the twentieth century.[1] The openness of his thought, the flexibility of his concepts, the preoccupation with the problems of ideology and culture in advanced capitalist societies, all converge to explain the recent fascination of many Marxist and non-Marxist scholars with Gramsci. His originality lies in having laid the foundations for a Marxist theory of the specific Western transition to socialism. Gramsci's work, thus, starts from this concern to develop a theoretical basis for a revolutionary strategy in the West, which takes into account the highlights of Western culture as well as the profound changes in the relations between state and civil society in the period of monopoly capitalism.

Most studies on Gramsci, in the English-speaking world, are historical in nature, or focus on specific aspects of his thought, such as the problems of hegemony, historical blocs, party organization, theory of the state. While there are good intellectual biographies of Gramsci, and very competent introductions to various aspects of his thought, there is no general introduction to the whole body of Gramsci's thought.[2] The present study attempts to provide a general and global interpretation of Gramsci's thought, a clear exposition of various aspects and concepts of his theory, focusing on the interrelationships between concepts and phenomena in the areas of Marxist theory, philosophy, political praxis, ideology, culture, science, aesthetics and linguistics.

This introduction provides a brief background of Gramsci's intellectual biography as well as a general characterization of his writings and the contemporary status of Gramscian studies.

Gramsci was born in Sardinia (Italy) in 1891 into a petit-bourgeois family. He completed his studies at the gymnasium of Santulussurgiu and the lycée in Cagliari. In 1911, benefiting from a scholarship, he was able to attend the Faculty of Letters and Philosophy of the University of Turin. For reasons of health he was obliged to abandon his studies. He joined the Socialist Party, in whose ranks he rapidly rose to a position of leadership. The socialist revolution of 1917, which brought the Bolsheviks to power, enabled him to see the important role that the working class could play in the Italian revolution. In May 1919, in co-operation with Palmiro Togliatti, he began the publication of a weekly review of socialist culture, the 'Ordine Nuovo,' championing the cause of the socialist revolution in

Italy. The program of the 'Ordine Nuovo' called for the organization of Councils in all Turin's factories and the democratic take-over of their administrations. Gramsci's political strategy received the approval of Lenin himself at the Second Congress of the Communist International, but was rejected by the majority of the members of the Italian Socialist Party. On 21 January 1921, at the 17th Congress of the Italian Socialist Party in Livorno, the left-wing of the party, under the direction of Gramsci, Togliatti and Amadeo Bordiga, broke from the opportunist majority and formed the Communist Party of Italy. In 1922, while Gramsci was representing the party at the Fourth Congress of the International in Moscow, the fascists came to power in Italy. To avoid the fascist repression Gramsci took refuge in Vienna, from where he continued to lead the party. In 1924 he was elected to the Chamber of Deputies and, protected by parliamentary immunity, he was able to re-enter Italy. All his efforts were then directed to unify the working class and the party seriously weakened by the fascist regime. In 1926 Gramsci participated in the Third Congress of the Italian Communist Party in Lyons, where he gained the support of the majority of its membership and was elected to the position of Party Secretary. Following the interdiction of the party by the fascist regime, Gramsci was arrested on 8 November 1926 and later condemned to twenty years in prison. While in captivity he wrote the famous 'Quaderni del Carcere.' He died on 27 April 1937.

After a long period of silence, only in the last twenty years have the personality and thought of Gramsci become the object of a passionate ideological and political debate in Italy. It is curious that the works of this greatest Marxist have remained in complete obscurity in countries other than Italy. The lack of diffusion of Gramsci's works has been commonly attributed to the fragmentary nature of his reflections, which precludes the reader from seizing the profound unity underlying the diversity and complexity of his thought. It has also been said that Gramsci's thought seems to be essentially 'national' in character, that is, elaborated in a specific Italian cultural climate, and addressing itself to specific Italian problems.

The above-mentioned reasons, however, could not fully explain the oblivion of Gramsci's writings among Western Marxists. His Marxism was so profoundly original and open that it could not be incorporated into the framework of a rigid, deterministic, and positivistic Marxism inherited from the Second International, which became crystallized in a dogmatic, Stalinized theory of historical development.[3] The lack of diffusion of Gramsci's thought was not accidental but intentional. Gramsci's political isolation in the last years of his life following his critical stance on Stalin's purges and the relations of the Italian Communist Party (PCI) with the Communist International, and probably his complete break with the Central Committee of the party and Togliatti himself, are well-known facts which explain

the slow diffusion of his writings and ideas in Marxist circles.[4]
After Gramsci's death, as we shall see, the PCI appropriated
his ideas and forced an interpretation of his writings in line
with the official positions of the leadership of the party.
   In order to understand the originality of Gramsci's theory
and praxis it is necessary to analyze them in the general context of the history of Marxism.

GRAMSCI AND THE HISTORY OF MARXISM

Gramsci's scholars generally seem to agree that the Italian
theorist has strongly defended the creative, activistic and
voluntaristic component of Marxian theory. Influenced very
early in life by the critical Marxism of Antonio Labriola,[5]
Gramsci deplored and vehemently opposed the empiricist and
deterministic interpretations of Marxism typical of Kautsky,
Plekhanov, Bukharin and the principal tenets of the Second
International. The theoretical and political shortcomings of the
Second International are well-known, but a Marxist explanation
of the deformations of Marxist theory is still in the making.
From Kautsky to Stalin an entire generation of Marxists upheld
the principle that the historical process obeys specific laws
of regularity and necessity - hence, the belief that the growing
numerical strength of the working classes would eventually
result in the automatic transition from capitalism to socialism.
Socialist transformation presupposed a high degree of capitalist
development. The masses were thus deprived of their preroga-
tive of initiating or accelerating such a process of transformation, while in the meantime they were immunized with a good
dosage of Marxist dogmas against bourgeois ideology. By the
end of the last decade of the nineteenth century, however,
industrialization and capitalist economic development did not
polarize societies into bourgeois and proletarian classes, and
revolutionary movements did not occur. Marxist revisionists,
such as Bernstein, realizing the growing strength and power
of capitalism and the appeasement of class conflict in the most
advanced industrial societies of the West, proposed a new
approach to the problem of socialist revolution. Socialist transformation could be brought about only in a democratic,
legalistic, and parliamentary manner. In contrast, orthodox
Marxists such as Kautsky continued to reaffirm strict allegiance
to Marxist scientific principles, economic laws being conceived
as historically necessary laws. Proletarian revolutions were
then understood as results of the inexorable concentration of
economic power in the hands of a diminishing number of
capitalist entrepreneurs.[6]
   This narrow theoretical framework meant the death of critical
Marxism and it generated political passivity among the masses.
Thus Marxism, divorced from revolutionary praxis, became
increasingly abstract and ineffectual in inspiring concrete

political strategies for the attainment of political hegemony.
Gramsci is among the few Western Marxist theorists to investi-
gate in a systematic fashion the place that such 'automatism'
of laws in the historical process leaves to the collective will of
the masses. A return to Marx provides him with the answer.
Marx, in fact, in his XI Thesis on Feuerbach, had written: 'The
philosophers have only interpreted the world, in various ways;
the point, however, is to change it.'[7] More generally, what is
the historical process if not the joint activity of individual wills
transformed into a 'collective will?' Certainly Marx predicted
that capitalist societies were doomed to final capitulation as a
result of necessary contradictions inherent in them; but he
also believed that the specific mode of socialist transformation,
as well as the time in which it would take place, would be
dependent primarily on the full development of political consciousness among the masses.

This 'human' element was completely lost after Marx. The
conception of the historical process began to be understood in
a deterministic framework, that is, on the model of scientific,
necessary laws which form the basis of all natural and physical
sciences. Responsible for this blatant deformation of Marxist
theory was Karl Kautsky, the leader of the German Socialist
Party before the First World War and the officially recognized
spokesman of orthodox Marxism after Engels's death in 1895.[8]

Marx and Engels recognized that revolutions are not made at
will. They come with inevitable necessity, when the conditions
which render them necessary exist, and are impossible so
long as those conditions, which develop gradually, do not
exist. Only where the capitalist methods of production are
highly developed is there the possibility of using the power
of the state to transform capitalistic property in the means
of production into social property....So it is that just as
the continuous expansion of capitalism necessarily and
inevitably goes on, so the inevitable antithesis to this expansion, the proletarian revolution, proceeds equally inevitably
and irresistibly.

The theory thus formulated, to the extent that it denies the
role of human intervention in the historical process, denies
consequently the possibility of creating historical alternatives.
Such an objectivistic conception of history became central in
the thought of Plekhanov and Bukharin, and culminated in the
absolute bolshevization of Marxism. The Bolshevik Party came
to be considered the only legitimate repository of Marxist
orthodoxy. History was believed to unfold itself according to
a strict ritual of mechanistic laws; every act of the socialist
state represented the expression of 'historical laws' and every
critique of the state constituted a direct attack on the 'doctrine'
of historical materialism.

In Gramsci, Marxism, from a theory of capitalist structure
and development, becomes the theory of the creation of new
historical formations, that is, new forms of human organizations

and institutions. Revolutionary change is an act of progressive forces, and new historical formations arise out of profound contradictions inherent within capitalism and the new rational order of revolutionary praxis. Gramsci's task, then, is that of restoring the unity of Marxist theory and praxis, grounding it on solid philosophical foundations.

Certainly it would be wrong to portray Gramsci as the first and only critic of the orthodoxy of the Second International. Lenin first, followed by Rosa Luxemburg, Lukács, and Korsch, have in their own ways attempted to formulate a theoretical Marxist interpretation of the Second International. Rosa Luxemburg, for instance, attributed the stagnation and the doctrinaire character of the Second International to the revisionism of the working-class leadership, no longer capable of conceiving itself as the expression of the feelings of the proletariat and increasingly viewing itself as the aristocracy of the working class. The revisionism of the leadership is explained in terms of the political and organizational immaturity of the masses. Despite Luxemburg's intention, mechanistic and deterministic elements are still present in her argumentation. Subscribing to the theory of crash, as many classical Marxists, she explained the political development of the masses as a function of the degree of maturity reached by the capitalist system. That is to say, the revisionism of the leadership is a phenomenon occurring in those historical conditions where the proletariat has not reached a state of political maturity; furthermore, its political maturity is attained only when capitalism reaches the final stage of its development.

It was Lenin who rejected the theory of the inevitable crash of capitalism and reformulated it as the theory of imperialism. To the extent that the revolutionary initiative of the proletariat is inextricably linked with the belief of an inevitable capitalist crash, Lenin noted, passive socialist strategy would inevitably perpetuate the stability of the capitalist system, modern capitalism having the capacity to eliminate progressively class conflict, to absorb gradually social contradictions. On the contrary, the exigency of direct confrontation and eventual overthrow of bourgeois domination are the result of intrinsic contradictions in capitalism during its imperialistic phase. Thus, the revolutionary activity of the proletariat is legitimated by the accumulation of the internal contradictions of capitalist imperialism. More specifically, the irregularity of capitalist development on the international level reveals the illusory foundations of orthodox Marxism and the theoretical positions of Bernstein and Kautsky. An 'organized' proletariat, Lenin concluded, has the capacity of accelerating the catastrophe of capitalism during its periodic crises, as in the case of the 1917 Revolution.

If Leninism represents a valid critique of the Second International and, at the same time, a valid justification of the Russian Revolution, it does not explain the failure of

revolutionary movements in Western countries. This was
Gramsci's task. Socialist revolutions have failed and will continue
to fail, Gramsci contends, as long as the subjective components
of Marxian theory and deficient. The failure of the proletarian
revolution is not the result of the immaturity of the working
class and the non-ripeness of objective conditions, rather of the
lack of a subjective realization of the ripeness of objective
conditions for socialist transformation. It is precisely the
insistence on such subjective aspects of Marxian theory that
differentiates Gramsci from Lenin. Gramsci's task in the West
is comparable to that of Lenin in the East. Lenin made the first
attempt to re-examine the classical foundations of Marxism and
rescue it from the objectivistic interpretation of the Second
International. This task was assumed by Gramsci in the West.
He pointed out that revolutionary change is a function of the
creative role of ideas and the revolutionary consciousness
attained by the masses. Hence derives the crucial role of the
intellectuals.

GRAMSCI'S WRITINGS

Gramsci's writings are voluminous. They span over a period of
more than twenty years. Two phases can be clearly discerned.
A political phase, which ranges from 1914 to 1926, before his
arrest, and a more theoretical one, which extends from 1929
until his death.

The political and cultural context of Gramsci's early writings
is pre-fascist Italy. As Cammett has well documented, Italy's
socio-economic conditions in the first decade of this century
had reached a state of crisis. Extremism had made dramatic
gains both on the right and the left of the political spectrum.
Italian socialists had vague ideas about the nature of socialism
and clearly lacked a strategy for revolutionary change.[9] It
became the task of the young socialists of the University of
Turin, Gramsci, Palmiro Togliatti, Umberto Terracini and
Angelo Tasca, all future leaders of the PCI, to work for the
rejuvenation of the tradition of Italian socialism. Under their
intellectual leadership, the Turin labor movement was transformed into an economic and militant force, and after the Revolution of 1917, Turin itself was cast into the role of the
Petrograd of the Italian socialist revolution. This role was
certainly tied to the vast expansion of Piedmont's new industries,
particularly the automobile industry.

Gramsci's pre-prison writings reveal a constant concern for
the cultural and theoretical aspects of socialism. At their base
is the firm conviction that a proletarian Enlightenment is the
best preparation for the socialist revolution in Italy, just as
the Enlightenment paved the way to the radical transformation
of society during the French Revolution. Gramsci wrote: 'every
revolution has been preceded by an intense labour of criticism,

by the diffusion of culture and the spread of ideas amongst masses of men.'[10]

This became his task during the pre-prison years. He left the University to practice philosophy and make the masses of backward Italy active participants in the elaboration of philosophy. In these early writings Gramsci asserted himself as the Marxist of the transition period to socialism, as the acute analyst of the contradictions of such a period.

The pre-prison writings can be grouped around three important phases. From 1914 to 1917 Gramsci established himself as a solid political commentator. He wrote on every subject ranging from theory, philosophy, linguistics, theater, and literature to various events of Turin social, cultural and political life. He wrote numerous articles in 'Il Grido del Popolo,' the Turin socialist newspaper, first as a columnist and from August 1917 as its only editor, in 'Avanti,' a socialist daily, and in 'La Città Futura,' a small pamphlet of the Socialist Youth Federation of Piedmont. All together, these early writings amount to more than 2,500 pages.[11] He became instrumental in creating a new style of socialist journalism, free of rhetorical pomposity, but with a strong taste for rational argumentation and for theoretical and practical coherence in the description and explanation of facts. Single events must clarify general concepts within a more general conception of the world.[12]

A quick glance at these journalistic writings reveals to the reader the basic conceptual framework of Gramsci's thinking, which was to remain unchanged in his 'Prison Notebooks.' The fundamental themes of these writings are: a flat rejection of the evolutionary and economistic interpretation of Marxism and acceptance of an historicist, humanist and voluntaristic Marxism. Marxism is a Weltanschauung, exerting a rational power of attraction over the masses and creating a new social consensus. Its task is that of creating an 'intellectual and moral reform' of society. The influence of Croce's philosophical idealism is here evident. Gramsci traced to the Hegelian Marx the origin of such conception. Hegelianism, Gramsci writes, is the major theoretical source of Marxism. Hence derives Gramsci's subjectivistic, idealist and voluntaristic interpretation of Marxism. A 'collective will' engenders a collective political praxis, and a collective praxis establishes a new historical reality. This praxis, in a creative dialectic with culture and ideas, engenders socialist transformation.

Gramsci's conception of the proletarian state is also delineated in its general traits in these early writings. The construction of a proletarian state is the end result of a gradual, molecular transformation of an 'economic' class into an 'historical' class, which is brought about by a dialectical relationship between the masses and the intellectuals. At the base of such a process is the concept of 'proletarian democracy,' the capacity of the masses to gain access to and exercise power autonomously. From here stems another constant theme, that of the subordination of the party to mass spontaneity and direction, categorically stated in the early writing and attenuated in a more subtle elaboration in his prison writings. The concept of 'proletarian democracy' is at the base of various interpretations of his ideas and explains his neglect during the Stalinization.[13]

Another phase in the development of Gramsci's thought is the experience of the 'Ordine Nuovo' group between 1919 and 1920. The 1917 Revolution had a distinct impact on Gramsci and the Turin labor movement. The Russian experience sharpened and polarized the theoretical and strategical positions of the various factions of the Italian Socialist Party. It taught the lesson that revolutions can be made when the 'objective' conditions are not ripe, and when a well organized and disciplined political avant-garde is present. On the right, the reformist group of Serrati disowned the method of armed struggle against the bourgeoisie to set up a dictatorship of the proletariat. On the extreme left, Bordiga's group fought for Marxist intransigency in theory and revolutionary tactics and was committed to mass organization on a national scale in order to smash bourgeois state power and set up a dictatorship of the proletariat. Gramsci led the centrist faction in clear opposition of the reformist and intransigent tactics of the right and the left. He argued that the revolution is not a 'thaumaturgical' nor a voluntaristic act. It is the necessary phase of a general develop-ment of the Italian history. It begins at the mass level in the factory and extends to the whole society. Proletarian conscious-ness and responsibility to lead the cultural and political pro-cess of history is a precondition to the conquest of power. At the base of the revolutionary process are the masses. Every-thing else exists in a critical relationship with this basic prin-ciple, which is Gramsci's hermeneutic canon of history. From this fundamental idea stems Gramsci's conviction of the inade-quacy of the major institutions of the workers' movement: the syndicate and the party. The unions and the party are capitalist institutions imposed by the capitalist rule of free competition. The first engages the proletariat to compete economically, the latter to compete politically with bourgeois institutions. Trade unionist tactics are capitalist responses by the workers and not autonomous formulation. So is party politics, if not subordinated to mass politics. The revolution can only be made through mass organization and mass institu-tions. To build a proletarian state, the proletarian movement has to become politically and culturally autonomous. Thus new institutions need to be created before the proletarian conquest of power as the condition for this transition.

In May 1919 Gramsci, together with Togliatti, Terracini, and Tasca, launched the weekly newspaper 'L'Ordine Nuovo,' which became the major Italian journal of Marxist theory and culture. The journal laid the theoretical foundations for the necessity of socialist revolution on the Russian model, but adapted to the political and cultural conditions of Italy. The

great achievement of the 'Ordine Nuovo' was the formulation
of the revolutionary strategy of the factory councils. Briefly,
such a strategy consisted in creating factory and farm councils.
An embryonic form of workers' government, comparable to the
Soviets in Russia, was already present in Italy, Gramsci noted.
They were the 'internal committees' ('commissioni interne'),
similar to the British shop stewards. All workers, whether they
were members of trade unions or not and regardless of party
affiliation and militancy, were to organize into democratically
elected and run workers' organizations, the factory and farm
councils. Their task would be that of gaining control of the
factories and creating their own political and cultural institutions. These councils, once established in every town, region
and provinces, would have become the basis for the creation
of a socialist state.

This is not the place to analyze critically the experience and
theory of the factory councils.[14] It suffices here to say that
Gramsci viewed the factory councils as a potential socialist
state based on a proletarian democracy, as autonomous mass
institutions, and as a spontaneous working-class reaction to
the situation created by the development of capitalism in
Italy.[15] Gramsci's theory of factory councils, as Leonardo Paggi
has noted, represents a creative effort to seek an autonomous
formulation of mass politics. More than a negation of syndicalist
and party tactics, this theory represents a critical evaluation
of their limitations.[16] The factory councils theory, in contrast
with the syndicalist theory, led the workers to view themselves
not as wage earners, but as producers. Syndicalism, for
Gramsci, degraded the worker, while socialism upgraded him.
The producer, in fact, far from viewing himself as an instrument of the productive process, is a master and creator of the
process of production. The subordinate role of the party in
Gramsci's theory of the councils is undeniable. The party,
Gramsci noted, is a 'voluntary' and 'private' institution like
the syndicate, whereas the council has a 'public' character,
being a truly representative organism. While allegiance to the
party is established through an act of consciousness, which
can be withdrawn at any moment, the latter is a representative
organization of workers in their work place, whatever their
beliefs. That is to say, its structure reflects the interests of
workers in the work place.[17] The subordination of the role of
the party to that of the mass movement of the councils can
also be explained if one keeps in mind the weakness of the
Italian Socialist Party in directing the course of the proletarian
revolution. With the creation of the Communist Party, the role
of the party becomes a more primary one. But at its base
remains the central idea of the councils' experience: proletarian
democracy.[18]

It is well known that the factory councils movement ended
in failure. The occupation of factories in Turin, attempted at
the end of August 1920, was shortlived. A solution was reached

a month later through trade unionist bargaining and personal intervention of the Prime Minister, Giolitti. The best explanation for the failure of the councils' experience was provided by Gramsci himself in 1926. Gramsci recognized the fact of its failure from the very beginning, just as Marx had foreseen the impossibility of success of the Paris Commune experiment. He defended, however, its historical significance for the workers' movement. The Turin experience, Gramsci noted, demonstrated the maturity of the Italian working class, its capacity to act, and revealed the wealth of the creative and organizational energies of this class. Its failure proved the incapacity of the Socialist Party to lead the process of revolution in Italy. Thus, the failure of the councils' revolutionary strategy demonstrated that the objective conditions for the revolution were potentially there. What was lacking was the intervention of a subjective element: the support of the party.

After the failure of the Turin councils movement, Gramsci's attention was concentrated on the organization of the subjective force of the revolution, the party. We enter the third phase of Gramsci's political thinking and revolutionary strategy characterized by the complete break of the centrist and left wing from the party and the foundation of the Communist Party of Italy in January 1921. No one can deny the impact of international events on Gramsci's thinking in the following years. The Second Congress of the Third International had concluded its work on August 1920. Social democratic movements turned against communist leaders in Germany, Hungary, Czechoslovakia and Rumania. The mot d'ordre was 'war on social democracy.' Revolutions are successful whenever revolutionary proletarian parties take the lead on their own as the Bolsheviks did in Russia.

The newly formed Italian Communist Party was far from homogeneous. The bitter rivalries between the centrist forces led by Gramsci and the leftist ones led by Bordiga have been amply documented.[19] Bordiga remained the unchallenged leader of the PCI. The emphasis was on purity of principles, discipline and sectarianism rather than mass action, proletarian democracy and grass-root organization. As the spectrum of fascism advanced daily, Gramsci began to analyze in the columns of 'L'Ordine Nuovo,' which reappeared as a daily newspaper in 1921, the real character of the fascist phenomenon. In 1922 the fascists took power and began a systematic campaign to liquidate opposition parties, their leadership and their press. In 1923, the Executive Committee of the Comintern, uneasy about the staunch opposition to its directives to create a united front with the socialists in the struggle against fascism, blamed the leadership of the PCI. A temporary leadership was installed, after Gramsci refused the Comintern offer to lead the party. Infights within the party continued over tactics against fascist power, PCI relations with the Comintern and concrete revolutionary tactics. After three years of fascist terror the idea of proletarian revolution began to appear very remote. Gramsci's concern was now the period of transition to socialism, the re-establishment of democratic order, and broad alliances with other leftist parties to face fascist power. The centrist forces were able to capture control of the party at the clandestine Congress held in Lyons in January 1925. Gramsci emerged as the leader of the semi-legal party. The Lyons theses characterized fascism as a new phase of capitalist development, proclaimed the hegemonic role of the Italian proletariat, upheld the principle of a democratic structure in the leadership of the party, and formulated the concept of a necessary alliance between the northern proletariat and the southern peasantry. They defined the period as one of transition to socialism.

A more detailed analysis of Gramsci's political thought will be made further on in this study. It suffices here to make some general observations on the evolution of Gramsci's thinking in the light of the events just sketched. All Gramsci's commentators seem to be in agreement in noting a significant shift in his conception of the role of the party. This role, in the writings of this period, appears as more direct and fundamental. It must be borne in mind, however, that the party of which Gramsci speaks is no longer the Socialist Party, but the Communist one. At its base remains, as we have noted, the conceptual framework of the councils' experience: a critical, dialectical, organic relationship between centralism and democracy, between the idea of direction and spontaneity. The ideas of mass participation, mass politics and democracy remain the necessary conditions for the role of direction exercised by the party and the spirit of discipline demanded by it. Party centralism is indeed a new element of Gramsci's thought in this period. However, this is not conceived in a mechanical sense, as the Bordiga's faction retained, rather in a dialectical sense. The role of the masses, in the ultimate analysis, is still pre-eminent. It is the autonomous organization of the masses which develops into a party. The party, Gramsci writes, is not a part of the masses, but an organ of them. Gramsci aptly distinguished the role of the party from the general revolutionary process. The first exerts an instrumental function but can never substitute itself for mass action. There is not opposition, then, between the Gramsci of the councils and the Leninist Gramsci of the 1920-6 period. The creative, idealist, intellectual Gramsci of the earlier period is fused in a creative synthesis with the Leninist Gramsci. Rather than submerge and disappear into a rigid, sectarian Leninism, Gramsci's thought creatively integrates Leninism. This results in a more mature conception of theory and praxis.[20] In this vein, Leonardo Paggi writes in his excellent study of the pre-prison writings of Gramsci: 'if in the years 1919-20 Gramsci's objective was that of directing and channeling the given revolutionary spontaneity, after 1924 his fundamental task will be that of removing through the activity of the party the ideological and political obstacles which impeded the political expression of the historical orientation of proletarian masses.[21] The element of continuity, the author continues, between the Gramsci of the two periods consists in the primary importance attributed to the organization of the masses. What changes profoundly is Gramsci's vision of the political process destined to accompany and promote such an organization. This vision becomes gradually more articulate the more Gramsci understands the capacity of the political and economic structure of capitalist society to contain the crisis present in the relations of production.

The years 1926-36 are Gramsci's prison years in the fascist jails of Italy. In these years socialism had suffered an outstanding defeat while fascism reigned supreme, and in various European countries reactionary forces had the upper hand. During the long prison years Gramsci's brain did not stop working as his prosecutor had hoped. He wrote 2,848 pages, the now classic 'Prison Notebooks.'[22]

In the 'Prison Notebooks' Gramsci reflected on the failure of socialist revolution and set out to analyze the conditions for the re-organization of socialist forces in a fascist state. He analyzed the history of Italy's institutions, its hegemonic and ideological system, and the mechanisms by which bourgeois hegemonies were formed in various European countries, as well as the processes by which they re-organized themselves in the face of political crises. He thus laid the theoretical foundations for the construction of socialist hegemonies in Italy and Western Europe well beyond the fascist era.

The central idea of Gramsci's work is that socialist revolutions do not occur spontaneously where bourgeois hegemony is well consolidated, but only where and when the cultural and political foundations of a new socialist hegemony have been solidly built. Political praxis is the basis for socialist transformation. Gramsci did not disregard the crucial problems of socio-economic change within the structure of capitalist societies. He presupposed them. But he ascribed to superstructural activities a primary role in Marxist theory. Following in Lenin's footsteps, Gramsci defended the primacy of political praxis. Lenin, however, did not analyze the theoretical foundations of such a praxis, that is, the place of political activity within an all-encompassing, systematic conception of the world. It was Gramsci who developed a theory of politics and founded a Marxist science of politics. This was part of a more ambitious task of systematizing and organizing Marxist theory into an integral, autonomous and universal Weltanschauung. That is why Gramsci dealt with such varied subjects as culture, science, objectivity, language, art, literature, theater, education, etc. These themes are not esoteric, nor an individual intellectual pastime. They are well integrated in Gramsci's central idea of hegemony and political praxis. If a revolution entails profound superstructural changes and a reform of human consciousness, then one understands Gramsci's dictum that a revolution is not an event to be awaited but one to be prepared well before the actual conquest of power. Only when subaltern classes transcend the corporate conditions of their origin and become hegemonic entities, Gramsci writes in the 'Prison Notebooks,' is a structural re-organization of society possible. The subaltern is by necessity reformist. Political praxis enables it to become hegemonic, that is, ideologically, culturally and politically dominant, the creator of a new Weltanschauung which, diffused throughout society, determines a new social order. A socialist revolution then, for Gramsci, begins before the conquest of power and goes on well after it has been attained. The socialization of the means of production is only one aspect of socialist revolution. There is also the important aspect of the socialization of the means of cultural and intellectual production.

These are some of the most important ideas of Gramsci's 'Prison Notebooks.' Before we plumb the depths of his reflections, an attempt will be made to provide a brief summary of the present status of Gramscian studies.

GRAMSCIAN STUDIES

The Gramscian bibliography is enormous, and most of it is written in Italian. Lack of reference to it renders Gramscian studies in English seriously handicapped and downright one-sided. Despite the vastness of the Gramscian bibliography, however, there have been few attempts to provide a global interpretation of his theory. The most recent ones are those of Paolo Spriano, L. Paggi, F. De Felice, M. Salvadori in Italian, C. Riechers in German, J.-M. Piotte, A.R. Buzzi, H. Portelli in French and J. Gammett in English.

This is not the place to review and analyze the various interpretations of Gramsci's Marxism. A brief summary of them is in order only to show the disparate interpretations to which Gramsci's thought has been submitted, to single out the most controversial aspects of his thought and to place into the proper perspective the nature of the present study.[23]

The major source of interpretation of Gramsci's thought for more than a decade has been Palmiro Togliatti, Gramsci's personal friend and collaborator and one of the most influential leaders of the PCI. Togliatti's discussion of Gramsci, in the form of speeches and occasional writings, encompasses a long period of three decades. During this period, the important changes in socialist Russia, the international strategy of the workers' movement and the PCI greatly influenced Togliatti's analysis of Gramsci's ideas.

In the Stalinist period, when party politics, party historiography and party propaganda were virtually fused, the praxis of the PCI became the sole frame of reference of Gramsci's theoretical and political thinking. Togliatti skillfully presented

and defended a line of continuity between Gramsci and the
tradition of the party. Continuous reference was made to non-
problematic aspects of Gramsci's thinking. The Gramsci of
the 'Prison Notebooks' received the most attention, while a
calculated silence was kept on Gramsci's critical stance on certain developments within the workers' movement, Stalin's famous
purges and the bureaucratization of the Communist Parties.
Following the de-Stalinization, the radical changes undergoing
the communist world and the tragic events of Hungary, the
PCI was confronted with the task of redefining its revolutionary
strategy and re-examining its own tradition and philosophical
foundations. Thus, in the 1950s, a more critical historiography
began to develop. The interest in Gramsci gained momentum
as his first writings made their appearance in print and party
scholars began to research critically the ideas of the founders
of the PCI. The 1950s were the important years in which the
intensive criticism of Stalinism culminated into the elaboration
of the strategy of the 'Italian road to socialism' through the
means of parliament and democracy.[24] Togliatti was quick in
linking the new praxis of the party with the best tradition of
the proletarian movement. The 'political' Gramsci was then
rehabilitated as the PCI response to the new changes in the
communist world, world politics and Italian new political
strategy. Togliatti's insistence was now on the Leninism of
Gramsci, who, faithful to the directives of the Third International, and against Bordiga's faction, defended the necessity
of the united front and elaborated the theory of a 'war of
positions' in the transition period to socialism. Following the
failure of the frontal attack strategy in various European
countries, Gramsci emerged as the theorist of the transition.
The originality of Gramsci, for Togliatti, consisted in having
assimilated Leninism and adapted it to the Italian conditions.
The Gramsci of the period of the councils is dismissed as
politically immature. The original concepts of 'hegemony,'
'historical bloc,' 'war of positions' and 'historicism' developed
by Gramsci in the 'Prison Notebooks' were appropriated by
Togliatti and interpreted in a Leninist perspective, as we shall
see further on.[25] The Togliattian interpretation of Gramsci,
however, did not remain unchallenged during the 1950s. The
challenge came from scholars to the left and the right of the
PCI and from non-communist intellectuals.

In 1953 appeared the first history of the party by Giorgio
Galli and Fulvio Bellini. Gramsci's political ideas and activities
were identified with the Stalinist praxis of the PCI. From
Bordiga's perspective, the authors severely criticized Gramsci's
councils movement and his approach to the theory of the
revolution as 'economistic' and 'productivistic,' avoiding the
central problem of the smashing of the bourgeois state.[26] In
the same vein, but from a rightist position critical of both
Gramsci and Togliatti, Angelo Tasca successfully documented
the non-homogeneity of the first leadership of the party in the

years of its formation. The myth of historical continuity
between Gramsci, Togliatti and the praxis of the PCI was
totally rejected. From this critical analysis, the thought of
Gramsci emerged as truly original and in contrast with Togliatti's
positions. The same conclusions were reached by Livio Maitan.
From a Trotskyite position, Maitan defended an interpretation
of Gramsci different from that of Togliatti. The experience of
the councils was interpreted as anti-Stalinist and in the best
Leninist tradition.[27] In the first years of the 1950s the originality of Gramsci's Marxism came to the fore in the works of
non-Marxist scholars. Nicola Matteucci and Aldo Garosci, for
instance, insisted on the 'national' sources of Gramsci's
thought: the philosophy of Benedetto Croce and Macchiavelli's
political thinking. The idealism and historicism of Gramsci's
orientation were deeply appreciated while the totalitarianism
and authoritarian aspects of his thought, present in the concepts of hegemony, and identification of politics and philosophy,
for instance, were clearly rejected.[28]

In 1958 the first conference on Gramsci took place in Rome.
Such a conference responded to the need of re-examining the
nature of Marxism and researching the national specificity of
proletarian strategy.[29] The major contributions to the study of
Gramsci were provided by Togliatti and Eugenio Garin. The
first developed the idea of the close relationship between
Gramsci and Lenin. The latter introduced a novel approach. He
defended the national character and originality of Gramsci's
reflections. Heavy emphasis was placed on the intellectual
context of Gramsci's Marxism characterized by a critical confrontation with the philosophy of Croce, the theory of intellectuals and, above all, the historicist, humanist and autonomous
conception of Marxian theory. From a critical standpoint, of
great interest were the contributions of Mario Tronti and Cesare
Luporini. In agreement with Garin, Tronti identified the
theoretical context of Gramsci's Marxism in the ideological and
critical debate with Crocean idealism. But great reservations
were made with regard to the problems of identification of
history and philosophy, the primacy of subjectivity in Marxist
theory and the problems of the reduction of being to thought,
and the general definition of Marxism as a Weltanschauung. In
the same line, Luporini, after having singled out the original
elements of Gramsci's theory (the autonomous and integral
conception of Marxism, the theory of intellectuals, the importance of the role consciousness, culture and the superstructure), was critical of Gramsci's underemphasis of the objective
dimension of Marxist theory. What was under attack was
precisely the historicism and humanism of Gramsci's Marxism
which constituted the theoretical foundation of the praxis of
the PCI. Needless to say, the criticism of historicism responded
to the concrete exigency posed by new capitalist developments
of elaborating a 'scientific' model on which to ground a correct
relationship between communist praxis and the proletarian

struggle. Such critique became more complex and sophisticated in the works of Althusser who, in defense of dialectical materialism and Marxist scientific orthodoxy, denounced the historicist and humanist approach of Gramsci along with the theoretical perspectives of Lukács, Korsch and Colletti.

In Italy, as Gian Carlo Jocteau observes, the critique of Gramsci shifted from a methodological to a more directly polemical plane.[30] While the defense of Gramsci's historicism by Togliatti served the purpose of providing the necessary conceptual background for the new strategy of the 'democratic road to socialism,' the criticism of it aimed at providing the theoretical justification for the rejection of the reformist strategy of the PCI by parties and individuals thinking and acting from the left of the PCI. Clearly in this direction are the works of Alberto Asor Rosa, Luigi Cortesi, Andreina De Clementi and Stefano Merli. De Clementi wrote about the heterodoxy of Gramsci's Marxism-Leninism and consequently denounced its reformist theory which culminated in the political praxis of the PCI in the 1960s. Cortesi compared Gramsci's reformism to that of Stalin, placing him outside the Marxist-Leninist tradition for his reformist interpretation of the concepts of state, revolution, and dictatorship of the proletariat. The same criticism is levelled by Merli.

In 1967 a second International conference was held on the thought of Gramsci.[31] Here the party interpretation of Gramsci was defended by Ernesto Ragionieri. He re-emphasized the Leninism of Gramsci, but was critical of the factory councils movement. Gramsci's concepts of the specificity of western conditions, hegemony and war of positions were analyzed in Leninist key. Garin, from another angle, defended a logical continuity in Gramsci's thinking from his early writings to the 'Prison Notebooks.' Gramsci's theory of intellectuals was recognized as his most original contribution to Marxism. A novel interpretation was put forward by Norberto Bobbio. In his scholarly paper, Bobbio demonstrated the originality of Gramsci's Marxism in relation to Marx and Lenin. Gramsci is said to have emphasized civil society over political society, the moment of the superstructure over that of the infrastructure, the subjective, ideological and political dimension of Marxist theory.

It was not until the early 1970s that the first serious attempts are made at the periodization and historicization of Gramsci's ideas. In this context the works of Leonardo Paggi, Massimo Salvadori and Franco De Felice are of extraordinary importance. Salvadori defended the underlying continuity of Gramsci's thinking before and after his arrest. The central theme is that of 'proletarian democracy.' The originality of Gramsci is seen in the re-evaluation of the importance of the subjective component of Marxist theory, and the defense of the necessity of a democratic consensus in revolutionary praxis.[32] In the same vein the works of Paggi and De Felice established a line of continuity between the early writings and the 'Prison Notebooks,'

documenting in great detail the centrality of the concept of
'democracy' in proletarian struggle and proletarian institutions
along with an historicist and humanist conception of history.[33]
An important contribution to Gramsci's studies is represented
by the work of Nicola Badaloni, who examined the contribution
of Gramsci to the development of Marxism in the context of the
crisis of socialism and theoretical Marxism at the turn of the
century. Gramsci's concepts are examined in the context of the
Marxist interpretations of Labriola and Sorel.[34]

Noteworthy are the first serious attempts made in the late
1960s and early 1970s at providing a global interpretation of
Gramsci's thought. Paolo Spriano, in his monumental history
of the Italian Communist Party, insists on the Leninism of
Gramsci in the early writings, but indicates important differences. While Lenin developed the revolutionary strategy of
the frontal attack, Gramsci in his theory of the factory councils
movement stressed a molecular, democratic and consensual
process in the proletarian struggle for power. Rather than
revolution from 'above' by means of the activities of a monolithic
party, Gramsci is said to have advocated a revolution at the
mass level in the work place as well as the creation of new
proletarian institutions before the conquest of power. The
Gramsci of the 'Prison Notebooks,' Spriano notes, is the more
original one. The central theme is that of hegemony, understood as the attempt by a class to become a national force,
capable of providing cultural and political direction to subaltern
classes and of obtaining a vast social consensus before the
assumption of state power.[35]

The work of Giorgio Nardone constitutes a major attempt to
reconstruct, through a rigid and systematic analysis, the
fundamental unity of Gramsci's thought. All major concepts are
well integrated into Gramsci's more general vision of the
development of the historical process. Incorporated into such
vision, revolutionary praxis is seen as the historical affirmation
of a collective praxis. Revolution is realized through the assertion of the liberating and progressive praxis of the present.
At the base of such a praxis, and new institutions emanating
from it, is an organic and dialectical relationship between
intellectuals and masses, party and masses. Great emphasis
is placed on Gramsci's concept of 'catharsis,' the transformation
of a class from an economistic to an hegemonic entity.[36]

The interest in Gramsci, outside Italy, has developed only in
recent times. The reasons are obvious. As Stalinist conformism
in theory and praxis is denounced and opposed, and as the
workers' movement adopted the strategy of 'national roads' to
socialism, the thought of a creative, original and potentially
heterodox Gramsci appeared as the most relevant source for a
renewal of both Marxist theory and praxis. Gramsci's concepts
of the specificity of Western conditions, of proletarian hegemony
before the conquest of power, of the importance of the role of
ideas, ideology, subjectivity and consciousness in the revolu-

tionary process, as well as the concept of proletarian cultural and political autonomy, are all concepts full of practical implications and relevance in today's socialist movements.

In J.-M. Piotte's work, the centrality of the role of intellectuals in Gramsci's theory is strongly analyzed. This concept, for Piotte, sets Gramsci apart from Marx and Lenin, and is rich in practical consequences for socialist transformation in Western societies. The intellectuals are, for Gramsci, not an homogeneous bourgeois class. They represent various strata 'organically' linked to various social classes. It follows that when they are 'organically' linked to the proletarian movement, they can become the creators and organizers of new political and cultural institutions. Piotte argues strongly that, for Gramsci, political power in the proletarian struggle for hegemony is the end result of a long and molecular development within civil society. The progressive acquisition of proletarian consciousness and the attainment of the active consensus of subaltern classes are the innovative ideas in Gramsci's theory.[37]

The same perspective is predominant in the works of another Gramscian commentator in France, Hugues Portelli. After demonstrating the original contribution of Gramsci to the development of Marxist theory, the author centers his analysis of the major themes of the 'Prison Notebooks' on the concept of the 'historical bloc.' Gramsci's originality is said to reside in having established an organic, dialectical relationship between the moments of structure and superstructure and having attributed to superstructural activities an autonomous role in relation to the structural ones. Hence the primary importance of politics, ideas, culture and intellectuals during the period of 'organic crises' developing within established political blocs is derived. The creation of a new historical bloc then restores the organic nexus between structure and superstructure.[38]

However, not all global interpretations of Gramsci developed in the 1970s are sympathetic. In Germany, Christian Riechers has elaborated the most sophisticated critique of Gramsci's theory and revolutionary strategy. Riechers dismisses Gramsci's thought as reformist and in the best tradition of social democracy. Gramsci's conception of Marxism as subjective idealism is attacked as a bourgeois appropriation of Marxism. Rather than emphasize the character of opposition of Marxian theory to all past systems of thought, Gramsci, according to Riechers, understood it unorthodoxly as the continuation, development and culmination of the cultural and intellectual achievements of the past. More serious is the heterodoxy of Gramsci with regard to the concrete problem of revolutionary praxis. Proletarian revolution is reduced to a bourgeois form of revolution, a struggle for a more rational, objective and scientific engineering of the system of production. The factory councils experience reveals the economistic, productivistic approach of Gramsci's vision of socialism. Having established the heterodoxy of Gramsci in relation to Marxism-Leninism,

the author severely criticizes and condemns the idealist and
bourgeois characterization of Gramsci's conception of a democratic and institutional transition to socialism not dissimilar from
that of the reformist Bernstein.[39] Although the main conclusions
of Riechers are wrong, his work remains an important source
for an interpretation of the originality and autonomy of
Gramscian Marxism.

In the English-speaking world, and particularly in the United
States, Gramsci has been dealt with as a footnote in the history
of Marxist thought for decades.[40] In the past few years,
Gramsci's writings have begun to stimulate a great interest
among a growing number of Marxist and non-Marxist scholars.
The first selected English translation of the 'Prison Notebooks,'
the very recent publication of a much larger selection of his
prison as well as his early writings, have contributed to the
development of Gramscian studies.

The major attempt to provide a serious study of Gramsci has
been made by J. Cammett in his book, 'Antonio Gramsci and
the Origins of Italian Communism,' published in 1967. This
study, together with A. Davidson's 'Antonio Gramsci' (1977),
is the first complete and authoritative biographical interpretation of Gramsci's thought and political activities. However, they
do not provide a substantive, interpretative contribution to
Gramscian studies. In their more theoretical aspects these
works emphasize the non-Leninist interpretation of the central
themes of his writings, such as the concepts of hegemony and
role of intellectuals in socialist transition. The short essays
by Hobsbawm, Genovese and the more recent books, 'Gramsci's
Marxism,' and 'Antonio Gramsci,' by Boggs and Joll, respectively, all provide a lucid introduction to Gramsci's thought.[41]
They indicate a general appreciation of the intelligence,
uncommon independence, and true originality of his theory,
but they do not provide a systematic, serious, global interpretation of Gramsci that matches those mentioned earlier.

More recently, the growing concern with understanding the
specific conditions of the West and the rise of 'eurocommunism'
explains the appearance of new works on Gramsci. 'Gramsci's
Politics' by Anne Sassoon-Showstack, provides a serious tex-
tual reading of Gramsci's writings in order to delineate
Gramsci's contribution to a Marxist theory of politics.[42] Very
informative and definitely a substantive contribution to
Gramscian studies in English is 'Gramsci and Marxist Theory'
by Chantal Mouffe. The author aims at familiarizing the English-
speaking public with the serious debate taking place in Italy
among the most renowned Gramsci's scholars on the compati-
bility of Gramscian conception of hegemony and the current
strategy of *pluralism* adopted by the Italian Communist Party.[43]
Finally, we have the invaluable contribution of two well-known
Marxist theorists, Christine Buci-Glucksmann and Perry
Anderson.

In her 'Gramsci and the State,' Buci-Glucksmann, having

established the basic Leninism of Gramsci, advances an interpretation of Gramsci which goes beyond Marx. Gramsci appears
as the theorist of the political forms of the transition, as he
attempts to analyze such a process as the product of a specific,
historical relation and combination of forces. Gramsci's well-
known concept of 'passive revolution' is interpreted as a process
of transition in which the transformation of society's structures
and institutions is undertaken by the state.[44] Such a process
entails a kind of 'enlargement of the state,' that is, a capacity
to assimilate all levels, strata and activities of society. The
originality of Gramsci, thus, for Buci-Glucksmann, lies in his
abandonment of all instrumentalist conception of the state either
as government (as in the liberal democratic tradition), or as
repressive apparatus (typical of most of the economistic tradition of Marxism which culminated in Stalinism). The thesis
of the 'enlargement of the state' enables Gramsci to reformulate
the problematic of the transition. Two types of transition are
then envisioned. There is a transition as a 'passive revolution,'
a transition brought about by the state without mass participation, which replaces the class as the hegemonic subject, resulting in a dictatorship without hegemony (Stalinism) where the
party and workers' associations become 'ideological state
apparatuses.' And there is a transition 'with a democracy at
the base,' entailing an hegemony without dictatorship. In such
a case, Buci-Glucksmann argues, the 'enlargement of the state'
takes the form of the socialization of politics and economics.
Having interpreted the phase of the transition in terms of a
dialectic of hegemony and domination, Gramsci's conclusion
is that the class must gain hegemony both before and after the
seizure of power in order to avoid being replaced by the state.
Gramsci's strategy for a successful revolution in the West
would then consist of an anti-passive revolution, a truly
democratic, mass-based revolution in contrast to Stalinism and
social democracy, the two forms of passive revolution in the
twentieth century.

    Buci-Glucksmann's book, however, has its limitations. It
does not show all the creative aspects of Gramsci's Marxism.
Gramsci's problems of culture, humanism, philosophy,
historicism are superficially analyzed and underemphasized.
As a result we have an apparent Leninization of Gramsci and,
under the influence of the Althusserian structuralism, a dismissal of any idealist interpretation of Gramsci.

    Perry Anderson's 'The antinomies of Antonio Gramsci'
contains the most sophisticated and influential dismissal of
Gramsci. From a Leninist and Trotskyist position, so clear in
his 'Considerations on Western Marxism,' lamenting Gramsci's
silence on the problems of capitalist economy, the author
detects in Gramsci an inhibition from theoretical confrontation
of major economic problems. As a result, obliged to proceed
beyond questions of method to matter of substance, Gramsci's
Marxism has no choice but to concentrate on the analysis of the

superstructures.[45] Thus the profound and original contribution
of Gramsci to Marxist theory is seen in the institutional analyses
of the functions of intellectuals, education, and ideologies
within historical blocs. Anderson's essay, though valuable
in tracing the historical background of Gramsci's ideas, engages
in an exegetical work to show the confusion of various versions
of Gramsci's concept of hegemony and the related revolutionary
strategy of 'war of positions' advocated for the West. The
apparent 'antinomies' in Gramsci appear because the author
has chosen not to relate Gramsci's central notions to his more
general vision of socialism and historical development, which
goes well beyond the categories of the Second International.
The clear intent of Anderson's essay is that of unmasking the
reformist implications of Gramsci's concept of hegemony, namely
the ideological nature of bourgeois power which has managed
to win the consent of the masses. The primacy of civil society
over political society, of consent over domination, and hegemony
over dictatorship, leads to the unorthodox strategy of the
'war of positions' similar to that of Kautsky, that is to social
democracy. Gramsci's war of position appears to justify the
parliamentary road to socialism pursued by eurocommunism,
which the author rejects from the standpoint of Marxist
orthodoxy.

The philosophical nature of Gramsci's Marxism, his analysis
of ideology, consciousness and subjectivity, the radical critique
of the economistic tradition within Marxism, the Hegelian source
of his Marxism, and the original analysis of the superstructures,
neglected in Anderson's treatment of Gramsci, are at the base
of the works of other Gramsci scholars not only in the United
States and Britain but also in Italy.[46]

THE NATURE OF THIS STUDY

The present study is not an intellectual biography of Gramsci,
nor a simple exposition of his theory. It is an attempt to provide an organic exposition of his thought by integrating the
central themes of his writings, such as hegemony, historical
blocs, intellectuals, with more peripheral ones such as those of
science, language, literature, aesthetics into the more general
vision of Gramsci's conception of the historical process. The
aim of this study is thus that of delineating in general traits
a global interpretation of Gramsci's work within the framework
of the sociology of political praxis and the sociology of knowledge. The method used is a structural rather than exegetical
one and the general perspective is that of sociological theory
more than that of philosophy and historiography. However,
there is no personal refrain to enter the philosophic and
historiographic universe of discourse when the treatment of
certain concepts required it.

No effort has been made to periodize Gramsci's ideas. This

transcends the limitations imposed by the present study. However, a general observation needs to be made in this regard. This work presupposes a line of continuity in Gramsci's thinking as contained in his early writings, the 'Ordine Nuovo's' experience and the 'Prison Notebooks' which has already been established by the works of Paggi, Salvadori and De Felice. There is an evolution in Gramsci's thinking. Such an evolution does not entail elements of rupture rather a gradual conceptual enrichment as new experiences and profound changes occurred in the international and national political scene during Gramsci's lifetime. Among elements of continuity, one finds the firm conviction that the ripeness of subjective conditions is the necessary precondition for the success of proletarian revolution in the West. That is, the maturity of the proletariat on the level of theory and praxis is a necessary condition for the attainment of political and cultural autonomy climaxing into the assumption by the proletariat of the historical task of directing civil society. As Gramsci became cognizant of the capacity of capitalism to contain the workers' movement – fascism being a new phase of capitalist development – he understood the crises of capitalism as 'organic crises,' that is, hegemonic crises. To be sure the conquest of power through the smashing of bourgeois state still remains the goal of proletarian struggle. The concept of state, however, undergoes a profound change in the 'Prison Notebooks.' It is no longer the 'state' in the bourgeois sense, but the state as civil society plus political society. The terminus ad quem of socialist hegemony is the reabsorption of political society into civil society. Given the solidity of civil society and the superstructures in societies where capitalism is fully developed, Gramsci delineated the new strategy of 'war of positions' for the proletarian revolutionary struggle. In so doing he laid the foundations for a new science of political praxis, a Marxist science of politics.

Political praxis, that is, in the most general sense, the affirmation of a collective will, is the hermeneutic canon of Gramscian historiography. The structure of such praxis is a dialectical unity of objective and subjective elements, of structural and superstructural activities, of materialism and idealism. Its major protagonists are the masses, the intellectuals, and the party. Its point of direction is the creation of hegemony. The philosophy of such praxis is Marxism, conceived by Gramsci as absolute historicism, as total immanence of thought. Historicism, as a conception-of-the-world based on political praxis, becomes, in Gramsci, more than a doctrine about history, an historical act, a modus operandi in history. As political praxis is both fact and truth within the development of history, one understands the importance assigned by Gramsci to the problems of Marxist sociology of knowledge. The superstructural phenomena of science, language, aesthetics, etc. are objectively analyzed to the extent that they are

historicistically tied to the dynamic context in which the
progressive praxis of the present struggles to become
hegemonic. Scientific prevision, in Gramsci's sociology of
knowledge, becomes then the practical way of creating a
collective will. The identification of historicity and political
praxis leads to the dialectical unity of theory and praxis, the
structural and cultural unification of mankind. In this respect,
the philosophy of praxis is also, for Gramsci, 'absolute
humanism,' marking the passage from the realm of necessity
to that of freedom. The historical affirmation of a collective
will within the realm of necessity thus coincides with the
birth of freedom.

The focus of this study is the 'Prison Notebooks,' which
contain Gramsci's most original ideas and which are regarded
as Gramsci's most ambiguous political testament. The 'Prison
Notebooks' are presented in the form of fragments, sparse
notes, and occasional reflections, at times contradictory, on
a wide range of subjects. It must be remembered that in
prison Gramsci worked in such conditions that it was virtually
impossible to obtain the necessary material to conduct his
well-planned research. To avoid the censorship of prison
authorities and the fascist state, Gramsci was obliged to
camouflage names of revolutionaries as well as Marxist concepts.
Thus, for instance, 'class,' 'Marxism,' 'Lenin,' 'Marx,'
become 'social group,' 'philosophy of praxis,' 'Ilich,' 'the
founder of the philosophy of praxis,' etc. This study thus
seeks to explore the complexity of Gramscian thought and to
establish the profound logic, coherence and unity underlying
Gramsci's concepts.

The first part contains an analysis of the fundamental components of Gramsci's Marxism: the assertion of absolute historicism and humanism over economic determinism, the primacy
of ideological over political hegemony, and the subjective over
the objective dimension in Marxist theory. Emphasis is placed
on the relationship between knowledge, ideology and political
praxis (chapter 1) and between Marxism and sociology in order
to delineate the basic framework of sociology within Marxist
theory (chapter 2).

The second part deals with Gramsci's sociology of political
praxis within the general conception of historical development.
Great emphasis will be placed on the concept of 'catharsis,'
that is, the process of transformation of the structure of a
given historical bloc. The totality of socio-cultural phenomena
will be understood in relation to Gramsci's hermeneutic criterion
of the critical consciousness of subaltern classes, which
develops in their ascendant movement toward ideological and
political hegemony (chapter 3). The discussion of the role of
intellectuals in the development of history and the process of
formation of hegemonic systems is central in Gramsci's thought.
The intellectuals, in dialectical relationship with the masses,
are agents of socialist transformation (chapter 4). In chapter 5

we will analyze the controversial notion of 'hegemony,' which will be understood in the present study as the unity of structure and superstructure, theory and praxis, masses and intellectuals, civil and political society. Hegemony constitutes the terminus ad quem of the historical process, the phase of the complete cultural and political autonomy of subaltern masses, of the structural and cultural unification of mankind, of the absorption of political society into civil society.

In the third part, we expound on Gramsci's historicist theory and its application to the analysis of superstructural activities. Chapter 6 examines the superstructural character of science, the notion of objectivity in the sciences of nature, history and culture. Chapter 7 deals with Gramsci's analysis of 'language,' a subject rarely investigated from a Marxist perspective. This study will conclude with a discussion of Gramsci's aesthetic reflections with regard to art and literature (chapter 8).

Part I
THE PHILOSOPHY OF PRAXIS
AND GRAMSCI'S SOCIOLOGY

1 MARXISM AS AN AUTONOMOUS AND INDEPENDENT WELTANSCHAUUNG

Marxism, for Gramsci, had been robbed of its philosophy and reduced to a simple method of explaining historical and political changes in terms of economic changes. Hence, the theoretical stagnation of the Second International, the economistic and mechanistic interpretations of historical materialism, and the consequent failures of the workers' movement in Europe. The re-examination of the philosophical foundation of Marxism, 'the philosophy of praxis,' responded to the necessity of restoring the philosophical dignity of historical materialism. Marxism is an autonomous conception of the world, capable of explaining the totality of the historical process and engendering an intellectual revolution in all fields of knowledge. Historically, the theoretical impasse of Marxism has been attributed to the emergence of ideological divisions and popular varieties of Marxism, each claiming to represent the 'orthodoxy.' At the origin of these historical divisions lies the issue of whether politics is a mere reflection of ongoing infrastructural processes or whether it plays an autonomous role in socialist praxis. It is not our intention here to analyze the historical circumstances which nurtured economistic and deterministic interpretations of Marxism. It suffices to say that Gramsci was among the first in the West to rescue Marxian theory from its positivistic and objectivistic interpretations. He attempted to restore to Marxian theory its historicist and humanist components and to socialist praxis the primary role of political praxis and superstructural activities.

In this chapter we will attempt to elucidate the nature of Gramsci's Marxism and to decipher the basic contours of a Marxist sociology of knowledge. But first a brief discussion of the ideological context of Gramsci's writings is in order.

THE IDEOLOGICAL CONTEXT

Gramsci's Marxist elaboration takes shape in the context of an ideological debate with Croce's idealist liberalism, Bukharin's positivist Marxism and Lenin's political strategy.

Critique of the idealist philosophy of Benedetto Croce
Croce represented in the Italian intellectual and cultural milieu what Hegel represented in Germany. He was the ideologist of

the liberal bourgeoisie, the lay pope, Gramsci writes, of
secularism and historicism in opposition to the positivistic
ideas dominating the intellectual life of Europe until the beginning of this century.[1] For a short period of time Croce professed
to be a Marxist but, soon disenchanted with the mechanistic
and deterministic orientation of Marxism, he defected from it,
and became the most outspoken critic of Marxist thought in
Italy. Gramsci engaged himself in a polemical debate with Croce
and ultimately launched his own attack against the ideology
destined to become dominant in a period of transition following
the crisis of fascism.[2] Croce exerted a decisive influence on
Gramsci during his formative years. He had resurrected against
positivism the values of culture, ethics, consciousness and the
individual in the process of history, and had developed a
conception of history with man at the center of its development.
The humanist and historicist components of Crocean philosophy
became useful conceptual tools in Gramsci's critical analysis of
the mechanicism of the Second International. Initially fascinated
by Croce's affirmation of the importance of human values and
rejection of passivity and acquiescence in history, Gramsci
separated himself from the Italian philosopher on the interpretation of man's role in the creation and process of history.
Idealism was evidently incapable of solving the conflict between
theory and praxis. By transposing the concrete reality of
social conflicts to the level of ideas, Crocean idealism became
an ideological apparatus justifying abstract, speculative, and
ahistorical values. When meta-historical values are elevated
to the status of absolute values, then theology, metaphysics
and pure theory replace real political conflicts among men.
Gramsci's work, thus, is intended to debunk Croce's ideological
and political pretensions, while accepting and incorporating
the healthy elements of his system into Marxist theory.

Gramsci's critique of Croce's idealism can be essentially
reduced to four basic points: the conception of historicism, the
definition of philosophy, the conception of the dialectic, and
the relationship between theory and praxis.

Gramsci and Croce are apparently in agreement on the
'immanent' and 'historical' role of ideas and on the refusal of
any theory that is not grounded in concrete, specific, historical
problems. But Croce was not consistent in making this his point
of departure. In fact, he elaborated a metaphysical conception
of history. When he affirmed that ideas generate action and
that man is the creator of history, he did not speak of an
historically determined man, that is, of a man who lives and
struggles in concrete historical realities and is confronted
with objective and social contradictions. Rather, man is
conceived as a 'universal' man, a metaphysical entity. The
Idea, the Spirit, is the meta-historical man which creates
history. In sum, the creation of history is nothing but a history
of ideas and concepts. For Gramsci, as for Marx, the historical
process is praxis, that is, practical activity. Ideas do not exist

by themselves but are concretized in objective social conditions. This signifies that the science of history is not metaphysics, as in pure Hegelianism, but rather an instrument for the creation of conscious history.

Historicism in Croce is the critique of transcendence. While for Hegel history is the unfolding of absolute Reason, for Croce it is the absolute becoming. Gramsci criticizes Croce's historicism for not being absolute. Croce's conception of history is impregnated with metaphysical, theological residues. The development in history is abstract development. Single concepts are hypostatized in eternal realities and become ahistorical noumena conditioning real, concrete history. Gramsci writes: '[In Croce] history becomes a formal history, a history of concepts, and in ultimate analysis a history of the intellectuals, more precisely an autobiographical history of Croce's thought.'[3] For Gramsci, as Leonardo Paggi notes, historicism from a critique of transcendence becomes an instrument for the comprehension and analysis of social facts, a form of comprehension and analysis of proletarian revolution.[4] Historicism, then, is understood by Gramsci as a form of consciousness of the role of history, as an instrument of action and political mobilization of the masses. It is precisely this conception of historicism that demonstrates the intellectual opposition between Marxism and idealism. While idealism negates the possibility of prevision of historical events, Marxism asserts it on the basis of organized collective will, that is, political praxis. The scientific nature of a theory resides in its capacity to offer a valid basis for action. Marxism is absolute historicism in the sense that it is capable of revealing the sociological context of all philosophical systems and ideologies.[5] It is just here that we can find the originality of Gramsci in relation to all other Marxist theoreticians. Marxism is a conception of the world, an ideology, the most encompassing ideology of all, which does not aim at mystifying human existence, but is rather the expression of human values. Marxism, Gramsci writes, is not 'an instrument of government of leading groups to obtain the consent and to exercise the hegemony over subaltern classes; it is the expression of these subaltern classes who want to educate themselves in the art of government.'[6]

The conception of dialectical development sets Gramsci and Croce further apart. As Norberto Bobbio observes, Gramsci levelled two types of criticism at Croce's dialectic. On the one hand, he denounces its speculative and conceptual character and unmasks its ideological functions; on the other hand, he rejects it as mystification of the Hegelian dialectic.[7] Croce, in fact, by understanding history as a history of ideas, and those who create such ideas, and not as a theory of real contradictions, replaces the real dialectic with a conceptual dialectic. For Gramsci, Croce's dialectic, as a dialectic between 'conservation' and 'innovation,' has immediate political implications. The philosophical error of such a conception of dialectic,

Gramsci writes, lies in the complete negation of conflict. Croce
would say that the thesis is not destroyed, but must always
be maintained by the antithesis. The fusion of contradictions
generates an historical synthesis. Gramsci rejects this dialectical
conception as a mystification and mutilation of the Hegelian
dialectic, which posits in real history a tendency within the
antithesis to destroy the thesis, the synthesis being an
'Aufhebung,' a transcendence of the initial form by new forms.
Croce's error then resides in the assumption that what will be
maintained in the synthesis is established a priori. Thus,
the negation, instead of being a phase in the totality of the
process, is a restoration of the totality. The Crocean dialectic
has a mere ideological function: to eliminate revolutionary
alternatives and justify the bourgeois order of the fascist state.
That is to say, all forces struggling against the conservatism
of the bourgeois state are bound to moderate the struggle and
conduct it according to rules established by the bourgeois
state. Croce establishes a priori the rules of the dialectical
process which respond to the interests of dominant groups
and dominant ideology. Such reformist historicism became the
ideology of the bourgeois state after Italian unification, and
subsequently, it became the ideology of the fascist state.

The reduction of the real dialectic of conceptual dialectic
minimizes the role of politics. For Croce, aesthetics, economics,
logic, and ethics constitute true sciences, pursuing respectively
what is beautiful, useful, true and good. There is no place for
a science of politics in such a system. Politics is merely
'passion,' an ideology; and ideology is not philosophy, Croce
concludes. The first arises from a given historical praxis; the
latter is pure theory and science. Croce's classification of
sciences, Gramsci would contend, has validity only in Utopian
societies, structurally and epistemologically unified, that is,
classless societies. Contemporary societies, however, are
characterized by class conflict. In such conditions 'political
passion' is a science. In contrast to Croce, Gramsci identifies
philosophy and ideology in a single historical category. He
posits only a difference of degree between them. The first is
a conception of the world which represents the intellectual
and moral life of a given social group in the process of its
development; the second is a 'particular' conception of a sub-
class aiming at the solution of immediate, specific problems.
Croce's philosophical system in this sense is the ideology of a
small but dominant group. Its lack of diffusion among the masses
indicates its closed, caste-like character. The history of
philosophy for Gramsci is the history of conflicts among classes
which oppose different Weltanschauungen. Thus, philosophy
is politics, and politics is the only science which can solve
societal conflicts.

If Gramsci and Croce seem to agree that philosophy has a
crucial role to play in the process of history, they are in total
disagreement over the nature of such a role. For Croce, the

initiator of historical movements is ideas; for Gramsci, it is praxis. For Croce, the creation of a new Weltanschauung is a function of the intellectuals who present it to the masses; for Gramsci, the intellectuals can only interpret the historical situation on the basis of praxis. Their opposite conception of the role of philosophy in the development of history derives from their opposite manner of positing the relationship between theory and praxis. Undoubtedly, for both, theory is related to specific historical conditions, but for Croce the function of theory is to understand and clarify social phenomena, while for Gramsci theory has the function of solving practical, concrete, socio-historical problems. Theory does not possess a value in itself, as Croce proposes; the real theory and ultimately the real knowledge is that which is contained dialectically in practical activity. This is what Gramsci means when he writes that philosophy must become political to be true and continue to be philosophy.[8]

Critique of Bukharin's Positivist Marxism
Gramsci arrived at a formulation of Marxism through a systematic critique of N. Bukharin's positivist Marxism. In his famous 'Theory of Historical Materialism: A System of Sociology,' published in 1921, Bukharin espoused clearly deterministic principles, such as the concepts of regular, necessary, and objective laws in history and society as well as the primacy of matter over human consciousness.[9] Reacting against the idealist tendencies of German social democrats, he fell into the same materialist philosophy which Marx so vehemently criticized. From such vulgar materialism the notion of the dialectical development of history disappears. The methods, canons and concepts characteristic of natural and physical sciences are applied to history; thus Marxist theory is reduced to a mere positivist sociology. Bukharin, Gramsci argues, falls into the same error of idealist philosophy, that is metaphysics. Abstract categories and the conceptual dialectic are replaced by empirical classifications and canons, in se abstract and ahistorical. Typical of this objectivistic conception is the notion of technique, that is, the instrument of relations of production. For Gramsci, the primary and decisive element of technical transformation is the economy defined as a network of human social production. For Bukharin, economic processes operate independently from human volition and outside history. Social phenomena can only be analyzed in terms of certain causalities which are objective and necessary. In the ultimate analysis, Bukharin, by eliminating the dialectical relationship between economic processes and human consciousness, eliminates the 'active' element from the historical process, which is the organized collective will. For Gramsci, as we shall see later, all laws are tendential laws; they reveal not what is fixed and immutable, but tendencies and possibilities. To admit

concepts of laws of regularity and causality is to capitulate to bourgeois positivist methodology.

The very attempt to develop a philosophy of praxis on the basis of common sense is highly questionable. Bukharin's Marxism is an a-critical acceptance of the masses' conceptions and notions. He refused to come to grips with traditional philosophical systems whose influence on common sense throughout history is undeniable. 'These systems influence the popular masses as an external political force, an element of cohesive force exercised by the ruling classes and therefore an element of subordination to an external hegemony.'[10] Positivist Marxism becomes a fatalist and determinist conception which tends to perpetuate the political and cultural passivity of the masses before the laws of history, thus becoming a fatalist doctrine of the 'inertia of the proletariat.' In this respect Bukharin is more reactionary than Croce. Marxism does not tend to leave the masses in their condition of cultural backwardness. Instead, it aims at elevating them to a critical conception of reality. As we shall see, the point of departure of Marxism is not common sense but critical common sense, which is transformed into a higher conception of the world. It is a matter of educating the masses, of diffusing among them the very culture which has been the privilege of the few throughout history. Culture is a process of human emancipation, a conquest of a critical and historicist method. Marxism is, then, for Gramsci, humanism and historicism.

Critique of Lenin's concept of hegemony
It can be said that the ideological debate within Marxism has focused on the well-known dichotomy, materialism versus idealism. On the one hand, materialist Marxism has stressed the primacy of economics over philosophy (pure theory), attempting to explain in a positivistic fashion the evolution of societies and history on the basis of empirical, scientific laws, thus formulating a mechanistic theory of causality which hampered the revolutionary process. On the other hand, the emphasis has been on the primacy of philosophy over economics, thus divorcing theory from its sociological context and creating a caste-like and abstract type of knowledge. Such a theoretical impasse has been overcome by Lenin with the assertion of the primacy of politics over both economics and philosophy. For Lenin, the Russian Revolution demonstrated the capacity of politics to mobilize vast masses for the creation of a new socialist type of society. In asserting the primacy of politics, Lenin established a reciprocal, dialectical relationship between the economic infrastructure and the superstructure.

Gramsci, following Lenin's intellectual lead, became the theoretician of the superstructures. He did not minimize the importance of the infrastructure. On the contrary he sought to establish a just equilibrium between the economic and

political processes.[11] The relations of production do not evolve
according to autonomous and self-generating laws, but act,
are regulated or modified by the human consciousness. The
economic moment of consciousness constitutes a negative phase
(realm of necessity) in the historical ascendancy of subaltern
classes toward political hegemony, which must be transcended
and replaced by a positive phase (realm of freedom) characterized by the creation of a new proletarian Weltanschauung
providing the masses with entirely new categories of thought
and behavior.[12]

However, Lenin did not fully analyze the 'practical' intervention and the influx of the 'popular element' in the revolutionary process. Gramsci, we think, completed and developed
further the Leninist theory of revolution, by insisting on the
concept of 'ideological hegemony' as distinct from that of
'political hegemony,' that is, the dictatorship of the proletariat.
In every concrete historical situation 'alternative forces' are
present (the working class in the bourgeois state), but they
exist in a state of disintegration. Once they are organized,
they give form to real historical alternatives. The political and
cultural development of subaltern classes is not spontaneous
but conscious. Consciousness grows, Gramsci notes, in direct
proportion to the cultural and political development of these
classes. For Gramsci, then, superstructural elements such as
consciousness, ideology, and culture are determining factors
of the nature, scope, and outcome of revolutions. It is precisely
in the attempt of analyzing the process of conscious organization
of the masses and the progressive acquisition of political self-
consciousness that he redefines the concept of 'hegemony.'
To be sure, such a term was common among Russian theorists,
but it was Lenin who elaborated it to mean the 'dictatorship
of the proletariat.' However, dictatorship of the proletariat is
a form of domination. No regime could sustain itself in power
by exercising control and domination over the masses; it will
need the 'ideological consent' of the masses. Hegemony becomes
in Gramsci 'cultural and ideological direction.' In contrast to
Lenin, asserting the primacy of political hegemony (seizure of
state power) over cultural and ideological direction of the
masses, Gramsci conceives hegemony as an ideological
phenomenon first, and only second a political one. More
specifically, in historical situations where the power resides
formally in the hands of the ruling classes, the working classes,
politically organized and conscious of their role, can and must
exercise an ideological hegemony by liberating themselves
from bourgeois ideology and progressively attracting into
their orbit all other subaltern classes. Ideological hegemony
(defined as 'intellectual and moral direction') is a preliminary
condition for the actual seizure of state power and the creation
of a new state. The proletariat, Gramsci contends, can and
must become a dominant class before a ruling class.[13]

The supremacy of a social group manifests itself in two ways, as 'domination' and as 'intellectual and moral leadership'.... A social group can, and indeed must, already exercise 'leadership' before winning governmental power (this indeed is one of the principal conditions for the winning of such power); it subsequently becomes dominant when it exercises power, but even if it holds it firmly in its grasp, it must continue to 'lead' as well.

The revolutionary experience that took place in Russia cannot be repeated in Western countries. The czarist state was not based on the consent of the masses; that is why it was easily overthrown by a small organized revolutionary group led by Lenin. In Western capitalist societies the bourgeoisie is all-powerful in so far as it has managed to secure and maintain the consent of the masses. Their aspiration, beliefs, needs, in sum their entire life, is impregnated with bourgeois ideology. These specific Western conditions will necessitate an ideological revolution as a precondition for political revolution.[14]

MARXISM: THE MOST INTEGRAL AND UNIVERSAL WELTANSCHAUUNG

Human activity is always embodied in and is an expression of a given conception of the world. A conception of the world denotes a conceptual, theoretical activity as well as a practical, conscious activity. Its historical validity is determined in terms of its impact on human activity. If it is true that a given philosophy is the expression of society, Gramsci writes, it should be able to react back on that society and produce certain effects. The extent to which it reacts back is the best indicator of its historical importance, of being an 'historical fact.'[15]

One could say that the historical value of a philosophy can be calculated from the 'practical' efficacity it has acquired for itself, understanding 'practical' in the widest sense.... The extent to which precisely it reacts back is the measure of its historical importance, of its not being individual 'elucubration' but 'historical fact.'

In contrast to Croce, for whom the historical value of a Weltanschauung is determined solely by the degree of rationality exhibited and by the authority of its expositors, Gramsci stresses its intrinsic capacity to mobilize, politicize, and reform the thinking and activity of the largest number of individuals. It follows that one cannot speak of a single absolute, universal Weltanschauung, but of Weltanschauungen in societies not structurally and culturally unified. The plurality of Weltanschauungen, furthermore, normally entails a problem of choice among them and of their diffusion in the total structure of society. Marxist sociology is called upon to analyze the criteria of how such a choice is made and how they diffuse in society. Analyzing the problem of their diffusion,

Gramsci observes, a given Weltanschauung can seduce the masses in virtue of its rational form (the form in which it is presented) and content. Such factors, however, account for its diffusion only among a limited number of intellectuals. Second, the authority of the experts facilitates its diffusion, but since their authority is normally subject to doubt and various interpretations, it cannot be considered a decisive factor in the process of diffusion. The above factors are subordinate to another more fundamental one: the solidarity of the group. Philosophy can be experienced in the masses only as a faith.[16]

> The most important element is undoubtedly one whose character is determined not by reason but by faith. But faith in whom, or in what? In particular in the social group to which he belongs, in so far as in a diffuse way it thinks as he does. The man of the people thinks that so many like-thinking people can't be wrong, not so radically, as the man he is arguing against would like him to believe; he thinks that, while he himself, admittedly, is not able to uphold and develop his arguments as well as the opponent, in his group there is someone who could do this and could certainly argue better than the particular man he has against him.

Such solidarity increases the degree of receptivity of the masses to specific political and philosophical principles. If one analyzes the diffusion of dominant ideologies, one will find the validity of such a criterion. Any dominant class employs a well-organized system of control to assure the maintenance of its ideological front. Such preliminary observations will aid the understanding of the specific mechanisms by which bourgeois society maintains its ideological, political, and economic control over the totality of the social body.

In this context it is of paramount importance to introduce Gramsci's original concept of 'historical bloc.'[17] Structures and superstructures form an historical bloc.[18]

> The realisation of a hegemonic apparatus, in so far as it creates a new ideological terrain, determines a reform of consciousness and of methods of knowledge; it is a fact of knowledge, a philosophical fact....Structures and super-structures form an 'historical bloc.' That is to say the complex, contradictory and discordant *ensemble* of the superstructures is the reflection of the *ensemble* of the social relations of production.

The historical bloc is not an alliance or amalgamation of various classes, but an hegemonic situation in which social cohesion is assured by a new conception of the world (superstructure) and a dominant social class (infrastructure).[19] A given social class maintains itself in power not by means of monopolization of the means of production and means of violence, but primarily through a more subtle process of winning the consent of all other subaltern classes to its ideology. What seems to interest Gramsci most, as Tamburrano observed, is not the organization

of class relations, but the mechanisms whereby such organization is created and perpetuated.[20] His contention is that
bourgeois domination is exercised on a deeper level through
a profound, unconscious transformation of human consciousness. Bourgeois Weltanschauung, diffused, popularized, and
finally internalized by the masses, becomes 'common sense'
knowledge. Bourgeois domination is essentially an ideological
and cultural fact; and this is original indeed in the history of
Marxist analysis of capitalism! Similarly, proletarian classes
struggling for socialist transformation need to develop a new
conception of the world which includes new ideas, new institutions, new culture, and new social arrangements to oppose
the existing dominant bourgeois Weltanschauung. Only through
the creation of a new 'intellectural order' can they de-alienate
the consciousness of all other subaltern classes and win the
consent to 'their' conception of the world. Marxism - which
Gramsci characterizes as the philosophy of praxis - is, then,
the Weltanschauung of subaltern classes aspiring to and
moving toward cultural and political hegemony.

From this standpoint, the process of rejuvenation of Marxism
in the Western world will depend on the re-assumption of its
historical role of 'ideological critique.' Of the two historical
objectives of Marxism, 'to combat modern ideologies in their
most refined form' and 'to educate the popular masses whose
culture is medieval,' the first has been neglected for the
benefit of the second. It has been the excessive concern with
the second objective, Gramsci argues, that has produced the
so-called historical deformation of Marxism. In fact, the new
philosophy, combining itself with popular culture, has fallen
into vulgarism and determinism, thus becoming 'absolutely
inadequate to combat the ideologies of the educated classes.
And yet the new philosophy was born precisely to supersede
the highest cultural manifestation of the age, classical German
philosophy.'[21] At present, Gramsci adds, Marxism is still in
its negative stage, in the romantic period of struggle, the
period of 'Sturm und Drang,' in which all interests focus on
the immediate and tactical problems of economic and political
nature. Such a phase has to be superseded by a positive one,
in which Marxism becomes a new intellectual, cultural, and
moral order.[22]

> But from the moment in which a subaltern group becomes
> really autonomous and hegemonic, thus bringing into being
> a new form of State, we experience the concrete birth of a
> need to construct a new intellectual and moral order, that
> is, a new type of society, and hence the need to develop
> more universal concepts and more refined and decisive ideo-
> logical weapons.

The task of resurrecting and rejuvenating Marxism requires
a radical redefinition of Marxism itself. Marx has to be read
in a new light and has to be considered as only a phase in the
evolution and elaboration of the 'philosophy of praxis.' Marxism,

by definition, is both historicism and humanism. Historicist
Marxism is intellectually opposite to scientific Marxism, the
brand of Marxism which degenerated into economism and
positivism. Scientific Marxism has obliterated the active,
conscious, and humanist components of Marx's thought. Historicist Marxism represents the most courageous attempt to
rescue Marxism from its historical impasse and to elevate
it once again to the status of a global, all-encompassing,
coherent, original, autonomous Weltanschauung.

A condition for the acquisition of a critical new conception
of the world is the consciousness of its historicity. A basic
historicist assumption is that any idea exists and develops
in dialectical relationship with praxis. Praxis is history;
it develops and transforms itself with history. Marxism as a
philosophy, then, is history becoming conscious of itself,
and since history is conscious activity, man becomes the
central focus of reality (humanism). In sum, in its very
essence Marxism is 'absolute historicism' and 'absolute
humanism.' Failure to lay the active and conscious human will
at the base of a Marxist Weltanschauung inevitably leads,
Gramsci writes, to solipsist theories (subjective idealism),
for which the self is the only object of knowledge, or
mechanistic theories (positivism and scientific Marxism), which
posit the existence of necessary laws and principles in the
historical process. In this respect, Marxism is the process
of historicization of human thought, which relocates ideas
and ideologies in their specific and concrete historical
framework, the process of relativization of existing social
structures and social arrangements. The philosophy of praxis,
Gramsci eloquently writes, is:[23] 'absolute historicism, the
absolute secularization and earthliness of thought, an
absolute humanism of history. It is along this line that
one must trace the thread of the new conception of the
world.'

Marxism is absolute historicism
The concept of relativity of social phenomena was certainly
not new in Gramsci's times. Historicist theories of knowledge
already had entered into the mainstream of philosophical and
sociological theories of the nineteenth century. However,
as Gramsci notes, such historicist theories, if well placed to
'criticize' the metaphysical nature of previous philosophical
theories, were no doubt incapable of conceiving themselves
as historical products reflecting given class interests. Marxism
is, on the contrary, total liberation from any form of abstract
'ideologism' in so far as it seeks to explain and justify
historically all the past as well as itself.[24] Every theoretical
system has validity within the limits of a specific historical
context, therefore it is bound to be superseded and deprived
of significance in the succeeding historical context. In sum,
whatever the rationality of a theory it cannot claim absolute

validity; ideas are continuously submitted to the test of emerging new historical conditions. The theory of eternal truths is the vestige of religious or para-religious systems; and the admission of the existence of objective reality outside human will is a blatant historical error. Laws of necessity, regularity, and causality are substitutes of old, transcendental, religious concepts such as God, Predestination, Providence, and so on.

Marxism as historicism signifies that within history is a theory of history, itself a transitory phase in the history of the development of human thought. As a historical product of a realm of necessity, it cannot imagine a world of freedom, a world in which all contradictions disappear without becoming a Utopia. In this regard, Gramsci writes:[25]

That the philosophy of praxis thinks of itself in a historicist manner, that is, as a transitory phase of philosophical thought, is not only implicit in its entire system, but it is made quite explicit in the well-known thesis that historical development will at a certain point be characterized by the passage from the reign of necessity to the reign of freedom.

Furthermore – and here we encounter an essential element – Marxism cannot be superseded by any other conception of the world since it contains in itself the principle of its disappearance; it is itself the result of and the theory of human consciousness. The philosophy of praxis is:[26]

a philosophy that has been liberated (or is attempting to liberate itself) from any unilateral and fanatical ideological elements; it is consciousness full of contradictions, in which the philosopher himself, understood both individually and as an entire social group, not only grasps the contradictions, but posits himself as an element of the contradiction and elevates this element to a principle of knowledge and therefore of action....If, therefore, it is demonstrated that contradictions will disappear, it is also demonstrated implicitly that the philosophy of praxis will disappear, or be superseded.

Gramsci's historicism differs from the most refined historicist approach of Karl Mannheim. Mannheim's concept of the 'general form of the total ideology' is an attempt to submit not only the adversary's point of view, but all possible points of views, and one's own, to the ideological critique. For Gramsci, the analysis of the social location of ideas does not preclude the assessment of the truth and the validity of such ideas. The validity is determined, as we have noted, by their capacity to mobilize and guide the masses toward the attainment of ideological and political hegemony. Furthermore, Gramsci's historicism has a direct relationship to revolutionary praxis. In this respect, it is opposed to any type of functionalist-structuralist theory of social phenomena. Functionalist economic theory, for instance, is a theory of the automatism of economic laws, as developed by Ricardo and Smith, seeking to discover 'decisive' and 'permanent' forces in the economic system of a 'determined market.' By focusing on the problem of variations of the economic structure, Gramsci's historicism fosters thought and action in terms of different and alternative strategies rather than necessary, constant, or immutable economic laws. Historicism is ultimately a revolutionary theory in so far as it seeks to free social structures from their 'objective facticity,' in the Durkheimian sense, and reveals new possibilities of existence. Any law of automatism admitted in the analysis of sociohistorical phenomena tends to stifle human will and human creativity and tends to mystify and alienate human consciousness. Historicism, on the other hand, is critical awareness of the 'historicity' of such laws of automatism. In sum, Gramsci's historicism has to be understood as: (1) a critique of all ideologies, (2) a theory of revolutionary praxis, which seeks to alter or transform existing social structures by focusing on their limitations and revealing new possibilities, (3) an ideological tool for the actualization of these new possibilities through the organization and politicization of subaltern classes.[27]

Marxism is absolute humanism

The philosophy of praxis is the bearer of an original, autonomous culture still in a state of incubation. Its historical mission is that of creating a new integral culture only attempted in past history by such movements as the French Revolution, Protestant Reformation and Greek classicism. The philosophy of praxis is humanism, that is a dialectical anthropology. Traditionally, humanism has represented an intellectual reaction against the increasing dehumanization of man entailed by the scientific-rational revolution as well as the emergence of new phenomena such as the bureaucratization and standardization of human activity. Within contemporary Marxism, humanism is an intellectual reaction against the process of bolshevization of Marxism and bureaucratization of socialism. Man, the subject of history, has become once again its object, an adjunct of impersonal institutions and processes, chief among them, the state, bureaucracy, technology etc. The bureaucracy and totalitarianism of socialism are the historical consequences of an a-human and a-historical scientific Marxism which Gramsci has been among the first to foresee and denounce.

Gramsci's humanism, more than a protest against the condition of human alienation, is an anthropocentric vision of reality. Humanism is a necessary component of historicism. It is the reduction of knowledge to historical social relations, the reduction of the *relations of production*, political and ideological social relations to *historicized* 'human relations,' to inter-human, intersubjective relations, to use Althusser's precise characterization of Gramsci's humanist conception.

The relations of production, objective socio-economic categories within scientific Marxism, are subordinated by Gramsci to man, the center of the cosmos. Thus, he broadens the traditional anthropology enunciated by Marx into a dialectical anthropology.[28] Humanism becomes a process of structuralization of human knowledge on the basis of the organized will of man. It affirms that man is the creator of history, the source of thought and practical activity. It is not a question of a hypostatized man as in traditional metaphysical philosophies, rather of a concrete man who is born and develops within the ensemble of historical relations, that is to say a reality immanent in history. Speculative philosophies have understood man in the same manner as the Christian religion, as 'an individual limited to his own individuality and of the spirit as being this individuality.'[29] From this standpoint history is reduced to individual histories and the individual becomes an 'absolute' entity in the development of universal history.

Man, by definition, is becoming, Gramsci writes; his history is that of his emancipation.[30]

Reflecting on it, we can see that in putting the question 'what is man?' what we mean is; what can man become? That is, can man dominate his own destiny, can he 'make himself' can he create his own life? We maintain therefore that man is a process, and more exactly, the process of his actions. If you think about it, the question itself 'what is man?' is not an abstract or 'objective' question. It is born of our reflection about ourselves and about others, and we want to know, in relation to what we have thought and seen, what we are and what we can become; whether we really are, and if so to what extent, 'makers of our own selves', of our life and our destiny. And we want to know this 'today', in the given conditions of today, the conditions of our daily life, not of any life or any man.

Man is not nature, but consciousness which develops through human activity within the given context of organized social relationships. Man is conceived in the philosophy of praxis as a series of active relationships, and individuality as consciousness of these relations. Gramsci does not deny the importance of the individual in history. Individuals are moments in the consciousness of mankind.[31]

each one of us changes himself, modifies himself to the extent that he changes and modifies the complex relations of which he is the hub....If one's individuality is the *ensemble* of these relations, to create one's personality means to acquire consciousness of them and to modify one's personality means to modify the *ensemble* of these relations.

The humanist preoccupation of Gramsci, Buzzi succinctly explains, is that of helping men to develop a new personality on the basis of new organic relations characteristic of a society without class antagonisms. The universality and autonomy of philosophy of praxis is, Buzzi continues, the universality and autonomy of subordinate classes, the subject of the new history.[32]

MARXIST HISTORICISM AND THE SOCIOLOGY OF KNOWLEDGE

It is not our purpose to survey the development of the sociology of knowledge and to expound on its relationship to Marxist
epistemology. But since the most consistent themes of Gramsci's
theoretical analyses are those traditionally discussed by the
sociology of knowledge, we will focus on some of the theoretical
issues that emerged in the process of its development, such as
the relationship between philosophy and sociology, theory and
ideology, and the problem of objectivity.

The basic contention of the sociology of knowledge, as Berger
and Luckmann have put it, is that social reality is socially
constructed and socially maintained in ongoing 'objective' social
processes, which constitute the specific object of empirical
investigation by social scientists. However, the relationship
between the sociology of knowledge and philosophy has not
been uniformly understood. For Berger and Luckmann,
philosophy asks questions pertaining to the ultimate status of
'reality,' sociology, on the contrary, investigates the variation
of types of knowledge and thus is forced to attribute it to
structural differentiation of societies.[33]

Along the same line, the French sociologist G. Gurvitch
argued that the sociology of knowledge never poses the problem of the validity of ideas, but that it attempts solely to
ascertain the effects of their 'presence,' their 'combination,'
and their effective 'functions.' Philosophy, on the other hand,
is concerned with the justification of the validity of ideas.[34]
The sociology of knowledge, Gurvitch continued, is limited to
the task of establishing 'functional correlations,' 'regular
tendencies,' and 'direct integration of ideas into the social
frameworks.' In contrast, Karl Mannheim has tended to
identify 'knowledge' and 'ideology.' In his view, the social
structure is the determinant factor, explaining not only the
diversity but also the content of human thought; consequently,
every mode of thought is ideological in nature.[35] Such identification of knowledge and ideology has given rise to a certain
disenchantment with the sociology of knowledge in recent
decades.[36] As an attempt to rescue the sociology of knowledge
from its theoretical impasse produced by Mannheim's identification of knowledge and ideology, Gurvitch has insisted
upon the empirical character of this discipline, whose object
must be the analysis of types of knowledge: perceptual
knowledge of the external world, knowledge of the Other,
political knowledge, technical knowledge, and common-sense
knowledge. Similarly, Werner Stark has proposed an important
distinction between the sociology of knowledge and the theory
of knowledge (ideological critique), further elaborated by
J. Gabel.[37] Gabel rejects the commonly held belief that
Mannheim's 'Ideology and Utopia' represents a work in the
sociology of knowledge and contends that it is rather an

exercise in 'ideological critique.'[38] The sociology of knowledge systematically analyzes 'types' of knowledge and attempts to establish their social origin, not their social determination. To speak of social origin of knowledge is simply making an empirical observation; in contrast, social determination of knowledge implies a critical posture toward it. More specifically, the social origin of knowledge emphasizes the relationship between knowledge and the totality of the social structure - presupposedly homogeneous - without any consideration of class structure and class conflict; social determination of knowledge emphasizes the relationship between knowledge and class structure, thus ultimately debunking its ideological pretensions and relativizing the validity of science and objectivity.

Gramsci, though he has never defined himself as a sociologist, has concerned himself with the most traditional problems of the sociology of knowledge, in particular the problem of the genesis of Weltanschauungen, their mode of formation and diffusion among social classes. He has not elaborated a system-atic theory of knowledge; nevertheless, he has formulated certain useful interpretative criteria for sociological analysis.[39]

Undoubtedly, Gramsci's approach to the study of knowledge shows similarities with the writings of the young Marx from his doctoral dissertation to the 'German Ideology.' In Gramsci as well as in Marx, men are the makers of history; they are not spectators of history, blind in the face of the development of technology, impotent in the presence of dominant ideologies, unarmed before the power of elites and grand theorists of bourgeois systems. On the contrary, history is the conscious activity of man in pursuit of his objectives, thus a political act. Gramsci is in agreement with Mannheim's identification of ideology and knowledge, but he has pressed to its limits the ideologization of knowledge to include scientific knowledge. He rejects any attempt to artificially separate the problem of social determination from the problem of social origin, as formulated by Stark and Gabel, while asserting the primacy of 'political knowledge' over any other type of knowledge, including scientific knowledge against the theoretical positions of Gurvitch and Scheler.[40]

Gramsci has ideologized sociology itself and has attempted to elaborate a humanist and historicist sociology of knowledge in which there is complete subordination of the totality of social phenomena to the 'critical consciousness' of the masses. Knowledge is not universal, and it cannot be as long as social structures are socially stratified. He seems to propose that the structural unification of society is the precondition for the de-ideologization, de-politization, and de-alienation of thought.

Gramsci certainly accepts Marx and Engels's principle of social determination of knowledge, the contention that ideas do not have an independent existence but are always grounded in specific socio-economic conditions, and that the dominant ideas of a given historical period are always the ideas of a

given ruling class. But can a given type of knowledge claim to
be objective? Marx's answer is that, knowledge being a function of class interests, there is no need to de-mystify it or
de-alienate it in a society that has reached the condition of
classlessness. More simply, the social determination of knowledge is not an obstacle to the attainment of objectivity. Such
a position has been criticized and rejected by Mannheim, for
whom all knowledge is partial, relative, and ideological in
nature. If for Marx, as Adam Schaff notes, the social factor
conditioning knowledge can determine the deformation of
reality only in historical conditions where the proletarian classes have not attained political hegemony (the proletariat is
the bearer of objectivity!), for Mannheim it *must* deform it
whatever the conditions.[41] Mannheim's thesis is far more radical
than Marx's in so far as it extends the principle of relativity
of knowledge to Marxism itself. Gramsci goes beyond Marx
and Mannheim. Marx, as we have noted, ceased to interest
himself with the problem of the social determination of knowledge
and the consequent deformation of thought in societies in
which the proletarian classes have become hegemonic. As for
Mannheim, the ideologization of thought is not total. Natural
sciences are exempted from the limitation of existential determination. For Gramsci, all thought is ideological, including
science. 'Without man, what would the reality of the universe
be? All science is tied to the needs, the life, the activity of
man.'[42] Reality, in fact, is always perceived and classified
according to human needs.[43]

> If reality is as we know it and if our knowledge changes
> continually - if, that is, no philosophy is definitive but all
> are historically determined - it is hard to imagine that rea-
> lity changes objectively with changes in ourselves. Not
> only common sense but scientific thought as well make this
> difficult to accept. In the *Holy Family* it is said that the
> whole reality is in phenomena and that beyond phenomena
> there is nothing, and this is certainly correct. But it is not
> easy to demonstrate. What are phenomena? Are they some-
> thing objective, existing in and for themselves, or are they
> qualities which man has isolated in consequence of his
> practical interests (construction of his economic life) and
> his scientific interests (necessity to discover things, a
> necessity which is itself connected to mediated and future
> practical interest).

If science is not a criterion for objective knowledge, is there
any other means for ascertaining the validity of thought
without falling into absolute scepticism or relativism? For Marx,
in classless society knowledge will be re-unified and objectivity
can be achieved; for Mannheim, a perspectivistic approach
(a plurality of perspectives) can lead to objectivity of thought.
For Gramsci, objectivity represents an inter-subjective
consensus among men; that is, objectivity is an historicized
and humanized objectivity.[44]

Objective always means 'humanly objective' which can be held to correspond exactly to 'historically subjective:' in other words, objective would mean 'universal subjective.' Man knows objectivity in so far as knowledge is real for the whole human race *historically* unified in a single unitary cultural system....There exists therefore a struggle for objectivity...and this struggle is the same as the struggle for the unification of the human race.

Marx, Mannheim, and Gramsci all agree on the necessity of identifying knowledge and ideology. What sets them apart from each other is the notion of ideology. For Marx, ideology denotes a set of ideas which reflects social existence in a deformed, illusory, and mystifying form. Gramsci gives to it a positive connotation and value. Ideology is a theory of human praxis; it is in fact on the level of ideology that man becomes conscious of social conflict. Consequently, ideologies have an historical value; they represent a tool for the understanding of socio-historical processes and a practical guide for the realization of a given political program. In this latter sense, ideologies also have a psychological value; in effect, they are capable of organizing human masses. The analysis of ideologies becomes, for Gramsci, the basis for the elaboration of a Marxist theory of knowledge. In this respect, ideologies have also and ultimately a gnosiological value, the determination of their historical and psychological value being the criterion for the establishment of objective thought.

Bourgeois sociological methodology attempts to describe, classify, and interpret socio-historical processes according to the criteria valid for natural and physical sciences. The apparent validity of such methodology presupposes and is the result of the masses' lack of critical consciousness and their political passivity. Critical consciousness is an obstacle, while political passivity is a favorable condition for the advancement of scientific knowledge. In contrast, for Gramsci, critical consciousness and organized human will are the only super-structural elements capable of impeding the 'objective' development of science and technology. Thus, Gramsci, in opposition to bourgeois positivism and scientific Marxism, minimizes almost to the point of denying the objective dimension of natural and social processes; he focuses instead on the subjective dimension of such processes. The subjective factor is of crucial importance for the comprehension of historical, as well as cognitive processes. But how can the role of the subjective factor in the cognitive process be understood? Certainly not in the Weberian sense of the individual's contribution to the process of knowledge. For Gramsci, the collective action of the subaltern classes is the basis and the most important criterion for the comprehension of history.

Marxist sociology of knowledge is then a form of critical consciousness, a form of ideological thought. It follows that the validity of sociological research resides not in its scientific function but rather in its ideological function, that is, in its capacity to organize the experiences of the masses.[45] To the extent that sociologists facilitate the process of organization of such experiences in an intellectual manner, their work can be considered legitimate within the framework of a Marxist theory of society, Gramsci would argue. Their role becomes that of changing the a-critical, a-political, a-philosophical, and superstitious 'conceptions of the world' prevailing among subaltern classes, such as 'common sense,' 'folklore,' and 'religion,' and guiding them to a conception of the world, historically more integral and universal, which is the philosophy of praxis.[46]

> The philosophy of praxis does not tend to leave the 'simple' in their primitive philosophy of common sense, but rather to lead them to a higher conception of life....Consciousness of being a part of a particular hegemonic force (that is to say, political consciousness) is the first stage toward a further progressive self-consciousness in which theory and practice will finally be one.

In this perspective, class conflict becomes for Gramsci the visible conflict of another more profound type of conflict, that is the confrontation between rival Weltanschauungen. The cognitive process thus becomes an integral part of social conflicts and cannot be analyzed independently from their reality.

2 THE SPECIFICITY OF MARXIST SOCIOLOGY IN GRAMSCI'S THEORY

Among Marxist theoreticians, Antonio Gramsci is one of the few to lament the theoretical degeneration of Marxist theory and predict its final demise resulting from its intellectual capitulation to the canons of Western positivism. It can be said that Alvin Gouldner's warning of the coming crisis of Western sociology and Marxism, as functionalism continues its victorious march to the East, had already been given and forecast more than forty years earlier by Gramsci in his 'Il Materialismo Storico,' written in a much different general intellectual, cultural and political context.[1] For Gouldner, the theoretical source of such a crisis in sociology is found in the culmination of classical positivism in Parsonian structural-functionalism – the most general theory of social systems legitimating the perfection of the capitalist social structure, and within Marxism in its sympathetic acceptance among those in the Soviet Bloc whose attention is centered on the problem of spontaneous mechanisms conducive to social stability.[2] For Gramsci, the theoretical crisis in Marxism is precipitated by the attempts made by some, such as Bukharin, to develop the most general 'model' of analysis of social systems according to the principles and deterministic laws of evolutionist positivism. Such attempts have obscured and eliminated the critical and revolutionary components of Marxist theory, and encouraged its 'schematization' and 'academization.'

Sociology and Marxism, in the view of Gramsci, have reached a state of intellectual stagnation. Both have abandoned their original ideological function and have embraced, or are in the process of embracing, a positivistic, framework. Positivist sociology, in particular, is engaged in detailed description of human behavior, institutional sectors of social systems, and ephemeral social phenomena. It has become a practical, useful and a-moral social science, an a-philosophical, a-critical, a-political and a-historical science of society. Gramsci characterizes it as the 'philosophy of non-philosophers.'[3] As a result, sociological thought is no longer dialectical, or a form of practical activity, but positivistic and scientific. Its ultimate validation is provided by the experience of carefully circum-scribed facts, analyzed according to the scientific laws and principles characteristic of the physical and natural sciences. Positivist thought is essentially affirmative thought, affirmative of a given state of affairs, totally committed to a given societal framework, and distrustful of the possibility of new social

arrangements.[4] This positivist thought, to be sure, does not
suppress critical ideas. Instead, it diverts the focus of the
critique from the whole to the parts of a given system, and
serves to defocalize the fundamentally ideological dimensions
of social reality. Thus, to use a well-known Marcusean expression, empirical, analytical sociology clearly assumes a thera-
peutic function. Endlessly engaged in minute analysis of
social reality, sociologists have necessarily become critical of
elements or parts of social systems, advocating changes or
modification in these parts. They have remained, as a consequence, apathetic or unintendedly sympathetic toward the
totality of the social structure, a totality which is either taken
for granted or at least conceived as non-problematic. The
French sociologist Raymond Aron has admirably described the
ideological implications of American analytical sociology. He
writes: 'when one undertakes a concrete, detailed study of
social institutions, one becomes critical in detail and forgets
about total negation.'[5]

These characteristic features of positivist sociology are
becoming increasingly apparent in Marxist sociology. Yet, as
social theorists have pointed out, Marxism from its origins has
constituted an intellectual system antithetical to positivism,
designed to cope with the phenomenon of radical transformation
generated by the French Revolution.[6]

The French Revolution undermined and liquidated the power
of traditional aristocracies, instituting in its place the power of
the new elite typified by the newly emerged industrial and
commercial classes. The institutionalization of such a technological elite entailed a polarization of society into bourgeois
and proletarian classes, and a radical transformation of the
nature of scientific thought, that is, a politicization of science.
If science, in nature, was capable of discovering certain
regularities and establishing necessary laws of development
ensuring order and predictability of physical events, could
not a 'science of society' reveal similar laws in the socio-
cultural universe? The precarious foundation of the new
industrial order then necessitated a sociology capable of stabi-
lizing its base. Positivist sociology thus became the theoretical
legitimation of the monopolistic political and economic practices
of the bourgeois social order. Similarly, Marxist sociology
emerged as a response to the needs of those classes which had
been betrayed by the ruling bourgeoisie. It sought, through
the establishment of a 'science of society,' to determine the
causes of existing class relations, as well as the laws of the
historical development, in order to bring about changes in the
established class-based social arrangements. Both sociologies
were then ideological systems affirming antithetical societal
frameworks.[7]

In this chapter our attention will focus on the old, but still
unanswered, theoretical question of the relationship between
sociology and Marxism. What is sociology in a Marxist sense?

What are its characteristic features and its dominant theoretical
and methodological concerns? Are sociology and historical
materialism, in the Marxist universe of discourse, identical
concepts? If not, what is the specificity of sociology within
the general framework of Marxist theory? Gramsci, we think
is among the first Marxist theoreticians to raise such questions,
and among the first Marxists to attempt to provide a systematic
answer to them. In his massive theoretical undertaking, he
developed a systematic critique of positivist sociology and
positivist Marxism with the purpose of rescuing 'critical'
Marxism from its state of theoretical degeneration.

We will first present the fundamental components of Gramsci's
critique of all social sciences in general, and sociology in
particular. Second, an attempt will be made to delineate the
basic framework of a Gramscian Marxist sociology.

THEORETICAL SPECIFICITY OF SOCIOLOGY WITHIN MARXISM: GRAMSCI'S CRITIQUE OF POSITIVIST THOUGHT AND METHODOLOGY

Gramsci knew only one type of sociology, that which had been
elaborated by classical social theorists such as Montesquieu,
Comte, Spencer, and Durkheim. The basic presupposition of
such organic, positivist, and evolutionist sociology is that
societies, despite the diversity of their cultures, traditions,
and forms of social organization, obey an essential, objective,
metaphysical order. They reveal a body of verifiable and fixed
laws which bind their structural elements into a harmonious
whole. Thus, sociological knowledge, by revealing such a body
of necessary laws, could enable man to determine not only what
is, but also, and more importantly, what should be and will
be.

Italian sociology, that which Gramsci knew, was dominated
by a vulgar brand of evolutionist positivism, a form of
a-historical and a-philosophical social Darwinism. Greatly
infatuated with the progress of natural and physical sciences,
Italian sociologists sought to explain socio-cultural phenomena
with criteria, concepts, and techniques derived from these
sciences. Gramsci notes that one needs only to read the
sociological works of Sergi, Sighele, Carli, Niceforo, and
Loria to convince oneself of the degeneration of sociological
theorizing.[8] A. Niceforo, for instance, attributed the general
backwardness of southern Italy to innate predispositions
and differences of the southern population. Problems of poverty,
crime, and illegitimacy were commonly explained in terms of
its 'organic' and 'biological incapacity' to develop higher forms
of social life. These widespread opinions 'were consolidated
and actually theorized by the sociologists of positivism...
acquiring the strength of "scientific truth" in a period of
superstition about science.'[9]

It was such degeneration of the social sciences that prompted Gramsci to pose the problem of their definition, methods, and relationship to Marxism.

For Gramsci, a global and structural Marxist analysis of society is characterized by three constituent elements: philosophy, politics, and economics. These intellectual activities are the 'necessary constituent elements of the same conception of the world,' and therefore, 'there must necessarily be, in their theoretical principles, a convertibility from one to the others and a reciprocal translation into the specific language proper to each constituent element.'[10] Historical materialism is the universal theory of history, assuming the concrete form of political economy, science of politics, and philosophy. It provides a common principle which unifies the specific theoretical principles of these activities. Such a unifying principle is, for Gramsci, the 'dialectical development of the contradictions between man and matter (nature-material forces of production).'[11] The unitary principle has to be apprehended in its specificity in the science of political economy, in the science of politics and philosophy. In economics the dialectical relation of man to nature is apprehended as the dialectical relationship between the worker and the productive forces of society. In the science of politics it is the dialectical relationship between the state and the civil society; that is to say, the dialectical struggle of man against nature for the development of productive forces takes the form of a political conflict between the ruling classes, organized as the state, and the civil society. Finally, in philosophy the dialectic between man and nature becomes the dialectic between theory and praxis for the intellectual domination of society.[12]

For Gramsci, then, the relationship between Marxism and these three activities is clearly that of a global theory to a specific, concrete theory. They are theoretically interdependent. Their specificity can be apprehended only on an intellectual and speculative level. Outside Marxist Theory, these activities claim an autonomous existence by adhering to strict scientific, positivist principles. Incorporated in a Marxist framework, however, they retain only a relative autonomy; they are historicized and transformed into 'critical economy,' 'critical science of politics,' and 'critical philosophy.'[13]

Bourgeois political economy, for instance, in analyzing specific economic systems seeks to determine 'specific decisive and permanent forces' and their 'spontaneous automatism,' that is, their independence from individual choices. Gramsci writes,[14]

> The scientist has, by way of hypothesis, rendered the automatism absolute; he has isolated the merely economic facts from the combinations of varying importance in which they present themselves in reality; he has established relations of cause and effect, of premises and conclusions; and he has thus produced an abstract scheme of a determined

economic society.

In contrast, critical economy, within Marxism, begins with the analysis of the historicist character of a 'determined market,' it analyses the relations of forces determining the market, that is, their contradictions, and, as Gramsci puts it, it 'evaluates the possibilities of modification connected with the appearance and strengthening of new elements and puts forward the "transitory" and "replaceable" nature of the science being criticized...'[15]

Similarly, a positivist science of politics is the science of political intrigues and compromises, the science of political maneuvers, while a critical science of politics, within Marxist theory, concerns itself with the problem of creation of new states, the mode of formation of 'collective will,' and new historical alternatives of political and intellectual hegemony. In sum, a critical science of politics is the science of political activity aiming at the creation of new hegemonic systems. The characterization of science as political activity is uniquely Gramscian:[16]

> The problem of 'science' itself has to be posed. Is not science itself 'political activity,' and political thought, in as much as it transforms men, and makes them different from what they were before?...And does the concept of science as 'creation' not then mean that it too is 'politics?' Everything depends on seeing whether the creation involved is 'arbitrary,' or whether it is rational - i.e. 'useful' to men.

What about sociology in Gramsci's conception of social sciences? What is its place within Marxist theory? It can be said that of all social sciences, sociology constitutes the target of the most rigorous critique in so far as it represents for him the most sophisticated intellectual system attempting to negate Marxism in its totality.

In the history of Marxist thought Bukharin has been among the first prominent theoreticians to posit a complete identification between Marxism and sociology. In his 'Manual of Popular Sociology' he defended the position that Marxism can be reduced to a sociology, in the sense that it can be schematized into a body of necessary, regular and objective laws capable of explaining the development of the historical process, a sort of catechism containing the basic concepts and rules of political conduct for subaltern classes aspiring to their political emancipation from bourgeois hegemony.[17] Such a theoretical position led to the development of positivist Marxism. For Gramsci, the acceptance of such a positivist branch of Marxism would legitimate the historical passivity of the masses. On the contrary, the real task of Marxism is that of raising the cultural and intellectual level of the masses and making them historically active and conscious participants in the process of political and social change.[18]

Gramsci's critique of positivist Marxism entails first, a critique of bourgeois positivist sociology, a critique of the very notion of science and the validity of statistical laws.

Critique of positivist sociology and its methodology
Positivist sociology, as it has been seen, has become the
'philosophy of non-philosophers,' in so far as it represents
an attempt to provide a schematic description and classification
of social facts according to criteria of established validity
among the natural and physical sciences, an attempt to derive
experimentally the laws of evolution of society. As Gramsci
notes, however, social phenomena cannot be analyzed in the
same manner as natural phenomena. Natural phenomena exist
and operate independently of any philosophical system, while
social phenomena emerge and develop in human conscious
activity. Sociology, then, has to explain the relationship
between consciousness and reality; that is, it has to occupy
itself with philosophical questions. The description and classification of social phenomena as advocated by early sociologists
such as Comte, Spencer, and Durkheim proves to be a futile
enterprise if it is not incorporated into a philosophical system.
Positivist sociology, unable to tackle the problem of the relationship between social consciousness and reality, limits itself
to the description and classification of social phenomena, which
necessarily requires a constant concern with the methodological
questions and a continuous preoccupation with perfecting
statistical operations.

In a general Marxist Weltanschauung, sociology can claim a
logic and a specific structure of its own only if it espouses a
'historical' methodology. Historicism does not preclude the
legitimate endeavor to search for the so-called laws of
uniformity and regularity, that is, statistical laws. As Gramsci
observes, however, statistical laws are not necessary laws as
positivists claim; they simply are approximations of constants
in the historical development. Sociological laws, to the extent
that they are a-historical and a-philosophical, are mechanistic, deterministic laws, implying the belief that human
behavior is regulated by forces operating independently from
human will. If sociology then is conceived as a science seeking
the establishment of necessary and objective laws, it tends
to eliminate from social analysis the most important deter-
minants of human behavior, to wit, human volition and human
initiative.

For Gramsci, sociological laws are essentially historical laws.
Their validity is directly proportional to the political involvement of the masses. Only when the masses are historically
unconscious, a-critical and inactive, do conditions exist for
the development of a science of social behavior. Put simply,
the political and social passivity of the masses enhances the
chances of predictability of their behavior. Consequently, the
triumph of positivist thought is a function of the general
passivity and unconsciousness of the masses. In those historical conditions in which the masses acquire 'political critical

consciousness,' the mechanicity of their behavior, and as a consequence the validity of statistical laws, is eliminated. Gramsci means precisely this when he writes:[19]

> It should be observed that political action tends precisely to rouse the masses from passivity, in other words to destroy the law of large numbers....But the fact has not been properly emphasized that statistical laws can be employed in the science and art of politics only so long as the great masses of the population remain (or at least are reputed to remain) essentially passive, in relation to the questions which interest historians and politicians....With the extension of mass parties and their organic coalescence with the intimate (economic-productive) life of the masses themselves, the process whereby popular feeling is standardized ceases to be mechanical and causal (that is produced by the conditioning of environmental factors and the like) and becomes conscious and critical.

Thus, the basic error of positivist sociology can be said to lie, for Gramsci, in the separation of 'cognition' from 'praxis.' Knowledge and scientific forecast are held to be neutral and value-free. But when knowledge becomes mass-produced, does it not determine fundamental changes in human conduct? Scientific knowledge is then not independent from reality, but is an element of it. The search for causal relationships, uniformities, and regularities in social analysis is connected with the need to resolve in a peremptory way the practical problem of predictability of social phenomena.[20] What science can predict is only the existence of conflicts and societal contradictions, Gramsci writes, and not the outcome, which always depends upon the fluctuation of organized collective will.[21]

> In reality one can 'scientifically' foresee only the struggle. ...In reality one can 'foresee' to the extent that one acts, to the extent that one applies a voluntary effort and therefore contributes concretely to creating the result 'foreseen.' Prediction reveals itself thus not as a scientific act of knowledge, but as the abstract expression of the effort made, the practical way of creating a collective will.

In sum, despite the pretensions of sociologists, laws of causation simply do not exist. Reality is a moving process, always changing under the pressure of contradictory forces. Dialectical development does not and cannot admit the existence of regular, necessary laws.[22]

> The so-called laws of sociology which are assumed as laws of causation...have no causal value: they are almost always tautologies and paralogisms. Usually they are no more than a duplicate of the observed fact itself. A fact or a series of facts is described according to a mechanical process of abstract generalization, a relationship of similarity is derived from this and given the title of law and the law is then assumed to have causal value. But what novelty is there in

that? The only novelty is the collective name given to a
series of petty facts, but names are not innovation.

In conclusion, Gramsci's general critique of bourgeois
positivist sociology seems to have a common denominator. The
notion of the existence of abstract forces in history is the
result of the political passivity of the masses. When there
is no collective will, there is no political activity but automatism of laws. Indifference and passivity foster fatalistic,
deterministic, and scientific outlooks. Gramsci's revolutionary
idea would then be the substitution of human passivity
with conscious critical activity, the only force capable of
breaking up the laws or pseudo-laws of social science in
general and sociology in particular. The radical implication
of this concept is that, for Gramsci, the final demise of
Western positivist sociology will occur when the masses will
acquire 'critical consciousness,' and act according to their
politicized will.

Positivist sociology, however, has outlived its usefulness,
but, Gramsci observes, Marxism recognizes and appreciates
the fact that it has played a historically useful role in giving
to European philosophical thought, enveloped in an abstract
and metaphysical idealism, a sense of reality and concreteness.
In so doing, positivist thought has fallen into the other
extreme of enclosing 'reality' in a body of fixed laws, making
it a 'dead thing,' an external facticity; it has reduced social
sciences to a form of materalist theology by elevating social
laws to the level of transcendental, metaphysical, and quasi-
religious status, that is, to the level of science.

To positivist sociology Gramsci opposes a historicist and
humanist Marxist Weltanschauung as the only conception
capable of historicizing the totality of social reality and asserting the primacy of human values over the automatism of social
laws predicated by science.[23]

As has been noted above, Gramsci's critique of positivist
sociology is not dictated by sheer academic intellectualism; it
has to be considered as the basis for a more systematic critique
of 'vulgar' Marxism.

*Critique of positivist Marxism: the doctrine of the inertia of
popular masses*

Any brand of Marxism which accepts implicitly or explicitly
all or any canon of positivism is for Gramsci a vulgar Marxism.
As we have briefly noted, the representative spokesman of
this trend of thought has been the Russian theoretician Nikolai
Bukharin. His interpretation and vulgarization of Marxian
thought is submitted by Gramsci to a theoretical and historical
critique.

Starting from the assumption of a necessary metaphysical
distinction between general laws and particular laws of
development, Bukharin attempted to establish a typology of
necessary laws in nature as well as in human societies. His

'Manual of Sociology' seeks to elaborate a body of universal
principles and laws of regularity and causality and proceeds
to establish a typology of societies and their relative development.[24]

The complexity of social reality, Bukharin argues, legitimates
the existence of a variety of social sciences within the Marxist
perspective. Two of them are of paramount importance: history
and sociology. History investigates and describes the current
life as it has flowed at a certain time and in a certain place;
sociology, on the other hand, attempts to explain the functioning of society by establishing the 'relation of various
groups of social phenomena (economic, legal, scientific) with
each other.' Sociology is then conceived as the most general
of social sciences, being a 'theory of the historical process.'
Thus, a close relationship is posited between history and
sociology. Sociology is the only methodology of history. 'Since
sociology explains the general laws of human evolution, it
serves as a method for history.'[25]

Gramsci refutes Bukharin's reduction of Marxism to sociology.
To admit the existence of concepts of law, causality, necessity,
etc., signifies acceptance of the positivist faith in the validity
of the scientific method, which implies the admission of the
existence of an extra-historical 'objectivity,' conditioning
human activity, but not being conditioned by it. Gramsci
argues that outside history there is not objective reality.
Objectivity is both historicist and humanist in its essence;
that is, objective reality is always a historical process constantly
subordinated to man's manipulation and classification. 'We know
reality only in relation to man, and since man is historically
becoming, knowledge and reality are also a becoming and so
is objectivity.'[26]

If Marxism is reduced to sociology, the very nature of its
doctrine and its conception of the proletariat as the protagonist
of history finds itself deformed. Thus Marxism becomes a
fatalist doctrine of the inertia of the proletariat. Positivist
Marxism's insistence on the idea that the historical process
develops according to objective, necessary sociological laws
tends to negate the unpredictability of human volition and
events. It becomes a doctrine latently functioning in such a
way as to maintain the masses in their simplicity, indifference,
and passivity. In contrast, critical Marxism is an ideological
system aiming at intellectually 'organizing' the experiences of
the masses, and 'transforming' their consciousness. In this
context Gramsci writes:[27]

> When you don't have the initiative in the struggle and the
> struggle itself comes eventually to be identified with a series
> of defeats, mechanical determinism becomes a tremendous
> force of moral resistance, of cohesion, and of patience and
> obstinate perseverance....The tide of history is working for
> me in the long term.

The ideological function of Positivism is analogous to that

of organized religions. The success of the Christian religion,
for instance, in monopolizing the process of legitimation of the
totality of the social order lies in its acceptance by the masses
as a necessity, as a necessary form of rationalization of the
world. That is to say, the strength of religion, its ultimate
power and authority in legitimating reality, is a function of
the passivity of the masses.[28] It is this kind of philosophy that
underlies Bukharin's intellectual reduction of Marxism to
positivist sociology. Positivist sociology represents the most
powerful contemporary theory aiming at restricting human
activity; it has become an instrument of control of the behavior
of the masses, a science which attempts to develop knowledge
not for the sake of restoring human values, but to further
predict and standardize human behavior. By explaining behavior
and social phenomena in socio-historical terms, it serves to
reduce and disperse individual responsibilities in a form of
abstract social responsibilities.

Gramsci's critique of positivist Marxism contains also a
unique evaluation of specific historical events. Positivist
Marxism proves itself unable to analyze the historical significance of proletarian revolutions in the world. Bukharin,
for instance, subscribing to the principles of the Second
International believed that revolutions materialize only in those
societies in which capitalism has attained the highest degree
of development; that is, socialism is the end result of internal
contradictions accumulated within the capitalist economy. The
Revolution of 1917 in Russia represents the most clear evidence
of such naive historical determinism, Gramsci writes.[29] The
Russian Revolution is the result, not of the explosion of
accumulated contradictions within the capitalist economy, but
rather the result of an organized collective action that no
sociological law could ever have foreseen. This event confirms
for Gramsci the validity of critical Marxism. In ultimate
analysis, science does not produce significant political changes,
only collective and conscious human activity can bring about
such changes. Gramsci's Marxism is unequivocably activistic
in so far as it celebrates and defends the active role of man in
shaping history according to his own needs.

In sum, within the Gramscian perspective, the real object
of all social sciences, and sociology in particular, is the
analysis of the formation of collective action of subaltern classes
in their attempt to conquer political and ideological hegemony.

THE STRUCTURE OF MARXIST SOCIOLOGY IN GRAMSCI'S THEORY

It would seem paradoxical at first glance to search for a basic
structure of Marxist sociology in the anti-sociological writings
of Gramsci. Nevertheless, the few sociologists who have studied
and analyzed the sociological aspects of Gramsci's theory have

pointed out that Gramsci's rejection of bourgeois sociology does
not entail a rejection of the possibility of the existence of
sociology within a Marxist perspective.[30] As it has been shown,
what Gramsci in effect criticizes is the abstract, reactionary,
and ideological function of positivism; therefore, sociology,
while it has to renounce its ambitions of elaborating a system
of absolute and objective laws, can significantly contribute to
the understanding of the origins, conditions, and importance
of socio-cultural systems. Every society possesses its own
system of rationality. Sociology is called upon to discover it,
ideologize it, and substitute it with a system of rationality
which benefits the entire civil society.[31]

> It is not a question of 'discovering' a metaphysical law of
> 'determinism,' or even of establishing a 'general' law of
> causality. It is a question of bringing out how in historical
> evolution relatively permanent forces are constituted which
> operate with a certain regularity and automatism.

Gramsci, it is worth noting, speaks of a certain regularity
and relative permanent forces in the development of history.
Therefore, nothing seems to oppose the possibility of existence
of an autonomous science of society, a critical sociology along-
side economics, and critical science of politics within the
general framework of critical Marxism. Such a sociology has to
be, Pizzorno explains, a political sociology, a science which
analyzes the conditions in which subaltern groups form,
crystallize, and function in a given historical bloc, more
specifically the process of formation of a given 'collective will.'[32]
Gramsci does not limit himself to the discussion of the definition
of a political sociology. He also suggests criteria, principles
of research and interpretation for such analysis. His approach
is best characterized as historical and dialectical. The best
illustration of his conception of an historical approach may be
found, in our opinion, in his study of 'relations of force,' the
analysis of specific historical blocs, and the problem of formation of new ones.[33]

Relations of forces within a given social structure

The genesis of any social group is always characterized by a
certain relationship to the means of production.[34] Its point of
arrival is always the conquest of cultural and political hegemony,
that concrete historical moment when a given social group
becomes the unifying and directing force of all other social
groups. The Jacobin experience can be characterized as the
global development of a specific social group (bourgeoisie),
which, born with a specific economic function in the world of
production, constituted itself in the process of its development
as an ethico-political will, a hegemonic force within the total
structure of French society.[35] At its inception, the representative of a specific social group (bourgeoisie) operated in virtue

of its advanced economic position; subsequently, once
constituted into an organized force, it tended to conceive
itself as the hegemonic group of all popular forces. The strength
and success of the Jacobin experience lay precisely in the
ability of such an avant-garde group to be perceived by all
subaltern classes as the representative of their aspirations,
and in its capacity to actually fuse its interests with the
interests of such classes. Jacobinism is for Gramsci the
political activity of an avant-garde revolutionary group aiming
at political hegemony. The Jacobin experience has always been
absent in the history of certain countries, such as Italy, and
yet it is the only force capable of organizing a 'national popular
collective will.' Marxism, of course, in Gramsci's view is called
upon to assume such an historical mission in the formation of
a new historical bloc.

The Jacobin experience demonstrates the fact that a social
class as an economic force alone is incapable of exercising
hegemony and creating a new state, in as much as it lacks
'intellectual and moral prestige.' A catharsis has to take place,
to wit, a passage from a mere economic, egotistical and
passional phase to an ethico-political one. This catharsis implies
the 'superior elaboration of the structure into the superstructure in the minds of men.'[36] Thus, any given social group
has to abandon the particularistic and economistic interests
characterizing its origins, and has to become a hegemonic
force over the national collectivity. In this respect, the acquisition of political consciousness by the subaltern classes, the
elaboration of their political and intellectual elite, the creation
of a political party, and the development of a new Weltanschauung
become clearly for Gramsci the superstructural elements of the
greatest sociological importance.

An historical analysis of the transition from infrastructural
to superstructural activity can be properly conducted only
if the study of relations of forces is taken into account. Such
relations of forces represent the various phases attained by
'essential' or 'fundamental' social groups in their development
toward hegemony.

Economic phase   Various social groups, as we have noted,
come into existence as economic-corporate entities with a specific
function and position in the world of production. The nature
of these relations varies, and depends upon the development
of the material forces of production. For Gramsci, the analysis
of the origin and development of the economic structure provides the necessary clues for the understanding of the problem
of the origin and development of fundamental social classes.
Nevertheless, this does not imply a one-sided economistic
interpretation of the historical process, the belief that the
demise of capitalism is the result of essential contradictions
within the economic system. Political transformation of society
and the realism of historical alternatives will always depend

upon the development of the modes of production, but the
economic phase has to be transcended by the political phase.[37]

Political phase   Relations of political forces permit the identification of various degrees of homogeneity and political consciousness attained by potentially hegemonic groups. The first is
the economic-corporate level. This represents the case in
which members of the specific professional groups (tradesmen,
manufacturers, etc.) become conscious of their unity and
homogeneity, but they do not feel any solidarity with other
professional groups of the same social class, for instance, the
tradesmen with the manufacturers. At this stage subaltern
classes are characterized by an elementary form of organization and autonomy, but their consciousness is still limited to
the economic interests of members of the trade. The second
level is that of class solidarity or trade unionism, in which
'consciousness is reached of the solidarity of interests among
all the members of a social class-but still in the purely economic
field.'[38] A negative element, the egotistical, economic interests
of class, is the basis of class solidarity. As a result, a given
class accepts the fundamental political, economic, and cultural
structures of dominant classes; it will participate in the
legislative process, and struggle for certain immediate, specific
reforms. This is a true reformist stage, in which not the power
of the state but the modalities of its exercise are questioned,
Gramsci writes.

Hegemonic phase   A class develops political solidarity: 'one
becomes aware that one's own corporate interests, in their
present and future development, transcend the corporate
limits of the mere economic class, and can and must become
the interests of other subordinate groups too.'[39] This is the
stage in which a given social group organized in a political
party becomes the state, and tends to expand throughout
the civil society by creating an intellectual, moral, cultural,
political, and economic unity.[40]

> It is true that the State is seen as the organ of one particular
> group....But the development and expansion of the parti-
> cular group are conceived of, and presented as being the
> motor force of a universal expansion....In other words, the
> dominant group is coordinated completely with the general
> interests of the subordinate groups.

This is the phase in which an historical bloc is created. An
historical bloc is precisely that situation in which a group has
become hegemonic and extends its hegemony over all other
subaltern groups.

Analysis of historical blocs
The concepts of 'organic integration' and 'organic crisis'
provide a useful theoretical framework for the understanding
of the dynamics of concrete social structures in relation to the

growth of a hegemonic group within them. Marx has been
among the first to explain the historical division of society into
classes in constant conflict with each other by attributing it
to their conflicting relation to the means of production. For
Gramsci, this contention is incomplete. The case of southern
Italy illustrates his point. The historical conflicts which have
opposed the industrial bourgeoisie and the proletariat, the
working class of northern Italy and the peasantry of the south,
have not been conflicts between groups with opposing economic
interests, but rather groups with global interests struggling
among themselves to assume the ideological and political control
of society. Their expansion has no limits; it tends to embrace
all civil society by gradually absorbing into their orbit all other
subaltern classes, and eventually proceeding toward the
realization of the structural and cultural unification of the
world. In sum, each class is a Jacobin force, a potentially
hegemonic force. A group can be said to be hegemonic when
it has succeeded in creating an organically integrated society.

Social integration is the result of organic relations established
between the state and the civil society. In the case of the
French Revolution, the bourgeoisie, by becoming the motor
force of political hegemony, was able to create an historical
unity precisely by attracting into its orbit all subaltern groups
and their respective elites by consensus rather than force.
Such a state of integration, created by the bourgeoisie
organized in the state, Gramsci notes, is only apparent since
the subaltern classes 'by definition are not unified and cannot
unite until they are able to become a "State": their history,
therefore, is intertwined with that of civil society, and thereby
with the history of States and groups of States.'[41] The masses,
whether they have been absorbed in the general ideology of
society (ruling class) or consented to it, are always a potentially disruptive force within a given historical bloc. They are
essentially a potential state within a state, constantly developing until they become a force of political activity, that is,
ideologically and politically hegemonic. More generally, any
social group which aims at its political autonomy constitutes
a potential danger to the organicity of any historical bloc, its
ultimate goal being the creation of a new historical bloc.

Organic crises thus occur as a result of contradictions which
accumulate over time within a specific historical bloc, offsetting
the institutionalized equilibrium of forces. Organic crises, in
Gramsci's theory, are always hegemonic crises. They are
produced by two types of situations: the failure of the ruling-
class politics and the sudden politicization of subaltern classes.
A typical example of the former is war. The Russian Revolution,
Gramsci writes, radically changed the psychology of the
peasants; it concentrated masses of individuals, thus fostering
working-class consciousness. The spontaneous mass revolt
of southern Italian peasants is an historical example of the
latter. Peasants have been traditionally a-political, passive,

and a marginal social stratum, typically lacking 'class consciousness.' Such spontaneous mass movements were inorganic
because they were characterized by a sudden transition from
an economic-corporate state to political activity without the
intermediary of a long process of organization, and development of class consciousness. Inorganic movements normally
fail under pressure from reactionary movements. In contrast,
only organic movements, organized, politically conscious,
equipped with an ideology, and hegemonic in their aspirations,
can resolve organic crises in favor of subaltern classes. In
this context Gramsci's distinction between conjunctural and
organic phenomena is heuristically useful.

Conjunctural phenomena denote a momentary period of crisis
which gives rise to a political strategy of limited significance,
consisting of 'minor political criticism,' and always subjected
to political leaders with government responsibilities. Organic
phenomena, in contrast, refer to a long-range strategy to
restore the political and ideological hegemony within a given
historical bloc. Revolutions will be successful to the extent
that they are based on organic movements of masses. Nevertheless, subaltern classes, before they attain political hegemony,
have to pose and solve the problem of the formation of a new
historical bloc.

*Superstructural activities and the process of formation of
a new historical bloc*
As has been noted, a historical bloc is an historical situation
in which a given 'essential' social group exercises ideological
and political hegemony. It follows that the problem of creation
of a new historical bloc is essentially that of creating a new
hegemonic system. The constitution of a new historical bloc
is not, for Gramsci, a mechanical, automatic process, but
rather a process of intense political activity of subaltern classes.
The revolutionary process takes the form of a struggle for
ideological hegemony as well as political control, that is, the
conquest of state power. In this context the role of intellectuals
and the political party are of fundamental importance.

Ideological hegemony   The problem of socialist revolution in
the industrialized countries of the West, for Gramsci, poses
itself as a struggle for ideological hegemony.[42] In those
historical conditions in which political power resides in the
hands of a well-organized dominant group, the subaltern classes
under the leadership of a politically organized working class
can exercise ideological hegemony well before attaining political
hegemony by a process of withdrawal from bourgeois hegemony.
The ideological erosion of the bourgeois society in all its
aspects - economic, political, and cultural - has to be accom-
panied by the creation of an all-encompassing Weltanschauung,
a new system of ideas, beliefs, and values. The type of
revolution, Gramsci observes, is always dependent upon specific

historical conditions. These conditions are not structural but superstructural in character. They consist of the varying degree of development of either the civil society or the political society (state).[43]

It is an historical fact that revolutions in the East have been successful, while in the West they have failed. The failure of revolutions in the West cannot be explained in terms of the non-ripeness of objective economic conditions. Gramsci's explanation takes into account the different degree of development of superstructural elements. He writes:[44]

> In Russia the State was everything, civil society was primordial and gelatinous; in the West, there was a proper relation between State and civil society, and when the State trembled a sturdy structure of civil society was at once revealed. The State was only an outer ditch, behind which there stood a powerful system of fortresses and earthworks.

As a result, in those historical conditions in which the civil society is strong, the struggle of subaltern classes had to take the form of a 'war of positions,' that of ideological confrontation with dominant classes. On the other hand, in historical situations in which the civil society is 'primitive and gelatinous,' the struggle has to take the form of a 'war of movements,' which is essentially a politico-military struggle. Both types of strategies involve an attack on two monolithic blocs. In Western countries the civil society is highly organized on the level of consciousness, and on the level of ideology, thus it has managed to absorb into its orbit the intellectuals and the leaders of subaltern classes. The struggle, therefore, has to be directed against the civil society and not the political society. Failure to adopt such a strategy will inevitably result in the defeat of the revolutionary process. Again, the French Revolution provides Gramsci with the model for proletarian revolutionary strategy. The struggle of the bourgeoisie against the aristocracy was, in fact, primarily an ideological struggle (Reformation-Enlightenment), aiming at the disintegration of the intellectual bloc of the dominant class well before it launched a political and military attack for the conquest of state power. Consequently, if in the West the struggle has to be primarily ideological, one understands the extreme importance that Gramsci attaches to the role of the intellectuals.

Organic intellectuals and traditional intellectuals   The intellectuals are the functionaries of the superstructure.[45] Born as specialized categories in the world of production, they become the deputies of the administration of social hegemony.[46] Their function is that of elaborating the ideology of the dominant group, of providing awareness of its role, and of transforming it into a conception of the world, which has to diffuse itself throughout society. These *organic* intellectuals – organic for they constitute an organic link between the social class they represent and the superstructure – are those of the dominant classes. In non-industrialized countries they are in opposition to *traditional* intellectuals who represent a historical continuity uninterrupted even by the most complicated and radical changes in political and social forms. Any social group attempting the conquest of power has to absorb such intellectuals. This process is relatively easy, Gramsci notes, in the case of 'isolated rural intellectuals,' organically integrated into the mass of peasants, and the petite bourgeoisie, not yet transformed by the capitalist system; but it encounters formidable resistance in the case of 'traditional' intellectuals, organized in a sort of caste such as the clergy, which the bourgeoisie has to confront for the control of the civil society. The case of the 'agrarian bloc' of southern Italy is Gramsci's favorite illustration of the organic integration of the intellectual bloc and a historical bloc.

The agrarian bloc of southern Italy at the beginning of the twentieth century consisted of three strata: the mass of peasants, the petite bourgeoisie, and the dominant landowning class. The petite bourgeoisie produced the organic intellectuals of the peasantry, but in effect they controlled it by imposing upon it a system which was that of the ruling bourgeoisie. They were not born out of the peasantry, but came from the ranks of the petite bourgeoisie; thus their economic function could not be but contrary to the interests of the class they represented. Their link with the dominant class is assured by a hierarchically structured intellectual bloc directly or indirectly controlled by a very limited number of influential intellectuals. Benedetto Croce and Giustino Fortunato were typical examples of such intellectuals. With their prestige, their cosmopolitan influence, they were able to control subaltern intellectuals, channel their aspirations, and assure the solidarity of the hegemonic system simply by preventing the disintegration of the intellectual bloc. It follows that any attempt by a subaltern class to create a new hegemonic system will be successful to the extent that it is able to create new 'organic' intellectuals.[47]

One of the most important characteristics of any group that is developing towards dominance is its struggle to assimilate and to conquer 'ideologically' the traditional intellectuals, but this assimilation and conquest is made quicker and more efficacious the most the group in question succeeds in simultaneously elaborating its own organic intellectuals.

The party: the 'collective intellectual'
The analysis of the nature and functions of the party in the process of formation of new historical blocs is generally considered the central theme of Gramsci's writings. Indeed, a large part of Gramsci's intellectual and political activities was devoted to the task of organizing a strong cohesive and well-

disciplined Communist Party in Italy. Gramsci's conception of the party, in our opinion, will be more fully understood if it is subordinated to more general and central themes. The party / masses relationship, which concerned most political theorists of the beginning of this century, namely Sorel, Michels, Mosca, Croce, and Lenin, is analyzed by Gramsci in a subtle and original manner. While Lenin emphasized the first element of the relationship, Gramsci, together with Sorel, although in an opposite perspective, emphasized the second one. Nardone has come the closest to this interpretation by noting that 'the real historiography of a party becomes the history of a reality other than that of the party.'[48] Gramsci's statement that the 'history of a party...can only be the history of a particular social group' is indicative of a novel way of posing questions concerning the problems of the nature and functions of political parties in the dynamics of the historical process.[49]

We have already touched upon the central themes of Gramsci's conception of history, that is the idea of the dynamics of the historical process is characterized by the process of formation of a collective will. The development of history is coextensive with the process of development of 'fundamental social groups' which, born in objective economic and social conditions, transform themselves into hegemonic agents by transcending the particularistic, economistic conditions characterizing their origin. The emergence of a party, in Gramsci's theory, marks the passage of a social group from an economic to a hegemonic phase. It follows that the party is an entity which is secondary to the praxis of a given fundamental social group. In Gramsci's words, it is the instrument by which subaltern groups assert their 'integral autonomy' within a new societal framework.[50]

The party, for Gramsci, Nardone observes, is an entity distinct from the mass or social group not politically conscious and active, but organically and dialectically linked to it in a subsequent phase, that of political consciousness and hegemony.[51] In the first phase the party is an elite, avant-garde, the anticipating experience and foretaste of a future totality, a history in fieri. Its distinction from the mass is greatest when the mass is amorphous, unorganized, not conscious of its universal interests and aspirations. But as soon as the mass becomes politically conscious and attains political and cultural hegemony, the party loses its avant-garde and elitist character. The realization of hegemony, which entails a restructuration and unification of the civil society, is the historical condition in which the party outlives its usefulness. The party loses its character of partiality as it universalizes itself, that is, it identifies with the global interest of society. Thus, what characterizes the party, for Gramsci, is more than a political program to be realized. It is the anticipating experience of the progressive society of the future, the instrument of diffusion of a conception of the world. The party, Gramsci writes, is the 'experimenter' of the new conceptions of the world.[52]

> One should stress the importance and significance which, in
> the modern world, political parties have in the elaboration
> and diffusion of conceptions of the world, because essentially
> what they do is to work out the ethics and the politics cor-
> responding to these conceptions and act as it were as their
> historical 'laboratory.'...For this reason one can say that the
> parties are the elaborators of new integral and totalitarian
> intelligentsias [intellettualità totalitarie] and the crucibles
> where the unification of theory and practice, understood as
> a real historical process, takes place.

Thus, political parties are historical necessities only for those
groups wishing to become hegemonic ones. In relation to the
problem of hegemony, the function of the party is that of
leading a fundamental and progressive social group to cultural
and political hegemony. Describing the political phase of class
consciousness, Gramsci writes:[53]

> it is the phase in which previously germinated ideologies
> become 'party,' come into confrontation and conflict, until
> only one of them, or at least a single combination of them,
> tends to prevail, to gain the upper hand, to propagate
> itself throughout society bringing about not only a unison
> of economic and political aims, but also intellectual and moral
> unity, posing all the questions around which the struggle
> rages not on a corporate but on a 'universal' plane, and thus
> creating the hegemony of a fundamental social group over a
> series of subordinate groups.

The originality of Gramsci's conception of the party becomes
more clear when contrasted with that of Michels, Sorel and
Lenin.[54]

Robert Michels devoted a large portion of his intellectual
activities to invalidating Marxist political theory. He pains-
takingly described the structure and tendencies of European
political parties in order to demonstrate the absurdity and
naïveté of the Marxist concepts of democracy and socialism.
There is an 'iron law,' Michels concludes in his 'Political Parties,'
and this is that 'democracy leads to oligarchy, and necessarily
contains an oligarchical nucleus.' The masses are incapable
of self-governing, for they lack expertise and experience.
'The incompetence of the masses,' he continues, 'is almost
universal throughout the domains of political life, and this
constitutes the most solid foundation of the power of the
leaders.'[55] As a result one will find a circulation of elites or a
reunion of elites in the political process. Gramsci does not
dismiss Michels's characterization of the political party as the
rallying point of masses of men around charismatic leaders.
But he sharply rejects Michels's interpretation of such
phenomenon. The individualist or charismatic analysis of
political parties is valid only when one describes the initial
phase of mass parties. Charismatic leaders, and more generally
oligarchical tendencies, prevail where a static equilibrium

exists, whose decisive factor is 'the immaturity of the progressive forces.'[56] To Michels's oligarchical conception of political
parties Gramsci opposes a Marxist conception of the party
based on an organic and dialectical relationship between the
leadership, the intellectuals and the masses. The party is the
Modern Prince, but in a different sense than that of
Machiavelli.[57]

> The modern prince, the myth-prince, cannot be a real person,
> a concrete individual. It can only be an organism, a complex
> element of society in which a collective will, which has already
> been recognized and has to some extent asserted itself in
> action, begins to take concrete form.

The nature and functions of Gramsci's party are profoundly
different from those theorized by Michels. The party, as conceived by Gramsci, is an association of men sustained by
universal ethical principles, directed by an elite linked by a
myriad of strings to a determinate social grouping and through
this intermediary to all mankind. It represents not an abstract
collectivity of men, in which case the tendencies toward
despotism, bureaucracy and political passivity of the masses
described by Michels would be real. Rather, it represents a
real collective will. 'The collectivity must be understood as the
product of an elaboration of collective will and thought reached
through the concrete effort of individuals, and not through
a fatalist process alien to the individuals: henceforth the
necessity of an internal discipline.'[58]

From a perspective radically different from that of Michels,
the French sociologist Sorel spoke of the masses as the basis
of all political activity, enjoying an integral autonomy and
independence from any form of centralized authority and
organized power, whether this is the state, the party or
political bureaucracy. The masses are opposed to any political
program and notion of party leadership and discipline. The
spontaneity of mass behavior is, for Sorel, the only rational
form of political activity. The proletariat is then a monolithic
bloc which develops spontaneously. It follows that socialist
revolution is a process which develops spontaneously and
molecularly underground and gradually asserts its autonomy
and independence from the existing societal framework.

In response to Sorel, Gramsci opposes the notion of the party
as a collective individual.[59]

> Critical self-consciousness means, historically and politically,
> the creation of an elite of intellectuals. A human mass does
> not 'distinguish' itself, does not become independent in its
> own right without, in the widest sense, organizing itself; and
> there is no organization without intellectuals, that is without
> organizers and leaders...

The modern prince is the most advanced consciousness of
humanity and the revolutionary process. It directs the historical
process through a synthesis of direction and spontaneity.
Spontaneous mass movements, Gramsci adds, are destined to

fail if they do not undergo a long process of organization and develop political leadership. The concept of 'collective intellectual' denotes the fact that the party plays the same role as the organic intellectuals, that of exercising cultural, ideological, and moral direction. The party is the intellectual organism par excellence, Piotte comments, in so far as it concretizes the very notion of the intellectual.[60] The party, however, is not a mechanism superimposed on the masses, as in Lenin, but the expression of popular feelings.

Lenin analyzed the party/masses relationship by emphasizing the crucial role of the party. At the very core of Lenin's revolutionary theory is the idea that the working class cannot spontaneously arrive at class consciousness. Left abandoned, the working class is only capable of developing a trade unionist consciousness, a consciousness of economistic-corporate interests.[61] Revolutionary theory is grounded on profound scientific principles. It developed out of Hegelian dialectics, classical political economy and French socialist theories through the intellectual elaboration of Marx and Engels. They became convinced that the inevitable contradictions of the capitalist system could only be resolved through revolutionary activity and by a class other than the bourgeoisie. Thus, political consciousness and revolutionary doctrine have to be brought to the working class from without, Lenin concludes in his celebrated 'What is to be Done?' Gramsci insists not on the spontaneity of the masses, as Sorel did, or the necessity of the party, as Lenin did, but rather on the dialectical relationship between them. Marxist revolutionary theory is born and develops out of a dialectic between the party and the masses. He writes, 'the popular element "feels" but does not always know or understand; the intellectual element "knows" but does not always understand and in particular does not always feel.'[62] Therefore, the success of the party in creating and consolidating a 'national-popular bloc' lies in the establishment of a dialectical unity with the masses.[63]

> If the relationship between intellectuals and people-nation, between the leaders and the led, the rulers and the ruled, is provided by an organic cohesion in which feeling - passion becomes understanding and thence knowledge..., then and only then is the relationship one of representation.
>
> One cannot make politics-history without this passion, without this sentimental connection between intellectuals and people-nation. In the absence of such a nexus the relations between the intellectual and the people-nation are, or are reduced to, relationships of a purely bureaucratic and formal order.

There has to be, then, integration between the intellectual function of the party and everyday struggles of the masses. The development of the party is dialectically related to the development of self-expression of popular masses. These two, although developing independently, have to converge.[64]

The intellectual stratum develops both quantitatively and qualitatively, but every leap forward towards a new breadth and complexity of the intellectual stratum is tied to an analogous movement on the part of the mass of the 'simple,' who raise themselves to higher levels of culture and at the same time extend their circle of influence towards the stratum of specialized intellectuals...

The crucial dilemma is how to conciliate spontaneity and direction. Gramsci advocates a dialectical unity of 'knowing' and 'feeling,' that is an emotional link between the party and the popular element. Without such a link Marxist theory loses its revolutionary appeal and becomes crystallized in a set of laws and dogmas characteristic of positivist Marxism. The masses provide the necessary feelings, sentiments and passion for action; they are in turn transformed by the intellectuals into comprehension and knowledge and become practical activity through the party's direction. Only the establishment of an organic and dialectical relationship between the party and the masses can avoid the dangers of elitism, oligarchy, and spontaneity inherent in the political theories of Lenin, Michels and Sorel. In sum, the mass, organized as a collective will, is the basis of historical transformation and the creator of new historical blocs. The party is the instrument of mass political activity, always subordinated to it. In fact, it ceases to exist when it has become a 'state' and has extended mass hegemony over the entire society, that is, it has realized a unified and homogeneous civil society, as we shall see in subsequent chapters.

To conclude, the structural analysis of Gramsci's sociological thought developed in this chapter has revealed two theoretical orientations which, at first glance, appear to be a contradiction in terms. On the one hand, Gramsci's approach to the analysis of social phenomena is characterized by 'absolute historicism' and 'absolute humanism.' From such a perspective, society is understood essentially as an historical process and its socio-cultural phenomena are explained as historically determined. Science itself is not exempted from Gramsci's historicist theory, being 'historical knowledge' and 'historical praxis,' the only form of knowledge, and the only form of praxis. On the other hand, as it has been shown, Gramsci admits the existence of certain regularities and necessities in the occurrence of social phenomena. Even if the facts are always unique and changeable in the flux of the movement of history, a theory of the historical process can be developed. These two orientations are mutually exclusive. In fact, if one reads Gramsci literally, one finds that his postulation of the principle of absolute historicization of social phenomena contradicts the idea in Marxist theory of 'absolute humanism.' Absolute historicism would tend to deny its basic presupposition that human conscious activity cannot be predicted through the mechanisms of scientific method. History is reduced to mere historical accidents.

An in-depth analysis of Gramsci's writings, however, reveals a certain unity underlying the complexity of his ideas. Gramsci's denial of positivist sociology, paradoxically, led to its critical acceptance, to the incorporation of its 'healthy elements' into the general framework of Marxist theory. In fact, what Gramsci seems to criticize is the naive orientation of classical positivism, according to which social laws are essentially 'causal laws,' ultimately constraining human conduct and human initiative in the process of historical development. As Costa, an Italian commentator on Gramsci, has admirably observed, what has attracted Gramsci to social sciences has been precisely the 'causal perspective' they have developed, while its misuse has forced him to reject them. Certainly not all contemporary sociologists accept the mechanistic, deterministic assumptions of the organistic or neo-positivist school of thought. Most of them search not for mechanical causes, but for the conditions and factors of social phenomena. It follows that what Gramsci clearly criticizes is the use of science as a means of predicting and controlling human events.[65]

Gramsci's critical sociology attempts to explain existing social arrangements and socio-political institutions in terms of their historical conditions. Such explanations are always made within the framework of a theory of the historical develop-ment, which is scientific to the extent that it can prove that under different conditions other conclusions can be drawn and other lines of development can occur. That is to say, the efficacy of sociological theory resides in its ability to establish 'relatively' permanent forces or 'certain regularities,' not for their own sake, but in order to create the preconditions for the possibility of a new social order or new social arrangements. What Gramsci ultimately advocates is an historical and humanist scientific theory of history and society. In this respect, his theoretical positions are not so divergent from certain orienta-tions of contemporary sociological thought. It has to be acknowledged, however, that Gramsci is among the first theoreticians in the history of Marxist thought to attempt to humanize and historicize the scientific enterprise with the purpose of rescuing the individual from the conditions of alienating existence created by the processes of scientific rationality.

To conclude, it can be said that Gramsci's negation of positivist sociology does not preclude the existence of a socio-logy as a concrete, autonomous science within Marxist theory, with principles, logic, and methods of its own. Such a socio-logy, however, is eminently a political sociology, as has been shown. The general methodological criteria of such a concrete political sociology were only summarily listed by Gramsci. He in fact prepared a very comprehensive plan for a Marxist political sociology, never completed because of his premature death. Gramsci writes:[66]

It is necessary to study: 1) the objective formation of the
subaltern social groups, by the developments and transformations occurring in the sphere of economic production...;
2) their active or passive affiliation to the dominant political
formations, their attempts to influence the programmes of
these formations in order to press claims of their own...;
3) the birth of new parties of the dominant groups, intended
to conserve the assent of the subaltern groups and to maintain control over them; 4) the formations which the subaltern
groups themselves produce, in order to press claims of a
limited and partial character; 5) those new formations which
assert the autonomy of the subaltern groups, but within the
old framework; 6) those formations which assert the integral
autonomy...

The general methodological criteria of Gramsci's sociological
theory are those of historical materialism. Sociology, thus,
studies not only the relationship of parts within a given social
structure, but also the interrelationship between the whole and
the parts. The whole can determine the qualitative structure
of the parts and the parts can determine the qualitative
structure of the whole. This signifies that all social phenomena
are autonomous and possess a structure and a dynamic development of their own. Gramscian sociology appears to be an attempt
to analyze the dynamic structure of society from the standpoint of its global development and the development of its parts.
Unlike positivist sociology, which reduces social laws to natural
laws and ignores the purposefulness of human activity, Marxist
sociology examines the role of human activity in consciously
shaping the development of the historical process. Unlike
positivist Marxism, which attempts to interpret social reality
by means of a set of objective, necessary, and scientific laws,
and understands historical development as the product of
economic forces, critical Marxist sociology understands history
and society as political praxis, as a process of subjectivization
of the objective dimension of reality. Finally, unlike structural-
functionalism, Marxist sociology does not focus on changes
within a given system, but changes of the totality of the social
system brought about by the development of conflicting social
groups aiming at the attainment of 'global hegemony.' Marxist
sociology, thus, analyzes the dialectical development of the
social structure, which embodies a unity of functions and
development understood in a sense different from that of
structural-functionalist analysis. Functions designate relatively
permanent forces. Development designates qualitative changes
undergone by the totality of social structures as the result of
the dynamics of its own substructures. It is to the major
components of such dynamics that we shall now turn the focus
of our analysis.

Part II
THE SOCIOLOGY OF POLITICAL PRAXIS

3 THE MASSES AND
THE DYNAMICS OF HISTORY

Gramsci's sociology can be rightly characterized as a political
sociology of history, a sociology which interprets universal
history from the standpoint of the particular history of the
subaltern masses. His sociology is historicist, macroscopic,
dialectical. It is a sociology which analyzes the socio-cultural
universe from the standpoint of the category of 'totality.'
In this respect, the similarities between Lukács and Gramsci
are striking. As Lukács, Gramsci conceives such a totality as
determining the object as well as the subject of knowledge.[1]
It is precisely this notion that separates Marxist from positivist
sociology. Positivist sociology seeks to establish relationships
among phenomena and arrive at their meanings from the context
of immediately given and apparent world of facts. In Gramsci,
as we have seen, facts are only aspects of an historical and
dialectical process. The analysis of a given phenomenon is
incomplete if the history of its development is not taken into
account. Similarly, the history of a given phenomenon is also
incomplete without the history of the interrelationships among
phenomena. It is from this general perspective that Gramsci
analyzes various problems. The analyses of the political and
cultural emancipation of subaltern masses and the nature and
role of intellectuals in the dynamics of history are, for Gramsci,
the most fundamental problems of Marxist theory.

In this chapter we shall examine the first of these problems
with emphasis on the historical role of the masses, then proceed
to present his analysis of the nature of their Weltanschauungen
and conclude with some general observations on the relationship between Marxism and common sense.

THE MASSES: PROTAGONISTS OF THEIR NON-HISTORY
AND HISTORY

No one has penetrated the deepest level of Gramsci's historiography and grasped the subtleties of his theoretical analysis
of historical development better than Nardone, a very original
commentator of Gramsci's intellectual work. He notes that for
Gramsci the historical truth is a political act par excellence
produced by a given political praxis. The hermeneutics of the
historical present, likewise, is a political act in the sense that
it depends upon a political praxis.[2] For Gramsci, in fact, social
reality is essentially a political reality. As a consequence, any

73

historical event is always dependent upon the political praxis
of present history. He writes: 'all history bears witness to
the present,'[3] and the present contains 'in nuce' all the past.[4]
   In fact every real historical phase leaves traces of itself in
succeeding phases, which then become in a sense the best
document of its existence. The process of historical development is a unity in time through which the present contains
the whole of the past and in the present is realised that part
of the past which is 'essential' - with no residue of any
'unknowable' representing the true 'essence'. The part
which is lost, i.e. not transmitted dialectically in the historical process, was in itself of no import, usual and contingent 'dross', chronicle and not history, a superficial and
negligible episode in the last analysis.
History, then, is for Gramsci a unitary process in which the
past, present and future fuse into a single category: the
political praxis of the present. The future is the transcendence
of the past through the political praxis of the present. Historical
praxis is the 'continuous struggle of individuals and groups
to change what exists in every given moment.'[5] Thus, it is a
great work of history which adheres to the praxis of the present, Gramsci concludes, that is, which aids the developing
progressive forces of the present history to become conscious
of themselves.[6] The truth of history, then, resides in the
political praxis of the present. It follows that historical analysis
is objective to the extent to which it provides not an abstract,
speculative system of interpretation, but a 'practical' knowledge for the realization of the political and philosophical
project of the most progressive social group, the subaltern
masses organized in a political collectivity.
   From this standpoint, Gramsci reviews the most important
phases of Italian and European history and arrives at a new
and original interpretation of history. In examining concrete
events, he seeks to establish which elements are progressive
or regressive in relation to the praxis of the most progressive
forces of present history. The hermeneutic criterion of Gramscian historiography is the degree of diffusion of a movement
or ideology among the popular masses or the extent to which
popular masses participate politically or culturally in the
hegemony exercised by non-subaltern groups, classes or
elites.
   Gramsci focuses his attention on three major phases of Italian
politics, the periods of communes, Renaissance and Risorgimento.
The first represents a progressive period in which a popular
movement affirms itself in politics, the second a regressive
period of reaction to communal liberties, and the third represents the period in which democratic liberties finally triumph
and modern states are constituted.
   The period between the eleventh and the fourteenth centuries
marked the beginning of a popular-bourgeois movement. The
constitution of various self-governing city-states, of prosperous

trading and manufacturing communes, is the first historical
prototype of a political-military organization involving popular
masses. But such movements were not politically and culturally
autonomous. The communes relied upon an economic-corporate
system. Their bourgeoisies failed to transcend the economic-
corporate phase of development and create a national state with
the consent of broad masses. The communal bourgeoisie, in
fact, was unable to go beyond feudalism and remained essentially a movement which pressed for timid economic and social
reforms. It was unable to develop a national consciousness
simply because it lacked, as we shall see in the next chapter,
'organic intellectuals.' The intellectuals of the communes were
absorbed by the traditional ones, the clergy which continued
to dominate the cultural, intellectual and political life of the
nation. The communal period, however, remains essentially a
progressive period in the history of Italy in so far as new
urban groups were able to develop in a molecular form as an
expression of the popular will.[7]

From 1300 onwards another movement followed, known as the
humanist and cultural movement of the Renaissance. Humanism
was an individualist movement, proclaiming the right to free
development and personal autonomy. It was the 'cultural
expression of an historical process in which there was created
in Italy a new intellectual class of European dimensions.'[8] This
cosmopolitan class advocated a return to the cult of the past,
romanitas, religion, authority in opposition to the communal
spirit which undermined the role of the papacy. With such
return to ancient *latinitas*, the separation between high culture
and mass culture became acute. While the Renaissance movement
outside Italy culminated in the foundation of national states and
in 'the world expansion of Spain, France, England, Portugal,'
in Italy it degenerated into 'the organization of the Papacy
as an absolute state.'[9] The intelligentsia of the Renaissance
movement was composed of a cosmopolitan stratum which
'exercised a cosmopolitan function in Italy linked to the Papacy,'
and another formed outside Italy 'from political and religious
exiles' which 'exercised a progressive cosmopolitan function
in the various countries where it existed, or participated in
the organization of the modern states as a technical element
in the armed forces, in politics, in engineering, etc.'[10] Because
of this cosmopolitan role, the traditional intellectuals were
able to contain the development of popular-bourgeois consciousness and actually assimilate it. This resulted in the separation
between intellectuals and masses, high culture and mass culture, and the absorption of a true popular-national movement
capable of undermining the feudal order legitimated by the
church.

The bourgeois movement resurfaced between 1750 and 1850
and finally triumphed in the Risorgimento, the period in which
Italian unity was realized and the Italian state was formed.
Gramsci devoted an important portion of his writings to the

interpretation of the Risorgimento. Briefly, the Risorgimento,
although progressive in relation to past history, was not
progressive enough, Gramsci observes. It did not mobilize the
mass of peasants and did not generate an agrarian revolution.
An analysis of the internal political forces of the Risorgimento
reveals that the new economic forces struggling to achieve
national unification were directed by a political and cultural
apparatus inherited from the past which prevented the full
realization of a true bourgeois revolution. The progressive
forces of the Italian Risorgimento consisted of a bloc of the
industrial bourgeoisie and large latifundists with no participation of the countryside. Consequently, the Italian bourgeois
revolution was not a popular revolution. It was guided from
above, by one particular state, Piedmont, and the Moderate
Party, the Liberal Party of Cavour, which conceived national
unity as the political expansion of Peidmont and the dynasty
of Savoy. It was a revolution without mass participation and
molecular transformation of social institutions, that is, in
Gramsci's terms, a passive revolution. Two political parties
were the major protagonists of the Italian Risorgimento: the
Popular Action Party and the Moderate Party. The first was the
true expression of popular-national forces, capable of expand-
ing its base to include the peasantry. But it failed, for it
lacked a solid class base, a Jacobin tendency, an ideology and
a well-defined political program. As a result, it underwent
structural modifications which led to its assimilation into the
politics of the party of the Moderates.[11] The Moderates, on
the other hand, represented an economic, political and cultural
front, an organic political force, attracting into their orbit
various social classes, and their intellectuals. Such cultural
supremacy had the effect of reorganizing all forces of the
nation. Cultural hegemony, hegemony over the intellectuals, and
through them over the process of education in the nation,
assured their political leadership. Thus, Gramsci concludes,
the Italian Risorgimento was not a truly national, popular and
progressive phenomenon.

In contrast to the Italian bourgeois revolution, the French
Revolution was for Gramsci a more total phenomenon. Here a
progressive class was able to transform the masses into a
collective will and a nation. The Jacobins were able to extend
on all strata of French society a new conception-of-the-world
and develop a clear political program which incorporated the
needs of all classes.[12]

> If it is true that the Jacobins 'forced' its hand, it is also
> true that this always occurred in the direction of real his-
> torical development. For not only did they organize a bour-
> geois government, i.e. make the bourgeoisie the dominant
> class – they did more. They created the bourgeois State,
> made the bourgeoisie into the leading, hegemonic class of the
> nation, in other words gave the new State a permanent basis
> and created the compact modern French nation.

The Jacobin group became the dominant, hegemonic class by assuming the avant-garde role in the revolution. It became the representative not only of the needs, interests and aspirations of the French bourgeoisie, but also of those of other social classes. The Jacobins became the embodiment of the revolutionary movement as a whole. Their success lay precisely in the fact that they were able to win the consent of the masses. Their political strategy, Gramsci writes, was twofold: annihilate the enemies to prevent the formation of a counter-revolution, and enlarge the cadres of the bourgeoisie. A political alliance between the peasantry and the most progressive elements of the Third Estate was the most politically expedient coalition to topple the old regime.[13]

> The Third Estate was the least homogeneous; it had a very disparate intellectual elite, and a group which was very advanced economically but politically moderate. Events developed along highly interesting lines. The representatives of the Third Estate initially only posed those questions which interested the actual physical members of the social group, their immediate 'corporate' interests (corporate in the traditional sense, of the immediate and narrowly selfish interests of the particular category)... Gradually a new elite was selected out which did not concern itself solely with 'corporate' reforms, but tended to conceive of the bourgeoisie as the hegemonic group of all the popular forces.

The phenomenon of Jacobinism for Gramsci meant first that a political force had been able to organize a collective will and insert the masses in the revolutionary process. Second, it represented a movement capable of transcending the economic-corporate interests of class and assuming more universal ones. The French Revolution, however, was not as progressive as the Russian Revolution. The two revolutions have similar characteristics: a class transformed itself in a collective and national will. Jacobinism was a historical event of great dimensions, the realization of a cultural-political bloc with popular consent. Likewise, the Russian Revolution realized a more global hegemony. The masses themselves became the hegemonic class. In this respect it was more progressive than the French Revolution. The only positive element in the Jacobin experience was its popular nature. But in the last analysis, Gramsci observes, it was not a truly popular phenomenon for the interests of the bourgeoisie were at variance with those of the subaltern classes.

From the analysis of these concrete events Gramsci arrives at a general conception and interpretation of historical development, the starting point of which is the emergence of fundamental social classes, and its point of arrival the attainment of their integral autonomy, that is, hegemony. Gramsci analyzes the process of development of such classes, the subaltern classes in particular, and formulates certain theoretical and methodological criteria for the study of these classes.

POLITICAL AND CULTURAL ASCENDANCY OF THE MASSES

The mobilization and organization of popular masses became
for Gramsci the most significant event of the twentieth century.
It was the experience of the Russian Revolution which prompted
him to ask fundamental questions: Why the popular forces
which appeared about the eleventh century did not develop
into a national collective will? By what mechanisms were the
Jacobins in France, the Moderate Party in Italy and the
Communist Party in Russia able to create a new hegemonic
system? Gramsci answers: they were able to develop an ideology
which unified such forces in an historical bloc, and create an
historical unity between the intellectuals and the masses, high
culture and mass culture.

The autonomous development or non-development of the
subaltern masses is the hermeneutic criterion of the historical
process. Important factors in history are not economic forces
but men who organize into a collective will. Human will 'becomes
the driving force of the economy and moulds objective reality.'[14]
But what is the role of the masses in the development of history? And in what consists the process whereby a given collective will is formed? The answer to these questions is to be
sought in the manner in which men organize into a political
collectivity and develop concrete programs.

Within the masses spontaneous movements occur and specific
attitudes are formed. They indicate 'the precise direction of
the historical development,' of new ways of thinking and social
forms as well as new historical blocs.[15] The development of
history, the formation of new institutions, of philosophical
systems and political ideologies are ultimately explained within
the context of a dynamics present among the masses. The
masses, being the very embodiment of the process of history,
are also the yardstick by which progress in history is measured.
They are the makers not only of their own history, that is,
the history to which they have given their assent, but also the
history made by others without their consent or their active
participation. Even in situations when they are politically and
culturally passive, 'What comes to pass does so not so much
because a few people want it to happen, as because the mass
of citizens abdicate their responsibility.'[16] What Gramsci means
by this is that the masses are not only the protagonists of
the history made by dominant groups, elites or individuals,
through their indifference, but also the non-history, that is,
of what did not happen for them, in a positive sense. The
entire history of Italy and Europe is the history of what actually
did not happen. The passivity of the masses, their indifference
and fatalist submission to an external, mechanical law of
necessity explains why given groups and institutions become
dominant. Gramsci writes: 'Indifference operates powerfully
in history.... What comes to pass... is due not so much to the
initiative of the active few, as to the indifference, the

absenteeism of the many.'[17] And what is more, the passivity
of the masses generates and sustains extra-historical or supra-
historical values and beliefs, such as religion, human nature,
science. On the contrary, an organized, active and conscious
mass is capable of creating new socio-historical worlds and
legitimating them with new and all-encompassing Weltanschauungen. Political praxis is the source of historical certitude! All
laws of necessity, causality and objectivity as well as the
processes of reification, alienation, fatalism, fetishism and
myths all disappear when the masses become politically and
culturally autonomous.

But how to explain the genesis of a political will? What are
the conditions affecting the process of its transformation?
Gramsci attempts to describe the various phases of the cultural
and political development of subaltern masses. As for their
origin, the material forces of production at various levels of
development are historically the primary conditions which
stratify politically, economically and culturally an amorphous
population and polarize society into classes. 'The level of development of the material forces of production provides a basis for
the emergence of the various social classes, each one of which
represents a function and has a specific position within production itself.'[18] Classes are born as economic entities, but in
the process of their development they undergo a profound
process of internal transformation. They transcend their
economic-corporate original conditions of existence and tend
to become hegemonic forces, agents of political and cultural
integration. The conquest of hegemony always presupposes
a dialectic among classes, best characterized as a dialectic
between a particularized sector of the civil society and the
totality. The 'particular' tends to expand throughout society,
to assimilate all other social groupings and become an hegemonic
force, a totality. Gramsci focuses his attention on 'fundamental
social classes,' those that aim at the attainment of hegemony
(bourgeoisie and proletariat) and analyzes the various phases
of their development. Any fundamental class undergoes a process of transformation from a negative to a positive stage. As
long as such classes remain an economic-corporate entity,
they are in a condition of historical primitivism, particularism
and egotism. Only when they transcend the particular interest
of class do they become the engineers of a new social consensus,
the agents of total transformation, and the creators of new
historical blocs. Hegemony, for Gramsci, as we shall see in
chapter 5, is the universalization of interests of all social
classes. In bourgeois systems, Gramsci notes, hegemony has
been achieved through a process of assimilation of the popular
will. In feudal society, dominant classes[19]

> did not tend to construct an organic passage from the other
> classes into their own, i.e. to enlarge their class sphere
> 'technically' and 'ideologically': their conception was that of
> a closed caste. The bourgeois class poses itself as an

organism in continuous movement, capable of absorbing the entire society, assimilating it into its own cultural and economic sphere. The entire function of the State has been transformed; the State has become an 'educator', etc.

If, on the one hand, the identification of social classes is the ultimate evaluative criterion of past history, and the individuation of fundamental classes the essential element of Gramscian historiography, the analysis of the subaltern classes is, on the other hand, crucial in the study of history to come. Gramsci distinguishes three types of classes. Fundamental classes are those which exercise cultural, political and juridical hegemony over the entire society; auxiliary classes are those which assent to specific programs and ideologies of dominant classes, and thereby form the basis of their hegemony; subaltern classes are those which either are excluded from participation in the hegemony of dominant classes or passively consent to it. While the 'historical unity of the ruling classes is realised in the State, and their history is essentially the history of States,' Gramsci writes, 'the subaltern classes, by definition, are not unified and cannot unite until they are able to become a "State": their history, therefore, is intertwined with that of civil society, and thereby with the history of States and groups of States.'[20]

The analysis of the level of historical and political consciousness attained by these progressive innovative forces involves the problem of assessing the degree of autonomy achieved and the degree of support acquired from groups which actively or passively assisted them.[21] Gramsci's principle of historical research can then be reduced to one: the degree of passivity or political consciousness of subaltern classes is the criterion by which the regressive or progressive character of hegemonic systems can be assessed. The degree of autonomy of popular masses is the criterion which enabled Gramsci to evaluate various hegemonic systems from the Middle Ages onwards. It is also the criterion by which he analyzes the internal development of subaltern classes. As long as popular masses remain in a subaltern condition vis-à-vis dominant groups, they lack political and cultural autonomy. Thus they are in a negative, primitive phase of development. To be sure, Gramsci notes, they do have a conception of the world, attitudes, beliefs and tastes of their own. But under closer examination such spontaneous popular manifestations appear to be the product of a powerful influence exerted from without. He writes: 'The question of mass attitudes cannot be posed independently from that of ruling classes....Spontaneous mass reactions help to indicate the "strength" of the domination exerted by the upper classes.'[22] Even when the masses revolt they are subject to the activity of ruling groups.[23] They are, in fact, the raw material of a history made by others. Negatively, they are the real protagonist of past history. As Nardone puts it, any mass activity is indicative of activities related to the interests of the dominant classes, and, on the contrary, the activity of dominant classes presupposes the non-activity and political passivity of the subalterns.[24]

Gramsci describes quite accurately the 'primitive' world in which the subaltern masses live. The masses live in a world of indifference, apathy, superstition, fatalism. Their political and cultural interests are so narrow that they barely go beyond the localistic world in which they live. Excluded from the high culture and intellectual life of the elites, they revert to a Ptolemaic, folkloric and naturalist conception of the world. Gramsci takes a strong position against Sorel's thesis that the spontaneity of the masses is the basis of correct political activity. Sorel's theory of myth and syndicalist strategy of revolutionary change is sharply criticized.

For Sorel, as we have noted in the preceding chapter, mass spontaneity is the basis of political action. Only by means of a general strike of all producers can capitalism be overcome. By opposing all political programs and all forms of mass organization Sorel abandoned politics to the impulses of the irrational, arbitrary and spontaneous mass activity. This a-critical acceptance of mass spontaneous feelings and attitudes constituted the major weakness of Sorel's theory, Gramsci wrote. Sorel refused to pose the problem of political activity and strategy as that of 'education' of mass spontaneity. But what are the implications of Sorel's theory? The masses are asked to act on an economic-corporate plane, to struggle for immediate, narrow social and political goals, not to organize into a collective force and strive to attain political and cultural autonomy. Sorel asks the masses, indirectly, to remain in their primitive condition of existence. Second, Sorel seems not to understand that spontaneity is typical of those classes which are subordinate to dominant ones. And the characteristic features of dominant classes are certainly not spontaneity and feelings, but rationality and conscious planning. One needs to examine history to find numerous cases in which spontaneous popular movements are followed by reactionary right-wing movements. 'Among the effective causes of the *coups* must be included the failure of the responsible groups to give any conscious leadership to the spontaneous revolts or to make them into a positive political factor.'[25] To be sure, mass spontaneity remains the basis of political activity in Gramsci's thought. But he does not speak of pure spontaneity, rather of an educated and directed spontaneity, a spontaneity 'purged of extraneous contaminations.' The masses are in need of the consciousness of 'being creators of historical and institutional values, of being founders of a State.' 'This unity between "spontaneity" and "conscious leadership" or "discipline" is precisely the real political action of the subaltern classes, in so far as this is mass politics and not merely an adventure by groups claiming to represent the masses.'[26] In the last analysis, Sorel's error lies in the fact of having presupposed the existence of a collective will within the masses prior to, and independent of, political organization. Whereas for Gramsci a collective will emerges in the process of political organization of the masses.[27] Sorel, thus, falls into a metaphysical and determinist conception of the political process, for he makes political praxis dependent on a 'myth.' For Gramsci, the formation of a collective will is a gradual, molecular process which entails a catharsis of the group in question, as we have previously seen. The party, the intellectuals, the ideology are all elements emerging in the process of development of subaltern classes. They constitute the cathartic moment, the point of transition from an economistic to a hegemonic phase of existence. In sum, subaltern classes cannot become agents of political transformation if they do not transcend the negative phase and conditions of their origin. The subaltern classes reach maturity when they attain hegemony, the terminal point of political emancipation.

Hegemony is also the culminating point of a concomitant process, that of cultural emancipation and cultural autonomy. The culture of subaltern classes is also characterized by negative traits. It is folkloric, commonsensical, religious and superstitious. In subaltern culture one finds layers of sedimentations of past historical epochs, indicating the cultural dependence of popular masses on dominant groups of past periods. Cultural transformation of subaltern classes then for Gramsci means a transformation from a condition of cultural immaturity to one of cultural autonomy. Popular culture has to be transformed into an integral, organic, all-encompassing Weltanschauung. This leads us into the central theme of this chapter, Gramsci's analysis of popular Weltanschauungen and their place in the Marxist theory and praxis.

Common sense and folklore: the Weltanschauungen of 'Subaltern' Masses

Gramsci's notes on popular culture make sense only if analyzed in the context of the notion of 'hegemony.' The leading question raised by Gramsci is this: How a given class passes from a subaltern to a hegemonic position. For Lenin the answer was simple. Once power is conquered and the dictatorship of the proletariat is established there follows a cultural revolution, an intellectual and moral reform of the masses, thus a transformation of human consciousness. For Gramsci, the proletariat must become a leading group before the actual conquest of political power. What really makes a group 'directive' is the creation of a Weltanschauung.[28]

> The foundation of a directive class [classe dirigente] (i.e. of a State) is equivalent to the creation of a Weltanschauung. How is the statement that the German proletariat is the heir of classical German philosophy to be understood? Surely what Marx wanted to indicate was the historical function of his philosophy when it became the theory of a class which was in turn to become a State?

If for Lenin the conquest of power alone is the condition for
the political and cultural supremacy of a class, for Gramsci
the question is how a group which has become a leading group
before the attainment of power can continue to be the leading
and directive group after political hegemony is reached.[29]
Hegemony is the 'intellectual and moral leadership' of subaltern
masses. It is realized when an 'intellectual and moral reform' of
society takes place. Revolution then is not a thaumaturgical act
but an organic and dialectical process which entails a subjective
transformation of the masses' conduct and thinking.[30] But
what are the Weltanschauungen of subaltern masses and what
are their characteristic features?

Common Sense
The notion of common sense in Gramsci is more subtle and
complex than that found in traditional philosophy or phenomenological sociologies. Common sense has been understood as 'the
general sense, feeling or judgement of mankind, more precisely
as a cluster of beliefs felt to be true by most people.' Some,
such as Thomas Reid and the Scottish School, have insisted
on the spontaneity of common sense and have defined it as 'the
totality of conceptions which is accepted in a given period and
a specific community spontaneously and by so many that they
are considered commonly known.'[31]
   Within the theoretical framework of various phenomenological
sociologies, the sociology of Schutz, Berger and Luckmann in
particular, common sense has been understood in opposition
to theoretical thought as 'what people "know" as "reality" in
their everyday, non- or pre-theoretical lives.'[32] In this respect
they revive the so-called common sense realism typical of the
Scottish school of philosophy, according to which the theory
of knowledge is elaborated from the standpoint and in support
of the realistic beliefs of the man in the street. Thus, common
sense knowledge has been regarded as either theoretically
more sound than philosophy (Santayana), or in opposition to
the 'critical nature' of philosophy and scientific methodology
but ultimately reconcilable with them (Henry Sidgwick), or
unmistakably superior to all types of knowledge because of its
taken-for-granted, massive and universal character (Berger
and Luckmann).
   A common element in all these philosophical and sociological
approaches to common sense is the reduction of its content to
an expression of a natural attitude, a conception-of-the-world
not rational or scientific, but practical and universal. Gramsci
rejects such approaches by insisting on the historical, ideological and political characteristics of common sense.
   Gramsci notes in an introductory remark that common sense
was virtually exalted in the seventeenth and eighteenth centuries
in the midst of an intellectual reaction to the absolutist
Aristotelian and biblical principles of authority and God. Science
saw in it a 'certain measure of "experimentalism" and direct

observation of reality though empirical and limited.[133] The
fascination with common sense in contemporary sociologies is
likewise ideological. Against positivist or pseudo-scientific
systems common sense is able to identify the clear causes and
produce judgments in an exact, simple and practical manner.

Common sense, Gramsci writes, is a conception of the world
mechanically imposed by an alien milieu, by 'one of the many
social groups in which everyone is automatically involved from
the moment of his entry into the conscious world.'[134] Common
sense is a product of history and must be analyzed as 'part of
the historical process.' As a matter of fact, there are many
common senses and not simply one. Every social stratum has
its own common sense and every current of thought leaves
behind a sedimentation of common sense which becomes crystallized in a contradictory way in popular consciousness. The
power of influence of dominant ideologies is visible in the content of common sense. Thus, all philosophies and sociologies
which make the common sense of the subaltern masses the
basis of objective thought need to understand the ideological
function of common sense in stratified societies.

Common sense is, for Gramsci, the philosophy of non-
philosophers, the conception of the world typical of subaltern
classes in the negative phase of their development, that of
political and cultural subordination to dominant groups and
ideologies. In contrast to 'philosophy,' an homogeneous,
coherent and systematic conception of the world, common sense
represents a negative, primitive form of intellectual order.[35]

'Common sense' is the folklore of philosophy, and is always
halfway between folklore properly speaking and the philosophy,
science, and economics of the specialists. Common sense
creates the folklore of the future, that is as a relatively
rigid phase of popular knowledge at a given place and time.
Common sense exists in opposition to philosophy and differs
qualitatively from philosophy, yet it is dependent upon it and
functions to integrate subaltern groups to dominant culture
and ideology. 'Its most fundamental characteristic is that it is
a conception which, even in the brain of one individual, is
fragmentary, incoherent and inconsequential, in conformity
with the social and cultural position of those masses whose
philosophy it is.'[136] Common sense is qualitatively inferior to
philosophy not only for the fragmentary, incoherent manner in
which it presents itself, but also for its content, which is an
accumulation of sedimentations of past epochs, a 'chaotic
aggregate of disparate conceptions' derived from various social
groups. For this reason 'one can find there anything that one
likes.'[137] Thus, Gramsci concludes, common sense is a 'rigid
phase of popular knowledge' yet 'continually transforming
itself and enriching itself with ideas, opinions derived from
metaphysical systems, mainly religion.'

For lack of critical consciousness, common sense is intrin-
sically incapable of thinking historicistically and dialectically.

Its conception of reality is, in fact, static, reified, naturalist, fatalist, and its beliefs are held by the masses as natural imperatives. In this context Gramsci rejects both the psychologistic approach of Sorel and the scientistic one of De Man. In Sorel there is no critical evaluation of common sense. It is important to accept and revere popular feelings, to bow to common sense, understand it and express it in rational and juridical form. Socialism is for Sorel a system of justice based on common sense.[38] For De Man, famous Belgian social democrat, equally opposed to revolutionary Marxism, a return to 'psychological and ethical values' of the working class assures the proper political strategy. His attitude toward common sense is labelled by Gramsci as 'scientistic.' He bows to common sense in order to 'theorise' their feelings and construct pseudo-scientific schemes much as a zoologist takes pride in observing the world of insects. 'His position is that of the scholarly student of folklore who is permanently afraid that modernity is going to destroy the object of his study.' He studies popular feelings, but 'he does not feel with them to guide them, and lead them into a catharsis of modern civilization.'[39]

Against Sorel and De Man, and certainly against all common sense sociologies, Gramsci proposes a political interpretation of common sense. It suffices here to mention that the fragmentary, incoherent, anthropomorphic character of common sense is the best documentation of its political and intellectual subordination and the 'primitive' nature of its content. Gramsci's aim is to prove that the political and cultural immaturity of subaltern classes is the basis of the political and cultural hegemony exercised by others. For this reason his analysis of common sense serves to demonstrate why popular masses failed to attain political hegemony throughout history. In analyzing the mechanisms by which dominant groups maintain themselves in power Gramsci emphasizes the function of traditional philosophical systems. He writes:

These systems influence the popular masses as an external political force, an element of cohesive force exercised by the ruling classes and therefore an element of subordination to an external hegemony. This limits the original thought of the popular masses in a negative direction, without having the positive effect of a vital ferment of interior transformation of what the masses think in an embryonic and chaotic form about the world and life.[40]

The history of philosophy . . . is the history of attempts made and ideological initiatives undertaken by a specific class of people to change, correct, or perfect the conceptions of the world that exists in any particular age and thus to change the norms of conduct that go with them; in other words, to change practical activity as a whole.[41]

But if common sense is essentially a chaotic aggregate of heterogeneous conceptions of the world sedimented in the consciousness of popular masses, it does not mean that it has to be dismissed as a source of knowledge and political action. Within common sense, Gramsci notes, there exists a positive nucleus, a creative element, which if developed can lead to the elaboration of an autonomous consciousness, and a renewed common sense. This is good sense, an embryonic critical thinking.[42] Autonomous development is then a transcendence of a primitive, negative common sense, and an elaboration of an integral conception of the world on the basis of good sense. Common sense purged of its a-critical elements can become the basis of a new conception of the world. The elaboration of Marxism, as the conception of the world of popular masses, rests on a critique and transcendence of common sense.

Folklore
As in the case of common sense, Gramsci's analysis of folklore responds to two exigencies. On the one hand, he intends to show the processes by which dominant classes exercise their cultural and political control. On the other hand, he searches within popular culture for an healthy nucleus of ideas and experiences which, educated, could become a superior conception of the world, able of superseding the most refined and elaborated philosophical systems prevailing in society. The negative characterization of common sense and folklore responds to the necessity of creating a new mass culture.

   Folklore is the lowest form of culture and philosophic thinking also typical of subaltern masses living at the periphery of dominant hegemonies. It is a by-product of the high culture of dominant classes and serves the function of maintaining popular culture in a subordinate position. At the same time, folklore is a conception which assures the maintenance of an ideological unity within the social bloc.[43] In folkloristic studies, 'folklore' is conceived as an object of erudition, an intellectual pastime, as something bizarre, strange or picturesque.[44] For Gramsci, folklore is instead an aid to an historical understanding of the general Weltanschauung prevailing in a given historical period. He considers it as a conception of the world linked to and subordinate to dominant culture and intellectual hegemonies, characteristic of certain popular strata. Folklore, he writes, is 'the entire system of beliefs, superstitions, opinions, ways of seeing things and acting.'[45] Three ideas seem to underline Gramsci's conception of folklore. First, it is a 'conception of the world' containing a specific body of beliefs, norms and values. As such, it is the reflection of the conditions of cultural primitiveness of popular masses. Second, it stands in opposition to the official conception of dominant classes. Third, it is characteristic of those classes which are excluded from participation in the cultural hegemony of the nation, mainly the peasantry. Gramsci proceeds with two series of observations on the nature and social organization of folklore.

As in the case of common sense, negative traits characterize
the phenomenon of folklore. It is a-systematic, unelaborated,
a 'disorganized conglomeration of fragments of all world-views
developed throughout history, most of which are found in
folklore as mutilated and contaminated surviving documents.'[46]
The unelaborated and a-systematic character of folklore stems
from the very nature of subaltern classes which by definition
are unable to develop elaborate, systematic, politically centralized and organized views.[47] By this Gramsci means that the
high degree of systematization and elaborateness of conceptions
of the world are the consequences and the expression of an
hegemony maintained on the entire social body. Conversely,
the a-systematic, unelaborate popular Weltanschauungen result
from a lack of hegemonic participation. Nothing is more
contradictory and fragmentary than folklore, Gramsci writes.
Elements from contrasting systems of thought have all con-
gealed in popular consciousness. They exist as fossilized values.
Religion itself is nothing but a 'folkloric conception of the
world' when contrasted with modern, rational and scientific
thought.[48]
Within religion one can distinguish various forms of religiosity.[49] On Catholicism Gramsci writes:[50]

there is one Catholicism for the peasants, one for the *petit-
bourgeois* and town workers, one for women, and one for
intellectuals which is variegated and disconnected. But
common sense is influenced not only by the crudest and
least elaborated forms of these sundry Catholicisms as they
exist today. Previous religions have also had an influence
and remain components of common sense to this day, and
the same is true of previous forms of present Catholicism -
popular heretical movements, scientific superstitions connected with past cults, etc.

Within folklore one finds a 'popular morality,' that ensemble of
maxims of practical conduct derived from the crudest religious
beliefs and superstitions. Modern science also feeds new elements into modern folklore. In fact, 'certain scientific ideas
and certain opinions, divorced from their whole context and
more or less disfigured, continually fall into popular knowledge
and are "inserted" into the mosaic of tradition.'[51]
The social organization of folklore seems to interest Gramsci
more than the problem of its nature. He examines it as a
phenomenon dependent upon dominant ideologies. He writes:
'So folklore has always been tied to the culture of the dominant
class, and, in its own way, has appropriated certain aspects
of it, which became part of preceding traditions.'[52] Most of
the essential elements of folklore are conservative. They are
retained by the masses as objective, reified ideas and serve
to perpetuate a cultural stratification in society. Again, as in
the case of common sense, Gramsci does not reject folklore
altogether. He individuates within it an 'healthy nucleus' of
positive and progressive elements which, if educated, can be

incorporated into a higher conception of the world, the philosophy of praxis. There are 'some imperatives' more tenacious
and effective than official morality, a 'series of innovations
often creative and progressive, determined spontaneously by
new forms and conditions of life opposite to or different from
the ruling-class morality.'[53] The masses do possess, however,
simple and orginal criteria of evaluation. Gramsci cites the
case of folksongs, popular songs written neither for nor by
the people, 'but adopted by them because they conformed to
their way of thinking and feelings.'[54]

> what distinguishes a popular song within the context of a
> country and its culture is not the artistic quality, nor the
> historical origin, but the way it sees the world and life, in
> contrast to the official society. In this and this alone can
> we seek the 'collective feeling' of the popular song and of
> the populace itself.

Such progressive and critical elements are potential forces
of change. Marxism is called upon to transform the folkloric
conception of the world of popular masses, by incorporating
and further developing its 'positive nucleus.' The creation of
a new culture entails a catharsis of folklore. It has to divest
itself of its particularistic, localistic elements and become a
truly national-popular phenomenon. Folkloric thinking, Gramsci
writes, is a provincial mode of thinking, in the sense of being
anachronistic and typical of a class lacking a universal character. And it is 'national-popular' when it attains a universal,
cosmopolitan level of culture.[55]

How then can the transformation of common sense and folklore
best be characterized? Gramsci, we think, seems to advocate
an aristocratization of popular thinking and feeling.

MARXISM AND THE PROCESS OF ARISTOCRATIZATION OF THE MASSES

More than any Marxist writers, Gramsci focuses on the problem
of popular consciousness and its relationship to hegemony. In
a very original fashion, and no doubt under the influence of
the idealist philosophy of Benedetto Croce, he defines Marxism
as an 'intellectual and moral reform' of the masses, as a continuous attempt at transcending primitive ways of thought and
conduct through the acquisition of a more universal conception
of the world. He speaks of the necessity to de-provincialize
popular culture, purify it and elevate it to the status of an
integral, autonomous and universal Weltanschauung.[56] Socialist
revolutions are the most progressive attempts by subaltern
masses to attain cultural and political autonomy.

Central to Gramsci's thought is the idea that the success of
a revolution lies in its capacity to confront and eliminate the
power of 'intellectual blocs.' Hence the need of 'organic
intellectuals' to confront 'traditional intellectuals,' and

assimilate them, as we shall see in the following chapter. Such confrontation entails an intellectual debate with dominant ideologies and all their components. An ideology is for Gramsci the Weltanschauung of a given social class. He focuses on 'hegemonic ideologies,' those that have succeeded in diffusing themselves throughout the social structure and have become manifest in each component of society, that is, in economics, politics, art, language, literature, science, etc. Born out of a particular political praxis of a socially progressive and fundamental group, such ideologies become the instrument of total reorganization of society. Their function is eminently political for their aim is to unify and homogenize all social strata. Ideologies are for Gramsci political historical facts. They create concrete political configurations, achieve a complex internal articulation and high degree of rationality which, diffused among all social groups and internalized by them, come to constitute a solid 'ideological bloc.' This prevents the formation and ascendancy of new and opposing ideologies.

Gramsci distinguishes various levels in hegemonic ideologies. They are: philosophy, religion, common sense and folklore, each representing qualitatively different conceptions of the world adhered to by various social strata. No clear distinction between them exists. Within philosophy, in fact, are present elements derived from common sense, religion and folklore. The same is true of common sense, folklore and religion, in which elements of the others are also visible.

Among all the components of ideology, philosophy enjoys the most privileged position in so far as it represents the most general, elaborate conception of the world, the most coherent, systematic and rational conception developed by an hegemonic group.[57] It is the ultimate frame of reference of an entire 'historical bloc.' Philosophy is an intellectual and ethical ordering of the world, an attempt to unite consciousness and conduct, theory and praxis. That is to say, it is a conception of the world capable of interpreting the totality of phenomena in a coherent, consistent and rational manner, and of generating a moral reform of the consciousness of the masses and becoming a source of practical conduct for a collectivity. Any philosophical system has a tendency to universalize itself.[58]

> The philosophy of an age is not the philosophy of this or
> that philosopher, of this or that group of intellectuals, of
> this or that broad section of the popular masses. It is a
> process of combination of all these elements, which culminates
> in an overall trend, in which the culmination becomes a norm
> of collective action and becomes concrete and complete
> (integral) 'history.'

Within an ideological bloc, philosophy exerts the most profound influence over the conceptions of the world of auxiliaries and subaltern classes.

Religion occupies in Gramsci's theory an intermediate position between philosophy and common sense. Unlike philosophy proper, religion does not constitute an intellectual order for it is an ensemble of practical norms of conduct. In its content, religion is characterized by heterogeneous notions not critically ela-borated and accepted by the masses as elements of 'faith.'

That the mechanicist conception has been a religion of the subaltern is shown by an analysis of the development of the Christian religion. Over a certain period of history in cer-tain specific historical conditions religion has been and con-tinues to be a 'necessity', a necessary form taken by the will of the popular masses and a specific way of rationalising the world and real life, which provided the general frame-work for real practical activity.[59]

Religion, or a particular church, maintains its community of faithful... in so far as it nourishes its faith permanently and in an organized fashion, indefatigably repeating its apo-logetics, struggling at all times and always with the same kind of arguments, and maintaining a hierarchy of intellect-uals who give to the faith, in appearance at least, the dignity of thought.[60]

In sum, religion tends to create social cohesion among groups demanding a praxis which conforms to a conception of the world, to a body of traditions and institutions. Thus, it serves to maintain an ideological unity in society on the levels of thought, conduct and history itself.

More important is the influence of philosophy on common sense. This is in fact the 'folklore' of philosophy, the 'con-ception of the world which is uncritically absorbed by the various social and cultural environments in which the moral individuality of the average man is developed.[61] By maintaining common sense in a 'Ptolemaic,' anthropomorphic condition and by preserving the fragmentary, incoherent, inconsequential and a-critical elements in mass spontaneous philosophy, the high philosophy assures its own intellectual superiority and dominance, and perpetuates the historical division between high and mass culture. Its historically produced 'truth' is adhered to by popular masses as a 'superstition' and has the force of a social 'imperative.'[62] Common sense, therefore, is an ideo-logical instrument of control and social integration. Together with religion and folklore it contributes to amalgamate and homogenize a collective will.

At the lowest level of the ideological bloc is folklore, the most heterogeneous conception of the world. As we have seen, folklore is not only unelaborated and a-critical, but also contradictory and ambiguous in its content. It is another ideo-logical instrument of control of the most marginal and peri-pheral strata of society. Miracles, for instance, are articles of faith for masses, but not for the intellectuals of the church.[63]

The relationship between common sense and philosophy is assured by politics, Gramsci writes. A paradigmatic example is that of the church, which has historically solved the problem

of the 'simple,' that is a split within the community of the
faithful not by raising the simple to the level of the intellectuals
'by imposing an iron discipline on the intellectuals so that they
do not exceed certain limits of differentiation and so render
the split catastrophic and irreparable.' In so doing the Catholic
church has tended 'to leave the "simple" in their primitive
philosophy of common sense.'[64]

Thus, the value of ideologies, Gramsci concludes, is not
determined by the intrinsic characteristic of rationality, but
rather by the degree of its diffusion in society.[65]

A conception of the world is unable to permeate a whole
society and become 'faith,' unless it demonstrates of being
capable of replacing preceding conceptions and 'faiths' at
all levels of social life...It must be noted that a faith unable
to be translated in 'popular terms' proves to be the characteristic of a certain social group.

Despite all attempts at social integration, subaltern classes
are not successfully integrated into the ideological bloc and
they cannot be, Gramsci notes, until they themselves become
the state. 'The history of subaltern social groups is necessarily
fragmented and episodic. There undoubtedly does exist a
tendency to ... unification in the historical activity of these
groups, but this tendency is continually interrupted by the
activity of the ruling groups.'[66]

In defense of his theoretical position on common sense
Gramsci engages in a critical debate with the positions of Croce
and Bukharin once again. From this debate emerges a clarifica-
tion of the role of Marxism vis-à-vis the spontaneous philosophy
of the masses.

Critique of the idealist conception of common sense
Gramsci views his debate with Croce as a confrontation between
Marxism and the neo-idealist philosophy prevailing in the
Italian intellectual climate, in order to eliminate it and dethrone
it from its position of cultural and intellectual supremacy. The
debate is complex, subtle and multifaceted. It involves a
discussion of the conception of history, philosophy, dialectics,
religion, politics and ideology. What interests us here is their
stance on the problem of common sense.

Idealist philosophy relegates common sense to a low level of
intellectual activity and excludes it from participation in the
high culture of intellectual elites. Marxism, as a philosophy of
the masses, comes, instead, to the rescue of common sense
attempts to transform it and raise it to the level of the highest
philosophical thought. Their contrasting attitude toward
common sense derives from the opposite philosophical nature
of idealism and Marxism. Gramsci was convinced that the
problem of Marxism in Italy was inextricably linked to that of
idealism and that the possibility of a socialist revolution in his
country was dependent upon the intellectual liquidation of
Croce's idealist philosophy. Such a philosophy, however,

represented a great step forward in the evolution of modern
thought. Croce's idealism, in fact, represented for Gramsci a
successful attempt at elaborating, against the vulgar evolutionist positivism, an historicist conception of the world which
negated all absolutes and all metaphysical, transcendent and
theological concepts posited in the understanding of historical
development. Yet, as we have previously noted, it did not go
far enough. It remained a 'speculative,' 'metaphysical'
philosophy, for it continued to view reality in terms of 'eternal
categories of thought,' universal and extra-historical concepts. For Croce, thought is historical and practical. Gramsci
accepted the equation, but in a different sense. For Croce,
history is a metaphysical concept, a history of ideas; for
Gramsci, it is concrete praxis. This implies that while for Croce
all problems are historical but their solutions universal, for
Gramsci they are both historical, that is dependent upon the
affirmation of a concrete political praxis. In Croce's historicism,
history and philosophy are identified. This identification must
be pressed to its extremes. History must be identified with
politics and ideology. As Nardone puts it, both Croce and
Gramsci agree on the necessity of historicizing knowledge, and
on two sets of equations: history=philosophy and politics=
ideology. But while Croce privileged the first, Gramsci
emphasized the latter. The theoretical and practical implications
of this are of great importance. For Gramsci, it is politics
which produces historical truths. In Croce theory is separated
from praxis, intellectuals separate from the masses, and pure
culture from popular culture. Gramsci goes beyond Croce by
identifying the two sets of equations: history=philosophy=
politics=ideology.[67] In a word, it is praxis which determines
the nature of philosophy. Croce's exclusion of politics and
ideology from the realm of pure thought, science and rationality
has the unintended consequence of transforming the stratum
of intellectuals into a priestly caste and culture into a phenomenon independent from politics.[68]

> What interests Croce is the fact that the intellectuals do not
> lower themselves to the level of the masses, but understand
> that ideology, a practical instrument of government, is one
> thing, and another thing is philosophy and religion which
> need not be prostituted in their priestly conscience.

Needless to say, Croce's rejection of ideology amounts to taking
a real 'ideological' position in Italian politics. It negates political conflict while it exalts a 'disinterested contemplation of
the eternal unfolding of human history.'[69]

As we have noted above, the value and practical importance
of a philosophy for Gramsci is proven by its becoming 'action.'
Now idealist philosophy is incapable of becoming a genuine
and integral conception of the world, for it is unable to leave
the narrow, restricted groups of intellectuals and become a
mass culture, or mass conception. The philosophy of praxis
alone can be considered as an integral philosophy because of

its popular and practical character. To repeat again, for
Gramsci, 'mass adhesion or non-adhesion to an ideology is
the real test of its rationality.'
   What is then the nature of philosophy of praxis? Gramsci
answers: it is a 'creative' and 'critical' intellectual order. It
is creative in the sense that it presents itself as liberation
from objectivistic and reified thought and modification of the
feeling of the many.[70] And it is critical activity in the sense
that it makes the mass thinking a coherent unity. In this
respect, Marxism stands in opposition to common sense. However, it accepts the most progressive elements present in
common sense which aid the process of autonomous development
of subaltern masses. In opposition to idealist philosophy, the
philosophy of praxis minimizes the 'individualistic' moment of
the elaboration of thought and insists on the process of diffusion of critical activity among all strata of the population. In
so doing, it tends to present a 'superior' conception of the
world.

   Philosophical activity is not to be conceived solely as the
   'individual' elaboration of systematically coherent concepts,
   but also and above all as a cultural battle to transform the
   popular 'mentality' and to diffuse the philosophical innovations which will demonstrate themselves, to be 'historically
   true' to the extent that they become concretely - i.e. historically and socially - universal.[71]

   Creating a new culture does not only mean one's own individual 'original' discoveries. It also, and most particularly,
   means the diffusion in a critical form of truths already discovered, their 'socialisation' as it were, and even making
   them the basis of vital action, an element of coordination
   and intellectual and moral order.[72]

Marxism is a criticism of common sense. But unlike idealist
philosophy, it does not tend 'to leave the "simple" in their
primitive philosophy of common sense.' It helps them to transcend common sense by developing the good sense present in
it. In this sense it can be said that Marxism is, for Gramsci,
a process of aristocratization of popular masses, a means by
which the autonomous development of the masses is made
possible.[73] Idealism, in contrast, because of its ideological
commitment precludes the process of massification of 'high'
philosophy and 'high' culture. Gramsci notes in this context
Gentile's and Croce's stance on the subject of the teaching of
religion in Italian schools, which is indicative of their elitist
approach to common sense. Gentile, for instance, wrote that
philosophy is reflective thought, an effort 'to gain critical
certainty of the truths of common sense.'[74] His interest in
common sense arises from the need of finding in it 'the confirmation of the truth,' the truth of his philosophical vision, Gramsci
comments. As in the case of Croce, he admits that religion
represents the primitive, infantile phase of modern thought.

Yet, as Minister of Education, he upheld the teaching of religion in the schools. This demonstrates the caste-like nature of idealist philosophy and its intent of leaving the masses in their primitive and backward world of religion, superstitions, in a word, of common sense.

Critique of the vulgar Marxist conception of common sense
If Marxism is a transcendence of popular Weltanschauungen and a superior elaboration of a new conception of the world which critically diffused and internalized by the masses is able to generate an intellectual and ethical reform of popular consciousness, it will not come as a surprise that Gramsci severely criticized the orthodox current of Marxian theory. In such a critique he was not alone. Many German Marxists in the late 1920s and early 1930s had criticized the simplistic theoretical formulation and political naïveté of the expositors of Soviet Marxism. Together with his political mentor, Antonio Labriola, Gramsci became the leading critic of such vulgar, dogmatic and positivist form of Marxism, which had rigidified Marxian theory to such an extent that any attempt at developing it was labelled 'heresy.'[175] Bukharin's theory of historical materialism became Gramsci's main target.

As we have seen, Gramsci took Bukharin to task for having separated philosophy from history and eliminated from Marxian theory its backbone, the notion of dialectics. As a result, Marxism was reduced both qua politics and history to a positivist sociology. It became a fatalist, metaphysical and objectivistic conception of reality and history and contributed to maintaining the political and cultural subordination and passivity of the masses. What was Bukharin's intended goal in publishing his 'Popular Manual of Marxism,' Gramsci asked. Apparently that of systematizing the theory of historical materialism and popularizing it among the revolutionary masses. Marxism then was conceived as a 'theory' complementing 'practice,' as an 'accessory of practice.'[176] Hence the need was felt to produce a manual of Marxist principles to be diffused among the masses. No mention or critical analysis is made of the crucial role of the intellectuals and the party and their relationship to the masses. The theoretical and practical implications of Bukharin's Marxist conception are evident. By reducing philosophical Marxism to the simplistic formulation contained in Marx's 'Manifesto,' Bukharin seems to believe that socialist revolutions occur even when the economic and social conditions are not ripe. Needless to say, this totally negated Gramsci's theoretical and political positions. For Gramsci, socialist revolutions are the product of a long, complex and molecular transformation of mass consciousness, the culmination of a long process of cultural emancipation of popular masses from the political and cultural hegemony of capitalist classes. We have examined elsewhere Gramsci's critique of Bukharin's positivism and mechanicism. We consider here another aspect of this critique, the relation of Marxism to common sense.

First of all, Bukharin engages Marxian theory in a critical debate with opposing intellectuals and their ideologies. He does this not from a position of strength. He seeks to demonstrate the superiority of Marxism on the basis of elements derived from common sense. Unknowingly, he capitulates to the same mistaken position of idealist philosophy, according to which the historical value of a theory resides in its internal, logical and rational coherence.[77] Cultural hegemony, thus, for Bukharin is achieved simply by substituting for one philosophy a superior one, mechanically and authoritatively. What makes a philosophy 'superior' is its adherence to common sense. By identifying Marxism with common sense, Bukharin, Gramsci argues, identifies it with the a-critical, incoherent, undialectical elements of common sense. His Marxism then becomes crassly dogmatic, a-historical and undialectical. 'It is felt that the dialectic is something arduous and difficult, in so far as thinking dialectically goes against vulgar common sense, which is dogmatic and eager for peremptory certainties and has as its expression formal logic.'[78] The equation of Marxism and common sense prevents Bukharin from going beyond traditional idealism and traditional materialism, 'philosophical expressions of past societies' and from arriving at a conception of Marxism as 'an integral and original philosophy which opens up a new phase of history and a new phase in the development of world thought.'[79] Bukharin's attempt to criticize past philosophies with conceptual tools derived from common sense is comical at best, Gramsci continues. He forgets that common sense is an historical product and represents 'the most typical case of the distance that has grown up between science and life, between certain groups of intellectuals - who are however in "central" positions of command in high culture - on the one hand, and the great popular masses on the other.'[80] Bukharin's capitulation to common sense is a capitulation to the very positions that he is eager to annihilate. He in fact attacks the metaphysical and speculative character of idealism, but ultimately he himself falls into a metaphysical position when he posits the existence of extra-historical laws of historical development. Likewise, he criticizes the 'subjective' conception of reality in the name of common sense. But he does not realize that common sense itself is characterized by a metaphysical orientation of religious origin, 'the conception of the objective reality of the external world in its trivial and uncritical sense.'[81]

The starting point of a new philosophy of the masses must be, Gramsci argues, a criticism of common sense as a first step toward a more general criticism of past philosophical systems. Criticism does not mean rejection, rather it means the transformation and transcendence of common sense, which implies the acceptance of vital, positive and progressive elements present in it. This is a precondition to Marxism's goal of cultural elevation of the masses. To substantiate this

Gramsci quotes Henri Gouhier:[82]
> There is but one sole movement of spiritualisation, be it in
> mathematics, physics, biology, philosophy or morals: it is
> the effort through which the spirit frees itself from common
> sense and from its spontaneous metaphysics which envisages
> a world of real sensible things and man in the middle of this
> world.

Thus the realization of Marxism for Gramsci is transposed to
the level of a cultural struggle to create a new culture, a
'single cultural climate.' Cultural unity, that is, unity of high
and popular culture, is not achieved through a systematic
exposition of a conception of the world, but through a dialectical
contact between the intellectuals and the masses. The real task
of Marxism is that of 'raising the tone and intellectual level of
the masses' and making them conscious and active participants
in the revolutionary process and critical elaboration of thought.
The task is that of aristocratizing the masses, of 'reforming
intellectually and morally social strata culturally backward.[183]
The renovation of common sense, however, is not the function
of intellectuals separated from common sense, but in dialectical
relationship with it. Any statement to the contrary would
amount to an a-historicist affirmation.[84]
> A philosophy of praxis cannot but present itself at the out-
> set in a polemical and critical guise, as superseding the
> existing mode of thinking and existing concrete thought (the
> existing cultural world). First of all, therefore, it must be a
> criticism of 'common sense', basing itself initially, however,
> on common sense in order to demonstrate that 'everyone' is
> a philosopher and that it is not a question of introducing
> from scratch a scientific form of thought into everyone's
> individual life, but of renovating and making 'critical' an
> already existing activity.

Gramsci and Bukharin are indeed at opposite poles in their
approach to common sense. For Bukharin, common sense is the
expression of the natural attitude of the masses, for Gramsci
it is a negative, primitive Ptolemaic conception of the world.
Equating Marxism with common sense is equivalent to demonstrating its inability to become a hegemonic conception. On the
contrary, by positing a critical relationship between them,
Marxism can be understood as the 'result and crowning point
of all previous history.'[85]
In concluding this chapter it is worthwhile to make a passing
reference to a considerable body of contemporary sociology, the
so called phenomenological and common sense sociologies, whose
general assumptions and methodological principles are seriously
criticized in an implicit manner by Gramsci.
Following positivism's loss of theoretical predominance,
various sociologies have emerged in recent years with a focus
on 'common sense,' and 'everyday life.' Phenomenology,
ethnomethodology, symbolic interactionism and critical sociology
are all manifestations of, and theoretical self-consciousness of,

the crisis of 'scientific objectivism.' It can be said that the
growing disenchantment with, and rejection of objectivism in
social science explains the popularity of various subjectivistic
theories. A point common to all these 'common sense sociologies'
is a return to the 'subject' and shared intersubjectivity as the
realissimum of social order, to subjectivity as the causal element
of social processes, and to intuitive evidence as the methodological canon of analysis.[86]

Alfred Schutz's phenomenological sociology represents one of
the first attempts to restore to human conduct the subjective
and intersubjective dimensions denied by the scientific objectivism of positivist sociology. Human experience, Schutz writes
in a perspective derived from Husserl, is always experience of,
and in a life-world (Lebenswelt), and consciousness is always
consciousness of something. The life-world is the sphere of
everyday life, of experiences, actions, in which individuals
act, think, and orient themselves toward others and pursue
their routine activities. Ultimately, it is society, culture and
language which provide the individual with a common stock of
knowledge made-up of specific recipes for acting and interpreting the very world he inhabits with other men. Everyday
knowledge, common sense knowledge and everyday life thus
become the most paramount reality in human existence. As
everyday knowledge is pre-given and pre-structured, individuals tend to assume a pragmatic and utilitarian (natural
attitude) toward it. They, in fact, Schutz argues, do not
question the meaningful structures of everyday life, but prefer
to be of it and in it as simple participants. The 'bracketing'
of underlying assumptions of everyday life becomes the principal
task of phenomenological sociology with little or no influence
on the 'natural attitude' typical of the man in the street. Living
in the world of everyday life is experiencing an intersubjective
world, and sharing with fellow men in part some zones of over-
lapping relevances. Common sense knowledge presupposes,
then, a minimum agreement of a 'world' within a common reach,
the dynamic element of which is a reciprocity of perspectives
and motives, allowing actors in a given situation to perceive
as others do.

By focusing on the problems of consciousness and life-world,
phenomenology rejects the classic concern with the externality
of social phenomena, central in Durkheim's and much of contemporary neo-positivist sociology, as well as the conflictive
basis of social order, the cornerstone of Marxian analysis.
Understanding social life comes to signify understanding the
processes by which reality is humanly constructed on the basis
of intersubjective experience.[87]

From Schutz's phenomenology two contrasting developments
emerged: a macro-phenomenological approach and ethnomethodology. The first is best typified by Berger's and Luckmann's sociology of knowledge. Here the central concern is
with the analysis of 'everything that passes for "knowledge"

in society,[188] more specifically, with processes by which any corpus of knowledge comes to be established as reality.[89] Of all types of knowledge, common sense knowledge is of paramount importance, for it alone is the most universally shared, massive and objective. The world of everyday life is a world which originates in the thought of ordinary members of society and is maintained as 'real' by them. It is through the processes of habitualization, objectivation and internalization that men find the remedy to an anthropologically built-in instability and proceed to create a stable environment, a shared, agreed-upon edifice of meanings. It is precisely the construction of such an edifice of meanings that makes social order possible, and not the ideas, the theorizing or Weltanschauungen elaborated by a limited group of people, Berger and Luckmann note.[90]

The other development of phenomenology is exemplified by ethnomethodology. Jack Douglas has singled out two varieties: the situational and linguistic ethnomethodological analysis.[91] The first focuses on the process of getting at the meanings of individuals in a given situation, or in Garfinkel's own words, on the study of the indexicality of everyday accounts and the manner by which participants in a situation go about sharing the 'rational account.'[92] Linguistic ethnomethodology, on the other hand, focuses more directly on linguistic phenomena, on concrete statements made by individuals in a situation and on the implications of these meanings to the action of individuals. Ethnomethodology in general becomes deeply concerned with penetrating normal situations of interaction to uncover rules and meanings that human actors take for granted. In this attempt the best research strategy is a purposeful disruption of real, everyday situations to expose underlying assumptions. Ethnomethodology restricts its inquiry to the relationship between the taken-for-granted meanings of participants in a situation and the routine patterns which emerge out of interaction. Thus it transforms itself into a science of man without society and history.

Ethnomethodology is not concerned, as Mennell has noted, with the problem of building theories or making all-encompassing generalizations, for it negates the 'trans-situational constancy of meaning.' Human interaction is always ambiguous and problematic, ethnomethodologists argue. Social order is then possible to the extent that individual participants in a situation arrive at a common agreement as to its definition.[93] It suffices here to note that, from a Marxist position, Marcuse has already denounced the ideological implications of linguistic philosophy developed by Wittgenstein, to whom ethnomethodologists are profoundly indebted. The ordinary universe of discourse, ordinary language, Marcuse writes, bereft 'of the means for expressing any other contents than those furnished to the individual by their societies,' is a 'purged,' and 'impoverished' language.[94] Marxist analysis, Marcuse continues, 'uncovers the history in everyday speech as a hidden dimension of meaning: the rule of society over its language.' [95] Thus, it can be said that if ethnomethodology accuses conventional sociology of misplacing concreteness, Marxist analysis rejects ethnomethodology for its commitment to false concreteness. The commitment to the common usage of words, and common universe of discourse is a commitment to leave everything as is. This implies a negation of the critical nature of prevailing behavior and the critical dimension of sociological analysis. Ethno-methodology thus capitulates to the power of positivist thought and methodology and comes close to accepting a behaviorist theory of human behavior.

Symbolic interactionist theory is also characterized by a rejection of the behaviorist approach in sociological analysis and the adoption of a subjective realist perspective. Like phenomenology and ethnomethodology, symbolic interactionism has consistently taken the perspective of the acting person. But it has focused more directly on the relationship between the individual and the social group to explain the emergence of meanings of objects, behavior and institutions. Through acquisition of common meanings derived from social interaction, individuals are integrated into social structures. Entire societies, Denzin writes, are created and function because of the 'ability of humans to join lines of action in a consensual and meaningful manner.'[96]

All these 'common sense sociologies' are theoretical mani-festations of the intellectual crisis existing in contemporary social thought, itself a consequence of the general alienation prevalent in contemporary industrial societies. That is to say, they represent on the level of consciousness and thought a crisis existing on the level of human praxis. These highly individuated sociologies are the theoretical legitimation of the retreat of the individual into a private sphere of activity and are forms of intellectual escapism, as Berger brilliantly observes. They are the intellectual counterpart of phenomena, such as counter-culture and youth culture in human praxis, themselves escapist forms of responses to the frustrations of functional rationality that technology imposes on all aspects of human life. It is the nature of modern societies which creates the socio-logical context of highly individuated persons, ideologies and ethical systems, Berger writes.[97]

The common element in all common sense sociologies is that they are developing not a science of man, but a science of atomized individuals committing the same fallacy of solipsistic philosophies. Their theoretical framework is a-political, a-historical and undialectical, similar to that of the conventional sociology they so sharply criticize. They are all concerned with consciousness and meaning in human conduct, to be sure. But their interest is limited to the consciousness of normal adults, of mature individuals capable of self-reflection and self-criticism. But, how does consciousness emerge and mature? How to explain the various forms of consciousness of men, groups, classes and societies? What are the forces that pit these forms of consciousness against each other? And more importantly, how to explain the relationship between the structures of societies and those of human consciousness? The answers to these questions, in Gramsci's sociology, are to be sought in the wider context of the dynamics of history. History is the history of the conscious freedom of subaltern masses, of their ascendant movement toward political and cultural autonomy.

Gramscian Marxism shares with common sense sociologies a common interest. They all advocate a 'return' to common sense as the foundation of knowledge. This amounts to a proclamation of the centrality of men in the process of history. However, unlike common sense sociologies, Gramscian Marxism does not limit itself to understand common sense, but to change it. That is, as we have seen, it is committed to liberate and purify it from past sedimentations, transform it and elevate it to the status of an integral Weltanschauung. Common sense sociologies leave common sense intact, which is the equivalent of saying, in Gramscian words, they leave the 'simple' in their primitive conditions of cultural and intellectual poverty. Gramscian Marxism, in contrast, aims at aristocratizing common sense, and ennobling popular Weltanschauungen. Furthermore, common sense sociologies, by eliminating the dynamics of history, produce a-political analyses of common sense. Gramsci's analysis of common sense is eminently political, in so far as it focuses on basic, objective contradictions, masses and elites, masses and intellectuals, ruling classes and subaltern classes, theory and praxis. Common sense, the process of its diffusion and renovation are all political acts. It follows that common sense is not viewed as an intellectual order containing greater truths, but as the basis for the search and creation of new historical truths. Thus, the relationship between Marxist theory and common sense is dialectical. As we have seen, Marxism is a criticism of common sense, at the same time as its content is derivative of common sense. Common sense is the typical Weltanschauung of the masses in their subaltern phase of development. Their assertion as hegemonic forces entails a process of transformation of the content of their language. Hence the necessity of a renewed common sense, which is the philosophy of praxis. The philosophy of praxis in Gramsci is simply a renewed common sense, the Weltanschauung of subaltern classes aspiring toward political and cultural hegemony. Socialist transformation is the process of political and cultural emancipation of the masses. We have called such emancipation, a process of aristocratization of masses; it is facilitated by the important role of organic intellectuals.

4 THE INTELLECTUALS AND THE DYNAMICS OF HISTORICAL BLOCS

The profound structural transformations taking place in contemporary industrial societies in the area of politics, economics and culture, and in the nature and functions of those in charge of their administration, have rendered the problems of Marxism and socialist revolution more complex on the level of theory and praxis. The Marxist critique of contemporary society has been thrown back, Marcuse notes, toward a high level of abstraction.[1]

It is commonly acknowledged that Gramsci's analysis of the role of intellectuals in connection with the more general problems of 'hegemony' and 'historical blocs' represents one of the most creative developments in the history of Marxist theory. Without doubt he is the only Marxist theoretician to have analyzed from a consistent standpoint the problem of intellectuals and ascribed to them a crucial role in the processes of formation and maintenance of past, present and future hegemonies. In our opinion, Gramsci's analysis, despite its fragmentary and sketchy nature, contains the most fundamental elements for the elaboration of a general theory of intellectuals.[2]

The social stratum of intellectuals has not been extensively investigated. Studies on the subject are sparse and limited in scope owing to some false assumptions underlying contemporary social thought. Among them are the widespread belief that the stratum of intellectuals has become a case of historical and political marginality running counter to the pragmatic development of the world of business,[3] and the belief shared by phenomenological and common sense sociologies that theoretical thought and 'ideas' are not that important in society, being reality constructed on a non- or pre-theoretical level.[4]

Traditionally, studies on intellectuals have focused on specific types, mainly academic intellectuals, bureaucratic intellectuals, technocrats and technicians.[5] Some of them have attempted to analyze the relationship between intellectuals and power and investigated the modes and problems of their access to power, prestige and status in society.[6] Others have concerned themselves with establishing ideal sociological types.[7] Approaches to the analysis of intellectuals have also varied. Some studies have dealt with the most prominent intellectual figures or movements in the history of social and political thought.[8] Others have investigated the integrating function of intellectuals in industrial societies and the process of diffusion of the intellectual phenomenon among the masses, or the specific role of intellectuals within the bureaucratic setting or their role in politics.[9] Most of these studies emphasize the phenomenon of marginality of intellectuals, the conditions and reasons for the emergence of alienated intellectuals in contemporary societies and their association with leftist or Marxist ideologies, often attributed to the rise of new types of intellectuals, the 'scientific intellectuals.'[10] It can be said that despite sporadic interest in the problem of intellectuals, a theory of intellectuals has not yet been elaborated.

Marx and Mannheim are to be considered pioneers in such an undertaking. Marx has the merit of first observing how the division of labor has engendered a special group of ideologists perfecting the illusions of ruling classes. One of the characteristic features of capitalism for Marx was the proletarianization of intellectual professions: 'The bourgeoisie has stripped of its halo every occupation hitherto honored and looked up to with reverent awe. It has converted the physician, the lawyer, the priest, the poet, the man of science, into its paid wage-labourers.'[11]

In the traditional Marxist analysis of intellectuals, there is no consistent line of development except the generally held belief that the intelligentsia is a consequence of stratified society. Intellectuals have not been totally held in contempt for their inherited or attained social standing nor acclaimed as potential defenders of the revolutionary cause of progressive forces. Marxism has regarded them with great suspicion and paradoxically wooed them as important elements in the process of erosion of the capitalist world. Kautsky, in fact, conceptualized the relationship between intellectuals and the proletariat as that of 'social antagonism' rather than 'economic antagonism,' for intellectuals per se are not bourgeois, but as their work has to be produced and sold, they have been exploited by capitalist entrepreneurs. Lenin also, despite his contempt for intellectuals, affirmed the necessity for the proletariat to create its own intellectuals. On this matter Mao Tse-tung wrote that 'a correct policy toward intellectuals is one important condition for the victory of the revolution.'[12]

The view that enjoys a certain prestige today in the non-Marxist world is that of Karl Mannheim. His sociology of knowledge, an approach based on the fundamental proposition of the 'existential determination of knowledge,' although it derogates knowledge, accords intellectuals a privileged position in the attainment of objective thought. He inconsistently postulates the existence of objective criteria for integrating and synthesizing the various particular views assured by the classless position of the 'socially unattached intellectuals.' As classless aggregates, intellectuals have the task of providing an interpretation of the world for the society they live in. They are able to comprehend the conflicting forces of historical situations with a synthesizing attitude, for they are 'recruited from constantly varying social strata.' In static societies, they are assured of a caste-like position (magicians, Brahmins, medieval clergy), enjoying a monopolistic control over the molding of global societal Weltanschauungen, which leads them toward 'scholasticism' and 'remoteness' from the open conflicts of social existence. In contrast, the open system of class societies, operated by the principle of competition, has undermined the monopolistic ecclesiastical interpretation of the world and enabled the emergence of a free intelligentsia or 'free-floating intellectuals.' They adopted 'the most various modes of thought and experience available in society and played them off against one another,' competing for the favor of the public 'no longer accessible to them without their efforts.'[13]

We might conclude that despite the number of studies on intellectuals, a sociology of intellectuals is non-existent for the simple reason that there is no consensus among sociologists on the definition of the term 'intellectual.' Divergent conclusions have been drawn as a result of divergent notion about intellectuals. Hundreds of definitions of the terms 'intellectual' and 'intelligentsia' have been proposed. All of them fall into certain categories. Shils ascribes to intellectuals the role of employing in their communication and expression 'symbols of general scope and abstract reference,' concerning man, society and the cosmos. Lipset ascribes to them the role of creating, distributing and applying culture, and Mannheim defines them in terms of their capacity to transcend the existing social structures and comprehend the totality of the historical phenomenon.[14]

Similarly, in the Marxist literature intellectuals have been variously categorized. Generally, they have been characterized in terms of the mental nature of their work and criticized on the level of their life-style and personal traits. In the second place, a segment of the intellectual stratum has been identified as ideologists. As such they are the servants of power, the intellectual instrument of oppression of subaltern classes. This category is the subject of criticism, their mystification is denounced and their class interests unmasked. Finally, there is the category of 'critical intellectuals' understood as constituting a smaller segment of the general stratum of intellectuals which tends to ally with and to support the ethos of 'progressive' revolutionary movements, providing them with the necessary intellectual weapons to assure their continuous development toward the assumption of power.

Common to all these categories of definitions is the assumption that intellectuals are characterized either by the nature of their work or the nature of their ideas. In either case, their functions are those of creating and diffusing high culture and ideologies. Both views account for a specific aspect of reality but do not provide precise characterization of the nature and function of the intellectuals in the dynamics of historical processes. Gramsci is the first theoretician to propose a definition of intellectuals in terms of their role in the process of development of specific historical hegemonic systems. For him history is not made by elites or the masses but by intellectuals in dialectical relationship with the elites or the masses in an historical development leading to the formation of ideological and political hegemonies.

In this chapter we will first examine the role of the intellectuals in the dynamics of 'historical blocs,' then proceed to analyze Gramsci's typology of intellectuals and the characteristic features of new intellectuals in a socialist society, followed by a discussion of the importance of Gramsci's theory of intellectuals within the framework of Marxist theory.[15]

THE INTELLECTUALS AND THE PROCESS OF FORMATION OF HEGEMONIC SYSTEMS

Intellectuals cannot be defined in terms of criteria intrinsic to intellectual activities, Gramsci writes, for in any form of physical labor, no matter how degraded and mechanical, there always exists a minimum of technical qualification, that is, a 'minimum of creative intellectual activity.' As in the definition of laborer, not the intrinsic characteristics of labor but the performance of work in 'specific conditions' and in 'specific social relations' is the constitutive criterion of distinction.[16]

The most widespread error of method seems to me that of having looked for this criterion of distinction in the intrinsic nature of intellectual activities, rather than in the ensemble of the system of relations in which these activities (and therefore the intellectual groups who personify them) have their place within the general complex of social relations.

Intrinsic criteria of distinction do not help to determine the nature of intellectual activity, for 'all men are intellectuals.' But it is also true that 'not all men have in society the function of intellectuals.' Thus, the criterion of distinction has to be located in the nature of such functions, that is, the 'general complex of social relations.' To be sure, non-intellectuals do not exist, first, because, as we have seen, intellectual activity is always in some degree inherent in any form of work, and second, because all men operate in a network of social relationships that are essentially intellectual in nature. Each man, in fact,[17]

outside his professional activity, carries on some form of intellectual activity, that is, he is a 'philosopher', an artist, a man of taste, he participates in a particular conception of the world...therefore contributes to sustain a conception of the world or to modify it, that is to bring into being new modes of thought.

Gramsci's analysis of the functions of intellectuals cannot be understood independently of the problem of the constitution of historical blocs and the dynamics of class relations.[18]

A given historical bloc is a global historical context or situation characterized by an organic link between a specific

structure, the ensemble of social forces and the world of
production, on the one hand, and the vast realm of an ideological superstructure, on the other hand. Such organic link
is realized when given 'essential' or progressive social groups
attain their ideological and political hegemony. In pre-industrial
societies the prevailing hegemonic system was that of various
forms of aristocracy; in capitalist societies it is that of technocrats and technicians, and obviously in socialist societies,
that of proletarian classes. The problem of the structure/super-
structure relationship is certainly one of the most delicate in
Marxist literature. It has generated a controversy between
those who assert the primacy of the structure or of the superstructure. In Gramscian perspective such a controversy is
sterile and out of focus. The real problem lies in the organic
link between structural and superstructural elements within
specific historical contexts. Such 'organicity' is always provided by a specific stratum of intellectuals, who, by virtue of
their function in the process of development of essential social
groups, are always dependent upon the structure and increasingly responsible for the elaboration of the entire complex of
superstructural activities. They are, in fact, the functionaries
of the superstructure.

A general theory of intellectuals needs also to take into
account the concrete form of the general development of the
historical process, that is, the gradual development of specific
social groups which, born as economic-corporate entities in
the world of production, develop into hegemonic systems as
they assume the intellectual, political, and ethical direction of
the totality of social activities. The development of a social
group in Gramsci's view is an historical development from a
negative condition characterized by partial, determinate class-
based economic interests to a condition in which it becomes
the instrument of new ethico-political forms. Such development
is, for Gramsci, a cathartic process from economy to politics,
more precisely from economism to political consciousness. The
transition from a mere economic to a political entity for any
social group implies that as long as it remains in the sphere of
economic activity (class as 'economic fact'), it is incapable of
becoming the subject of ideological and political hegemony, in
other words, of becoming a state. Hence, the importance of
intellectuals in the realm of superstructure becomes clear. The
process of internal transformation of an essential social group
from economic to hegemonic entity is the product of the stratum
of intellectuals, and inversely, the acquisition of political
consciousness by potentially hegemonic groups generates a
transformation of the nature and function of the intellectual
stratum.

Subaltern groups are characterized by a condition of cultural
and political immaturity. By definition, Gramsci writes, they
are incapable of elaborating integral conceptions of the world.
On the cultural level, as we have seen, the masses' world views

are spontaneous, irrational, folkloric, superstitious, in a word,
'common sense.' Common sense contains essentially negative
elements as its state of disintegration and lack of intellectual
coherence demonstrate. Subaltern groups are the repository
of past cultural sedimentations which have accumulated in their
consciousness. Mass consciousness is 'false consciousness' in
so far as it lacks critical thinking and fosters an attitude of
general passivity which prevents the masses from thinking
and acting historically and dialectically. On the level of political
consciousness, subaltern groups are characterized by a lack
of political will, or political autonomy; they form the raw
material for the history made by others. Their history is impregnated with localistic, naturalistic and fatalistic attitudes. The
most important aspect of their immaturity is their separation
from the intellectuals, and most significantly their inability to
produce intellectuals. Marxism, then, for Gramsci is the most
integral conception of the world aiming at raising the intellectual level of the masses through the establishment of a new
organic and dialectical relationship between intellectuals and
the masses.[19]

It is precisely in this unique conception of the historical
process that Gramsci's discussion of the intellectuals has to be
analyzed. For Gramsci, the creation and maintenance of hegemonic systems depend on the realization of an organic and
dialectical relationship between intellectuals and the masses,
a relationship which will be fully established in socialist
societies. He finds in history several examples of such attempts
at creating this unity. But these are incomplete or negative
models compared with the one Marxism can produce. An illustration of this point is furnished by the history of the Roman
Catholic church. It has been a constant preoccupation of the
church to preserve the ideological unity of the entire religious
body and ensure that the higher intellectual stratum did not
separate from the base. Such a model of organic unity is
negative in as much as 'it is politics that assures the relationship between the Catholicism of the intellectuals and that of
the simple,' preventing the appearance of a split within the
community of the faithful. Such a split has been healed,
Gramsci writes, not 'by raising the simple to the level of the
intellectuals,' but only 'by imposing an iron discipline on the
intellectuals so that they do not exceed certain limits of
differentiation and so render the split catastrophic and irreparable.'[20] As a result, the masses have been kept in their
native world of passivity and superstition. In contrast, the
organic unity between intellectuals and the masses postulated
by Marxism is antithetical to that of religion.[21]

The philosophy of praxis does not tend to leave the 'simple'
in their primitive philosophy of common sense, but rather to
lead them to a higher conception of life. If it affirms the
need for contact between intellectuals and simple it is not in
order to restrict some scientific activity and preserve unity

at the low level of the masses, but precisely in order to
construct an intellectual-moral bloc which can make politically possible the intellectual progress of the mass and not
only of small intellectual groups.

It seems that from a Gramscian perspective the fundamental
problem facing any cultural, political, and ideological movement
is that of creating and preserving the 'ideological unity' of
the entire bloc. If movements such as those of the immanentist
philosophies, Renaissance, Reformation, and idealism have
failed, in the sense of not having become universal and integral
conceptions of the world, the reason lies in their inability 'to
create an ideological unity between the bottom and the top,
between the "simple" and the intellectuals.'[22]

The modern history of Italy is also a case in point. The
Italian intellectuals have traditionally been cosmopolites. Cosmo-
politanism is for Gramsci the process by which a vertical
relationship with the base (masses) is substituted by a hori-
zontal one connecting intellectual elites among themselves on
the national and international scale. Thus, separated from the
masses, the intellectuals feel the need to assert themselves
as an uninterrupted continuity in history. The abstractness
of their theories or systems of thought increases proportionately to their withdrawal or detachment from the reality of
social conflicts. In effect, Gramsci observes, such autonomy
is denied by history.[23]

> Every social group, coming into existence on the original
> terrain of an essential function in the world of economic
> production, creates together with itself, organically, one
> or more strata of intellectuals which give it homogeneity
> and an awareness of its own function not only in the economic
> but also in the social and political fields.

This passage is of paramount importance since it contains
'in nuce' the whole Gramscian theory of the intellectuals. They
do not constitute a class, but 'strata' produced by each social
group.[24] The most important of them are formed when essential
groups come into existence. That is to say, any given fundamental group in the process of its development creates its own
intellectuals with a function directly related to the position
it occupies in the world of production. The capitalist entre-
preneur, Gramsci notes, has created with himself 'the industrial
technician, the specialist in political economy, the organizer
of a new culture, of a new legal system,' an intellectual elite
with 'a certain technical capacity, not only in the limited sphere
of his activity and initiative but in other spheres as well....He
must be an organizer of masses of men.'[25] The notion of
'intellectual' is thus expanded. The intellectual function is not
exercised by any given professional group, but is inherent
in the intellectual strata organically linked to a social group.
Consequently, Gramsci's sociology of intellectuals concerns
itself with the problem of identifying the group which, in varying historical contexts, exercises the intellectual function.

The stratum of intellectuals normally exercises economic and
hegemonic functions. At the onset of the development of essential social groups, intellectuals help elaborate the consciousness
of common economic interests. They actively participate in
the process of constitution of social groups from an amorphous
collection of individuals into a homogeneous structure. Furthermore, they help the cathartic transformation of the groups'
trade unionist condition into a hegemonic one. In the process
of such transformation the nature and function of intellectual
strata also expand to embrace the entire realm of superstructural
activities. Any social group, then, which aspires toward
hegemony needs, in order to be successful, to create its own
stratum of intellectuals capable of exercising such global
functions. Without intellectuals performing hegemonic functions,
a group is doomed to remain an economic corporate entity.
Normally, all social groups produce intellectuals who defend
their class interests, but only fundamental groups produce
intellectuals with hegemonic functions. Thus, the intellectual,
for Gramsci, becomes not only the generator of class consciousness, but also the elaborator of homogeneous and autonomous
conceptions of the world which expand to include the entire
society on the level of production and distribution of knowledge.
A group, then, is said to be dominant when it is able to produce a great number of specialized intellectuals for all specialized activities and a conception of the world more integral
and homogeneous.

In conclusion, the fundamental functions of intellectuals are
structural but more importantly superstructural. In fact, from
mere '"specialisation" of partial aspects of the primitive activity'
of the new social group, the intellectuals become 'the functionaries of the superstructure,' the engineer of the masses'
consent to the ideology of dominant classes.

TYPOLOGY OF INTELLECTUALS AND THE DYNAMICS OF INTELLECTUAL BLOCS

Organic intellectuals and the constitution of bourgeois hegemonies

Gramsci distinguishes two major types of intellectuals: organic
and traditional intellectuals. Organic intellectuals are those
whose origin coincides with that of the group they represent.
They are defined in terms of the functions attributed to them
by the social group from which they originate, first in the
sector of economic activity and subsequently in that of ideology,
politics and culture. The process of development of intellectuals
is not one-sided, in the sense of being a mere reflection of
class interests, but dialectical. Born from a group having an
important function in the world of production, they act back
on it by transforming it into an organized collective will. Thus,
they are a function of class interest but also an instrument of

class transformation. As we have seen, to each mode of production corresponds a fundamental social group and a specific type of intellectual. In capitalist societies, for instance, the development of industry has introduced a new type of intellectual: the industrial technician and the various specialists of applied science. These are the 'organic intellectuals' of the industrial bourgeoisie. In the course of their development they encounter another stratum of intellectuals, the 'traditional intellectuals.'

The traditional intellectuals present themselves as an 'uninterrupted historical continuity' much as ecclesiastical hierarchies legitimate their status by tracing their origin to the apostles and Christ, Gramsci writes. The raison d'être of their existence is the autonomy of their past and their caste-like position in society.[26]

> every 'essential' social group which emerges into history out of the preceding economic structure... has found... categories of intellectuals already in existence and which seemed indeed to represent an historical continuity uninterrupted even by the most complicated and radical changes in political and social forms.

These intellectuals share a common characteristic, an avowed independence from the activity of the new social group. What really defines traditional intellectuals, as a Gramsci scholar has noted, is the 'dialectically negative politics with regard to the new social group.'[27] Their self-proclaimed autonomy stands in direct opposition to the global aspirations of new progressive social groups. They do have in reality a true 'monopoly of the superstructure' as the history of various historical blocs demonstrates. The central problem of Gramscian analysis, then, becomes the distinction between these two types of intellectuals and the study of concrete 'intellectual blocs' within the context of historical blocs which vary from country to country. As an illustration of Gramsci's thesis we will briefly mention the case of the initial development of bourgeois revolutions in France, Italy, England and Germany.[28]

The case of bourgeois hegemony in France   The crucial element in the struggle of the French bourgeoisie against the landed aristocracy has been the conflict between the organic intellectuals of the bourgeoisie and the church. A progressive bourgeoisie has gradually been able to erode the feudal institutional structure with the creation of the capitalist mode of production. The ascendant movement of the bourgeoisie encountered in the struggle against the aristocracy, its powerful monolithically organized ally, the clergy, that is, a stratum of traditional intellectuals, ideologically autonomous and independent from the new dominant social group. Despite their pretensions to the universality of their mission, spiritual or ethical in character, the ecclesiastics were the monopolizers of social institutions, of 'religious ideology, schools, education,

morality, politics, charity etc.[29] They were, in fact, the
organic intellectuals of the landed aristocracy. To be sure,
they were not aristocrats, but because of their possessions and
privileges they did enjoy a social status similar to that of the
aristocracy. Classic bourgeois tactics in regard to these
traditional intellectuals have been either their liquidation or
their assimilation. The French Revolution, for instance, knew
a series of conflicts between the organic intellectuals of the
bourgeoisie and the church for the ultimate direction of the
civil society, conflicts which led to various compromises,
concordats and finally the Dreyfus affair, signaling the victory
of anti-clerical forces against the powerful clergy-monarchy
coalition.[30]

These historical events demonstrate the process by which
an essential class has been successful in progressively assuming ideological control over the civil society by assimilating
the traditional intellectuals and winning the consent of popular
forces. The bourgeoisie equipped 'for all its social functions'
conducted a struggle for total domination of the nation. Such
a hegemonic intellectual bloc was so integrated that any attempt
by the Action Française to restore the ideological adhesion
of the Catholic masses to the ideologies of the clergy and
aristocracy always failed. The case of the bourgeois revolution
in France induces Gramsci to draw this important conclusion:[31]

> One of the most important characteristics of any group that
> is developing towards dominance is its struggle to assimilate
> and to conquer 'ideologically' the traditional intellectuals,
> but this assimilation and conquest is made quicker and more
> efficacious the more the group in question succeeds in simul-
> taneously elaborating its own organic intellectuals.

Assimilation or liquidation of traditional intellectuals seems to
be for Gramsci the key factor in the success of various bourgeois revolutions.

The case of bourgeois hegemony in Italy   The Italian bourgeoisie began to develop about the eleventh century, the epoch
of medieval communes, of autonomous city states. The communal
bourgeoisie managed to displace the political domination of
the aristocracy but was unable to transcend the 'corporate
phase,' to create a state 'with the consent of the governed,'
that is, unable to create political and ideological superstructures
for lack of organic intellectuals.[32] Intellectually disarmed before
the ideological influence of traditional intellectuals, the clergy,
instead of assimilating it, the new group capitulated to it.
The short-lived period of communal bourgeoisie was then
followed by the formation of principalities administered by the
old aristocracy. The failure of the Italian bourgeoisie is attributed to the power of the Italian clergy which exercised a
true integral hegemony and politically controlled vast terri-
tories enabling it to dominate ideologically vast populations.
Conversely, the success of the clergy in its hegemonic struggle

against the bourgeoisie lay precisely in preventing the creation of bourgeois organic intellectuals through a molecular process of assimilation of these potentially disruptive strata into the international community of the church. As Piotte, a contemporary Gramsci scholar, noted, the Italian traditional intellectuals integrated (de-nationalized) the intellectuals of the bourgeoisie or forced them to emigrate if they refused to submit.[33] The caste-like position and power of traditional intellectuals retarded considerably the process of development of the Italian bourgeoisie until a century after the French Revolution, that is, the Italian Risorgimento when it was finally able to attain its hegemonic pre-eminence through the political activity of the Moderates and the Action Party which 'exercised a power of attraction "spontaneously", on the whole mass of intellectuals of every degree who existed in the peninsula, in a "diffused", "molecular" state,....'[34]

The strategy of the Italian bourgeoisie fundamentally differed from that of the French bourgeoisie. The latter, in its struggle against the aristocracy, managed to obtain the consent of subaltern classes, the peasantry in particular, by detaching them from the sphere of influence of the clergy and assimilating them. In contrast, the Italian bourgeoisie did not seek the support of popular elements; it used instead Piedmont, a northern monarchical state, as the instrument of Italian unification.[35] This is a case of domination and not hegemony. The strategy of the Italian bourgeoisie has been rightly called by Gramsci 'transformism,' the process of assimilation of intellectuals of the subaltern classes by the dominant political class, depriving them of their organic intellectuals. Molecular transformism, the incorporation of individual political figures issuing from revolutionary parties, was followed by a politics of transformism, a process by which entire groups were assimilated into the dominant camp.[36] Moreover, the ideological assimilation of large masses seems to have been a more effective mechanism as in the case of the famous southern Italian question.

This case illustrates the importance that Gramsci attributes to the concept of traditional intellectual.[37] The south produces traditional intellectuals, the north organic intellectuals of a progressive bourgeoisie. Rural intellectuals, because of their petit bourgeois origin, exercised functions economically opposed to the interests of the class they were supposed to represent. They were organically linked to the dominant class through their participation in a tightly knit 'intellectual bloc.' Round and about the dominant class there existed an ideological bloc dominated by the thinking of great intellectuals (the intellectuals of the intellectuals), among them Benedetto Croce, the Hegel of the Italian philosophy. His influence was of historical importance. Because of his international prestige and influence, Croce had been able to separate southern Italian intellectuals from the mass of peasants, integrating them into the mainstream of national and international high culture. The

assimilation of the intellectuals of subaltern classes, for
Gramsci, represented a process of neutralization of the revolutionary aspirations of subaltern classes. A politics of transformism was adopted, that is, the molecular process of incorporation of the most active and articulate spokesmen of subaltern
classes into the judiciary and the administration of the state.

The case of bourgeois hegemony in England and Germany   The
development of the English bourgeoisie offers a model essentially different from that of Italy and France. Here, bourgeois
revolution was characterized at its onset by a fusion between
old and new hegemonic groupings. The old aristocracy remained
a governing stratum with certain privileges, but became the
intellectual stratum of the English bourgeoisie. The bourgeois
group is induced 'not to struggle with all its strength against
the old regime, but to allow a part of the latter's facade to
subsist, behind which it can disguise its own real domination.'[138]
Thus, the leading personnel of the dominant bourgeoisie is
constituted by elements of old feudal classes which, dispossessed
of their economic pre-eminence, found new forms of economic
power in the world of industry and banking.[39] How, then, can
such industrial development be accounted for in terms of a
dialectic between organic and traditional intellectuals? Gramsci
himself provides a tentative hypothesis for research. The
English bourgeoisie created organic intellectuals on the economic-
corporate level, but was not powerful enough in its ability to
exercise the political and intellectual functions of a more global
nature. Thus, the bourgeoisie incorporated the old landed
aristocracy into the state's administration. As a consequence,
deprived of its economic supremacy, the landowning aristocracy
preserved its position of virtual monopoly in the form of
political-intellectual prominence; it is assimilated, Gramsci
writes, as a stratum of 'traditional intellectuals and as a directive [dirigente] group by the new group in power. The old
landowning aristocracy is joined to the industrialists by a kind
of suture which is precisely that which in other countries
unites the traditional intellectuals with the new dominant classes.'[40]

The industrial development in Germany presents an analogous
pattern. Here the bourgeoisie asserted itself within the context
of a quasi-feudal society, showing a similar fusion between old
and new hegemonic groups. The German bourgeoisie assumed
the industrial and economic direction, leaving to the Prussian
Junkers the political and intellectual direction of the country.
To counter the Junkers, the progressive German bourgeoisie
lacked, as in England, organic intellectuals with hegemonic
functions. The Junkers became the traditional intellectuals of
the German industrialists, but retained the functions of direction
and organization as well as an economic base of their own,
special privileges and a strong consciousness of being an
independent group.

In conclusion we might say, these four cases of bourgeois hegemony constitute, for Gramsci, three models of successful bourgeois revolution brought about by three different strategies employed by bourgeois organic intellectuals against their respective traditional intellectuals.[41]

Hierarchization of intellectuals within the complex of the superstructure
Within the context of a hegemonic system Gramsci's socio-historical analysis of the functions of intellectuals focuses on the relationship between the intellectuals of dominant social groups and those of subaltern groups, that is, organic and traditional intellectuals. From this standpoint, all groups possess a stratum of intellectuals. The important problem is how the organic quality of such strata can be measured. It will then be necessary to establish a qualitative hierarchy of intellectuals within the framework of the complex of the superstructures.[42]

The relationship between the intellectuals and the world of production is not as direct as it is with the fundamental social groups but is, in varying degrees, 'mediated' by the whole fabric of society and by the complex of superstructures, of which the intellectuals are precisely the 'functionaries'. It should be possible both to measure the 'organic quality' [organicità] of the various intellectual strata in their degree of connection with a fundamental social group, and to establish a gradation of their functions...

Intellectuals are structured according to the qualitative value of their function in the creation, organization and administration of the complex of superstructures. At the highest level one finds the creative intellectuals, those who create various sciences, global theoretical systems and ideologies, and at the lower level, those charged with the function of administration and diffusion of 'pre-existing, traditional, accumulated intellectual wealth.[43] At the intermediate level there is a category of intellectuals charged with organizational functions of all superstructural activities essential to the survival of the dominant ideology and hegemony. This hierarchized structure of intellectuals constitutes, for Gramsci, the core of any hegemonic system.

This qualitative structure of intellectuals provides new progressive social groups with the necessary strategies for the attainment of their hegemony. In historical situations in which the struggle among social groups takes the form of an ideological struggle, as in Western capitalist societies, where the civil society is strong and well organized, the role of creative intellectuals, as Gramsci calls them, is more decisively strategic. In this case, socialist struggle has to concentrate its efforts on a systematic ideological confrontation with this type of intellectuals, 'leaving aside the men in the second rank, the regurgitators of second-hand phrases.'[44]

On the ideological front, however, the defeat of the auxi-

liaries and the minor hangers-on of all but negligible
importance. Here it is necessary to engage battle with the
most eminent of one's adversaries. Otherwise one confuses
newspapers with books, and petty daily polemic with scientific work. The lesser figures must be abandoned to the
infinite casebook of newspaper polemic.

While in those historical situations in which the struggle takes
the form of a political military struggle, that is, in those
situations in which political society is strong and well organized:
'it can be correct tactics to break through at the points of
least resistance in order to be able to assault the strongest
point with the maximum forces that have been precisely made
available by the elimination of the weaker auxiliaries.'[45]

The strategic importance of the 'great intellectuals' is
explained by Gramsci in terms of the specific functions they
play in the articulation of historical blocs, as in the case of
southern Italy. The role of subaltern intellectuals (intermediate
and lowest), however, cannot be minimized in the process of
revolutionary transformation. As we have seen, in the case
of southern Italy, their dependence and assimilation into the
dominant intellectual bloc assures the smooth functioning and
perpetuation of the capitalist hegemonic system; but they are
strategic elements, always potentially disruptive forces. Their
massive withdrawal of allegiance from the dominant hegemony
can facilitate 'organic crises' ultimately leading to its collapse.
Their consensus and dissensus can therefore entail stability
or revolutionary change.

In conclusion, the distinction between intellectuals as an
organic category of essential social groups and intellectuals as
a traditional category generates a 'whole series of problems and
possible questions for historical research.'[46] Historically,
Gramsci writes, the formation of traditional intellectuals is the
most interesting problem. Their presence helps determine the
intellectual strata which a new, progressive social group must
assimilate if it wishes to assure itself of complete hegemony over
all other groups in a given social structure. The characteristics
of such intellectuals have been well summarized by Piotte.[47]

They are constituted by intellectuals organically linked to a
social group emerged from within an old system of mode of
production.

They are the intellectuals dependent on classes which have
disappeared or are in the process of extinction, but are not
organically linked to the new dominant classes.

They present themselves as independent and autonomous social
categories.

They produce ideologies by which their class origin and class
position is mystified along with their intellectual hegemony over
the total social structure.

In concurrence with Piotte, we conclude that Gramsci emerges
as the first Marxist theoretician to develop a new and original
line of research on the nature and function of ideologies.

Traditionally, Marxism has attempted to explain the problem
of survival of old ideologies and treated them as economic and
political vestiges of ancient modes of production or as false
systems of beliefs legitimizing past social stratifications. In
contrast, Gramsci attempts to understand the reasons for the
survival of old ideologies in terms of the strength and power of
influence of traditional intellectuals. Their importance can be
seen in their function of articulating and strengthening the
entire complex of superstructural activities, thus preventing
or retarding the process of revolutionary change. Such is the
case of Europe, where 'there exists a whole series of checks
(moral, intellectual, political, economic, incorporated in specific
sections of the population, relics of past regimes which refuse
to die out) which generate opposition to speedy progress.'[48]
As a result in these historical situations, the task of new
progressive social groups has to be that of absorbing or assimilating such traditional intellectuals. This necessity is intrinsic
to the more fundamental process of creating organic intellectuals,
both essential to the constitution of new historical blocs. These
two processes have significant strategic implications for the
creation of a socialist hegemony.

Our focus will now shift to the analysis of the role of new
intellectuals in the dynamics of socialist society.

NEW INTELLECTUALS AND SOCIALIST TRANSFORMATION

The emphasis on the class nature and functions of intellectuals
in classical Marxism had the effect of obliterating the revolutionary role of intellectuals in socialist transformation and
further increasing the opposition between intellectuals and
proletarian classes. The relationship between them was conceptualized on the level of theory and socialist praxis as that
of a politically expedient alliance for the conquest of political
hegemony. The dogmatic posture of various communist parties,
as Macciocchi has noted, has further contributed to workers'
lack of interest toward the problem of intellectuals.[49] Thus,
serious contradictions emerged in Marxist theory and socialist
strategy. On the one hand, intellectuals are regarded with
great suspicion, hostility and contempt, and on the other hand,
an alliance with them has been repeatedly and openly advocated
in the official circles of communist parties. To this one has to
add, Macciocchi continues, the un-Marxist stance assumed by
communist parties in certain countries, defending the autonomy
and independence of individual intellectuals. Picasso, for
instance, is admired for his talent and communist ideals, but
exempted from criticism for his lack of political involvement
and contact with the laboring classes. Failure to understand
the crucial role of intellectuals in socialist revolution and
socialist hegemony has weakened the revolutionary potential
of communist parties in the industrialized countries of the West.

This is one of Gramsci's most original ideas. Intellectuals are denied any organic contact with the masses on the grounds that only the leadership of the party is the ultimate expression of working-class consciousness. This explains the common lack of interest in the problem of intellectuals, and, more seriously, the inability of Western communist parties to come to grips with Gramsci's analysis of intellectuals, which demands a creative reformulation of Marxist theory and socialist revolutionary strategy.

Gramsci - and on this point we are in full agreement with Macciocchi's observations - has reversed the classic Marxist approach to the problem of intellectuals. The relationship between the intellectuals and the masses is an organic component of socialist revolution. The intellectuals have to become the organic intellectuals of subaltern classes. This concept entails a redefinition of the notion and function of the party, aptly called the collective intellectual. The sense of this expression is profound and original indeed in the history of Marxist thought. The party, organically linked to and in dialectical relationship with the masses, is the point of convergence of a multiplicity of creative minds and at the same time the instrument of cultural, moral renovation of the masses.[50]

The concept of autonomy of intellectuals derives implicitly from Hegel's idealist philosophy. For Hegel, in fact, the historical process is the manifestation of the gradual unfolding of reason which objectifies itself in society by the process of fusion of contradictions. Each thesis engenders an antithesis. Both are resolved in a synthesis, whose architects and arbitrators are the intellectuals.[51]

In real history the antithesis tends to destroy the thesis, the synthesis will be a transcendence, but no one can establish *a priori* what element of the thesis will be 'preserved' in the synthesis....One can observe that such a way of conceiving the dialectics is typical of the intellectuals, who view themselves as the arbitrators and mediators of concrete political conflicts, those who personify the 'catharsis' from the economic to the ethical-political sphere, that is the synthesis of the dialectical process itself, synthesis which they 'manipulate' speculatively in their minds....This position justifies their complete 'non involvement' in the historical act and is undoubtedly a comfortable one: it is the position of Erasmus in regard to the Reformation.

For Gramsci, intellectuals are directly dependent on a given social group; such dependence is both organic and dialectical. Any change in their structural base (group) entails a transformation of their nature and functions. Thus, as long as the bourgeoisie is a progressive group, its intellectuals remain organic intellectuals, but once it loses its progressive character its intellectuals become traditional in relation to the new group ascending toward hegemony. The historically progressive groups exercise 'such a power of attraction' over the intellectuals of other social groups that they eventually assimilate them. This is one of Gramsci's methodological criteria of socio-historical analysis. But what are the criteria for assessing the progressive nature of social groups?

A given group is said to be progressive when it possesses the capacity not only to develop society's productive forces, but also to elaborate the entire complex of the superstructure. These two processes take place in a dialectics between the social group in question and its intellectuals, which is a dialectic between structure and superstructure. As the development of the superstructure is not an autonomous process, but a process limited and conditioned by the structure, so intellectual activities develop always within the limits imposed by their structural base. At the same time, through the activity of organic intellectuals they become the force of transformation of the base (group) from a corporate-economic condition to a hegemonic one. It is in this context that Gramsci's insistence on the necessity for proletarian classes to elaborate their own organic intellectuals must be explained. Organic intellectuals have been a key factor in all bourgeois revolutions. They are also of strategic importance in socialist transformation.

In fact, at their onset, progressive industrial classes have been capable of autonomous development climaxing into a true hegemony precisely because of their ability to produce 'new' intellectuals. The industrial revolution, in effect, not only created technicians, but also a stratum of technical intellectuals in charge of global societal organizational activities, that is, of activities well beyond the world of business itself.[52] This unique pattern of development can be theoretically stated as follows: political-intellectual-cultural activities are an integral part of industrial activity and are always articulated by a stratum of intellectuals. Thus, productive classes in Gramsci's view tend to become not only the organizers of economic activities, but also, and more importantly, organizers of all systems of social relationship, in a word, the organizers of economic, ideological and political hegemony.

The problem of socialist transformation is, then, posed by Gramsci as a problem of disintegration of the intellectual bloc sustaining the capitalist order and as a process of development of critical consciousness among the masses. The elaboration of this form of consciousness is the primary function of the new intellectuals. 'Critical understanding of self takes place therefore through a struggle of political "hegemonies" . . . first in the ethical field and then in that of politics proper, in order to arrive at the working out at a higher level of one's own conception of reality.'[53]

The strategic importance of the new intellectuals in socialist revolution lies in the nature of the struggle against capitalism, which is essentially an ideological struggle. The organic intellectuals of the bourgeoisie for the mass of subaltern classes have become traditional intellectuals to ideologically assimilate.

We have here a process of erosion of the capitalist hegemony at all levels and in all areas, leading to an 'organic crisis,' which proletarian forces precipitate by means of their organic intellectuals. The ideological and cultural disintegration increases proportionately to the progressive acquisition of critical consciousness by the masses. By themselves, the masses cannot elaborate critical consciousness. They need organic intellectuals.[54]

> Critical self-consciousness means, historically and politically, the creation of an elite of intellectuals. A human mass does not 'distinguish' itself, does not become independent in its own right without, in the widest sense, organizing itself; and there is no organization without intellectuals, that is without organizers and leaders, in other words, without a theoretical aspect of the theory-practice nexus...

The characteristics of the new intellectuals are clear, then. They perform intellectual, political and technical functions. The necessity of direct contact between the intellectuals and the masses entails a convergence of intellectual and political functions. Thus, the new intellectuals are those who distinguish themselves from the masses to become the organizers of a new collective will. Technical education will still remain an important function of the new intellectuals. Technique, however, has to be superseded by politics. 'From technique-as-work one proceeds to technique-as science and to the humanistic conception of history, without which one remains "specialised" and does not become directive (specialised and political).'[55] The new intellectuals abandon the pursuit of abstract knowledge, transcend the narrow sphere of their specializations by politicizing them and become the organizers of the consciousness of the masses. As a result, their 'directive' functions ensure that technical activities are transformed and incorporated into a humanistic conception of the world. 'The mode of being of the new intellectual can no longer consist in eloquence, which is an exterior or momentary mover of feelings and passions, but in active participation in practical life as constructor, organizer, "permanent persuader".'[56]

The intellectuals of the bourgeoisie are nothing but technicians; those of progressive proletariats are technicians plus active participants in a conception of the world which transforms the world of nature as well as the social world. Of the two elements, intellectuals and masses, neither is privileged, for both are necessary constitutive elements of a dialectical relationship. The specialist and *elitist character that Gramsci attributes to the new intellectuals seems to respond to the exigencies of the immediate political conditions, but such necessity is transitory.*[57]

> But innovation cannot come from the mass, at least at the beginning, except through the mediation of an elite for whom the conception implicit in human activity has already become to a certain degree a coherent and systematic ever-present awareness and a precise and decisive will.

The process of development of the new intellectuals is the product of an organic and dialectical unity between the intellectuals and the masses, between theory and praxis. To the extent that subaltern groups increase their level of critical consciousness, they expand also the stratum of their organic intellectuals, and to the extent that their intellectuals extend the sphere of influence on larger sectors of the social structure, they expand the socialist ideological hegemony. In other words, there is no one-sided activity of intellectuals, but reciprocal activity between them and the masses. The political party becomes the unifying force of these elements.[58] Its function within the ambit of civil society is that of assuring the fusion between the organic intellectuals and the traditional intellectuals. But once proletarian classes constitute themselves as hegemonic states, such fusion among intellectuals becomes juridically legitimated. In Gramscian perspective, political parties are the elaborators of new, unified and all-absorbing intelligentsia, the 'crucibles where the unification of theory and practice' takes place.[59]

THE SIGNIFICANCE OF GRAMSCI'S THEORY OF INTELLECTUALS

Gramsci's originality in the history of Marxist thought lies, as we have seen in the preceding chapters, in the insistence that revolutionary change can occur only on a plane higher than that of economy.[60] 'It may be ruled out that immediate economic crises of themselves produce fundamental historical events; they can simply create a terrain more favourable to the dissemination of certain modes of thought.'[61]

Analyzing concrete historical situations, Gramsci largely employed Marx's classic structure/superstructure dichotomy, but emphasized the primacy of superstructure over structure.[62] In so doing, he did not deviate from classical Marxism, rather returned it to its idealist beginnings.[63] Marxism, Gramsci writes, came into existence as a form of ideological critique of the most advanced and refined ideology and as an instrument of education of the masses. In the process of its development all effort was concentrated on the latter at the expense of its primary task of affirming itself as the highest cultural manifestation of Western civilization, an integral conception of the world elevating the intellectual level of the masses. The result was, on the one hand, the elaboration of a form of primitive, vulgar Marxism slightly superior to the cultural forms characterizing the conceptions of the world of the masses, and, on the other hand, the formation of the higher culture and idealist philosophy enveloped in abstract and theoretical schemes restricted to narrow intellectual circles, thus incapable of creating a 'popular culture.'[64] Gramsci attempted to conciliate these two extremes. The analysis of the mode by which dominant

classes established their hegemony induced him to believe that
only through intellectual activity could the masses be elevated
to the role of agents of historical transformation. In formulating
these theses, Gramsci privileged a subjective dimension absent
in the bulk of Marxist literature up to his time. For this reason he became one of the first Marxist theorists of human
creativity and mass consciousness as necessary elements for
the success of socialist revolution. His theoretical position could
be stated as follows: while the structure underwent quantitatively a profound process of transformation, the quality of the
superstructure remained undeveloped.[65]

Marxism, for Gramsci, becomes essentially a cultural, ethico-
political movement, aiming at the cultural unification of the
world, structurally divided, and at the creation of a new
historical bloc. 'Every revolution has been preceded by an
intense labour of criticism, of cultural penetration and diffusion.'[66]

The importance of the historical role assigned by Gramsci
to the intellectuals is not determined by the intellectuals'
strategy to bring to the socialist movement the notion of their
own elitism and authoritarianism as Feuer contends,[67] rather,
it is a response to the exigency of aristocratizing popular
culture and the intellectuality of the masses. It is in this
perspective that one understands why Gramsci has been led to
emphasize the formation of organic intellectuals in the process
of development of mass consciousness. The key to socialist
transformation lies in the superstructure, since only the power
of the intellect and the ethico-political function of the intellectuals can transform human consciousness. They, in fact,
represent the 'critical consciousness' of social groups which is
the real world-shaking and world-transforming force. 'Above
all, man is mind - that is, he is a product of history not
nature.'[68] Knowledge, as the comprehension of the historical
process, becomes the mechanism of winning 'intellectual
autonomy' and 'his own freedom in the realm of ideas by struggling against fatigue, against boredom and against the mono-
tony of a job that strives to mechanize and so kill his inner
life.'[69]

Socialist transformation aims at 'raising the intellectual tone
and level of the masses' through the actualization of a dialectical
unity of the intellectuals and the masses. Without such a
unity both elements are unable to comprehend. 'The popular
element "feels" but does not always know or understand; the
intellectual element "knows" but does not always understand
and in particular feel.'[70] The masses' feelings allow passionate
adherence to ideologies; they are ultimately a controlling force
upon the abstract conceptions elaborated by intellectuals.[71]

One cannot make politics-history without this passion, without this sentimental connection between intellectuals and
people-nation....The relationship between intellectuals and
people-nation... is provided by an organic cohesion in

which feeling-passion becomes understanding and thence
knowledge...

Perhaps the absence of such a nexus between intellectuals and
the masses provides a better explanation of why anti-intellectualism in modern times has become a way of life and why
intellectuals have become a marginal stratum, whose knowledge
is not wanted by society at large, as Berger and Luckmann
put it.[72]

The superiority of Marxism over all other philosophical systems
consists for Gramsci in this: it extols the power of the intellect,
will and consciousness in a meaningless, mindless and alienating
world. Long before the Frankfurt school, Marcuse and Ellul,
Gramsci pointed out that the tyranny of society lies precisely
in having co-opted intellectuality and transformed it into the
servant of dominant power. It follows that only when knowledge
is restored to the service of the collectivity can radical change
occur. But this runs counter to the present trend of bureaucratization of knowledge.

It is a truism in contemporary sociology that the intellectual
phenomenon has been transformed into a bureaucratic phenomenon.[73] Max Weber has understood the bureaucratic phenomenon
as a necessity inherent in all technocratic societies, technocracy
and bureaucracy being interdependent. Complementing Marxian
theory, the Weberian thesis states, as Zeitlin has pointed out,
that the most important consequence of contemporary capitalism
is its tendency to concentrate not only the means of production,
but also the means of administration, violence, and knowledge
in the hands of a few organisms of power, known as the process
of bureaucratization.[74] Such a process, although it generates
dysfunctions, is deemed a necessary one simply because it is
technical, rational and most efficient.[75]

Shil's macro-sociological analysis of the intellectuals in some
respects comes closer to that developed by Gramsci. Both speak
of the diffusion of the intellectual phenomenon among the
citizenry and proliferation of intellectual roles in contemporary
societies. Shils, however, attributes such processes to the
differentiation of functions and tastes in civil society, while
Gramsci, from a Marxist perspective, uncovers the monopolistic
hegemonic functions of a hierarchically organized 'intellectual
bloc,' as we have shown. Shils focuses on the quantitative
character of the stratum of intellectuals, Gramsci, in contrast,
examines the qualitative nature and functions of such a stratum.
For Shils, intellectual activity 'in humanitarian and democratic
societies' has become more diffused throughout society, extended
so to speak from a 'small group of wealthy and traditionally
ascendant families, first to the wider reaches of the property-
owning classes and then to the citizenry at large.' 'The more
complex the structure,' he continues, 'and the larger the scale
of undertaking, the more likely it is to involve a component
of intellectual action.'[76] Shils does not ask important sociological
questions: who are those who perform hegemonic intellectual

functions? To which group are they attached and whose interest
do they serve? How are various categories of intellectuals
assimilated, integrated or subordinated to culturally dominant
ones? And finally, what type of relationship exists between the
latter and the highest organisms of power? Gramsci's answer
is: an organic one. There is always a socio-structural base for
any intellectual activity and, therefore, a conflict among
intellectuals. Berger and Luckmann seem to agree with Gramsci:
'power in society includes the power to determine decisive
socialization processes and, therefore, the power to produce
reality....Rival definitions of reality are thus decided upon
in the sphere of rival social interests whose rivalry is in turn
"translated" into theoretical terms.'[77] But Gramsci would qualify
such statement by adding that the social base itself is incapable
of resolving intellectual rivalry without a stratum of organic
intellectuals transforming its nature and interests.

Max Weber was among the first to point out the alienating
consequences of the process of bureaucratization. He hoped for
the emergence of charismatic leaders to humanize the world.
Overall, Gramscian analysis contrasts sharply with that of
Weber. The latter does not take into account the dynamics of
social classes or the ascendant movement of new progressive
groups which, throughout history, have been able to topple
old hegemonic systems and establish new ones with the help of
intellectuals.

The problem of the bureaucratization of the intellectual
phenomenon for Gramsci is one aspect of the general problem
of the intellectuals and a consequence of the degeneration of
democratic systems. More precisely, it is the result of bureaucratic centralism, a tendency of political organizations or any
type of voluntary organism to select individuals and groups
around an 'infallible bearer of truths' or one who is 'enlightened
by reason' through a process of co-optation.[78] Bureaucratic
centralism is a phenomenon which occurs in situations where
groups, parties or organizations are no longer progressive
or receptive to waves of innovation stemming from below. In
such conditions, the relationship of single individuals to the
collective organism, of parts to the whole, is essentially a
fetishist relationship, in the sense that individuals come to
perceive the organism in question as an entity external to
themselves, thinking and acting independent of their intervention.[79] Bureaucratic centralism is the result of the absence
of 'organicity' between the intellectuals and the masses, Gramsci
concludes. It comes out for lack of initiative and responsibility
at the bottom as well as for lack of political maturity of
peripheral forces.[80] Gramsci speaks of 'democratic centralism,'
a system in which stability and movement coexist without
solidifying mechanically into a bureaucracy. Democratic
centralism is:[81]

a 'centralism' in movement i.e., a continual adaptation of the
organization to the real movement, a matching of thrusts from

below with orders from above, a continuous insertion of
elements thrown up from the depths of the rank and file into
the solid framework of the leadership apparatus which ensures
continuity and the regular accumulation of experience.

To the negative features of bureaucratic centralism, Gramsci
opposes not the authority of charismatic leaders as Weber and
Michels but the establishment of centralized but democratic
relations, which he calls 'integral democracy.'[182]

Democracy... is an ideology that cannot fully establish itself
in capitalist societies. The part of it that can be realized is
liberalism, through which all men can become *authority* from
time to time as minorities circulate: all men can be capitalists,
but not all at the same time, rather, a minority at a time.
Integral democracy maintains the principle of 'all at the same
time.'

Gramsci's analysis does not provide a complete theory of
intellectuals. It contains, however, the fundamental components
for the elaboration of such a theory. His analysis remains
abstract and rigid, lacking flexibility of application to the
structure of contemporary societies. Nevertheless, Gramsci
remains the first Marxist theorist to have investigated the
profound structural modifications undergone by intellectual
strata as changes in economic and political conditions occurred
in various historical situations. He did not foresee, for instance,
the extent to which scientific and technical revolutions in our
times would affect the totality of the superstructure and its
dependence on the structural base. The scientific-technical
revolution has rendered obsolete the classic distinction between
economic and political components of social structures so rigidly
maintained by classical liberalism.[83] By necessity, political
organisms have been pressed to intervene at an increasing rate
in the operation of the economic sector and industrial organizations equally induced to concern themselves with the global
functioning of the economic system, which implies direct involvement in political affairs.

A new stratum of intellectuals has been created, composed
of technocrats and technicians. Both are, as we have seen, the
organic intellectuals of contemporary capitalist hegemony, the
monopolizers of the functions of power and knowledge. What
is important to note is that these new types of intellectuals are
linked not to any fundamental class, but to a general process,
that of scientific and technical development. As Bon and Burnier
note, there is a difference between technocrats and technicians,
a difference closely resembling Merton's distinction between
policy-makers and technicians.[84] Technocrats are intellectuals
who exercise hegemonic functions in societies based on science
and technology; technicians, on the other hand, represent
the ensemble of scientific and technical personnel. The first
control the direction of science and technological progress, the
latter are the instrument of administration and application of
science. The technocrats are close to the seat of power, their

goals and means to achieve them are not economistic but hegemonic. In contrast, the technician does not possess power and
lacks an ideology and organization of his own. The powerlessness
of this stratum will result in its proletarianization, as the means
of administration and decision-making process will be increasingly concentrated in the hands of fewer technocrats. Thus,
the possibility of revolution in the Western world is becoming
greater as the crisis among the organic intellectuals deepens.[85]
The stratum of technicians is destined to become more dominant
and powerful in societies in which automation reduces proletarian classes to marginal phenomena. These new developments
in capitalist societies do not alter significantly Gramsci's
analysis of intellectuals, but pose new problems on the level of
socialist strategy for the conquest of hegemony. For instance,
should the organic intellectuals of the new progressive groups
proceed to assimilate the intellectual stratum of contemporary
capitalism, as Gramsci proposes, or, rather, should they join
forces with the proletarianizing group of technicians as Bon
and Burnier have recently advocated? On the possibility of
socialist revolution in affluent and industrialized societies, some,
such as C. Anderson, have recently voiced the viewpoint that
the increasing radicalization of the productive sector of the
working class in the next decade will lay the foundation for
socialist revolution. Such radicalization, it is said, is the result
of new contradictions developing in neo-capitalist societies
and the work-specific problems of alienation and exploitation.[86]
We do know, however, that the American working class is
anti-socialist and anti-revolutionary and is engaged in a 'politics
of interest groups and the economics of state manipulation.'[87]
From a non-Marxist framework, Irving Horowitz argues that
the most vigorous critique of the bourgeoisie, as a class of those
who are neither engaged in managerial work nor in production,
but simply absorb profits, will spring from a segment of the
new managerial sector. As this sector moves into labor, a left-
wing movement is likely to emerge.[88] Horowitz, of course,
does not explain the nature of such a shift to the left, the
reasons for the radicalization of the managerial class and what
portion of this sector will be pressed to radicalize. His analysis,
however, seems to lend some support to Bon-Burnier's thesis,
which from a Marxist perspective contends that the nature of
the increasing radicalization of technicians consists in their
proletarianization. This results not from their necessary
pauperization, but rather from their growing sense of powerlessness in the face of the arbitrariness of technocratic power.
Gramsci emphasizes the need to politicize the consciousness
of subaltern groups and bring about a revolution which takes
the form of a total reconstruction of the civil society and
culture. His revolutionary plan calls for an ethico-political
revolution leading to the conquest of ideological and political
hegemony. All bourgeois revolutions have been carried out
with the support of civil society. The intellectuals played the

crucial role of articulating civil society on the level of ideology and consciousness. They performed hegemonic functions in the complex realm of the superstructure. Likewise, the intellectuals are essential in the process of construction of socialist hegemony. To this controversial notion we now turn the focus of our analysis.

5   HEGEMONY IN MARXIST THEORY AND PRAXIS

Having examined the nature and role of masses and intellectuals in Gramsci's general conception of historical development and in the specific process of formation of historical blocs, we now discuss the problem of the nature of historical blocs. No doubt this is one of the most controversial aspect of Gramsci's thought. It is controversial in a double sense. First, it entails a discussion of the complex and delicate problems of hegemony, structure and superstructure, and political and civil society still debated among Marxists and non-Marxists alike. Second, it has given rise to various interpretations of Gramsci's ideas and sharply divided Gramscian scholars. However, most of Gramsci's commentators seem to agree that the notion of hegemony represents his more lasting contribution to Marxian theory and revolutionary strategy for socialist transformation. It provides, in fact, an original theoretical framework for a Marxist analysis of the problem of revolution in advanced capitalist societies as well as the process of consolidation of socialism in those countries where proletarian forces have become victorious. All concepts developed around the notion of hegemony are indeed original, subtle and fluid. Any attempt at defining them would rigidify them, and thus lead to oversimplification and downright distortion. In an effort to maintain the original fluidity and complexity of Gramsci's thought, we have preferred to examine the notion of hegemony in relation to other concepts, particularly those of structure and superstructure, political and civil society, ideology and culture.

As a way of introduction, two observations need to be made. First, the notion of hegemony in Gramsci represents a standpoint from which he critically examines all Marxist literature and revolutionary activity, and critically evaluates all past historical developments, and the contemporary phase of proletarian history.

In a word, it is the viewpoint which provides coherence and profound unity to all elements of his theory. Second, the notion of hegemony constitutes the focal, terminal point of the history of subaltern classes. If the organization of the masses in a collective will marks the beginning of a new history, the attainment of hegemony represents the terminus ad quem, the point of arrival of the revolutionary process. The hegemonic phase of the new history is the phase in which civil and political society, structure and superstructure, theory and praxis, society and culture, intellectuals and masses, philosophy, history, politics and ethics, are all historically unified in a common whole.[1]

In this chapter we shall first examine the notion of hegemony in relation to socialist revolutionary praxis, and then deepen the philosophical meaning of Gramsci's concept of hegemony.

HEGEMONY AND MARXIST PRAXIS

The twin concepts of structure and superstructure are the cornerstone of Marxist analysis. The way people organize society's productive forces gives shape to all social, cultural, legal and political institutions. The ruling ideas of a given society and a historical epoch, Marx wrote, are those of ruling groups. Yet, no consensus has ever been reached on the exact nature of 'structure' and 'superstructure,' and the relationship existing between them. This has resulted in a general confusion in Marxist theory and socialist praxis. Is Marxism a determinist or voluntarist theory? The theoretical source of such confusion is the absence in classical Marxism of a theory of politics and political praxis. A theory of revolutionary praxis is barely sketched in Marx. Revolutionary praxis, in Marx, develops under conditions inherent in capitalism. The growing contradiction between the forces of production and the relations of production generates social and political antagonisms whose solution requires political revolutions by the very subject of capitalist exploitation, the working classes. After Marx other Marxist theoreticians, such as Engels, Plekhanov, Kautsky and Luxemburg, displayed a lack of interest in Marxist theorization of politics. They occupied themselves with organizational and strategic means to bring about the 'revolution.' As Hobsbawm notes, the lack of a theory of politics and a systematic theory of the relationship between 'structure' and 'superstructure' is understandable if one considers the absence of the 'experience' of the revolution.[2]

As we have noted at the outset, it was Lenin who brought to an end the sterile debate taking place among the theoreticians of the Second International which centered around the idea of the historical inevitability of proletarian revolutions or the necessity of full capitalist development for the final crash of the bourgeois state. Lenin freed human conscious will from the servitude of the inexorable laws of historical necessity. Consciousness, will, revolutionary activity and tactics became the decisive mechanisms of the revolutionary process. Lenin's major contribution to theoretical Marxism was a non-mechanistic and non-deterministic understanding of the relationship between structure and superstructure. The categories of consciousness, politics, and ideology became primary and determinant.[3] The October Revolution marked the beginning of a new phase in the development of Marxist thought. It provided the sociological basis for a Marxist theory of politics and political praxis. The debate among the theoreticians left the speculative plane and became more concrete. The discussion centered around the character of social and political institutions in socialist societies and the correct strategy to bring about a socialist revolution in the industrialized countries of the West. The concept of 'hegemony' became the focus of concern of Marxist theory of politics. Lenin had realized a proletarian revolution in the East, Gramsci theorized about its nature and possibility of realization in the West. In an article written at the occasion of Lenin's death, Gramsci asserted: 'Bolschevism is the first movement in the international history of class struggle to have developed the idea of proletarian hegemony, to have applied the principal revolutionary problems sketched by Marx and Engels.'[4] Gramsci paid tribute to Lenin and celebrated the October Revolution as the most important event which radically transformed the thinking of the world. 'One can affirm that the theoretization and realisation of hegemony carried out by Ilich [Lenin] was also a great "metaphysical" event.'[5] The principle of hegemony, Gramsci writes in another passage, was Lenin's 'greatest theoretical contribution to the philosophy of praxis.'[6] However, as we shall presently see, Gramsci is to be credited more than Lenin for refining the concept of hegemony and laying a solid theoretical foundation to the Marxist analysis of hegemony.

Hegemony and the problem of revolution in the West
The first issues that Gramsci confronted regarded the correct strategy for the success of socialist revolutions in Italy and western Europe and, more generally, the various modes of access to power. It became obvious that structural differences between Russia and the West necessitated a different political strategy. He developed the concepts of 'war of movement' and 'war of position.' The first denotes the conquest of power through direct confrontation, the second, the gradual, molecular process by which progressive socialist forces prepare the conditions for the conquest of power. Central to his conception of revolution is the notion of the relationship between its two phases, destruction and reconstruction. All revolutions carried out in two phases, Gramsci notes, have ended in failure. For instance, in the cases of Austria, Germany, Hungary, Bavaria 'the revolution as a destructive act has not been followed by the revolution as a process of reconstructing society on the communist model.'[7] Hence the necessity of posing the problem of revolution in the West in a different manner. In Russia, the state was centralized and concentrated in the hands of the Czar. Its civil society, composed of a ruling elite of feudal, bourgeois and intellectual strata on the one hand, and a vast mass of peasants peripheral to the political life, on the other hand, was extremely weak. The correct revolutionary strategy was clearly that of conquering the state and assuming the political direction of the nation. In contrast, in Italy the state was firmly entrenched in a powerful and complex civil society.

The state derived its strength and support from a network of
private organizations, schools, churches, urban and rural
associations, northern industrialists and southern latifundists,
all reinforcing its power and preventing communist penetration
and domination in the countryside. In addition, Italian and
Western capitalism was successful in creating a well-articulated
political bloc, assimilating some elements of the working class
and integrating the popular masses into its hegemonic structure.
Given these political realities and a more complex social stratification in Western societies, a 'war of movement' was virtually
impossible.

Gramsci opposed the revolutionary strategy advocated by
Rosa Luxemburg, the theoretician of the 'war of movement.'[18]
For Luxemburg, economic crises in the capitalist system provoke
spontaneous waves of reaction, eruption and insurrection which
lead to its final demise. Implicit in such a view, Gramsci argues,
is an element of determinism, the belief that structural elements
are the mechanical cause of the transformation of the superstructure. With regard to a concrete revolutionary strategy,
Luxemburg proposed a general strike involving the party and
various workers' syndicates. Gramsci insisted on the idea
that revolution is an organic, molecular process requiring the
organization of conscious activity and theoretical critical consciousness. This implies that the intellectual, cultural and
political preparation of the working class was a necessary
prerequisite for the success of proletarian revolutions. The
essence of the debate between Luxemburg and Lenin, more
than the emphasis on the role of mass spontaneity vs party
discipline and direction, was a different conception of capitalist
development. For Luxemburg, 'objective' conditions are the
primary cause of the crash of the bourgeois state. For Lenin,
capitalism has the capacity to overcome internal crises through
imperialist practices. Thus, the only strategy for successful
revolutions was proletarian organization, discipline and militancy
under the leadership of a strong communist party. In the last
analysis, while Luxemburg emphasized objective conditions and
mass spontaneity, Lenin put the stress on organization, direction, consciousness and theory.

Gramsci accepted Lenin's criticism of the spontaneity of
Luxemburg's revolutionary theory. Mass uprisings do not lead
to the creation of new socialist order. For Gramsci and Lenin,
spontaneous revolutions are economistic revolutions, characterized by short-range goals. They both stressed the need to
transcend the empirical, limited, economic corporatism of class
and pose the problem of the revolution in terms of conquest
of political hegemony. Gramsci, however, did not accept Lenin's
conclusion that class consciousness is brought to the workers
from above. Despite Lenin's efforts the problem of the nature
and role of consciousness in the revolutionary process remained
unexplained. Both the spontaneist and party strategies of
Luxemburg and Lenin did not deal systematically with such a

problem. Gramsci's question was this: how the economic-corporate phase of proletarian consciousness is transformed into class consciousness, and how from class consciousness the proletariat arrives at the phase of 'hegemony.' Lenin's solutions apply to the Russian conditions. The proletariat organized in a Party, through a war of movement can attain political hegemony. In Italy, and more generally in the West, only a war of position can lead to such hegemony. Are Gramsci's positions divergent from those of Lenin? Gramscian scholars are divided on this issue. It is known that Lenin himself envisaged a specific revolutionary strategy for the West. At the 7th Congress of the Russian Communist Party, Lenin spoke of the serious difficulties in repeating the Russian experience in the West, and dismissed as naive the thought of beginning a revolution without a long period of preparation. This explains the slogan of the Third International: nationalization of the revolution, and its adopted strategy of the united front, that is the politics of class alliances. Comparing Gramsci's notion of war of position with Lenin's politics of the united front, Jean-Marc Piotte demonstrates the profound differences existing between the two. His conclusions are the following: (1) the strategy of the Third International is transitory and valid in all countries; Gramsci's strategy is permanent and implies the coexistence of two world strategies for socialist revolutions, one valid for the West and the other for the East. (2) Gramsci defends the national character of socialist revolutions, their conditions and their direction. (3) By implication the admission of two world strategies to achieve socialist revolutions is a rejection of a unitary communist movement direct by a centralized international organism and leadership, and an affirmation of the autonomy of national communist parties.[9] Piotte's conclusions, although justifiable in terms of isolated Gramscian texts, do not concur with the general sense of Gramsci's thought and his conception of the historical development of subaltern classes. Gramsci's emphasis on the national character of socialist revolutions has to be understood from the international perspective of the working-class struggle. National revolutions are the concrete realization of a phase of the historical development of subaltern classes. The point of departure of the revolution, Gramsci writes, is 'national,' while its terminal point is 'international.'[10]

> The point which seems to me to need further elaboration is the following: how, according to the philosophy of praxis (as it manifests itself politically) - whether as formulated by its founder [Marx] or particularly as restated by its most recent great theoretician [Lenin] - the international situation should be considered in its national aspect. In reality, the internal relations of any nation are the result of a combination which is 'original' and (in a certain sense) unique: these relations must be understood and conceived in their originality and uniqueness if one wishes to dominate them and

direct them. To be sure, the line of development is towards internationalism, but the point of departure is 'national' - and it is from this point of departure that one must begin.

Yet the perspective is international and cannot be otherwise. The relation between the national and international dimensions of revolutions is, then, for Gramsci, a dialectical one. It is true that Gramsci took position against Trotsky on the question of 'permanent revolution' in order to assert the original character of national revolutions, as Piotte notes.[11] But it is also true that what Gramsci criticized in Trotsky was his 'superficially national and superficially Western or European' positions. 'Ilitch [Lenin] on the other hand was profoundly national and profoundly European.'[12]

But, how should Gramsci's note on 'the transition from the war of manoeuvre to the war of position' be understood? Unduly forcing the analogy between political and military strategy, Piotte has not understood the historical significance of Gramsci's note. For Piotte, in Gramsci the war of position precedes the war of movement, that is to say, the frontal attack on state power has to be preceded by the domination of the civil society. The struggle for hegemony, he writes, must prepare the military struggle.[13] The transition from the strategy of 'frontal attack' to that of war of position indicates rather an historically necessary change in revolutionary praxis. As Gerratana observes, the choice between a violent or gradual and peaceful conquest of power is for Gramsci a matter of tactics determined by the political realities of a given historical moment.[14] More correct seems to be Auciello's interpretation, for whom the concept of war of position indicates not only the necessity of a change in strategy in Western socialist revolutions, but also a general modification of the direction of proletarian struggle, valid for all countries, in the West and the East. He writes: '"the war of movement" represented the form of struggle appropriate to an historical phase which came to an end in 1917-1921, with the triumph of the Russian Revolution and the defeat of the revolutionary movements in the West.'[15] To understand fully Gramsci's revolutionary strategy the notion of 'hegemony' needs be analyzed in great detail.

Ideological hegemony and political hegemony
Despite the attribution of the notion of hegemony to Lenin by Gramsci, almost all commentators agree that its elaboration is Gramsci's creation and represents his major contribution to theoretical Marxism.[16] The notion of hegemony is initially defined in the 'Southern Question' and distinguished from that of 'dictatorship of the proletariat.' In this essay, written just before his incarceration, hegemony is defined in terms of the proletariat's role during the revolutionary phase of the conquest of power. Two ideas are predominant. First, the proletariat presides over a system of class alliances. Thus, proletarian hegemony refers to the political direction which the

proletariat exerts over allied social groups, above all the
peasantry. The conditions of such hegemony are: the transcendence of the economic-corporate interests of class and the
acquisition of a global vision, which include the problems of
the state, civil society and effective representation of the
interests and aspirations of all subaltern social groups. Second,
proletarian hegemony is achieved through the enlargement of
a social consensus around the political program and philosophical
conception of a fundamental and progressive social group. This
consensus is obtained actively and spontaneously. Subaltern
groups come to recognize the fundamental group as the most
historically progressive class in the political, economic and
cultural realms.[17] In support of such ideas we cite the following
Gramscian texts:

> The Turin Communists posed themselves concretely the ques-
> tion of the 'hegemony of the proletariat', in other words, of
> the social basis of the proletarian dictatorship and the
> Workers' State. The proletariat can become the leading and
> ruling class to the extent to which it succeeds in creating a
> system of class alliances which enables it to mobilise the
> majority of the working population against capitalism and
> the bourgeois State; this means, in Italy, in the actual rela-
> tions existing in Italy, to the extent to which it succeeds in
> obtaining the consent of the large popular masses.[18]

> No mass action is possible unless the mass itself is convinced
> of the ends it wants to reach and the methods to be applied.
> The proletariat, in order to be able to rule as a class, must
> rid itself of all corporative hangovers, of all syndicalist
> prejudices and incrustations... they must think as members
> of a class which aims at leading the peasants and the intel-
> lectuals, of a class which can conquer and can build socialism
> only if aided and followed by the great majority of these
> social strata.[19]

From these passages it is clear that the prevailing sense of
hegemony is further refined and developed. It refers primarily
by the proletariat.[20] In the 'Prison Notebooks' the concept of
hegemony is futher refined and developed. It refers primarily
to the cultural intellectual and moral direction exercised by
fundamental classes over the entire social body and the diffusion
of a new conception of the world among the popular masses.
Gramsci then distinguishes the moment of hegemony from that
of political domination.[21]

> the supremacy of a social group manifests itself in two ways,
> as 'domination' and as 'intellectual and moral leadership'.
> A social group dominates antagonistic groups, which it tends
> to 'liquidate', or to subjugate perhaps even by armed force;
> it leads kindred and allied groups. A social group can, and
> indeed must, already exercise 'leadership' before winning
> governmental power (this indeed is one of the principal con-
> ditions for the winning of such power); it subsequently

becomes dominant when it exercises power, but even if it
holds it firmly in its grasp, it must continue to 'lead' as
well.
Briefly, hegemony designates the intellectual and moral direction of a combination of social groups struggling to attain
political and cultural autonomy.

The interpretations of Gramsci's concept of hegemony are
various. They are all dictated by the commentators' own political
convictions. As Portelli notes, the real object of such divergent
interpretations is the exegesis of Marx and Lenin rather than
that of Gramsci.[22] We shall briefly review such interpretations
in the hope of clarifying the roots of the controversy.

There is the Leninist interpretation of Gramsci's concept of
hegemony, proposed by the Italian Communist Party and defended
by Togliatti and Luciano Gruppi, among others. Togliatti was
one of the first to equate Gramsci's concept of hegemony with
Lenin's concept of the 'dictatorship of the proletariat' and to
characterize Gramsci's distinction between civil and political
society as innovative only on the plane of methodology.[23] In
Gramsci, as in Lenin, Togliatti argues, the party is the collective
intellectual which directs the proletarian struggle to conquer
the state power, and utilizes the state to create a new social
order. 'The state is a dictatorship, and all dictatorship presupposes not only the power of a class, but also of a system of
alliances and compromises, by which one arrives at the domination of the entire social body and the world of culture itself.'[24]
For Togliatti, Gramsci's originality consists in having applied
Lenin's revolutionary theory to the conditions of the Italian
society. Luciano Gruppi has argued that there is a convergence
between Gramsci's and Lenin's concepts of hegemony. For both,
hegemony comprehends the moment of direction and domination.
He points out that there is an evolution in Gramsci's concept
of hegemony. In his early writings (1921-3) Gramsci did not
articulate the relationship between the party and the revolutionary movement. Such articulation appears in the 'Southern
Question.' Here, hegemony is understood clearly as the dictatorship of the proletariat and refers to both the moment of
direction and domination.[25]

Both Togliatti and Gruppi deny the importance of a distinction
between hegemony and domination. Without such distinction
Gramsci's analyses of past hegemonic systems are not fully
understood. The Risorgimento, as we have seen, is the typical
example where a dictatorship without hegemony existed. 'It is
one of the cases in which these groups have the function of
"domination" without that of "leadership": dictatorship without
hegemony.'[26] Analyzing past revolutions Gramsci focused on
the relationship between a fundamental group and the mass.
Where such relationship was not organic or did not exist at all,
he did not hesitate to call the revolution a 'passive' one and
speak of dictatorship rather than hegemony.

More prevalent among Gramsci's commentators is a beyond-

Lenin interpretation. The studies of Paggi, Auciello, Cambareri, Portelli, Piotte and Macciocchi, among others, seem to point in this direction. All these authors insist, in varying degrees, on the crucial importance of Gramsci's distinction between hegemony and dictatorship, and on the primacy of the former over the latter. Cambareri, for instance, characterizes Gramsci's notion of hegemony as a further elaboration of Marxism-Leninism. He notes that in Lenin, hegemony denotes a guiding system in the struggle to topple the old regime, that is it functions as a revolutionary strategy. The problem of popular consensus is posed only when the proletariat has been successful in establishing its dictatorship. In Gramsci, Cambareri continues, the concept of hegemony is elaborated from a critically conscious standpoint. It presents itself as an intellectual and moral reform of the entire society, prior to the conquest of power. Gramsci underlines the ethico-political aspect of politics and places at its very center the ethical and intellectual leadership of the proletariat. Understood in this sense, hegemony becomes the condition for the conquest and exercise of power. That is why he insists on the crucial role of the intellectuals in socialist revolutions.[27] This interpretation of Gramsci's hegemony, however, does not deny the common elements between Gramsci's and Lenin's positions. In fact, as Portelli puts it, both Gramsci and Lenin are in agreement on the point of the class base of hegemony. Proletarian hegemony is based on a system of alliances and implies an element of coercion and domination. The conditions of Russia in the Czarist period were such that proletarian hegemony could not be achieved without force and coercion. However, the differences between Gramsci's and Lenin's concepts of hegemony are profound. Gramsci, Portelli concludes, gives pre-eminence and primacy to the cultural and ideological dimension of hegemony. Lenin focuses on the political aspect of hegemony, its objective being the seizure of the state. No objection is raised by Gramsci to such a political formulation of hegemony, since the political and not the civil society was strong in that country. In the West, as we have seen, the struggle is against a powerful civil society on which a weak state is firmly entrenched. Therefore, proletarian hegemony entails an ideological domination of the civil society.[28] Piotte also insists on the differences between Lenin and Gramsci. Hegemony in Lenin is a means to and end, the conquest of power; for Gramsci, instead, it is the very end to be attained, the moral and intellectual reform of society.[29]

A non-Leninist interpretation of Gramsci's hegemony has been proposed by Tamburrano and Bobbio. Both emphasize a shift in Gramsci from a Leninist to a uniquely Gramscian concept of hegemony. Tamburrano views the distinction between civil and political society, hegemony and domination, as central in Gramsci's thought. The domination of a society, be it feudal or bourgeois, is the domination of a Weltanschauung which, diffused among the masses, generates a consensus on the norms

and institutions of that society. Likewise, proletarian hegemony
is the establishment of proletarian direction of a new historical
bloc on the level of ideology and culture. Hegemony is attained
through 'democratic consensus.' The primacy of consensus
over coercion is deduced from the privileged position given by
Gramsci to civil society over political society. The first is
based upon consensus, the latter on force, coercion and
domination. For Tamburrano, the conquest of power is above
all the attainment of mass consensus rather than the coercive
apparatus of political society. Hegemony, in Gramsci, must
be realized before the seizure of the state power.[30] In the same
vein, Norberto Bobbio points to a shift in Gramsci's concept
of hegemony from the sense of political direction to that of
both political and cultural direction. The first is present in
his writings of 1926, the latter is predominant in the 'Prison
Notebooks.' For Bobbio the differences between Gramsci and
Lenin are substantial. He argues that: (1) hegemony denotes
a cultural direction, in the sense of intellectual and ethical
reform of culture and society; (2) as a consequence of the
subordination of the political to the civil society, the moment
of domination, force and coercion is subordinate to that of
hegemony. In Lenin dictatorship and hegemony are equally
important, but the first, the moment of force, is decisive and
primary in relation to that of the consensus. (3) While in Lenin
the conquest of power precedes that of hegemony, in Gramsci
it is the hegemony which must precede the other. (4) The notion
of hegemony is more extensive and in its functions more
encompassing than that of Lenin. In fact, Bobbio argues, the
agent of hegemony in Gramsci is not the party only, as in
Lenin, but all the institutions of the civil society in charge of
the elaboration and diffusion of culture.[31]

   All of the above interpretations of Gramsci's notion of
hegemony have fixed specific concepts and isolated one or
another aspects of Gramsci's thought to the point of obfuscating
the real sense of hegemony derived only from his general conception of historical development. Most of them are colored by
the commentators' own political prejudices and still riddled
with old Marxist categories. Gramsci excels among Marxist
theoreticians for his dialectical and historicist qualities of mind.
He is far from a blind adherence to Marx, Lenin or Croce. He
arrives at an elaboration of concepts through a critical evaluation of their positions. More than dependence on Lenin's
theoretical positions, one has to emphasize the dialectical relationship between them, Auciello brilliantly notes.[32] Thus a
perfect understanding of Gramsci's hegemony is possible only
if the concept is defined as a process in continuous movement
within the movement of history itself. No writer has yet defined such a concept in all its complexity and fluidity. For instance, when Gramsci describes the subject of hegemony he not
only speaks of the proletariat, but also the party, 'any social
group,'[33] the bourgeoisie,[34] the Jacobins and the Italian Popular

Action Party,[35] the philosophy of praxis,[36] as Nardone aptly
observes.[37] What we propose is a 'für ewig' interpretation of
hegemony.

Hegemony is that phase of history in which an organic unity
is realized. Such unity is intellectual, political and social.
History is characterized by various processes all tending toward
unity. The masses develop, form a collective will, a party,
become a state, and ultimately a nation. The party evolves in
dialectical relationship with the masses until it reaches an
organic unity with them. Theory and praxis, likewise, tend
toward unification. The same is true of all intellectual and
political movements and Marxism itself which fuse into the most
progressive ones. Structure and superstructure are dialectically interrelated until they reach a unity. All these ideas
are present in Gramsci's notion of hegemony. Nardone, in our
opinion, is the only scholar who has treated the concept of
hegemony from this perspective. The subject which realizes
the most integral hegemony is the mass in its process of political
and cultural development. The realization of hegemony, Nardone
notes, is the realization of a qualitative and quantitative
totality. Qualitative in the sense that various social groups,
all differentiated on the economic, cultural and political levels,
are progressively assimilated by a fundamental, hegemonic
group into its new, autonomous and integral Weltanschauung.
Quantitative in the sense that it leads to the structural and
cultural unification of the world.[38] The universal character of
hegemony is present in the following text:[39]

> It is true that the State is seen as the organ of one particular
> group, destined to create favourable conditions for the lat-
> ter's maximum expansion. But the development and expansion
> of the particular group are conceived of, and presented, as
> being the motor force of a universal expansion, of a develop-
> ment of all 'national' energies.

Hegemony is thus the point where all social relationships cul-
minate. Again, in Nardone's words, 'the realization of hegemony
marks the transition from the sector of the structure to that
of superstructure, from economism to politics, from corporatism
to universalism, from distinction and opposition between groups
to their unification around a fundamental group.'[40] Close to
this particular understanding of Gramscian hegemony came the
British scholar G. Williams. Hegemony is:[41]

> an order in which a certain way of life and thought is
> dominant, in which one concept of reality is diffused
> throughout society in all its institutional and private mani-
> festations, informing with its spirit all taste, morality,
> customs, religious and political principles, and all social
> relations, particularly in their intellectual and moral
> connotations.

HEGEMONY AND THE SUPERSTRUCTURE OF HISTORICAL BLOCS

Gramsci's emphasis on 'consciousness' as the basis of socialist revolutions, on the creative role of intellectuals, the moral function of culture and the ethico-political moment of hegemony, Williams writes, are the end result of a strong, independent and creative reflection on the problem of the revolutionary praxis in the West. He found Lenin's elaboration of the concept of hegemony somewhat deficient.[42] He gave primacy to the moment of consciousness in the elaboration of concepts. The philosophy of praxis is conscious critical activity, revolutionary praxis is conscious praxis.[43] Hegemony itself is a fact of consciousness and of knowledge. 'The realisation of a hegemonic apparatus, in so far as it creates a new ideological terrain, determines a reform of consciousness and of methods of knowledge: it is a fact of knowledge, a philosophical fact.'[44] Gramsci was fully aware that revolutionary forces are generated from society's economic structure. Objective conditions have been ripe for decades, yet no revolution ensued. As we have seen, he focused on the superstructure, made it more autonomous and more conditioning than classical Marxism ever admitted. Proletarian hegemony is a creative political act. Almost alone among Marxists, Gramsci became absorbed in the problem of the superstructure. It was in the superstructure that Gramsci found the key to socialist transformation. Hegemony entails a dialectical unity of civil and political society, of structure and superstructure.

Hegemony as dialectical unity of civil and political society
The concept of 'civil society,' the product of a long process of philosophical elaboration from Hobbes, Locke, Rousseau to Hegel, became the central focus of Hegel's systematic philosophy. As the bourgeoisie became politically independent and autonomous, and as its dominant position became consolidated, the need was felt to separate state from society, political from social phenomena. Hegel became the theoretician of the modern bourgeois state.
   The main achievement of Hegelian philosophy is the attempt to bridge the gap between the 'rational' and the 'actual' and to develop a science of the state, apprehended as something inherently rational. 'What is rational is actual and what is actual is rational,' is Hegel's starting assumption.[45] The absolute rationality of the state resides in its ability to realize an organic unity in which the individualistic and particularistic self-interests fuse with those that are more universal, typical of the collectivity, the state. 'The state is the actuality of concrete freedom. But concrete freedom consists in this, that personal individuality and its particular interests not only achieve their complete development... but... also pass over of their own accord into the interest of the universal.'[46]

Within political society Hegel distinguishes two conflicting
spheres: civil society (bürgerliche Gesellschaft) and the state.
Philosophically, civil society denotes that state of social life
in which the needs and interests of the individual regulate his
relationship to others. It is 'the battlefield where everyone's
individual private interest meets everyone else's,' the locus
where private and common interests are in conflict with each
other, and together in conflict with the interests of the state.[47]
Sociologically, civil society refers to a concrete corporatist
structure. The unity of civil and political society is realized
in the modern state through the political institutions of the
monarchy, the vast bureaucracy of salaried civil servants,
embodying the interests and values of the state, and the
Assembly of Estates, composed of representatives of the Crown
and civil estate. Civil society tends toward absorption into the
state. As the process of rationalization of life continues, so
does the transition from civil society to the state. Men come to
realization that conflicts between them are objectively resolved
when they are subordinated to the state, which realizes the
concrete unity of particularity and universality.

Marx, in his 'Critique of Hegel's "Philosophy of Right",'
submitted Hegel's theory of the state to a very systematic
critique. The state and political institutions are not the embodiment of universality. They only mask the particularistic and
egotistic interests of civil society. The state is, in Marx, a
coercive apparatus, the instrument of domination of civil society.
The historical development does not proceed from civil society
to the state, as in Hegel, but rather from the state to civil
society. Hence the necessity of the withering away of the state.
But what is civil society in Marx? It is the realm of economic
relations, to which political institutions are subordinated. 'The
state - the political order - is the subordinate, and civil
society - the realm of economic relations, the decisive element.
The traditional conception, to which Hegel, too, pays homage,
saw in the state the determining element, and in civil society
the element determined by it.[48] On Marx's conception of civil
society it is important to cite the famous text of the 'German
Ideology':[49]

Civil society embraces the whole material intercourse of
individuals within a definite stage of the development of
productive forces. It embraces the whole commercial and
industrial life of a given stage and, insofar, transcends the
State and the nation, though, on the other hand again, it
must assert itself in its foreign relations as nationality, and
inwardly must organize itself as State. The word 'civil'
society [bürgerliche Gesellschaft] emerged in the eighteenth
century, when property relationships had already extricated
themselves from the ancient and medieval society. Civil
society as such only develops with the bourgeoisie.

Marx accepts Hegel's distinction of civil and political society
but not the postulate of the absorption of the first into the

latter. The distinction between them is overcome not in the abstract and outside history, as in Hegel, but in the establishment of true democracy. Democracy represents the unity of the universal and the particular, a 'state of society where there is no alienation between man and the political structure,'[50] no separation between the citizen of the state and the member of the civil society. Both the state and the civil society must disappear, that is, be abolished and transcended (aufgehoben).

Gramsci's concept of civil society radically differs from that of Marx. As Norberto Bobbio notes, civil society is not part of the structure but of the superstructure in Gramsci.[51] In support of this thesis the following text is cited:[52]

What we can do, for the moment, is to fix two major superstructural 'levels': the one that can be called 'civil society', that is the ensemble of organisms commonly called 'private', and that of 'political society' or 'the State'. These two levels correspond on the one hand to the function of 'hegemony' which the dominant group exercises throughout society and on the other hand to that of 'direct domination' or command exercised through the State and 'juridical' government.

Civil and political society are distinguished in terms of two superstructural functions exercised by dominant groups within them, that is, those of hegemony and domination. Civil society is characterized on the conceptual level by an ideological sphere which permeates and directs the entire social body, and on the organizational level by groups and organisms in charge of the maintenance and development of the ideological front, church, schools, army, courts and all the media influencing public opinion.

The exercise of functions of domination, coercion and force typifies instead the political society. As Portelli notes, political society represents the political-military aspect of the civil society. In this respect it is the prolongation and concretization of the economic and ideological direction exercised by a dominant class.[53] The principal agents of the political society are a military organization, a juridical system and the state apparatus, all maintaining the established socio-political order through constraint. This function of coercion, Portelli comments, is exercised habitually against those groups which do not consent to the direction of the fundamental class, and exceptionally in the period of organic crises, when the dominant class loses control of the civil society and calls on the state to maintain its dominance.[54]

The relationships between civil and political society are multifaceted and complex. Between them, Nardone writes, there is a relation of opposition, dependence and partial identification. As for the first, it must be recalled that civil society is based upon consensus, political society on force. However, the separation between them is not organic. Gramsci notes that they are intimately related and complement each other. There is no society based exclusively on consensus or force. The

complete separation of political society is impossible to sustain.
The state is born in the civil society and acts back on it.[55]
  In this multiplicity of private associations... one or more
  predominates relatively or absolutely – constituting the
  hegemonic apparatus of one social group over the rest of
  the population (or civil society): the basis for the State in
  the narrow sense of the governmental-coercive apparatus.
Given this partial identification between civil and political
society (the state as expression and instrument of assimilation
and domination of one group within civil society), Nardone
continues, the civil society becomes the battlefield where
conflict among various groups takes place. The state is then
the instrument of homogenization of civil society. As one group
becomes the state, the entire civil society is transformed.
Complete hegemony is achieved not when the particular is
absorbed by the universal, the absolute state, as in Hegel,
but rather when the state disappears. The existence of the
state reveals a conflict still occurring within civil society and
the presence of coercion and force as well.[56] The state is 'the
entire complex of practical and theoretical activities with which
the ruling class not only justifies and maintains its dominance,
but manages to win the active consent of those over whom it
rules.'[57] The state is, then, for Gramsci, not only the 'apparatus
of government' but also the '"private" apparatus of "hegemony"
or civil society.'[58] On this ground he criticizes liberalism for
having conceived the distinction between civil and political
society as organic, thus affirming the identification of economic
activity and civil society and negating any form of state
intervention in it.[59]
  Thus it is asserted that economic activity belongs to civil
  society, and that the State must not intervene to regulate it.
  But since in actual reality civil society and State are one
  and the same, it must be made clear that *laissez-faire* too
  is a form of State 'regulation', introduced and maintained
  by legislative and coercive means.
In the same vein, Gramsci rejects the economic-corporatist
theory for confusing civil and political society. Its result is the
identification of hegemony and dictatorship, consensus and
force.[60]
  Gramsci's conception of civil society has important theoretical
and strategic implications. Bobbio examines the first, Portelli
the latter. For Bobbio, civil society is, in Gramsci, no longer
part of the structure, but of the superstructure, that is,
it is no longer the complex of material and economic relations,
but rather the complex of ideological and cultural relations.
In this respect, Gramsci departs from Marx. In addition, civil
society and not the state is the most positive element of the
historical process. On this Gramsci and Marx are in perfect
agreement. The very notion of civil society is actually derived
from Hegel and not Marx. As we have seen, for Hegel in the
civil society are included not only 'economic relations,' but

also political and syndicalist associations and the corporations
all constituting the 'ethic content of the State.' Likewise,
'private organisms' are in Gramsci the content of civil society.[61]
   Gramsci's affirmation of the primacy of civil society over
political society has strategic implications. To establish proletarian hegemony, both civil and political society need to be
developed and organically linked, Portelli comments.[62] The
dominant class could utilize them alternately to perpetuate its
domination. As we have previously seen, in Western societies,
where the civil society is strong, bourgeois domination is
intellectual and ideological. Thus any attempt to establish a
new historical bloc requires a long process of disintegration
of the civil society. The struggle is against the civil society.
On the contrary, in those countries where the political society
is all-powerful and civil society weak and underdeveloped, the
revolutionary struggle aims at the conquest of power, followed
by the process of construction of a civil society. In these
situations a period of statolatry (primacy of political society)
is justifiable momentarily. The primacy of the civil society must
be restored if dictatorship is to be avoided.[63]

> For some social groups, which before their ascent to auto-
> nomous State life have not had a long independent period of
> cultural and moral development on their own... a period of
> statolatry is necessary and indeed opportune. This
> 'statolatry' is nothing other than the normal form of 'State
> life', or at least of initiation to autonomous State life and to
> the creation of a 'civil society' which it was not historically
> possible to create before the ascent to independent State
> life. However, this kind of 'statolatry' must not be aban-
> doned to itself, must not, especially, become theoretical
> fanaticism or be conceived of as 'perpetual'. It must be
> criticised, precisely in order to develop and produce new
> forms of State life, in which the initiative of individuals
> and groups will have a 'state' character, even if it is not
> due to the 'government of the functionaries' (make State life
> become 'spontaneous').

The problem of the primacy of civil society is linked to that
of the withering away of the state. Marxian theory of the
withering away of the state, as understood by Lenin, refers to
a socialist society without classes and without state. Gramsci
speaks of regulated society, of 're-absorption of the political
society in the civil society.' While for Hegel the distinction
between civil society and political society is resolved by the
absorption of the first into the latter, for Gramsci it is political
society that recedes to the point of total disappearance. This
takes place in two distinct phases. Before and after the conquest of power by proletarian classes the new hegemonic system
unifies political and civil society, the political and ideological
superstructures. This unity is realized in the party and the
socialist state. The socialist state, however, is transitory and
must give way to the regulated society, that is, a civil society

where individuals are capable of self-government.[64]

The assertion that the State can be identified with individuals (the individuals of a social group), as an element of active culture (i.e. as a movement to create a new civilisation, a new type of man and of citizen), must serve to determine the will to construct within the husk of political society a complex and well-articulated civil society, in which the individual can govern himself without his self-government thereby entering into conflict with political society - but rather becoming its normal continuation, its organic development.

As civil society expands, so does social consensus and hegemony. Political society disappears when the civil society occupies the space of political society. Only a universally hegemonic class which aims at the elimination of the moment of force and coercion can liberate civil society from political society.[65]

Hegel's conception belongs to a period in which the spreading development of the bourgeoisie could seem limitless, so that its ethnicity or universality could be asserted: all mankind will be bourgeois. But, in reality, only the social group that poses the end of the State and its own end as the target to be achieved can create an ethical State - i.e. one which tends to put an end to the internal divisions of the ruled.

As Bobbio notes, while in classical Marxism the extinction of the state is a structural process, entailing the suppression of class antagonisms, in Gramsci it represents a superstructural process, that is, the universalization of the civil society. Likewise, while in classical Marxism the transition is from class to classless societies, for Gramsci it is a transition from a civil society with political society to civil society without political society.[66] In a situation of universal hegemony there is no need for the state, for there are no groups on which coercion need be applied. The state, thus, is born in civil society, it becomes the instrument of its transformation and ends in a renewed civil society.

Hegemony as dialectical unity of structure and superstructure
The problem of the relationship between structure and superstructure, the vexata quaestio of Marxian theory, is also treated by Gramsci in relation to the notion of hegemony.

Marx wrote in the 'Preface to the Critique of Political Economy' that 'the mode of production of material life conditions the social, political and intellectual life process in general.'[67] Ever since, Marxists have written extensively about it as if economic relations are the sole determinant of various elements of the superstructure. Marx and Engels made it clear that the apparently one-sided relationship between them was stressed polemically by those who denied it. In actual reality, a reciprocal relationship between them exists. In a letter to J. Bloc, Engels wrote:[68]

if somebody twists this into saying that the economic element

is the *only* determining one, he transforms that proposition
into a meaningless, abstract, senseless phrase. The economic
situation is the basis, but the various elements of the superstructure...also exercise their influence upon the course of
the historical struggle and in many cases preponderate in
determining their *form*...and we had not always the time,
the place or the opportunity to allow the other elements involved in the interaction to come into their rights.
Marx and Engels never explained the nature of the relationship
between structure and superstructure. They were concerned
with the problem of the origin of the superstructure and not
its influence upon society. They assigned a secondary and passive role to the superstructure. Gramsci, on the contrary,
was concerned with the analysis of the role of the superstructure in socialist transformation. He elaborated a theory
of the superstructure from an original perspective. Again
Norberto Bobbio needs to be cited for his interesting interpretation of Gramsci's concept of superstructure. He demonstrates that Gramsci departs from Marx in transposing civil
society to the level of the superstructure and making it
determinant in relation to political society. As a consequence
the relation of structure and superstructure is decisively
altered. Whereas in Marx the 'structure' is primary and a
'determining' factor, for Gramsci it is the superstructure which
is primary and determinant. Such interpretation, Bobbio adds,
does not place Gramsci outside Marxism, for the basic tenets
of Marxian theory are still maintained. The basis of Bobbio's
thesis is Gramsci's concept of catharsis, which indicates the
passage from a mere economic moment to an ethico-political
one.[69] 'The term "catharsis" can be employed to indicate the
passage from the purely economic (or egotistic-passional) to
the ethico-political moment, that is the superior elaboration of
the structure into the superstructure in the minds of men.
This also means the passage from "objective to subjective" and
from "necessity to freedom".'[70] The relationship between
structure and superstructure is not mechanistically understood by Gramsci, that is, as a relationship of cause and effect,
but rather as a means to an end. Material conditions are the
instrument for the creation of an ethico-political phase of
history.
   In opposition to Bobbio, Texier has formulated an interpretation of Gramsci not very different from the traditional,
orthodox one. In this interpretation, the socio-economic structure of historical blocs remains the determining factor of
superstructural activities in Marx and Gramsci.[71] Several texts
are cited in support of this interpretation, which is claimed to
be in consonance with the sense and conception of history
developed by Gramsci. Texier's analysis is based on a
mechanistic interpretation of Marx's dichotomy and term of
'reflex.' For Texier, the primacy of structure over superstructure is only questioned by Gramsci in certain periods of

history (Gramsci's periods of organic crisis) when superstructural elements, namely political activity and consciousness,
become decisive. The only difference between Gramsci and
Marx, in the opinion of Texier, lies in the fact that Gramsci
emphasizes the study of superstructure while Marx that of
the structure. Very recently, Portelli, refuting both Bobbio
and Texier, argued that what differentiates Gramsci from Marx
is not the primacy of either element of Marxian dichotomy,
but rather the rendering of the two elements equally determinant. The relationship between structure and superstructure
is organic and dialectical, Portelli states, when viewed from
the standpoint of the articulation of the historical bloc. In
support of his interpretation he cites the following passage:[72]

> The analysis of these propositions tends, I think, to rein-
> force the conception of the *historical bloc* in which precisely
> material forces are the content and ideologies are the form,
> though this distinction between form and content has purely
> didactic value, since the material forces would be incon-
> ceivable historically without form and the ideologies would be
> individual fancies without the material forces.

The superstructure, we think, is the terminus ad quem of
hegemony. No doubt both elements of the dichotomy exist in
a dialectical and organic relationship within a given historical
bloc. The conquest of hegemony is not only the result of
transformation within the structure, that is of the explosions
of contradictions between productive forces and relations of
production, but also, as we have seen in the preceding chapters, the result of the superstructural process by which
subaltern classes develop toward political and cultural autonomy
and consciousness. Both structure and superstructure, Gramsci
writes, form an organic whole which, adopting Sorel's concept,
he calls an 'historical bloc.'[73] 'Structures and superstructures
form an "historical bloc". That is to say the complex, contradictory and discordant *ensemble* of the superstructures is the
reflection of the *ensemble* of the social relations of production.'[74]
Gramsci opposes any deterministic interpretation of such
dichotomy, which leads either to economism or ideologism.
Economism, typical of mechanical historical materialism, assumes
that every political act is determined immediately by the structure and that 'every fluctuation of politics and ideology can
be presented and expounded as an immediate expression of
the structure.'[75] Economism leads to syndicalism and trade
unionism, or to the belief that the evolution of the structure
will entail a corresponding radical transformation of the
superstructures. The other theoretical error is that of ideologism, typical of the neo-idealism of Croce in Italy. In this
case, history is conceived as the product of the superstructures,
it is the history of mere ideas. It excludes the reality of
'structure' from history. As Portelli puts it, both economism
and ideologism underestimate or deny the organic nature of
the relationship between structure and superstructure.[76]

For Gramsci, the structure, defined in the classical sense
as the ensemble of productive and social forces, has an essential function within concrete historical blocs. 'The ensemble
of the material forces of production is the least variable element
in historical development: it is the one which at any given
time can be ascertained and measured with mathematical exac-
titude.'[77] Yet, it is difficult, Gramsci adds, to identify sta-
tically the structure. 'A structural phase can be concretely
studied and analysed only after it has gone through the whole
process of development, and not during the process itself...
Politics in fact is at any given time the reflection of the tendencies of development in the structure.'[78] That is to say,
the variation of the ensemble of material forces of production
can be measured with precision only when its development
becomes 'qualitative.'[79] How then must 'structure' and 'superstructure' be understood? First, 'structure' is not something
immutable, fixed, absolute, an 'unknown God' as Croce
understands it, but a reality in continuous movement to be
analyzed not in a speculative manner, but historically.[80]
Second, 'superstructures' are not mere illusions, appearances
and mystifications, as Croce also believes. In characterizing
superstructures as appearances, Marxists have simply utilized
a metaphorical language in a polemical manner against dogmatic
conceptions to affirm their historicity. Ideologies are not
arbitrary; they are not illusions and mystifications either,
but 'real historical facts' that need to be attacked and unmasked
as instruments of domination.[81] In genuine Marxism, 'superstructures are an objective and active reality' in so far as:[82]

it explicitly affirms that men become conscious of their social
position thus of their roles in the realm of ideologies... The
philosophy of praxis itself is a superstructure, it is the
terrain on which determined social groups acquire a consciousness of their social existence, their power, their roles
and their own development.

Gramsci analyzes the relationship between structure and
superstructure from a philosophical and historical perspective.
Marxism is not for him a science, a system of beliefs and
tactics as in Lenin, and, in a sense, in Marx and Engels, but
still a philosophy in the process of development. The problem
of 'structure' and 'superstructure' in Gramsci involves the
totality of the historical process, as Nardone has pointed out.
The general direction of history is the passage from a phase
of necessity to a phase of freedom, from common sense to
Weltanschauung, from economic-corporatism to hegemony, from
passivity to consciousness, from quantity to quality, from
force to consensus, from objectivity to 'collective subjectivity.'
The first element of the dichotomy, 'structure,' characterizes
the moment of negative existence to be transcended by that of
hegemony. The realization of new history and hegemony indicates the passage from structure to superstructure. The
ethico-political moment, Gramsci writes, is 'the superior

elaboration of the structure into superstructure.' It follows
that superstructure is not only primordial, that is, the condition
for the appearance of the structure, but also the end toward
which history tends. It is the terminus ad quem of proletarian
hegemony.[83] Proletarian hegemony is the new historical praxis
in which the unity of structure and superstructure is realized.
In this context, Nardone rightly observes:[84]

> structure is seen by Gramsci already as expressive of super-
> structural values 'implicit' in it, and the 'passage' to the
> superstructure signifies the progressive affirmation of free-
> dom which has begun to operate in the forms of economic
> activity. The dialectic structure-superstructure becomes the
> genesis of freedom in a necessary distinction and opposition
> of moments. Structure is the historical 'past', and the super-
> structure the terminal phase of the movement. Past and
> future are unified and historically realized by the human
> will.

The structure embraces the whole world of necessity and
objectivity. It is all that cannot be wished away in nature and
history, such as economy and the historical past. 'The ensemble
of the material forces of production is at the same time a
crystallisation of all past history and the basis of present and
future history: it is both a document and an active and actual
propulsive force.'[85] The structure, thus, conditions, coerces
and disciplines human will. The superstructure is the conscious
realization of a collective will, the world of conscious praxis.
Hegemony signals the advent and triumph of consciousness
and responsibility over necessity and fatalism.[86] How can the
structure of past history be ascertained? It is the superstructure, the conscious political praxis of a collectivity, which is
able to ascertain the new progressive force of development
within the structure. Scientific analysis cannot ascertain the
past. There are, in fact, as many pasts as groups that become
hegemonic in history. It is the praxis of the present which
determines the true historical past. Structure becomes a
means to an end, the conquest of hegemony. 'Structure ceases
to be an external force which crushes man, assimilates him to
itself and makes him passive; and is transformed into a means
of freedom, an instrument to create a new ethico-political form
and a source of new initiatives.'[87] Economic activity does not
condition political activity, it is the instrument of political
activity. The analysis of objective material conditions is not
sufficient in creating revolutionary praxis. Only the conscious
organization of man to achieve a determined end is primary
and decisive. Structure does not determine superstructure
mechanically, rather it channels and limits the development of
the superstructure. Gramsci, in this context, quotes Marx's
interpretative criteria of historical analysis: 'No social order
ever perishes before all the productive forces for which there
is room in it have developed; and new, higher relations of
production never appear before the material conditions of their

existence have matured in the womb of the old society itself.[88] Is economy reduced to politics in Gramsci? He limits himself to asserting that political praxis is the determinant of any praxis, the catharsis of economic praxis.[89]

AMERICANISM AND SOCIALIST HEGEMONY

There is another aspect of Gramsci's concept of hegemony, that of hegemony as a new pedagogy to create a new form of universalism, a new type of man, a 'collective man.'

As we have noted in chapter 3, not the individual but a collectivity is the subject and object of hegemony. The collectivity is in fact the agent of historical transformation, and the very reality to be transformed. Historical acts are performed by a collective man. Through conscious participation in a collectivity, the individual actively participates in the creation of his own history. Hegemony is, then, that project which presses men to think and act in a universalistic manner, and societal institutions to adapt to a new collective man.[90] 'Every relationship of "hegemony" is necessarily an educational relationship and occurs not only within a nation, between the various forces of which the nation is composed, but in the international and world-wide field, between complexes of national and continental civilisations.'[91] By definition, man is not an individual, Gramsci writes, but the ensemble of social relations. And the process of becoming a man is dependent upon that which modifies the ensemble of concrete social relations.[92]

> Man is to be conceived as an historical bloc of purely individual and subjective elements and of mass and objective or material elements with which the individual is in an active relationship. To transform the external world, the general system of relations, is to potentiate oneself and to develop oneself.

This amounts to saying that the process of socialization is an historical process. As a child grows into an adult by means of active and reciprocal relationship established with the social world, so man is what he is by participating in the creation of the world he inhabits. Gramsci's 'collective man' is Marx's 'universal man,' that is, not the alienated subject, but the hegemonic man, master of his destiny, history and the institutions he creates. The ideal collective man is, for Gramsci, Leonardo da Vinci, in whom one finds an original and creative individuality as well as 'mess elements,' the qualities of an American engineer, German philosopher, French politician, and the Italian Renaissance humanist man.[93] The collective man is formed through discipline, in the Gramscian sense of dynamic, active and creative conformism.[94] An Italian sociologist has noted that Gramsci's conception of man bears striking similarities to that of Durkheim. Both advocate social controls to integrate the

individual into a collective society.[95] Certainly not. While in
Durkheim the individual loses his individuality in the paramount objective reality of society, in Gramsci social constraints
aid the development of independent, autonomous, conscious
and critical individuals. Discipline is not, for Gramsci, a
mechanism to facilitate the submission of masses to society, as
was the case with idealism and Catholicism, but an instrument
to accelerate the development of subaltern masses and transform them into an hegemonic subject.[96] 'We are all conformists
of some conformism or other, always man-in-the-mass or
collective man. The question is this: of what historical type is
the conformism, the mass humanity to which one belongs?[97]
Collective man arises out of a dialectical relationship between
discipline and spontaneity. Discipline instills in men a conception of the world, free from magic and folkloric elements,
from past sedimentations and localistic, individualistic elements
typical of common sense and the child's world-view. A conception which is historical, dialectical and all projected into
the future.[98] This explains Gramsci's great interest in the
revolutionary pedagogy of Fordism and Taylorism, the constitutive components of the new phenomenon called
'Americanism.'

Paradoxically, an individualist superstructure in American
capitalism has been able to realize a complete emancipation of
man on the basis of a progressive and rational mode of production. 'In America rationalisation has determined the need
to elaborate a new type of man suited to the new type of work
and productive process.'[99]

Massimo Salvadori has analyzed in great detail the historical
and intellectual context of Gramsci's notes on Americanism
and Fordism. He recalls the great interest and debate generated
by the publication of Taylor's 'The Principles of Scientific
Management' in 1911, later developed by the American industrialist Henry Ford and adopted as the philosophy of American
industry. Greater productivity can be assured only through
a scientific organization of the work process, and rigid separation of functions and responsibilities between managers and
workers. The worker must be the object of rational planning
and motivated to maximum production through the system of
graduated income and raises determined on an individual basis.
The rationalization of work soon became an important issue in
the communist world. In Russia, Lenin pronounced himself in
favor of the adoption of the essence of Taylor-Ford's method,
representing an objective-rational innovation, after it had been
purified of capitalist incrustations. In Italy, the anarchist
Carlo Petri also proposed adoption of the scientific nucleus of
Taylorism-Fordism and rejection of its non-scientific covering,
to offer to the world a concrete model of smooth transition
from capitalist to communist economy.[100] Gramsci's notes on
Fordism are an attempt to solve the debate on the relationship
between communism and the Taylor-Ford method. For Salvadori,

Gramsci's final recommendation was a flat rejection of any use
of such method in the socialist system. Fordism, for Gramsci,
Salvadori continues, represented a revitalization of American
capitalism in the face of pressing demands advanced by organized
working-class movements in the world. It was a progressive
proposal, 'the ultimate stage in the process of progressive
attempts by industry to overcome the law of the tendency of
the rate of profit to fall.'[101] Salvadori's interpretation of
Gramsci's analysis of Americanism is not correct. Gramsci
advocated a full-scale introduction of Americanism in Italy to
abolish the last residues of feudalism and shake the political
superstructures of fascism, as G.N. Smith also notes in the
introduction to the translation of Gramsci's notes on Americanism and Fordism.[102]
    Gramsci's notes on 'Americanism and Fordism' must be
analyzed in relation to the concept of hegemony. Fordism
represents, for Gramsci, another model of 'passive revolution'
to be utilized and completed in the process of transition to
communism. Gramsci writes: 'Hegemony here is born in the
factory and requires for its exercise only a minute quantity
of professional political and ideological intermediaries.'[103]
    Americanism contains the essential traits of mass revolutionary
movements. It is a conception of the world and a practical norm
of conduct capable of modifying all society's structures, culture and man himself. What is the progressive revolutionary
force of change within Americanism? The rationalization and
mechanization of the system of production has created a new
collective man, a new culture on a new economic basis. Such
rationalization has affected all economic and human activities.
It has created a particular civil society and a particular type
of government, marginalized or eliminated parasitic strata and
activities. All demographic forces of the nation have been
restructured on the basis of the Taylorized social structure.[104]
    Americanisation requires a particular environment, a parti-
cular social structure (or at least a determined intention to
create it) and a certain type of State. This State is the
liberal State, not in the sense of free-trade liberalism or of
effective political liberty, but in the more fundamental sense
of free initiative and economic individualism which, with its
own means, on the level of 'civil society', through historical
development, itself arrives at a regime of industrial concentration and monopoly.
    An important question can be raised: why does Gramsci
praise Americanism and Fordism, the most advanced capitalist model, and not the socialist model? Buzzi suggests that
Russia lacked an economic rational plan capable of developing
a new collective man from its industrial and productive world.
It needed a juridical apparatus to direct from above the process of formation of the new collective man. Fordism, in contrast, had been able to form such a man from within the work
process itself. This was very close to the program and

revolutionary theory and strategy of the movement created by Gramsci's weekly 'L'Ordine Nuovo,' the factory councils, for which the real development of the revolutionary process occurs in the obscurity of the factory.[105] It is true that Gramsci understood the 'significance and objective import of the American phenomenon, which is also the biggest collective effort to date to create, with unprecedented speed, and with a consciousness of purpose unmatched in history, a new type of worker and of man.'[106] Taylor's slogan of making every man a 'trained gorilla' is significant to Gramsci. It expresses a need for[107]

> developing in the worker to the highest degree automatic and mechanical attitudes, breaking up the old psycho-physical nexus of qualified professional work, which demands a certain active participation of intelligence, fantasy and initiative on the part of the worker, and reducing productive operations exclusively to the mechanical, physical aspect... A forced selection will ineluctably take place; a part of the old working class will be pitilessly eliminated from the world of labour, and perhaps from the world *tout court*.

Ford's method is not an original method. It is the product of the objective development of industrialism, Gramsci notes. The mechanization of the worker and the rationalization of work are inherent in industrialism.[108]

> The history of industrialism has always been a continuing struggle... against the element of 'animality' in man. It has been an uninterrupted, often painful and bloody process of subjugating natural (i.e. animal and primitive) instincts to new, more complex and rigid norms and habits of order, exactitude and precision which can make possible the increasingly complex forms of collective life which are the necessary consequence of industrial development.... The selection or 'education' of men adapted to the new forms of civilisation and to the new forms of production and work has taken place by means of incredible acts of brutality which have cast the weak and the non-conforming into the limbo of the lumpen-classes or have eliminated them entirely.

Gramsci thus accepts Americanism for various reasons. It is rational; it is the generator of radical changes in all aspects of life; it is the only progressive force capable of revolutionizing Italy's and Europe's feudal structure. In Europe, liberal capitalism had created a protectionist liberal state, dominated by economically parasitic classes, opposed to the new American method of production.[109] Against traditional European Bohemianism, Gramsci advocates acceptance of the new work systems.[110]

> We Europeans are still too Bohemiam; we think we can do a certain job and live as we please, in Bohemiam fashion. Naturally, mechanization crushes us, and I am taking mechanization in the broad sense, to include the scientific organization of brainwork. We are absurdly romantic, and

in our efforts not to be bourgeois, we fall into Bohemianism,
which is in fact the most typical form of bourgeois behavior.
In America, the absence of the 'leaden burden' of parasitic
classes and 'great historical and cultural traditions' has
facilitated the development of industry and commerce. To this
one has to add a skilful combination of force (destruction of
the working-class trade unionism on a territorial basis) and
persuasion (high wages, various social benefits, extremely
subtle ideological and political propaganda) which also facilitated
the process of rationalization of production. In Europe, Gramsci
continues, the existence of parasitic classes prevented the
generalization of a rationalized and mechanized system of
production.[111]

> This past history has left behind a heap of passive sedimen-
> tations produced by the phenomenon of the saturation and
> fossilisation of civil-service personnel and intellectuals, of
> clergy and landowners, piratical commerce and the profes-
> sional...army. One could even say that the more historic a
> nation the more numerous and burdensome are these sedi-
> mentations of idle and useless masses living on 'their ances-
> tral patrimony', pensioners of economic history.

One understands, thus, Gramsci's acceptance of Americanism.
It would accelerate structural changes in European economy
(Gramsci was writing in 1929!). Unlike the dominant class,
fearful of being crushed by the new work and productive
systems, the European working classes were not frightened
by the spread of Americanism. Gramsci insisted that the
working class could bring about a new civilization, a new order,
only by accepting the new bases of material production.[112]

> What is today called 'americanism' is to a large extent an
> advance criticism of old strata which will in fact be crushed
> by any eventual new order and which are already in the
> grips of a wave of social panic, dissolution and despair. It
> is an unconscious attempt at reaction on the part of those
> who are impotent to rebuild and who are emphasising the
> negative aspects of the revolution. But it is not from the
> social groups 'condemned' by the new order that reconstruc-
> tion is to be expected, but from those on whom is imposed
> the burden of creating with their own suffering the material
> bases of the new order.

Gramsci's acceptance of Americanism is not, however,
uncritical. He rejects its brutal and inhuman aspects. In
Americanism one has to separate what represents an objective,
rational, technical exigency from the interests of dominant
classes in it. 'Technical exigency can be thought of not only
independently from the interests of the dominant class, but also
in combination with the interests of the class still subaltern.'[113]
Americanism is a progressive program of a particular social
force working against the interests of the subaltern classes
'which have to be "manipulated" and rationalised to serve new
ends.' The process of socialist reconstruction entails, thus,

acceptance and transcendence of Fordism, the creation of a
'humane Americanism.' Americanism is not concerned with
human and spiritual processes. In Americanism 'humanity and
spirituality' cannot be realized except in the world of production and work and in productive 'creation.' 'Puritanical
initiatives simply have the purpose of preserving, outside of
work, a certain psycho-physical equilibrium which prevents
the physiological collapse of the worker, exhausted by the new
method of production.'[114] Such equilibrium is mechanical and
external, imposed through force and coercion, iron discipline
exerted externally. In socialist Fordism, 'it can become
internalized if it is proposed by the worker himself and not
imposed from the outside, if it is proposed by a new form of
society.' Ultimately, conformism is unavoidable. Rationalization
of production always entails a restructuring of intellectual
and structural activities. The problem is that of creating a conformism that stems from below and from self-discipline. In the
ultimate analysis, the new conformism is a dynamic conformism.
There is a conflict between two types of conformism, Gramsci
notes, and this is part of the more general conflict between
two types of hegemonies.[115] While the social conformism created
by Taylor-Ford's method is mechanical, external and denies
spiritual and human activities, that advocated by socialist
Fordism is spontaneous and conscious. It balances maximum
social utilitarianism and maximum individuality.

In concluding this chapter, we make some very general
observations. It has been rightly said that hegemony is in
Gramsci what the idea is in Hegel. Hegemony is, in fact, the
concrete realization of the dialectical process of history. It is
a dialectical and on-going process. History is the history of
struggles between hegemonies, Gramsci would say. Socialist
hegemony has a concrete historical origin within the bourgeois
hegemony. It comes into existence at that cathartic moment
in the historical development of subaltern classes when the
proletariat transcends the limits of its corporate-economic
origin and begins its march toward 'becoming the State.'
Hegemony expands as its sociological basis (fundamental group)
expands. The point of arrival of hegemony is the realization
of a totality. This totality is in Gramsci intellectual, political
and ethical and coincides with the structural and superstructural unification of society. The condition sine qua non
for the realization of such totality is the disappearance of the
subject of hegemony, the party and the state. Succinctly,
three phases can be distinguished in the development of
socialist hegemony. First, hegemony (cultural and ideological
direction), realized before its subject conquers political power.
Second, hegemony (cultural and political direction), realized
when its subject become the state. Third, hegemony (structural
and superstructural unification of society), realized when the
state, and therefore the subject of hegemony, disappears within
civil society. This third phase is achieved when the civil society

absorbs political society, or, as Gramsci puts it, when the
political state becomes an ethical state. 'In reality, only the
social group that poses the end of the State and its own end
as the goal to be achieved can create an ethical State.'[116] The
presence of the state within civil society indicates a 'particularity' still present in it, thus the incomplete realization of
Gramscian totality. From this perspective, Gramsci examined
the development of past history. He identified regressive and
progressive hegemonic systems. Proletarian hegemony is the
most progressive in so far as the masses themselves assert
themselves autonomously in the political and cultural spheres.
Hegemonies are progressive as long as their subject, the
fundamental group, is progressive. When fundamental groups
cease to be progressive then hegemony becomes dictatorship.
Hegemony is the model adopted by the bourgeoisie and the
proletariat alike. Proletarian hegemony develops because of
the failure of the first to realize a structural and cultural
unification of societies.

Part III

POLITICAL PRAXIS AND THE SUPERSTRUCTURES

6 SCIENCE, POLITICAL PRAXIS AND HISTORICISM

The problem of the relationship between history and nature, historical thought and scientific thought has been at the center of philosophical inquiry for centuries. Medieval thought hypostatized the universal and dealt with the material world from the universal and absolute perspective of God. The natural and human world were deprived of autonomy. They were subordinated, shaped and governed by the objective purpose of God. Renaissance historical thought placed man at the center of the natural and social universe. History maintained its central position, but it was no longer divine history, rather human history, the history of man's actions emanating directly from human 'nature.' Seventeenth-century thought dethroned history from its dominant position in the realm of knowledge. The overwhelming concern became 'natural science.' Descartes rejected history as 'fantasy-building' activity and became instrumental in the foundation of a movement toward 'rational philosophy' and exact science. With him the divorce between history and philosophy was sanctioned. The seventeenth century gave birth to 'scientific materialism.' For Hobbes, all phenomena, natural, individual and social, can be explained with 'geometrical precision.' Everything that exists in nature and society is a mode of 'motion.' The weight of Locke's philosophy was on the side of empiricism. He marked the beginning of the estrangement of science from philosophy. There are no innate or absolute ideas. Knowledge is acquired through experience. Ideas, rights, laws, are not historical categories, they derive from sensuous experience. In the course of the eighteenth century, the Enlightenment thinkers, impressed by the spectacular achievements of science in the natural and physical world, adopted scientific concepts and methods to explain social phenomena. Data of experience alone and the method of systematic deduction do not guarantee the attainment of objective knowledge. Methodical observation and reason enable men to establish patterns of regularity and relations among phenomena. If Newton was able to establish a general law of attraction in physics, so should a science of society be able to comprehend the diversity of natural and social phenomena in terms of a single universal law. The Enlightenment thinkers assumed that a static, immutable human nature underlines the course of historical events. Thus, they searched for a science of human nature. In so doing, Collingwood writes, 'they made it impossible for themselves to arrive at the conception of a history of human nature itself.[1]

Hegel approached history not from the standpoint of nature. For him, the only history is the history of thought. It is the development of the consciousness of the idea and its realization. Hegel, thus, separates the processes of nature and those of history, and gives pre-eminence to the latter. As a consequence, the only universal history is philosophical history. Such history is in the ultimate analysis the history of the cosmic unfolding of Absolute Reason. It follows that history cannot be ascertained 'empirically;' it can be understood and known only as the outward expression of ideas. Historical development, Hegel concludes, is not accidental, but a logical and necessary process. The priority of thought over nature, and the distinction between history and nature, posited by Hegel, were flatly rejected by positivism. History and nature are once again identified. The concepts and methods of natural science became those of the science of history and society. Sociology, for Comte, became that science which attempted to ascertain facts, discover causal relationships between them, and frame inductively general laws of the dynamics of social systems. History became the knowledge of autonomous, individual facts, each studied in and for itself, in a positivistic manner, independently from the knower. The only facts are empirical facts. As a consequence, positivist history is the history of external happenings, and not, as in Hegel, the history of ideas from which they derive. Toward the end of the nineteenth century the interest in the theory of history was revived, as well as the old problem of the distinction between history and nature. This issue was treated by the German philosophers Windelband and Rickert.[2] The failure of positivism and idealism, Lucio Colletti writes, lies in their monistic approach: 'they reduce the unity-distinction of thought and being to a mere *identity*, one in the Idea, the other in Matter *as such*. The effective result of this abstract monism is, in both cases, a *de facto dualism*.'[3] This dualism between historical and natural process also prevailed in the thought of Simmel, Dilthey and Spengler.

The history-nature problem was approached in a novel way by the philosophical movements founded by Marx and Croce. The primacy of history over nature was re-established, although in a radically different sense. Much has been written on the historicism of Marx and Croce. It is important to differentiate their respective views.

Helmut Fleischer has rightly identified three approaches to the concept of history in the writings of the founders of Marxism. History is a process of humanization (anthropological approach); history is praxis (pragmatological approach); history is a natural process developing according to definite and objective laws (nomological approach).[4] The emphasis on one or the other of these approaches led to either an objectivistic or subjectivistic interpretation of Marxist historicism.

On the one hand, we have the orthodox Marxism which is the
official doctrine of Soviet Marxism, based on the nomological
approach, and on the other hand, the subjectivistic Marxism
of Lukács, L. Kofler, etc., which stresses the importance of
the anticipatory function of consciousness.

Croce's historicism is a vindication of the autonomy of history.
The major problem of philosophy was its emancipation from
the domination of natural science. All reality is history, and
all knowledge is historical knowledge. The implications of Croce's
historicism are far-reaching. First, the traditional distinction
between universal and contingent truths is false. Only thought
can distinguish between truth and falseness. Second, reality
is not contained in the particulars, but in universal concepts
from which the particulars emanate. Finally, a necessary distinction must be made between the concepts of science and the
concepts of philosophy. The first are pseudo-concepts and
arbitrary constructions, the latter universal, necessary and
logical.[5]

Gramsci's discussion of the relationship between history and
nature makes sense only if viewed in the intellectual context
just surveyed. He attempts to reconstruct an historicist approach
to the problem of knowledge and an historicist methodology.

In this chapter we shall first analyze Gramsci's historicism
and then attempt to expound upon the problems of science and
objectivity.

HISTORICISM AND THE THEORY OF NATURE

Gramsci's task was not simply that of elucidating partial aspects
of theoretical Marxism. He attempted to analyze it in its
entirety, seize its essence, and further develop it so as to
spur its rejuvenation. He saw in Marxian theory only the basis
of a new conception of the world. Much remained to be done
to arrive at an elaboration of Marxism as the most integral,
universal and autonomous conception of the world. This was
precisely Gramsci's complex task. Marxism, as a theory, had
not been systematically exposed by its founders. It was born
in the form of aphorisms, which needed further elaboration
and systematization.[6]

> The philosophy of praxis was born in the form of aphorisms
> and practical criteria for the purely accidental reason that
> its founder dedicated his intellectual forces to other problems,
> particularly economic (which he treated in systematic form);
> but in these practical criteria and these aphorisms is implicit
> an entire conception of the world, a philosophy.

Gramsci rejected, in a sustained polemic against Bukharin, the
general interpretation of Marxism as historical materialism/
dialectical materialism or historical-economic determinism as a
distortion of Marx's thought. Marxism is a philosophy, Gramsci
argues, an historicist conception of the world, knowledge,

history and all reality. This was the thesis he intended to
demonstrate.

The definition of Marxism as a conception of the world is
already in itself a radical way of approaching the problem. It
implies that like any Weltanschauung, it is a unity of theory
and praxis. It is a theory, but also a praxis, much like Christianity, which contains fundamental theoretical precepts as well
as a morality of its own, demanding a specific religiosity in its
adherents. In its essence, thus, Marxism is an historicist
theory, a philosophy of praxis. This notion derives from Hegel,
for whom philosophy is the history of philosophy, the self-
conscious historical realization of the Spirit. Following Marx,
Gramsci reinterprets historicism as a concrete philosophy of
historical development, as the self-realization of concrete man,
struggling to change concrete historical situations. Gramsci
characterizes it as immanent philosophy, a philosophy identified
with human praxis. In so doing, Gramsci ultimately denies any
reality pre-existent to human initiative and will, be it nature
or spirit. We have then, as we have seen, a complete identification of history, philosophy and praxis.

To assert that knowledge is concrete knowledge is not enough.
In order to respond to the criticism levelled by all quarters
that Marxism is simply another angle from which history can be
analyzed, one has to insist on the idea that it is an autonomous
and complete theory of knowledge. Orthodox Marxism, for
Gramsci, is unable to meet this criticism by insisting that the
philosophical foundation of Marxism is dialectical or historical
materialism. Such a notion was introduced by Engels in his
'Anti-Dühring' and further developed by Lenin and his followers.[7]
The formula, dialectical materialism, contains the idea that
Marxist conception of reality is 'materialist' and its methodology
'dialectical.' More specifically, it implies the primacy of matter
and being over spirit and consciousness. With regard to the
problem of the 'reality of the external world,' for instance,
it affirms that it exists objectively, independently of human
consciousness and will. In short, all knowledge is a reflection
of the objective world. The admission of such a position, Gramsci
observes, signifies that Marxism is not self-sufficient and is in
need of another philosophical system to complete itself, in our
case, the 'materialist philosophy,' developed before Marx by
naturalist philosophy. In this respect, Croce's characterization
of Marxism as a simple interpretation of history, as another
perspective from which to approach the problems of reality,
would be correct. On the contrary, the widespread belief that
Marxism is simply another moment in the evolution of modern
thought must be dispelled, Gramsci writes. And this can be done
by defending its original and universal character against all
other philosophical systems. Gramsci has words of praise for
Antonio Labriola, his intellectual mentor, for having understood
this exigency.[8]

Labriola distinguishes himself from both currents by his

affirmation ...that the philosophy of praxis is an independent
and original philosophy which contains in itself the elements of
a further development, so as to become, from an interpretation of history, a general philosophy. This is the direction in
which one must work, developing Antonio Labriola's position.

As Jacques Texier has demonstrated in his systematic exposition of Gramsci's thought, the conception of Marxism as an
autonomous, integral and universal Weltanschauung in itself
represents an original idea in the history of Marxist thought.
It establishes new criteria in solving the so-called question of
Marxist 'orthodoxy' and it provides a new interpretation of
various 'revisionisms.'[9] Not only is the right-wing movement
of Bernstein revisionist, who, in opposition of the theoretical
tendencies of the Second International, abandoned the revolutionary ethos of Marxist doctrine, but so is the 'orthodox'
Marxism of Kautsky, Plekhanov and Bukharin, who, against
the positions of Bernstein and in line with the scientistic
and positivistic positions of the time, developed the idea of
Marxism as a 'philosophical materialism.' Also, Gramsci notes,
all attempts made by Sorel, Croce and Gentile are revisionist.
While Sorel distorts Marxian theory, Croce and Gentile attempt
to liquidate it by incorporating some of its healthy elements
into their idealist philosophical framework.[10] In this respect,
Gramsci redefines the notion of Marxist 'orthodoxy.'[11]

> Orthodoxy is not to be looked for in this or that adherent of
> the philosophy of praxis, or in this or that tendency con-
> nected with currents extraneous to the original doctrine, but
> in the fundamental concept that the philosophy of praxis is
> 'sufficient unto itself', that it contains in itself all the funda-
> mental elements needed to construct a total and integral con-
> ception of the world, a total philosophy and theory of natural
> science, and not only that but everything that is needed to
> give life to an integral practical organisation of society, that
> is, to become a total integral civilisation.

Marxism is historicism. The essence of historicism is that
history is praxis. It is praxis which creates historical facts and
historical truths.

We have already dealt elsewhere with the notion of historicism.
We now occupy ourselves with the problem of how Marxism
becomes, in Gramsci, the theory of reality, of a totality which
encompasses the realm of nature, without falling into the
dualism of idealism/materialism and subjectivism/objectivism.

Marxism is not mechanical materialism
Lenin reduced Engels's materialist philosophy to epistemological
realism. He emphasized the idea that materialism recognizes
beyond phenomena a reality existing independently from the
human subject. Materialism meant ontological priority of nature
over spirit, matter over mind, body over consciousness.
Thought being the product of matter, it became logical to assert
that thought is a reflection of the external world (copy theory).

These ideas entered Marxian theory under the pressure of the scientific achievements of natural science. By separating being and thought, matter and history, orthodox Marxism pronounced itself for the objectivity of the external world. For Gramsci, this philosophical dualism leads to philosophical realism, and in the last analysis to a new form of metaphysics and mysticism typical of traditional religion, which posits the existence of the natural world outside and prior to the cognizing man. The consequences of such realist conception are that truth and objectivity become extra-historical and extra-human categories. Man confronts reality not as his own production, but as a given facticity. One of the political consequences of materialism was the rendering of men passive before reality and nature.

Gramsci attempted to solve the old problem of being/thought and history/matter within a Marxist perspective, without falling into the error of both materialism and idealism, by historicizing reality, matter, science and knowledge.

Let us take, for instance, the notion of matter. Lenin wrote: 'The sole "property" of matter with whose recognition philosophical materialism is bound up is the property of being an objective reality, of existing outside our mind.'[12] Gramsci rejects Lenin's objectivistic characterization of matter, passed on under the name of scientific materialism, for it is mechanistic, determinist, anti-historical, anti-human, in a word, un-Marxist. Gramsci re-establishes the primacy of man over matter by redefining it in an historicist sense, and humanizing it, so to speak.[13]

Clearly, for the philosophy of praxis, 'matter' should be understood neither in the meaning that it has acquired in natural science (physics, chemistry, mechanics, etc. - meanings to be noted and studied in the terms of their historical development), nor in any of the meanings that one finds in the various materialistic metaphysics. The various physical (chemical, mechanical, etc.) properties of matter which together constitute matter itself... should be considered, but only to the extent that they become a productive 'economic element'. Matter as such therefore is not our subject but how it is socially and historically organised for production, and natural science should be seen correspondingly as essentially an historical category, a human relation.

Matter is then, for Gramsci, the ensemble of material forces socially organized by production, denoting specific social relationships. It is an historical reality. To be sure, there is a definition of matter in natural and physical sciences, but this is of no importance to man. The philosophy of praxis studies a machine not in its natural components but 'only in so far as it is a moment of material forces of production... and expresses a social relation which in turn corresponds to a particular historical period.'[14] To illustrate this point, Gramsci makes the following observation: 'As an abstract natural force electricity

existed even before its reduction to a productive force, but it
was not historically operative and was just a subject of hypo-
thetical discourse in natural history (earlier still it was historical
"nothingness", since no one was interested in it or indeed knew
anything about it).[15]

The same historicist perspective is applied by Gramsci to
the so-called 'objectivity of the external world.' For Lenin, the
answer to such a question is consequent on that of the primacy
of matter over spirit. If matter is understood in the physical
sense, then it is clear that matter alone constitutes objective
reality. 'Sensation reveals objective truth to man,' Lenin writes.
There is nothing uniquely Marxist in this statement, Gramsci
would reply. Such a notion could be accepted without any
reservation of Hegelian philosophy, as well as by the pheno-
menalist and naturalist philosophy of Berkeley and Mach. Idealism
has solved the problem of the objectivity of the external world
by asserting its fundamental subjectivity. The reality of the
world is the creation of the spirit. Marxism, Gramsci continues,
has critically rectified idealism with an historicist interpretation
of the superstructures. To be sure, historical materialism does
not deny the objective reality of the world. In opposition to
metaphysical materialism it interprets it in the sense that
reality is known only in relation to man. To avoid the solipsistic
conclusions of idealism and at the same time the metaphysical
dualism of common sense and orthodox Marxism, Gramsci analyzes
external reality in its practical relationship to man.[16] 'We know
reality only in relation to man, and since man is historical
becoming, knowledge and reality are also a becoming.'[17]

Idealist philosophy has proposed a subjectivist theory of
knowledge and reality in opposition to the 'realist' one of
philosophical materialism. Its merit is that of having criticized
preceding 'receptive' conceptions of knowledge and affirmed the
creative role of man in the production of knowledge and reality.
Idealist philosophy, however, has fallen into solipsism and
metaphysicism. Thought becomes creative of itself and by itself
And any form of metaphysics is anti-historicist.

The starting point of Marxism is idealism completed by Marxist
historicism. 'It is surprising that there has been no proper
affirmation and development of the connection between the
idealist assertion of the reality of the world as a creation of the
human spirit and the affirmation made by the philosophy of
praxis of the historicity and transcience of ideologies.'[18] Gramsci
notes that mechanical materialism in its opposition to idealism
has not utilized its positive nucleus, the affirmation of the
creative role of man and creative nature of intellectual activity.
In detaching theory from praxis, materialism has dichotomized
being and thought, separated the subject and object. In so
doing, it has departed from Marx's important contribution that
the truth is demonstrated in practical activity. In Marx, in
fact, the object is always a product of human practical activity.
This means, as Mario Tronti writes, that the object, on the one

hand, must be conceived subjectively (knowledge is critical-practical activity), but also, on the other hand, that the subject must be conceived objectively as concrete reality.[19] Strangely, both Lenin and Gramsci base their respective theoretical conclusion on Engels's famous text: 'the unity of the world consists in its materiality.' Materiality, for Lenin, simply means 'objective reality' existing outside man. Engels's phrase that 'the materiality of the world is demonstrated by the long and laborious development of philosophy and natural science' should be analysed and made more precise.[20] It represents the starting point of the philosophy of praxis, of a Marxist historicist theory of knowledge. Only through recourse to history and man can objective reality be demonstrated. While materialism hypostatizes and deifies 'matter,' Gramsci historicized it and humanized it. There is no 'nature' independent from man, nor man independent from nature, but an historical and dialectical relationship between them. By acting historically, man also modifies nature. The world of things, Gramsci writes, is always dependent upon concrete human interests.[21]

> If reality is as we know it and if our knowledge changes continually – if, that is, no philosophy is definitive but all historically determined – it is hard to imagine that reality changes objectively with changes in ourselves... What are phenomena? Are they something objective, existing in and for ourselves, or are they qualities which man has isolated in consequence of his practical interests (the construction of his economic life) and his scientific interests (the necessity to discover an order in the world and to describe and classify things, a necessity which is itself connected to mediated and future practical interests). Accepting the affirmation that our knowledge of things is nothing other than ourselves, our needs and interests, that is that our knowledge is superstructure (or non-definitive philosophy), it is difficult not to think in terms of something real beyond this knowledge... in the concrete sense of a 'relative' ignorance of reality, of something still unknown, which will however be known one day when the 'physical' and intellectual instruments of mankind are more perfect, when, that is, the technical and social conditions of mankind have been changed in a progressive direction.

The notion of the historicity of nature implies that the history of men and history of nature are intertwined; there is a dialectic for the history of men and the history of nature.[22] By historicizing nature, thus, Gramsci is able to reject materialism and by historicizing knowledge, as we shall see, he is able to distinguish Marxism from idealism. Yet, idealism remains the philosophical basis of Marxism.

Marxism and the subjectivist conception of reality
Materialism has the merit of being anti-speculative and anti-metaphysical. Yet, for lack of dialectics it needs to be rejected,

Gramsci writes. In contrast, idealism is dialectical, but speculative and metaphysical. Marxism was born out of Hegelian
philosophy and transcended it. Idealism still remains the foundation and point of arrival of Marxian philosophy in the form of
historicized philosophy. 'What the idealists call "spirit" is not
a point of departure but a point of arrival, it is the ensemble
of the superstructures moving towards concrete and objectively
universal unification and it is not a unitary presupposition.'[23]
Hegel is credited for having resolved the dualism of idealism
and materialism by positing a dialectical relationship between
them.[24]

> Hegel, half-way between the French Revolution and the
> Restoration, gave dialectical form to the two moments of the
> life of thought, materialism and spiritualism, but his syn-
> thesis was 'a man walking on his head'. Hegel's successors
> destroyed this unity and there was a return to materialist
> systems on the one side and spiritualist on the other. The
> philosophy of praxis, through its founder, relived all this
> experience of Hegelianism, Feuerbachianism and French
> materialism, in order to reconstruct the synthesis of dialec-
> tical unity, 'the man walking on his feet'. The laceration
> which happened to Hegelianism has been repeated with the
> philosophy of praxis. That is to say, from dialectical unity
> there has been a regress to philosophical materialism on the
> one hand, while on the other hand modern idealist high cul-
> ture has tried to incorporate that part of the philosophy of
> praxis which was needed in order for it to find a new elixir.

A work of reconstruction of Marxism requires the re-establishment of dialectical unity between the subjective and objective,
being and thought, matter and spirit, not in the speculative
sense, as in Hegel and Croce, but in an historicist one. Two
questions are posed: what is the relationship between idealism
and Marxism? When historicist Marxism denies the objectivity
of the world and whatever exists outside human consciousness,
does it fall into idealist positions which Marx systematically
criticized?[25]

> Without doubt the subjectivist conception is proper to modern
> philosophy in its most achieved and advanced form, in that
> it gave birth to, and was superseded by, historical materialism,
> a philosophy which, in its theory of superstructures, poses
> in realistic and historicist terms what traditional philosophy
> expressed in speculative form.

To combat mechanical materialism, Gramsci appropriates the
historicist and humanist components present in idealist philosophy. The latter has the merit of positing the centrality of
man with regard to the problem of 'reality,' and the centrality
of 'history' among all experimental, physical and natural
sciences. Does this mean capitulation to idealism?[26]

> It must be demonstrated that while the 'subjectivist' con-
> ception has had its usefulness as a criticism of the philo-
> sophy of transcendence on the one hand and the naive

metaphysics of common sense and of philosophical materialism on the other, it can find its truth and its historicist interpretation only in the concept of superstructures.

Marxism, then, accepts the notion of historicism from Croce's idealist philosophy, but proceeds to historicize all reality and all thought. It demonstrates the practical character of knowledge, and the unity of theory and praxis. On the problem of the relationship between being and thought, praxis and theory, while idealism reduces the first to the latter, materialism falls into the opposite error of reducing everything to matter. Gramsci posits a dialectical relationship between them. Dialectical unity, in Gramsci, means the unity or identity of opposites.[27] If one element of the relation is denied we have either an idealist monism or materialist monism. To be sure, Gramsci adds, the philosophy of praxis will also be a 'monism.' But in what sense?[28]

> It will certainly not be idealistic or materialistic monism, but rather the identity of contraries in the concrete historical act, that is in human activity (history-spirit) concrete, indissolubly connected with a certain organised (historicised 'matter' and with the transformed nature of man).

In conclusion, when examined in its relation to idealism, Marxism is the historicist interpretation of the subjectivist conception of reality. The only way that the subjectivist idealist conception can be salvaged is by giving to it an historicist interpretation. Hence the importance of the superstructures.

HISTORICISM AND SCIENCE

The essential characteristics of Marxism during the period of the Second International were lost. Marx's followers were not able to come to grips with the problem of 'science.' At a time when scientific achievements in all fields of knowledge astounded the world and the positivist method dominated the realm of thought, Marxists did not attempt to articulate in a systematic way the relationship between science and Marxism. Dialectical method and science were thought to be incompatible. Bernstein, for instance, rejected dialectical thought in the name of positivist science and revised Marxian principles on the basis of empirical facts.[29] Similarly, orthodox Marxists, particularly Kautsky, Plekhanov, Bukharin, etc., infatuated with the results of natural science, proceeded to scienticize Marxian theory. Kautsky, in fact, was attracted by Darwin's biologism, and Plekhanov by Spinoza's monism. Scientific Marxism was, in fact, an attempt to elevate Marxian theory to the high status achieved by positivist science.

It is true that Lenin re-emphasized the dialectical and superstructural components of Marxism in opposition to the theoreticians of the Second International. But it is also true, as Z. Jordan has noted, that he conceived dialectics as a means to an

end, that of realizing socialism. He modified the laws of
dialectics, reducing its three laws, negation of negation, doctrine of the leaps, and unity of opposites, into one, the third
one;[30] and this for several reasons. The negation of negation
recedes from Lenin's conception of the dialectics as socialism
consolidates in communist countries. Of Engels's laws of
dialectics, Lenin retained the idea that 'the revolutionary
advance preserves or reproduces the stage already passed in
the ascent from lower to higher levels of development and incorporated it into the unity of opposites.'[31] Likewise, Lenin formulated a materialist interpretation of natural science under pressure from the latest discoveries in the world of science. It
was Lukács who extended the category of the totality to natural
science and refused to reduce history to nature.

In the same vein, but independently of Lukács, Gramsci
refused to exempt the sciences of nature from historical analysis.
On the one hand, he was confronted with Croce's idealism,
which downgraded the 'science of nature' to the lowest form of
knowledge, and on the other hand, with the vulgar Marxism of
Bukharin which uncritically equated Marxism with positivist
science. Both conceptions separated science from history and,
in Gramsci's view, overlooked the strategical importance of
'scientific knowledge' in controlling and humanizing nature.[32]
Gramsci thus asserts the fundamental unity of history and nature. In this he echoes Marx: 'History itself is a real part of
natural history - of nature developing into man. Natural science
will in time incorporate into itself the science of man, just as
the science of man will incorporate into itself natural science;
there will be one science.'[33] There is a history of 'scientific
knowledge and scientific achievements,' Gramsci writes, and this
is part of 'human history.'

The superstructural character of science
Gramsci laments the position of quasi-fetishism that exact
sciences acquired within the philosophy of praxis. They came
to be regarded as the only 'true philosophy or knowledge of
the world.'[34] He concluded that if Marxism aims at becoming an
integral conception of the world - as it should - then it has to
develop a total philosophy and 'theory of natural sciences.'[35]

It should deal with all the general philosophical part, and
then should develop in a coherent fashion all the general
concepts of a methodology of history and politics and, in
addition, of art, economics and ethics, finding place in the
overall construction for a theory of the natural sciences.

Gramsci certainly did not develop a systematic historicist
theory of scientific knowledge and activity. He limited himself
to analyzing the philosophical assumption of the scientific problem and its role in socialist reconstruction of society. One of
his major observations on the nature of science is its instrumental value, its subordination to a general conception of the
world. From this derives the historicist, that is, the practical,

ideological, superstructural character of science.[36]
   To place science at the base of life, to regard science and
   the world view *par excellence*, as the one that clears the
   eyes from every ideological illusion, and which places man
   in front of reality as it is, means to fall again into the idea
   that the philosophy of praxis needs philosophical props outside of itself. But in reality science, too, is a superstructure, an ideology.
It should be clear, however, that not science, but scientism is
what Gramsci rejects. Gramsci was aware of the dangers involved in his theory of complete historicization of the sciences
of nature. As we shall see, he proceeded to press to the
extremes the logic of historicism without compromising the
integrality of the historicist method and the autonomy of the
scientific methodology. Let us first review his treatment of
science. If one chooses to analyze the evolution of science
throughout history or to examine the nature of scientific
research, one is forced to accept the conclusion that science
is a 'historical category.'[37] It suffices to take into consideration
the historical variation of the relationship between science,
magic and religion to convince oneself. It is from an analysis
of the nature of science that the ideological character of science
can best be demonstrated. 'Concretely science is the combination of the objective fact with an hypothesis or a system of
hypotheses which surpass the mere objective fact.'[38] In experimental investigation one finds concepts pre-existing the
scientific activity proper which are, in fact, part of the history
of man and culture. The affirmation that the progress of
science depends upon the development of the instruments of
science is, for Gramsci, wrong.[39]
   The principal 'instruments' of scientific progress are of an
   intellectual (and even political) and methodological order,
   and Engels has written that 'intellectual instruments' are not
   born from nothing and are not innate in man, but are acquired, have developed and are developing historically. How
   great a contribution to the progress of science was made by
   the expulsion from the scientific fields of the authority of
   Aristotle and the Bible?
The influence of Croce on Gramsci is here apparent. Gramsci
and Croce are in agreement that the essence of natural science
consists of thoughts, concepts and intuition.[40] Thus science
cannot and does not offer an absolute gnosiology for the simple
fact that 'if scientific truths were definitive, science would
have ceased to exist as such, as research, as new experimenta-
tion, and scientific activity would reduce to the diffusion of
what had already been discovered.'[41] Gramsci subordinates
science to man: 'All of science is tied to the needs, the life,
the activity of man. Without man's activity, which creates all
values, including the scientific ones, what would "objectivity"
be? Chaos, that is nothing.'[42] What is, ultimately, the object of
science? Not natural phenomena per se, but their relationship

to men.

All Gramsci's observations on the 'sciences of nature' do not make sense unless they are incorporated in the general context of the problem of the relationship between man and nature. Is man the point of departure or the point of arrival? Marx provided Gramsci with the proper answer. Man is the complex of his social relations. 'Thus Man does not enter into relations with the natural world, just by being himself part of the natural world, but actively, by means of work and technique.'[43] For Gramsci, it is not a question of seeking to establish absolute truth, rather of grasping the dialectics between men and nature in order to participate in the transformation of reality. The purpose of science, Gramsci concludes, is not that of knowing things, but of subordinating things to man. What is, then, the value and what are the functions of experimental sciences within the philosophy of praxis?

Philosophy of praxis and science

The problem of the relationship between Marxism and science is for Gramsci one of the most complex and delicate ones. What is at stake is the very definition and autonomous status of Marxism and science. Can science become an integral philosophy? If not, what are the functions of science within a given conception of the world? And given the superstructural character of science, in what does its specificity consist? These are the questions Gramsci raises.

First of all, the very definition of science shows its character of instrumentality and partiality. The very meaning of science, Gramsci writes, is that given by only a restricted number of sciences, natural and physical sciences. The natural sciences became sciences par excellence and any method similar to that of these sciences was called 'scientific.' Gramsci reflects: 'Sciences *par excellence* do not exist, and neither method *par excellence*, a "method *in se*". Every scientific research creates its own method, its own logic, whose generality or universality consists in its being 'related to an end.'[44] As ends change throughout history so do the methods. Thus, in reality,[45]

'scientific' means 'rational', and more precisely 'rationally in relation to an end' to be attained, that is that of producing the maximum with minimal effort, of obtaining the greatest economic efficiency, etc. by choosing and fixating rationally all the operations and acts toward the attainment of a goal.

The identification of Marxism and positivist science, maintained by Bukharin, deprives the first of its independent and universal character. Gramsci, in contrast, reduces science to the philosophy of praxis without compromising the specificity of the scientific methodology. 'There can be no doubt that the rise of the experimental method separates two worlds, two epochs, and initiates the process of dissolution of theology and metaphysics and the process of development of modern thought

whose consummation is in the philosophy of praxis.[46] From this
perspective, science is not denied, as in idealism, but assigned
positive functions. Science constitutes a liberating and universalizing force. Despite the incapacity of experimental sciences
to seek to establish a universal objectivity, scientific activity
realizes a partial universality in so far as it is an instrument of
unification in the world of things and the world of men.[47]

> Up to now experimental science has provided the terrain on
> which a cultural unity of this kind has reached its furtherest
> extension. This has been the element of knowledge that has
> contributed most to unifying the 'spirit' and making it more
> universal. It is the most objectivised and concretely univer-
> salised subjectivity.

The universalizing character of science, which Gramsci praises
in science and incorporates into the philosophy of praxis,
resides in its ability to create a consensus by means of a shared
set of principles (induction and deduction) and of a complex
of material and logical instruments distinguishing in sensations
what is necessary and what is arbitrary and transitory.[48] But,
Gramsci cautions, this consensus is always human and subjective, never an ontological and extra-historical one.[49]

> What interests science is therefore not the objectivity of
> reality, but man, who elaborates his methods of research,
> who continually improves his material instruments that
> strengthen his sensory organs and the logical (including
> mathematical) instruments of analysis and of proof; that is
> to say, culture, one's view of the world, and the relation
> between man and reality with the mediation of technology.

Such a universalizing function of science, though partial and
limited to the scientific community, can be integrated into the
philosophy of praxis. Science represents a liberating force,
capable, that is, of generating qualitative transformations. As
cited in a text, Gramsci sees in science a tendency to modify
continually the 'mode of knowledge' and establish what is necessary and not arbitrary in social reality.

However, a practical interest is at the basis of science.
Science is always dependent upon a certain political praxis.
From a Marxist perspective it has to transcend its caste-like
character and participate in the creation of a universal consensus of much wider scope. Scientific praxis must always be
dependent upon political praxis. This follows from the principle
of the historicity of nature and knowledge.[50]

Gramsci's analysis of science is consistent with his theory
of absolute historicism and humanism and avoids the pitfalls of
idealist and materialist positions. He is able to assert the
principle of objectivity of science and at the same time its
historicist, human and practical character. He rejects the narrow
definition of science, typical of positivism, but accepts the
wider one, that of science rationally conforming to an end.
Having accepted the wider definition of science, Gramsci proceeds to analyze its ideological, practical and instrumental

character and its dependence upon a political praxis. He finally arrives at an historicist conclusion, opposite to that of Bukharin. It is not the philosophy of praxis which is reduced to science, rather it is science which is reduced to the philosophy of praxis. If the history of nature is part of the history of men, it follows that the history of scientific praxis is part of the philosophy of praxis, of a philosophical and political project in the process of realization. As Nardone observes, Gramsci does not contest the scientific aim of discovering new truths, and creating new knowledge, provided this knowledge remains within history. The possibility of a new knowledge is dependent upon the possibility of creating a new history.[51]

With regard to the relation between historicism and science, Roberto Guiducci has noted that Marxism not only respects the autonomy of scientific praxis, but acts on it, by providing it with new conceptual tools, a historical and socially responsible consciousness. Natural sciences discover new 'material forces' for the benefit of men; these are complemented by socio-economic sciences which render them 'economically-productive' and finally integrated into a coherent, integral Weltanschauung, the philosophy of praxis.[52]

It remains for us now to follow Gramsci's elaboration and application of the historicist theory to the problem of objectivity.

HISTORICISM AND OBJECTIVITY

The Marxist historicist gnosiology of Gramsci extends, as we have seen, to all knowledge, whether historical or scientific. All knowledge is dependent upon man, who creates and transforms the world (Marxism is absolute humanism) and develops in a dialectical relationship with a given political praxis in history (Marxism is absolute historicism). It follows that the objectivity of knowledge cannot be a-historical and a-human, that is, sought outside history and man. Truth cannot be hypostatized for it is impossible for man to judge it from an absolute point of view, transcending history. Gramsci proposes a dialectical conception of objectivity. More than any other Marxist theoretician, he examines the subjective dimension in the process of knowledge and objectivity, and man's active role in their formulation and elaboration.

The problem of objectivity has not been seriously analyzed in Marxist literature. Marx and Engels, to be sure, spoke of the relative nature of knowledge, but, as we have seen in the first chapter, they ceased to be interested in this problem once classless societies were created. Lenin modified the theory of relativity of knowledge. For him, the affirmation of the relativity of knowledge does not preclude the attainment of absolute truth. He arrives at this conclusion through an un-Marxist operation, that of reducing the subject to an object, thus eliminating the active and subjective components from objective knowledge. For Marx, the relationship of subject and object is fundamental in the process of knowledge. Knowledge is in fact the result of subjective and objective factors as well.

Traditionally, the sociology of knowledge has analyzed the subjective factor in knowledge. Mannheim, above all, following Marx's footsteps, spoke of the subjective dimension of knowledge when he focused his attention on the ideological character of human thought. Both Marx and Mannheim have insisted upon the social context in which knowledge arises. When they, in fact, attempted to analyze the vested interests present in ideas themselves, they actually underlined the subjective dimension in the cognitive process. As Schaff notes, the demarcation line between the subjective and the objective within knowledge is blurred. The 'subjective' is social in origin, external, thus objective. And the 'objective' manifests itself always subjectively.[53] The problem of objectivity is formulated by Mannheim as a process by which the subjectivity is surmounted. The fundamental problem in his sociology of knowledge is how a socially conditioned knowledge can attain objectivity; how the partiality and limitations of knowledge can be overcome. Mannheim's answer is well-known. Possession of a plurality of perspectives enables one to gain a detached point of view, ultimately possessed by the intellectuals. The problem of 'subjectivity,' that is, the role of the subjective factor in the cognitive process, is posed by Marx differently. It is examined in relation to human praxis. Marx wrote: 'The chief defect of all hitherto existing materialism – that of Feuerbach included – is that the thing, reality, sensuousness, is conceived only in the form of the object or of contemplation, but not as human sensuous activity, practice, not subjectively.'[54] Gramsci bases his analysis on Marx, but further clarifies the nature of the subjective and the objective phenomenon.

Praxis as the determinant of thought
The nucleus of Gramsci's discussion of objectivity is contained in one formula: 'reality does not exist on its own, in and for itself, but only in an historical relationship with the men who modify it.'[55] Put differently, knowledge always exists in a practical relationship with history and is always dependent upon the intervention of human will, organized in a political will. Knowledge, being 'practical,' is also political. Two ideas are crucial.

First, knowledge is for Gramsci a 'creative' activity and not a 'receptive,' ordering activity, which describes or systematizes the external world. At the basis of knowledge there is a 'will.' 'No, the mechanistic forces never prevail in history; but men, consciousness, spirit which mold the external appearance and always triumph in the end....The pseudo-scientists' natural law and fatal course of events has been replaced by man's tenacious will.'[56] The notion of knowledge as creative active is a

derivation from classical German philosophy. Gramsci accepts
it not in its speculative sense, but in an immanentist, historicist
sense. It is 'creative' only in that knowledge 'modifies the way
of feeling of the many and consequently reality itself, which
cannot be thought without this many.'[57]
   A second point follows. Knowledge is historical, that is, it
is the product of history. This is also a derivation from idealist
philosophy. Gramsci accepts it as the cornerstone of his theory,
but in an immanentist sense. History is praxis. Knowledge is
the truth of praxis. The contemplative, transcendental and
detached character of knowledge is replaced by an absolute
immanence. Historicism and humanism, pressed to their extremes,
produce a knowledge which is not outside history, society and
praxis. In short, knowledge is an historical act. In an historical
act, Gramsci writes in 'Scritti Giovanili,' 'man and reality' are
identified.[58] This can be interpreted to mean that objective
knowledge is established by a given political praxis of a collective will becoming 'hegemonic.' Thus, for Gramsci, as we
have shown in the first chapter, the problem of objectivity
cannot be independent from that of hegemony. Any theory of
knowledge cannot but be a theory of ideology. More importantly,
the problem of objectivity cannot be formulated apart from that
of political conflict and human subjectivity. Knowledge being
praxis, objectivity is part of struggle between groups to attain
the hegemony. Conflict among groups is a struggle for an
objectivity. 'There exists therefore a struggle for objectivity
(to free oneself from partial and fallacious ideologies) and
this struggle is the same as the struggle for the cultural
unification of the human race.'[59] Objectivity is not a terminus
a quo, but a terminus ad quem, which can be attained only
when the human race is structurally and culturally unified.[60]
   Man knows objectively in so far as knowledge is real for the
   whole human race *historically* unified in a single unitary
   cultural system. But this process of historical unification
   takes place through the disappearance of the internal contradictions which tear apart human society, while these contradictions themselves are the condition for the formation of
   groups and for the birth of ideologies which are not concretely universal but are immediately rendered transient by
   the practical origin of their substance.
The identification of knowledge and praxis entails another
consequence, the formulation of the problem of objectivity in
terms of men's subjectivity, well elaborated in the idealist
philosophy of Benedetto Croce. Gramsci *historicizes objectivity,*
and as such incorporates it into the philosophy of praxis. He
does so by maintaining the unity of the subject-object, sub-
jective-objective, theory-praxis established by Marx, and the
historicist and humanist essence of Marxist theory. The objective, nature and economy, is transformed into the subjective,
necessity into freedom and possibility. In this sense, scientific
knowledge, in Gramsci's Marxist gnosiology, is the 'most

objectivised and concretely universalised subjectivity.[161] Two
important ideas are contained in this pronouncement. Objectivity
is a human and dialectical process. The objective designates a
reality which is ascertained by all men, independently from any
particularistic perspective. Furthermore, it is dialectical. 'We
know reality only in relation to man, and since man is historical
becoming, knowledge and reality are also a becoming and so is
objectivity.[162] Of paramount importance in objectivity is the
process of universal diffusion and affirmation of knowledge. As
Nardone explains, this means that the necessity and universality
of scientific knowledge is dependent upon the historical affirmation of a social collectivity.[163] The more subjective knowledge
universalizes itself, the more it becomes a rational necessity
for society. This process is obviously a political one. The
problem of objectivity thus formulated by Gramsci avoids the
dualism of materialism and idealism as well as solipsism. By
historicizing and humanizing objectivity, that is, by negating
the necessity and objectivity of historical laws of development
and by affirming the fundamental role of praxis in history,
Gramsci is able to avoid the dogmatic and deterministic positions
of mechanical determinism. By historicizing subjectivity, that
is, by placing man (not man in general), concrete, collective
man, at the basis of the cognitive process, Gramsci is able
also to avoid the metaphysicism, speculativity and mysticism of
idealist philosophy. Finally, by accepting the very notion and
possibility of objectivity, he avoids scepticism and nihilism.

It remains for us to explain further the subjective dimension
of objective knowledge by following more closely some Gramscian
texts. The 'subjectivist' conception of reality, formulated by
classical idealist philosophy, remains the best way of approaching the problem of objectivity only if understood as the 'historical subjectivity of a social group.[164]

> The philosophy of praxis is not only tied to immanentism, but
> also to the subjectivist conception of reality, in so far as it
> transcends it, by explaining it as a historical fact, as 'his-
> torical subjectivity of a social group', as a real fact... prac-
> tical act, the form of a concrete, social content.

For Gramsci, not the individual but a collectivity is the
bearer of objectivity. As the collectivity expands and tends to
become hegemonic, so does the objectivity. Historical objectivity
is the historical subjectivity which diffuses throughout society,
modifies the 'mode of knowledge.' The more knowledge becomes
a 'norm of collective action' and becomes concrete and complete
(integral) 'history,' the more it approximates universal objectivity. The conversion of thought into action is the measure of
the degree of objectivity reached in Gramsci's historicist theory.
This said it will not be difficult to understand the following
assertion: 'Objective always means "humanly objective" which
can be held to correspond exactly to "historically subjective":
in other words, objective would mean "universal subjective".[165]
More properly speaking, objectivity denotes in Gramsci, as

Guiducci notes, an intersubjective consensus among men,
amply criticized by Gramsci's commentators.[66] As Badaloni
explains, objectivity is not reduced to subjectivity. Rather,
the subjectivity is enriched by elements transferable to it.[67]
  With the historicization of objectivity Gramsci's gnosiology
is complete. Marxism is the philosophy of praxis, an absolute
historicism and humanism, a theory of the totality of the natural
and socio-historical phenomena, at the basis of which there is
the organized collective will, the motor force of history. This
gnosiology in its constitutive elements is based on Marx, but
is further developed and systematized and represents another
original contribution of Gramsci to the development of Marxian
theory. If one compares the humanism of Gramsci with that
of Marx, one finds in Marx a conception of man that is more
'naturalist,' so to speak. Not that Marx was a naturalist. It
was precisely naturalism which he criticized in Feuerbach! But
in Marx the relationship of man to nature is of central importance. Nature, Marx wrote, is the 'inorganic body of man,' if
man is alienated, estranged from himself, it is because he is
estranged from nature. Gramsci occupied himself with the
relationship of man to nature for polemical reasons. If he
de-emphasized the 'natural component' of materialism within
Marxism, it was because of his opposition to vulgar Marxism.
To those who adhere to a scientific Marxism, Gramsci's historicism and humanism obviously appear to be a distortion of
Marxian theory. Among the few to criticize the historicist
gnosiology of Gramsci is the French Marxist theoretician, Louis
Althusser. Some Italian commentators of Gramsci also reproach
him for having undermined the scientific basis of Marxism.
Among them, Tronti, Graziani, Gruppi, Agazzi, Luporini.
Under Croce's influence, Gramsci emphasized philosophical
knowledge over scientific knowledge, it is said. Gramsci did
not emphasize philosophical knowledge, as his critics claim. He
opposes praxis to philosophy and science. We shall review
briefly the most severe criticism of Gramsci's historicism, that
of Althusser. In this attempt we shall discuss another component
of Gramsci's theory of objectivity: the relationship of theory
and praxis.

Dialectical unity of theory and praxis: Althusser's critique
of Gramsci's historicism
The thesis of Althusser is well-known: Marxism is not a historicism. He writes: 'theoretically speaking, Marxism is, in a
single movement and by virtue of the unique epistemological
rupture which established it, an anti-humanism and an anti-
historicism.'[68] The historicist interpretation of Gramsci leads
to the 'practical negation of the distinction between the science
of history (historical materialism) and Marxist philosophy
(dialectical materialism).'[69] What remains of Marxism if philosophy
is identified with history? It would be, Althusser continues,
'the philosophy of the philosophy-history identity, or the

science-history identity.[170] Similarly, the humanism of Gramsci
is severely attacked on the level of concepts and its theoretical
implications. Gramsci's humanism leads to a reduction of the
relations of production to human relations, 'to historicized
"human relations", i.e. to inter-human, inter-subjective
relations.'[171] Hence the denial of their scientific character.
Marxism and humanism are, for Althusser, incompatible. The
first is science, the latter ideology. 'In the couple "humanism-
socialism" there is a striking theoretical unevenness: in the
framework of the Marxist conception, the concept "socialism"
is indeed a scientific concept, but the concept "humanism" is
no more than an *ideological* one.'[172]

Althusser's critique of Gramsci's interpretation of Marxism
revolves around the distinction between science and ideology.
He criticizes Gramsci's reduction of Marxism to an integral
conception of the world, an idea foreign to Marxism. On the
contrary, Marxism is science, and as such it distinguishes
itself from all past intellectual movements. What is in question
here is the definition of science and, on the contrary, that of
ideology. The two are radically different in Althusser's system.
For Althusser, an ideology is[73]

a system (with its own logic and rigour) of representations
(images, myths, ideas or concepts, depending on the case)
endowed with a historical existence and role within a given
society... ideology, as a system of representations, is distinguished from science in that in it the practico-social function is more important than the theoretical function (function
as knowledge).

Gramsci's Marxism is ideological in this sense. In Gramsci,
Marxism and ideology are certainly identified, but in a sense
different from that of Althusser. For Althusser ideology in a
class society is the relay whereby the 'relation between men
and their conditions of existence is settled to the profit of the
ruling class,' whereas in a classless society it is lived to the
benefit of all.[74] Thus, against Gramsci, there can be no autonomous proletarian ideology within bourgeois society. For
Gramsci, Marxism is not simply an ideology, but an organic
ideology. Organic ideologies, he writes, are those that are
necessary for a given structure, those that are capable of
organizing human masses and creating 'the terrain on which
men move, acquire consciousness of their position.'[75]

This polemic around the concept of ideology stems from the
complete disagreement on the manner of conceiving the relationship between theory and praxis. Althusser defines theory as
a specific form of praxis, 'any theoretical practice of a scientific
character.'[76] The criterion of the scientificity of a theoretical
practice lies, for Althusser, in the theory itself. He reduces
Marxism to axiomatics, whereby the criteria of verification of
a theory are to be sought in its internal coherence. For Gramsci
the criterion is external to theory. We quote:[77]

in the masses *as such*, philosophy can only be experienced

as a faith... Mass adhesion or non-adhesion to an ideology
is the real test of the rationality and historicity of modes of
thinking. Any arbitrary constructions are pretty rapidly
eliminated by historical competition, even if sometimes,
through a combination of immediately favourable circumstances,
they manage to enjoy popularity of a kind; whereas constructions which respond to the demands of a complex organic period of history always impose themselves and prevail
in the end...

What is unorthodox is not Gramsci's ideological Marxism, which
makes praxis the criterion of verification of theory, but rather
Althusser's interpretation of Marxism, according to which the
truth of Marxism lies in Marxism itself. Theory, thus, celebrates itself! Althusser writes:[78]

for *theoretical practice* is indeed its own criterion, and contains in itself definite protocols with which to *validate* the
quality of its product, i.e., the criteria of the scientificity
of the products of scientific practice. This is exactly what
happens in the real practice of the sciences: once they are
truly constituted and developed they have no need for
verification from *external* practices to declare the knowledges they produce to be 'true', i.e., to be *knowledges*....
It has been possible to apply Marx's theory with success
because it is 'true'; it is not true because it has been applied
with success.

In Althusserian Marxism the revolutionary essence of Marxism
is lost. How does Gramsci examine the relationship between
theory and praxis? As we have seen, he speaks of a dialectical
unity of theory and praxis. The problem includes several
aspects. In practice, in history, what is the role of theory?
How has the unity of theory and praxis to be understood? Is
it possible to establish a conceptual hierarchy between them?
On all these questions the most meaningful Gramscian text is
the following:[79]

If the problem of the identification of theory and practice
is to be raised, it can be done in this sense, that one can
construct, on a specific practice, a theory which, by coin-
ciding and identifying itself with the decisive elements of
the practice itself, can accelerate the historical process that
is going on, rendering practice more homogeneous, more
coherent, more efficient in all its elements, and thus, in
other words, developing its potential to the maximum: or
alternatively, given a certain theoretical position one can
organize the practical element which is essential for the
theory to be realised.

Theory is, for Gramsci, necessarily contained in praxis, in the
sense that it is a factor in social change. From this it cannot
be deduced that theory is subordinated to praxis, as vulgar
materialism claims. Gramsci, in fact, criticizes those who speak
of theory as a 'complement,' and 'accessory,' the 'handmaid
of practice.'[80] Such a conception is mechanistic and deterministic.

It subordinates the superstructures to structural activities.
In what sense, then, does theory determine praxis? In the
sense, Gramsci answers, that ideas have the same power as
material forces when they penetrate the consciousness of the
masses. Any conception of the world determines praxis when
it transforms itself in an ensemble of practical norms of conduct for a given collectivity and generates a new historical
reality. Gramsci sees in the Protestant Reformation the best
examples of such cathartic passage from theory to concrete
action. The Calvinist notion of predestination became 'one of
the greatest impulses to practical initiative the world has ever
known.'[81] 'One could say therefore that this is the central nexus
of the philosophy of praxis, the point at which it becomes
actual and lives historically (that is socially and no longer in
the brains of individuals), when it ceases to be arbitrary and
becomes necessary - rational - real.'[82] No hierarchy can, then,
be established between theory and practice. In certain historical situations one can have primacy over the other. We
have seen that during the economic-corporate phase of the process of development of subaltern classes, it is practice that
takes precedence over theory, practical considerations over
long-range perspectives.[83]

Insistence on the practical element of the theory-practice
nexus, after having not only distinguished but separated and
split the two elements (an operation which in itself is merely
mechanical and conventional), means that one is going through
a relatively primitive historical phase, one which is still
economic-corporate, in which the 'structural' framework is
being qualitatively transformed and the appropriate quality-
superstructure is in the process of emerging, but is not yet
organically formed.

In situations in which a social group attains hegemony, theory
and praxis are unified. The philosophy of praxis in this case
becomes the expression of a dialectical unity of theory and
praxis. It is a real theory, Gramsci would say. Not the product
of the elucubrations of intellectuals, but an organic conception
of the world. The philosophy of praxis aims at transforming
the world, and acting on human praxis. It is man's activity
which tends to realize the unity of theory and praxis.

The unity of theory and praxis is not a philosophical a priori.
It is not a mechanical fact, but 'part of the historical process.'
Marxist theory, Nardone observes, is oriented toward the
future. It is the study of the past and the historical present
directed toward a concrete political action.[84] The unity of theory
and praxis, thus understood, is the basis of scientific pre-
diction.[85]

In reality one can 'foresee' to the extent that one acts, to
the extent that one applies a voluntary effort and therefore
contributes concretely to creating the result 'foreseen'. Pre-
diction reveals itself not as a scientific act of knowledge,
but as the abstract expression of the effort made, the

practical way of creating a collective will.

In concluding this chapter, we can say that Gramsci's attempt at elaborating a complete Marxist gnosiology remains another original contribution to theoretical Marxism. If the reduction of Marxism to an economic deterministic theory represents a negative development in the history of Marxian thought, its identification with historicism represents an important step in the process of its rejuvenation. Gramsci fills a void in Marxian thought by producing a theory of knowledge and the super-structures. As we have seen, revolution is, for him, not a negative but a positive act. It implies the affirmation of a new intellectual, moral and cultural order. No new intellectual order can ever be affirmed without confrontation and eventual elimina-tion of old intellectual and cultural forms. All Gramsci's intel-lectual energies were thus concentrated in revitalizing Marxian thought, bringing it to the most advanced level of modern thought and proceeding in the direction of its full autonomy. He individuated in historicism and humanism the essence of the philosophy of praxis. The philosophy of praxis is a philosophy of history, a theory and methodology of history with practical intentions, that of directing all forces of society, intellectual and material, to change the world. No Marxist theorist has analyzed the relationship of history to the future. Gramsci's historicism, we think, represents an effort to arrive at such future in the praxis of the present. Historicism is not, as Popper suggests, the theory of the inevitability of the historical laws of development, the determinist theory of history which subordinates men to the irrational forces of history. Rather, we learn from Gramsci, it is the affirmation of the absolute im-manence of knowledge. Its practical intention is that of free-ing man's thought from the tyranny of metaphysics and deter-minism, and stimulating men to act and gain mastery of the world. Consciousness is the basis of past history made by elites, consciousness remains the basis of the new history made by the masses. The course of history is not, then, predetermined; it depends on the development of human consciousness and will. Gramsci's historicism enables one to foretaste the beauty of the future intellectual order in the historical present. Unlike most Marxists, Marcuse above all, who emphasized the power of the negative forces in socialist reconstruction, Gramsci stresses the importance of the positive in socialist transition. All his intellectual elaboration constitutes a courageous effort to formulate positive ideas about the new socialist intellectual order. This explains his interest in building a Marxist gnosiology, which asserts independent principles and methods in all areas of knowledge. He devoted most of his writings to the analysis of the superstructures because of their importance in the process of the revolution, and future socia-list society. All intellectual activities are integrated in the philosophy of praxis, and become meaningful within it. But they do not lose their autonomous status. As we have seen, nature, science and objectivity are subordinate to man, but their existence is not denied. To further illustrate the autonomy of certain intellectual activities, we now turn to the analysis of language and art by Gramsci.

7 LANGUAGE, POLITICAL PRAXIS AND HISTORICISM

The great emphasis placed by Marxist theorists and their critics on economic and political issues obfuscated the 'global' nature of Marxism. As we have seen, Gramsci sought to restore the original flexibility of Marx's theory and reformulate its 'global' claims. He elaborated a gnosiological, historiographic and political theory. At the forefront of his political theory are the problems of the masses, intellectuals and hegemony, and those of historicism and humanism in his historiography and gnosiology. Gramsci also placed a great emphasis on the analysis of cultural phenomena. The reason is simple. Socialism meant to him above all a reorganization of culture. A great portion of his writings deals with the problems of art, theater, literature, literary criticism, poetry, and language. He certainly did not analyze systematically all these cultural phenomena, nor did he elaborate a Marxist theory of aesthetics, art, literature and language. He did, however, as Anglani and Petronio have noted, delineate the fundamental framework of a Marxist analysis and theory of literary criticism, art and language.[1] Gramsci analyzed all these phenomena from the more general perspective of the philosophy of praxis, and the practical goal of the conquest of hegemony. His analysis of cultural phenomena is, then, political and historicist. All cultural phenomena are essentially historical phenomena, thus, instruments in the process of transformation of the world. We choose to examine Gramsci's analysis of language and art to show the centrality of cultural politics in Gramsci's thought. We shall attempt in this chapter to present in an organic manner the key concepts developed by Gramsci in regard to the problem of language, often neglected in Marxist literature.

Marxists themselves admit that linguistics and most problems related to language have been almost exclusively the concern of non-Marxist sciences.[2] As a matter of fact, very little has been written on the subject by the founders of Marxism. Two pronouncements by Marx and Engels have generally been considered the basis for the elaboration of a Marxist analysis of language. For Marx, in fact, the essence of language is social. It is a form of consciousness which arises from social relationship. As such, it is a superstructural activity. He writes: 'Language is as old as consciousness, language *is* practical consciousness that exists also for other men, and for that reason alone it really exists for me personally as well; language, like consciousness, only arises from the need, the necessity, of intercourse with other men.'[3] Engels mentions, in a passing remark, the other aspect of language, the system of signs, and declares it autonomous, that is, independent of the determination of structure and superstructure. This is the meaning that can be derived from the following passage: 'Without making oneself ridiculous it would be a difficult thing to explain in terms of economics the existence of every small state in Germany, past and present, or the origin of the High German consonant shifts, which widened the geographical wall of partition.'[4]

Until 1950 the whole field of Marxist linguistics was monopolized by the works and theories of Nikolai I. Marr (1864-1934).[5] The major idea of Marr's linguistic theory is that all Indo-European languages descend from a single language spoken by a single race. Thus linguistic evolution is determined by the economic basis, and society's class structure. As a result, language, as a system of signs, is ideological and super-structural. Marr's position was opposed to that of Engels, which recognized the autonomous status of language, as a system of signs. At a time when Russia was undergoing an internal process of language unification, comparative linguistic studies began to flourish, arriving at conclusions opposite to those of Marrist linguistics. Stalin's intervention in 1950 put an end to the controversy between Marrist and comparative linguistics.

Stalin, in his historic essay 'Marxism in Linguistics,' rejected the theories of Marr and affirmed the autonomy of the linguistic system, its independence from superstructural institutions and the determination of the economic structure.[6] The thrust of Stalin's arguments is the fact that while Russia had undergone profound structural changes in its transition to communism, various national languages and systems of Russian language remained unaffected and continued to develop according to their own laws. Stalin's intervention was followed by the re-emergence of the 'neo-grammarian' approach to the study of language, whose major concern was the formulation of phonetic laws and its strict application to linguistic phenomena. This approach separated language, thought and history. It became anti-historicist. This explains the general anti-semantic and anti-ethnolinguist orientation of Soviet linguistics after Stalin's death. Only after de-Stalinization did Soviet linguistics experience a profound change in the direction of structural linguistics.[7]

Gramsci is among the few Western Marxist theorists to take an active interest in the study of language and arrive at a general theory of language, not dissimilar from contemporary structural linguistics.[8] He developed an interest in linguistic studies while attending the courses of the well-known linguist M. Bartoli at the University of Turin, who, as Gramsci writes in his 'Letters from Prison,' saw in him the 'archangel sent to destroy the neo-grammarians once and for all.'[9] He has left

only a few notes on the problems of language and history of
language, sufficient to delineate the major components of a
Marxist sociology of language. They are the product of his own
reflections on the subject. He was not acquainted with the
German Ideology and certainly not aware of developments in
Soviet linguistics. Before we pass to an exposition of his notes
on linguistics, it is appropriate, we think, to discuss the
status of linguistics in Italy.

GRAMSCI'S HISTORICIST APPROACH TO THE PROBLEM
OF LANGUAGE

The idealist philosophy of Croce was no doubt the reigning
philosophy in Italy. It dominated all fields of inquiry, particularly history, philosophy, aesthetics, literature, art and
language. Gramsci took upon himself the task of writing the
most systematic critique of Croce as Marx did with regard to
Hegel and Engels with regard to Dühring. The only common
element between Croce and Gramsci is the historicist approach
in the analysis of socio-cultural phenomena. This is apparent
in their treatment of language. The concepts of language as
a Weltanschauung, of its historicity and relation to the 'national
spirit,' are a derivation from Crocean philosophy. These ideas
were indeed dominant in the philosophy of language not only
in Italy, but also, and above all, in Germany. They were the
cornerstone of the philosophical school of thought which
included Herder, Humboldt, Vossler, Trier and Weisgerber.
They were all in agreement on the creative role of language in
the cognitive process and the definition of language as a
Weltanschauung. They analyzed the linguistic phenomenon in
relation to the German national character, the Volkgeist and
Weltgeist. Language was conceived as a means of understanding
reality and a given Weltanschauung. Language creates symbols
and, through them, reality itself. The subjectivistic tendency
of this approach is beyond doubt.[10]
   In Italy, in opposition to the positivist, neo-grammarian
school of thought, Croce posed the problem of language as that
of aesthetics. Every language is a subjective art of expression.
As in art, 'intuition' is the essence of language. Thoughts,
in their deepest level, are free from specific linguistic structures. They derive from a very general, abstract and universal
human experience. One can understand Croce's famous assertion that a language, as art, can never be translated. Only
through intuitive understanding can the inner essence of
language be grasped. How influential such an approach became
in linguistics is demonstrated by the fact that Croce greatly
influenced the noted German Philosopher of language, Vossler,
and the American ethnologist Edward Sapir. The latter expres-
sly acknowledged his indebtedness to Crocean aesthetics. Sapir
noted that deep symbolism in language does not rest on the

'verbal associations of a particular language,' but 'on an intuitive basis underlying linguistic expression.' The phonetic, rhythmic, symbolic and morphological elements of language constitute a set of aesthetic factors which make every language unique.[11]

To Croce's subjectivist conception of language Gramsci opposed an historicist one. Language is a social product, the expression of the culture of a given society. The essence of language is history. It follows that the major concern of linguistics is the history of language. Given the historical character of languages, the identification of art and language is useless. An historicist linguistics studies the languages 'not as art, but as the material of art, as a social product, and cultural expression of a given population.'[12] Linguistic innovations are to be understood, in an historicist perspective, as collective innovations become part of the 'history of languages.' 'The history of languages is the history of linguistic innovations, but these innovations are not individual (as in the case of art). They are innovations of a social collectivity which has renewed its culture, and progressed "historically".'[13]

As Rosiello notes, Gramsci saw in the neo-linguistic methodological approach the empirical confirmation of his linguistic historicism. Such neo-linguistics, propounded by Matteo Bartoli, combined an objectivistic and historicist methodological approach. It sought immanent causes in linguistic phenomena, but always from a historical perspective. Its goal, in the words of Bartoli, was that of establishing a chronology and causes of linguistic innovations. Bartoli's observation that innovations are caused by the influence of culturally and historically superior languages indicated to Gramsci the serious 'historicist perspective' present in neo-linguistics, thus its superiority in relation to Croce's abstract and subjectivistic approach and that of the neo-grammarians.[14]

The neo-linguistics of Bartoli, to which Gramsci adheres, was in effect influenced by the more important linguistic tradition of the Geneva school, founded by Ferdinand de Saussure (1857-1914), whose impact on contemporary linguistics is universally acknowledged.[15] Saussurean linguistics and Durkheim's school are the indirect intellectual sources of Gramsci's historicist linguistics. Durkheim's conception of language as a spiritual phenomenon transcending individuals and historical societies was concretized and historicized by the more prominent spokesman A. Meillet. A sociology of language was thus born, based on the assumption that language is a social process by which a community of men establish an institution as a collective means of communication. This approach had the merit of establishing an intimate relationship between language and culture of societies. Malinowski's studies of primitive societies are an example of how difficult it is to understand primitive languages apart from their cultural and social context.

Durkheim-oriented linguistics did not press further the pro-

blem of the historicity of language. It limited itself, because of
its positivist orientation, to search for the linguistic laws of
development not in history, but in society. Societal structural
changes became the real condition for linguistic changes. It was
Saussure who combined historicism and objectivism into an
historical objectivism, which Bartoli's neo-linguistics whole-
heartedly accepted. Saussure's distinction between language
and speech (langue and parole), a universally accepted fact in
linguistics nowadays, had the effect of establishing two types
of linguistic analysis: the synchronic and diachronic. The first
deals with linguistic systems as independent and autonomous
systems. The latter concerns itself with the general, societal,
historical context in which linguistic systems develop. The two
complement each other. Language can be analyzed in its static
and dynamic aspects.

How dependent Gramsci was on the Saussurean method is
indicated by the fact that he too postulated a static-dynamic
approach to language. Grammar is at the same time a photograph
of a phase in the historical evolution of language, and the
historical affirmation of a linguistic system over others, as we
shall see further on.

Italian neo-linguistics developed in close affiliation with
Saussurean linguistics, and together with Crocean idealist
philosophy was instrumental in the liquidation of the neo-
grammarian method from Italian linguistics. Yet, neo-linguistics
was unable to topple Croce's theoretical dominance, Gramsci
notes. To be sure, Gramsci acknowledged the theoretical
superiority of Bartoli's method over Croce's intuitive approach.
Neo-linguistics is a new, original and progressive method of
linguistic analysis. Gramsci writes: 'The innovation of Bartoli
is exactly this: he made linguistics, conceived narrow-mindedly
a natural science, a historical science, whose roots are sought
"in space and time" and not in the phonetic apparatus, in the
physiological sense.'[16] Despite a strong historicist orientation
in Bartoli's method, Gramsci was quick in perceiving a serious
weakness in it. Bartoli did not develop, on the basis of his
empirical acquisitions, a theory of language. His remained an
empirical method, committed to the task of ascertaining only
technical laws in linguistic development. And rightly so. He
could not arrive at a theory of language for he lacked a philosophical perspective, such as that of Marxist historicism. This
perspective would have rendered linguistics theoretically
independent from, and superior to, Croce's system. Instead,
neo-linguistics capitulated to, and was theoretically undermined
by, Crocean linguists, such as G. Bertoni. In a critical assessment of Bertoni's work, Gramsci brings to the fore and ridicules
the shallowness of his linguistics. Bertoni's linguistics as a
'subtle analysis discriminating the poetic sounds from the
instrumental ones' is a return to the old rhetorical conception
of language. It is concerned with isolating 'beautiful' words
from the 'bad' ones, and establishing what in language is poetic,

non-poetic, or anti-poetic. Thus, Bertoni's linguistics re-
introduces the old and naive distinction and classification of
languages in 'beautiful or bad,' 'civilized or barbarian,'
'poetic or prosaic.'[17] Bertoni's insistence on the definition of
language as aesthetics fell into a vulgar form of positivism,
which Croce himself criticized and rejected. Refuting Bertoni,
Gramsci asks: 'What are words when they are isolated and
abstracted from a literary work? No longer an aesthetic element,
rather an element of history and culture, and as such the linguist studies them.'[18]

   Neo-linguistics, thus, came to a standstill. It did not develop
a theory of knowledge. What is worse, Gramsci notes, it
accepted the theoretical framework of Bertoni. Hence its capitulation to Croce's philosophical perspective.[19] In prison, Gramsci
planned to revive the neo-linguistic method and complete it with
an organic, systematic historicist theoretical perspective. But
before we embark on a discussion of Gramsci's notes on linguistics, some general observations are in order on the characterization of Gramscian linguistics.

   Luigi Rossiello, an analyst of Gramsci's linguistics, has
critically evaluated his linguistic notions and contrasted them
rightly with those of the Saussurean school and the contemporary
school of structuralist linguistics. He has established the common points between Gramsci and Saussure, such as their
emphasis on the importance of history in linguistic analysis and
the social character of language. Yet an incomplete image of
Gramsci emerges from Rossiello's essay. Gramsci is viewed as
the precursor of contemporary structuralism, the eager defender
of objective, concrete and scientific linguistic analysis. What
is more serious, the linguist Gramsci is seen as a detached,
neutral academic man, distinct from Gramsci 'the revolutionary
Marxist theoretician.' Important questions have not been asked:
how is Gramsci's analysis of language related to and integrated
in his more general theory of 'absolute historicism?' What is
the nature and place of a 'science' of language within his
historicist theory of science? How consonant is Gramsci's
adhesion to neo-linguistics, and its objectivistic orientation,
with his humanist (anti-science?) Marxism? How can a disinterested study of language be justified given the *practical*
interest of Gramsci in not writing the history of an aspect of
culture, but attempting to modify it?[20] The association of
Gramsci's linguistics with structuralist linguistics is forced and
exaggerated, we think. Certainly linguistics has a method
and an objective of its own. Gramsci was interested in developing an historicist theory and methodology of the linguistic
system. He was interested in the 'history of language' from the
standpoint of political history. The empirical investigation of
phonetic and morphological aspects of language does not concern Gramsci. It is relegated to non-history, but not denied,
however. Gramsci writes: 'the absence of a critical and historicist conception of the phenomenon of language, can lead to

many errors in both the scientific and the practical field.[21] We
will concentrate in the following section on analyzing this
'critical and historicist' conception of language, of which Gramsci
speaks.

THE LINGUISTIC FACT AS A POLITICAL ACT: THE ESSENCE OF GRAMSCI'S SOCIOLOGY OF LANGUAGE

Language, as a system of signs, cannot be analyzed apart from
the study of ideologies. Meanings embodied in words are ideological. That is to say, ideologies are signs. Gramsci, however,
avoids Marr's error of equating language and superstructure.
He was aware of the necessity of rendering language 'autonomous' from both structure and superstructure. He distinguished
within language, a form and content, that is, a linguistic
system proper (organization of signs), from a linguistic content (semantic values). The first develops and is governed by
its own internal laws, and thus is independent from the determination of the structure. The latter is superstructural, and
as such should be analyzed in terms of ideologies and political
praxis. Gramsci chose to analyze this second aspect of language,
of primary importance in socialist transformation. The linguistic
content of languages indirectly can affect the external form.
He writes: 'no new historical situation, however radical the
change that has brought it about, completely transforms
language, at least in its external formal aspect. But the content
of language must be changed, even if it is difficult to have an
exact consciousness of the change in immediate terms.'[22]
   The most important aspect of language is, for Gramsci, then,
its cultural content. He agrees with the Saussurean principle
of the arbitrariness of signs, by speaking of the metaphoricality
of language. Every language is metaphorical, Gramsci writes,
in so far as it contains 'meanings' which derive from past
periods of civilization. It was the concept of the metaphoricality
of language that led the Italian sociologist Vilfredo Pareto and
Italian pragmatist Vailati, among others, to conceive of languages
as a source of error, and linguistic explanations as non-logical
explanations. They set about eliminating metaphors from
language and replacing them with new meanings, and scientific
concepts. In contrast to Pareto, Gramsci argues that metaphorical meanings cannot be eliminated from language. The
transformations of these metaphors is eminently a political fact
and is associated with the transformation of whole civilizations.[23]

> Language is transformed with the transformation of the whole
> civilisation, through the acquisition of culture by new classes
> and through the hegemony exercised by one national language
> over others, etc., and what it does is precisely to absorb in
> metaphorical form the words of previous civilisations and
> cultures....The new 'metaphorical' meaning spreads with the
> spread of the new culture, which furthermore also coins

brand-new words or absorbs them from other languages as
loan-words giving them a precise meaning and therefore
depriving them of the extensive halo they possessed in the
original language.

The historicity of language: its practical and political character
If in language there is a continuous process of formation and
transformation of metaphors it is because the 'history' of culture
transforms itself. Language is a political fact and instrument of
politics. It aids the development of a cultural social unity
through the welding together of a multiplicity of dispersed wills
in a common conception of the world. In this political context,
Gramsci writes, 'great importance is assumed by the general
question of language, that is the question of collectively attaining a single cultural "climate".[124]

Important methodological observations can then be made. Linguistic facts are not individual but collective and cultural facts.
This has for Gramsci a great political significance. By characterizing language as a 'collective' phenomenon, one stresses the
social and dialectical nature of language. Language is social,
that is, a social product, in the Durkheimian and Saussurean
sense. But it is also dialectical, Gramsci adds. Within a given
language there is a dialectic between the individual and collective language, individuals' language contents being absorbed
by cultural ones.[25]

> It seems that one can say that 'language' is essentially a
> collective term which does not presuppose any single thing
> existing in time and space....At the limit it could be said
> that every speaking being has a personal language of his
> own, that is his own particular way of thinking and feeling.
> Culture, at its various levels, unifies in a series of strata,
> to the extent that they come into contact with each other, a
> greater or lesser number of individuals who understand each
> other's mode of expression in differing degrees, etc.

This signifies that far from being the subjective realization and
expression of culture, language is the expression of concrete
interests of given groups. The difference between the Gramscian
historicist approach to language and that of Durkheim's school
of linguistics is fundamental. While for Durkheimian linguists
linguistic changes are the product of changes in society, for
Gramsci they are the consequence of the hegemony of a social
class or group over society's culture. Gramsci insists on the
interrelationship between linguistic stratification and social
stratification. Each class has its own language and a Weltanschauung of its own. Linguistic innovations are to be explained
in terms of the molecular influence of the new hegemonic class
over all others. In this respect, Gramsci writes:[26]

> Every time the question of language surfaces, in one way or
> the other, it means that a series of other problems are begin-
> ning to emerge: the formation and expansion of the ruling
> class, the necessity of establishing closer and firmer ties

between the leading groups and national-popular masses,
that is of reorganizing cultural hegemony.
The most important linguistic changes, Gramsci continues, are
caused by external factors. A given language mirrors more profound changes that have occurred in the cultural, political,
moral and sentimental milieu. 'In language also there is no parthenogenesis, that is the phenomenon of language producing
another language, but innovation through the influences of
diverse languages....The interference and "molecular" influence
can take place within a nation, between various strata.[127]

From the texts cited above and from the general context from
which Gramsci approaches the study of language, an organic
set of propositions can be established:
Linguistics concerns itself with the history of languages.
The history of languages is the history of semantics, itself an
integral part of the history of culture.
The source of 'meanings' in language is history, more specifically, the political praxis of a given group.
Meanings are always 'ideological,' they reflect the interests of
a given group.
Meanings are 'critical' in so far as they indicate the presence
of elements derived from old or new conceptions of the world.
There is a dialectics of meanings, reflecting a dialectic taking
place in society.
Linguistic truths are established by the political praxis of a
dominant group.

The theoretical and practical implications of Gramsci's historicist perspective in linguistics will be discussed further on.
It suffices here to say that for Gramsci, an historicist linguistics
is not concerned with discovering immanent laws, specific
changes or new directions occurring in the linguistic system.
Rather, it focuses on the 'practical reasons' why a given law,
a certain development or direction, finally prevailed. From a
practical standpoint, that of socialist revolution, for instance,
the problem of language is crucial. A revolutionary change
must be preceded by a transformation of meanings, a 'linguistic
conformism,' to use a Gramscian term. As new meanings are
developed, the old ones become metaphors. 'Usually, when a
new conception replaces the previous one, the previous language
continues to be used but is, precisely, used metaphorically.
The whole language is a continuous process of metaphor, and
the history of semantics is an aspect of the history of culture.[128]
Linguistic conformism is dictated by praxis. Marcuse's thesis of
one-dimensionality in language, a process by which critical
meanings and concepts are eliminated by technological praxis
and replaced with scientific, operational ones, is very close to
Gramsci's ideas. The difference between them lies in the fact
that any praxis for Gramsci engenders a 'linguistic conformism.'

Historical and political character of grammar
From what has been said, language in its content and history
belongs to the realm of the superstructures, and as such it does
not escape the determination of the structure. Grammars, however, within languages are autonomous systems. This needs
further elaboration. In a series of notes on 'Grammar,' sound-
ing like an introductory guide to the study of grammar, Gramsci
posed several problems, some partially answered, others
barely hinted at. His discussion of grammar is also conducted
from an historicist perspective, from the practical perspective,
that is, of how to teach a grammar historically.

The first question raised in his polemic with Croce was that
of the definition of grammar. Croce wrote a provocative essay
entitled: 'This Round Table is Square.' This sentence, he
concluded, is wrong from the standpoint of aesthetics and logic,
but correct from the point of view of the grammarians. It must
be remembered here that the essence of language is, for Croce,
aesthetics. Gramsci criticized Croce's misconception of grammar,
characterized as a 'technical' system. For Croce, a grammatical
error is a technical error. Not so for Gramsci. A grammatical
error denotes a lack of 'discipline to the historicity of language,'
or simply a lack of knowledge of the historical reasons for
grammatical norms.[29] Thus, what is grammatically exact can also
be justified from the point of view of aesthetics and logic,
Gramsci concludes. What is in dispute is the definition of
grammar.[30]

> The grammar is 'history' or a 'historical document': it is the
> 'photograph' of a specific phase of a (collective) national
> language, which was formed historically and continues to
> develop, or it is the fundamental traits of that photograph.
> The question, in the practical sense, can be: what is the
> purpose of such photograph? To write the history of one
> aspect of civilisation or to modify an aspect of civilisation?

Defining grammar as a 'historical document,' Gramsci draws
a distinction between two types of grammar: immanent and
normative. The first is inherent in language, in the technical
sense. Everyone speaks according to grammar and is influenced
by it. As a matter of fact, every cultural expression, moral
or intellectual activity, Gramsci notes, has an historically
determined language. The second consists of a system of norms
derived from reciprocal controls, reciprocal teaching, reciprocal
'censorship.' 'This whole complex of actions and reactions
contributes to determine a grammatical conformity, to establish
"norms", and standards of correctness or incorrectness.'[31]
'Normative grammar,' especially when written, is instrumental
in creating a national or regional linguistic conformity.

Rosiello has seen in Gramsci's distinction of grammars an
initial formulation of the structuralist method, associating the
concept of 'immanent grammar' with that of 'generative grammar,'
of which N. Chomsky speaks. Gramsci's recourse to a structuralist form of linguistics has been explained in terms of his

opposition to the idealist subjectivism of the Crocean school.[32]
In effect, Gramsci opposed Croce not by resorting to an objec-
tivist, scientific linguistic method. Rather, he opposed him on
historicist grounds. Historicism, as we have seen, is the
scientific method par excellence! In fact, distinguishing between
'immanent' and 'normative' grammar, Gramsci proceeds to discuss the relationship between history and grammar. The best
grammarians are the historians of language, and the best type
of normative grammar is the historical grammar.

Teaching a particular grammar means teaching about a particular phase of the history of language, from a certain class
position. And learning a grammar means learning a particular
interpretation of the historical past. This is the sense of the
following text:[33]

> It is evident that a writer of normative grammar cannot ignore
> the history of the language, of which he wants to propose an
> 'exemplary phase' as the 'sole' one worthy of becoming
> 'organically' and 'totally' the 'common' language of the nation,
> in struggle and competition with other 'phases' and types or
> schemes already in existence (tied to traditional developments
> or inorganic and incoherent attempts of forces, which, as has
> been seen, operate continually in spontaneous and immanent
> 'grammars' of the language).

From the historicist point of view, Gramsci continues, the
historical grammars par excellence are the comparative grammars, the only ones capable of grasping the essence of language. 'Historical grammar cannot but be "comparative", an
expression which, analyzed in depth, indicates the profound
consciousness that the linguistic phenomenon, like any other
historical phenomenon, cannot have narrowly defined national
boundaries, but that history is always "world-history".'[34] The
political context is thus central in Gramsci's analysis of grammars. With no hesitation he states that a normative grammar
is a political *act*.[35]

> Written normative grammar thus always presupposes a 'choice',
> a cultural orientation, and is therefore always an act of
> national-cultural politics. There can be discussion of the best
> way of presenting the 'choice' or 'orientation' so that they
> could be accepted willingly, that is a discussion of the most
> suitable means to attain the end; there can be no doubt that
> there is an end to attain, which necessitates proper and
> suitable means, that it is a question of a political act.

By insisting on the historical and political nature of grammar,
Gramsci attempted to develop a Marxist approach to various
theoretical and practical problems. First, he sought to argue
against Croce and Gentile, the representatives of the dominant
philosophy and political liberalism in Italy, that a grammar is
more than a 'technique.' It is an 'historically determined' mode
of expression. As such, it should have a place in a general
theory of knowledge. Second, the identification of grammar and
technique made by Croce had the effect of excluding the

grammar from history, philosophy and theory, and relegating
it to practical activity. His position justified Gentile's educational
policies in Italy, which opposed the teaching of grammar in
school, and proposed a laissez-faire practical stance: grammar
is learned from speaking! This is a politically reactionary position, Gramsci notes. It strengthens the existing social stratification, it prevents the accession of the popular masses to
the high culture of intellectuals and cultivated social strata,
which is learned and transmitted orally from generation to
generation in a caste-like manner. Hence, the necessity of
teaching an historical grammar, whose purpose is to facilitate
the attainment of an homogeneous culture with the active
participation of the masses. The teaching of a grammar as a
'technique' and as an 'historically determined' mode of speaking
would, in fact, enable socialism to accomplish its goal, previously discussed, of elevating the cultural and intellectual
level of the masses, and transforming their Weltanschauungen,
common sense and folklore into a superior one.[36]

Only from this perspective can Gramsci's notes on linguistics
and the study of language be truly understood. They must be
analyzed in relation to the central themes of the 'Prison Notebooks,' the notion of hegemony and the socialist construction
of a new intellectual order. Gramsci's interests in linguistics
are diametrically opposed to those of contemporary structuralist
and positivist linguistics. He is concerned with the political
context of language, the place of the study of languages in a
general historicist theory of knowledge, and the role of
language in socialist transformation.

We now pass to the discussion of a related theme, Gramsci's
analysis of the history of the Italian language, a case which
historically confirms the general methodological and theoretical
criteria we have just presented. Gramsci's analysis of the
history of the Italian language is an attempt to elaborate a
Marxist sociology of language whose objective is that of demonstrating the practical and historical relationship between language and the cultural and political hegemony of a given class
and its intellectuals.

The linguistic conflict as a political conflict: the case of the
origin of the Italian language
Leonardo Paggi has observed that the interest in linguistic
studies leads Gramsci to examine the historical function of the
intellectuals in Italy.[37] Simply by reading his notes on the
Italian Risorgimento one can see how interrelated the problem
of language and that of the intellectuals are. Various phases
of Italian history are determined by a specific relationship
between the popular language and that of the intellectuals.
When the intellectuals wrote and spoke in a language that was
not understood by the masses, there existed a separation
between a high culture and popular culture.

Gramsci notes that a real history of the Italian language has

not been written. He outlined such a history, to include a
discussion of language as an 'element of culture' and thereby
of a 'general history.'[138] Already in an earlier essay, examining
the question of language in Manzoni, Gramsci raised the issue
of how a unified language could be created in Italy. Manzoni
had stated that the linguistic unification was possible only
after the realization of the political unification of Italy and the
creation of a unified state; that is, only when all Italian regional
dialects had been eliminated and replaced by that of Tuscany
through the intermediary of the unified state.[39] In contrast to
Manzoni, Gramsci argued that the creation of a common national
language is not an artificial process. The diffusion of a language
is due to literary production and commercial activities conducted
in that language.[40]

> In the period between the 14th and 16th century, Tuscany
> produced writers such as Dante, Boccaccio, Petrarca, Mac-
> chiavelli, Guicciardini who diffused the Tuscan language;
> it had bankers, artisans, manufacturers, spreading in all
> Italy Tuscan products and the names of these products;
> afterwards the productivity of goods and books, and there-
> fore, of language was limited.

Very early in life, then, Gramsci was convinced of the intimate
connection of linguistic history and political history.[41] 'Every
new social stratum, which emerges to history, organizes itself
for a struggle, instils in the language new currents, new
usages, thus breaking up the fixed schemes which grammarians
established for practical and opportunistic reasons.[42] This is
true of the origin of the Italian language during the early period
of Italian history, particularly the Renaissance and Humanism,
between the eleventh and fifteenth centuries.

From 600 AD to about 1200, a period of 600 years, Europe
experienced a complete separation between the masses and the
culture of the intellectuals. There was the literary Latin of
cultured men and ecclesiastics, and the vulgar Latin, from
which various neo-Latins developed all over Europe. The
crystallization of these two types of Latin is the historical result
of the monopolization of knowledge and ideas in general in the
hands of the ecclesiastic class of intellectuals. Religion, which
dominated the whole culture of Europe, became increasingly
abstract and understood, studied, discussed and preached in
literary Latin among clerics and monks.

At the beginning of the eleventh century, various dialects
developed. In France, while the country underwent great
political, economic, religious and cultural changes, the literature
of langue d'oc and langue d'oil began to develop. Likewise, in
Italy, as popular movements began to assert themselves in
political life, various regional dialects emerged. During the
period of the Communes, various dialects were already in
existence. Among them, only one, the volgare illustre, prevailed, due to the expansion of the intellectual hegemony of
Florence.[43] A characteristic of this dialect of Tuscany, known

as Florentine, which became the Italian language in the twelfth
century, was that while it developed a vocabulary and phonetics
of its own, it remained Latin in its syntax. This is due, Gramsci
writes, to the pre-eminence of traditional intellectuals, the
ecclesiastics, who were not national, but cosmopolitan, intellectuals, writing for a Christian European audience. Let us
sketch the successive developments of the Italian language
with Gramsci's words.[44]

> With the fall of the Communes, the advent of Principalities,
> and the creation of a governmental caste removed from the
> people, this dialect crystallizes, in the same manner in which
> the literary latin had crystallized. Again, Italian is a written
> but not spoken language, a language of literati, and not of
> the nation. There are now two cultural languages in Italy,
> the latin and the Italian. The latter finally prevails and be-
> comes completely dominant in the 20th century with the separ-
> ation of the lay intellectuals from the ecclesiastics...

How to explain these linguistic developments? Gramsci makes
two important observations. The birth of various dialects marking the historical break with medieval culture and the affirmation of a dialect, the Florentine, over all others result from
the concentration of intellectual groups. Gramsci strongly
rejects the interpretation of linguistic developments advanced
by the historian Vittorio Rossi as well as the general interpretation of the Renaissance period. According to Rossi, the early
Renaissance marks a smooth transition from one intellectual
world to another. The Renaissance movement is the culmination
of, and the spontaneous manifestation of, creative energies
springing from the depth of man's consciousness, eager to feel
and live the 'antiquity.' Gramsci argues instead that the
emergence of new dialects represents a dramatic break with
medieval culture and feudal institutions and values. The conflict between the Latin language and the new dialects was the
manifestation of a more profound conflict between two conceptions of the world. On the one hand, there was an aristocratic-
feudal intellectual world, attached to the Roman antiquity and
expressing itself in Latin; on the other hand, there was a
new, progressive bourgeois-popular civilization expressing
itself in new languages to affirm new exigencies and values.

The spontaneous Italian Renaissance of the eleventh century
was a bourgeois reaction against the feudal regime, which
affected all aspects of society, particularly the economic,
political and cultural life. The new bourgeois class developed
the agriculture, industry and commerce, which culminated in
the phenomenon of the Communes.

This spontaneous Renaissance was followed by the humanist
and cultural Renaissance, which extended into the fifteenth
century. It represented a rebirth of Latin, as the language
of the intellectuals in opposition to new dialects. The progressive bourgeoisie, after the fall of the Communes, was contained
and finally suppressed by regressive-reactionary forces, an

aristocracy separated from the masses.

The new Italian culture, which emerged in the eleventh century, was not a 'national,' but 'regional,' and 'communal culture.' The linguistic unification of Italy took place in the fourteenth century. The bourgeoisie reacted against a European, catholic, abstract universalistic culture, and expressed its practical interests through the new dialects. Yet, Gramsci continues, the newly emerged bourgeoisie could not create a 'national language' precisely because its intellectuals were absorbed by the traditional and reactionary ones. Humanism, with its cult of classical antiquity, is, for Gramsci, a reactionary period. It demonstrates how strong 'Latin' was, and how powerful were the intellectual strata attached to the feudal-aristocratic world.[45]

But how to explain the crystallization of the volgare illustre? In Gramsci's words, why was the Florentine dialect able to become hegemonic in literature and culture while the new popular-bourgeois classes lacked a socio-political hegemony? Gramsci himself answered the question by sketching a brief analysis of the role of the intellectuals during the Renaissance and humanist period.

The period of the Communes, of communal liberties, Gramsci writes, was characterized by a political ascent of popular masses. New intellectuals, attached to the bourgeoisie, issued from the popular (-bourgeois) classes, prospered and developed to such an extent that they were able to create a new Italian literature, written and spoken in the new dialects. In the post-communal period, these intellectuals were absorbed into the traditional caste of the aristocracy. To be sure, the intellectuals continued to issue from the popular classes, but they were individually selected and assimilated into the traditional caste of intellectuals, the ecclesiastics. The limited success of communal bourgeois, and popular literary activities, can be explained, Gramsci continues, only if one considers the ambivalent role of the intellectuals. Petrarch, for instance, was a poet of the bourgeoisie and wrote in the Florentine dialect. But he wrote also in Latin in matters of politics. Thus he was the intellectual of the anti-bourgeois reaction in the period of the principalities. The Renaissance period, in which the new dialects emerged, is for Gramsci a progressive period in the history of Italy. At this time, new popular forces made their appearance in history, but could not affirm themselves politically, for their intellectuals were unable to maintain their political autonomy vis-à-vis the traditional intellectuals, the social stratum of clerics, intimately attached to the old feudal-aristocratic regime. Humanism is a reactionary period, the period of the restoration of the old feudal world and lost cultural unity. The humanist movement prevailed both politically and ideologically. Politically through the containment and repression of the revolutionary bourgeois classes; intellectually through the assimilation of the ideological principles of the bourgeoisie. The return to the

'Latin' language and cult of the classics was thus a political and ideological movement which led to the Counter-Reformation. The triumph of the cult of romanitas is to be explained in terms of the re-assertion of the political power of the popes, and the re-establishment of the Holy Roman Empire.[46]

It is all this history that Gramsci had in mind when he wrote that language is a political phenomenon and that an historical grammar has not yet been written. The Italian language is the dialect of a class; it asserts itself, in reaction to the feudal, aristocratic and universal interests, and in defense of the newly emerged popular-bourgeois interests.

In conclusion, there is no organic and systematic analysis of language to permit one to speak of a sociology of language in Gramsci. However, from all his notes on language, a Marxist perspective, from which the phenomenon of language can be analyzed, has certainly been developed by Gramsci. Every grammar reflects the history of class in its ascendancy toward political and cultural hegemony. Gramsci searched for an empirical, historical confirmation of this idea. The history of the origin of the Italian history provided him with the best illustration of his thesis. Linguistic conflicts are always part of a struggle among groups, classes aiming at cultural and political hegemony. This is the objective of a Marxist sociology of language.

8 AESTHETICS, POLITICAL PRAXIS AND HISTORICISM

Gramsci's notes on the subject of art and literary criticism
have been systematically analyzed and widely commented upon
by Italian Marxist and non-Marxist scholars. They have
influenced prominent historians of literature and Italian critics.
However, partly because they are fragmentary and unfinished,
and partly because they are polemical in nature and formulated
in the context of specific problems of Italy's literary history,
they have remained untranslated and generally unknown outside Italy. To this, one has to add the fact that no systematic,
objective treatment of Gramsci's ideas on the subject of art
and literary criticism has been developed. More than everything else, these notes have also become the object of a moot
controversy between Marxist and non-Marxist aestheticians.
    There are those who see in Gramsci's notes a general metho-
dology for a Marxist theory of art and aesthetics, and there
are those who deny such an intent in Gramsci and insist on
the obvious dependence of Gramscian aesthetics on Croce's
aesthetic philosophy. Generally, Marxists adhere to the first
position, although in various degrees and dependent upon their
respective political convictions, and non-Marxists, and some
Marxists of Crocean tendency, to the second one. Even among
Marxists, one finds a diversity of opinions with regard to
Gramsci's notes. There are those who have found no original
theory of art and literary criticism in them, and there are
those who, from the general sense of these notes, have derived
original elements for a theory of aesthetics in Gramsci.
    In this chapter we shall briefly review the formulation of
the problem of aesthetics in the history of Marxism and Crocean
philosophy, then proceed to analyze the central problem of
Gramsci's aesthetic theory, that of the historicity and autonomy
of art. We will conclude with some observations by Gramsci on
the important problems of the relationship between aesthetic
criticism and political criticism, popular art and proletarian
art.

GRAMSCI AND MARXIST AESTHETIC THEORY

Gaetano della Volpe, almost universally known as the founder
of Marxist aesthetics in Italy, has insisted that the specificity
of Marxist aesthetics consists of a 'rational' and 'structured'
nucleus of ideas, possessing a logic of its own within Marxist

theory. From this perspective, art, despite its determination
by culture, society and history, is characterized by a 'concrete
historicity,' a coherent system of thought and structure of its
own. Gramsci, he concludes, has been able to articulate the
idea of the historicity of art and its autonomy within Marxist
theory.[1] Other analysts of Gramscian aesthetics speak of a
methodological sociology of literature, or of cultural politics
in Gramsci, and not of a Gramscian aesthetic or art theory.
Among them one finds Guiducci, Scalia, Sapegno, Anglani,
Stipcevic and Petronio.[2] The latter comes the closest to recog-
nizing Gramsci as the Marxist theoretician of art par excellence.
    In general, those who have proposed a distinctly Marxist
interpretation of Gramsci and speak of a complete theory of art
and literary criticism have been pressed by the need to elaborate a Marxist aesthetics, barely sketched by the founders
of Marxism, to oppose the 'socialist realism' characteristic of
the Stalin period, as well as the Crocean aesthetics still dominant
in Italian culture. Before we embark on a discussion of Gramsci's
aesthetic notes, it is necessary to briefly review the problem
of aesthetics in classical Marxism and Crocean philosophy.

The problem of aesthetics and art in classical Marxism and
Crocean philosophy
It is well known that because of the lack of any systematic
theory of aesthetics in Marx, his successors felt free to put
forward the most disparate theories on this subject, and particularly on the subject of art and literature. Marx, in fact,
though aware of the importance of the aesthetic phenomenon
and actually personally eager to write a book on Balzac after
the completion of 'Das Kapital,' concerned himself only marginally
with this problem.
    Marx's few observations on aesthetics are to be understood
in the light of Hegelian aesthetics. Hegel's thesis on the transcendence of art is well known. In the progression of the spirit
toward absolute knowledge, art represents a temporary and
incomplete phase of development. It is an ideality existing
above 'the objectivity of the human ethical world,' revealing
the absolute in an intuitive form. It is a thing of the past, an
outmoded means to accede to reality. In Hegel's view, art
reached its apex in ancient Greece, but it has been superseded
once and for all by religion in the form of Christianity, and in
modern times by philosophy. It is philosophy, in its rational
form, that reveals the true essence of phenomena.
    Marx historicized art not in the speculative sense, as did
Hegel, but in a materialist sense. He translated Hegel's
aesthetics into the language of sociology. Marx established a
correlation between social, material forms and artistic forms.
While Hegel analyzed art from a distant, abstract, universal
standpoint, Marx focused on the relationship of art to the
concrete stages of historical evolution. It suffices here to recall
the famous text on Greek art in the 'Introduction to the Critique

of Political Economy.' Artistic expression reached its apogee in Greek art because of specific social conditions prevailing at a low stage of historical development, thus restricted to a determined period of history.[3]

> As regards certain forms of art, as e.g., the *epos*, it is admitted that they can never be produced in the world-epoch-making form as soon as art as such comes into existence; in other words, that in the domain of art certain important forms of it are possible only at a low stage of its development....All mythology masters and dominates and shapes the forces of nature in and through the imagination; hence it disappears as soon as man gains mastery over the forces of nature....Greek art presupposes the existence of Greek mythology, i.e., that nature and even the form of society are wrought up in popular fancy in an unconsciously artistic fashion.

Hegel and Marx agree, but in a different sense, on the principle of the historicity of art. They depart from each other, however, on the evaluation of aesthetic enjoyment. While for Hegel art has completely lost its truth in the present phase of historical evolution, for Marx art can, despite its historicity, continue to exert a trans-temporal attraction and generate a permanent pleasure in various phases of history. He attempted to reconcile the temporal and a-temporal character.[4]

> But the difficulty is not in grasping the idea that Greek art and *epos* are bound up with certain forms of social development. It rather lies in understanding why they still constitute with us a source of aesthetic enjoyment and in certain respects prevail as the standard and model beyond attainment.

It is a matter of knowing, then, how the idea of the historical determination of art does not deny the existence of aesthetic values transcending both society and history. Greek art continues to exert an eternal charm because it represents the social childhood of mankind, an age that will never return.[5]

> The charm their art has for us does not conflict with the primitive character of the social order from which it had sprung. It is rather the product of the latter, and is rather due to the fact that the unripe social conditions under which the art arose and under which alone it could appear can never return.

Marx and Engels did not elaborate a systematic theory of aesthetics. As Henry Arvon writes, three aspects are discernable in their aesthetic reflections without knowing which one is more important 'for at times they view art as totally dependent on the social situation, at times as completely autonomous, and at times as an instrument of political action.'[6]

It was the Russian theoretician, G.V. Plekhanov, who rigidified the Marxian approach to art. He was an opponent of the 'art for art's sake' movement in Russia, rejected the idea of the absolute autonomy of art and insisted upon objective

criteria to analyze the aesthetic phenomenon. In so doing, he
eliminated the subjective component of art. Art is essentially
a social phenomenon. It is progressive or reactionary depending
on whether or not it accepts the revolutionary principles of
the proletarian classes. Art is thus deprived of autonomous
status in Marxist theory and made dependent upon the status
of the productive forces of society.[7] Lenin carried Plekhanov's
arguments a step further and concerned himself more directly
with the problem of creating a socialist art and socialist literature. In his virulent essay of 1905 on 'Organization and Party
Literature' in the name of Marxism and the proletarian revolution, he denounced any form of uncommitted literature, and
declared the total subordination of cultural life to the partignost
(party spirit).[8]

> What is this principle of party literature? It is not simply
> that, for the socialist proletariat, literature cannot be a
> means of enriching individuals or groups: it cannot, in fact,
> be an individual undertaking, independent of the common
> cause of the proletariat. Down with non-partisan writers!
> Down with literary supermen! Literature must become *part*
> of the common cause of the proletariat, 'a cog and a screw'
> of one single great Social-Democratic mechanism set in
> motion by the entire politically-conscious vanguard of the
> entire working class. Literature must become a component
> of organized, planned and integrated Social-Democratic
> Party work.

Lenin proceeded to denounce the illusion of artistic freedom in
bourgeois society as the expression of capitalist anarchy and
advocated a critical approach to past art. Socialist art is given
the task of debunking and exposing the hypocrisy of bourgeois
art. Art is thus denied an autonomous existence and becomes
the instrument of political action and party glorification.

Trotsky was among the few to oppose the 'partitization' of
art. In his book, 'Literature and Revolution,' he rejected the
idea of a 'proletarian' culture which meant a qualitatively
inferior culture and defended the principle of the autonomy of
art both in its content and form.[9]

> It is very true that one cannot always go by the principles
> of Marxism in deciding whether to reject or accept a work of
> art. A work of art should, in the first place, be judged by
> its own law, that is, by the law of art. But Marxism alone can
> explain why and how a given tendency in art has originated
> in a given period of history.

Trotsky encouraged all kinds of experiments in art, even
futurist ones. Because of this he was accused by Stalin of being
the proponent of formalism in art, a tendency which considers
techniques for their own sake and stresses the priority of form
over content in artistic phenomena. It has been argued, of
course, that the separation of form and content presupposes
the separation of thought and praxis which is characteristic of
idealist philosophy.

The more socialism was consolidated in Russia, the more
Marxist aesthetics rigidified. Russian novelists Belinski and
Chernyshevski subordinated art to reality. The more art reflects
reality, proletarian life and Russian life, the more it approximates perfection. They thus denied the subjective component
in artistic phenomena. The 'socialist realism' approach came
to be identified with Marxist aesthetics tout court. Gorky,
Stalin and Zhdanov became the staunch defenders of the 'social
realist' method, which considered art as the ideological instrument for the education of the masses to socialism. Art, they
wrote, must be the concrete representation of reality in its
revolutionary development.[10]

Two opposite directions can thus be distinguished in Marxist
aesthetics. One based on the sketchy aesthetics of Marx and
Engels, the other associated with Lenin, Stalin and Zhdanov,
and known as 'socialist realism.' In the first tradition, one
finds the critical theory of the Frankfurt School, Sartre,
L. Goldmann, and Lukács, among others.

The Frankfurt School is known for its opposition to the
analysis of artistic forms as an expression of individual creativity in the Kantian sense. The 'critical theorists' of this
school, above all, Theodor Adorno, Walter Benjamin, Max
Horkheimer, Herbert Marcuse, have been pioneers in the sociological analysis of aesthetics. They all shared the belief that
all works of art are the expression of objective tendencies
unintended by their creators. Artistic creation and subjective
appreciation of art, they argued, are limited by social factors.
For instance, industrial society, by gradually eliminating the
'autonomous' subject, has undermined the notion of individual
'tastes.' The result was the emergence of 'mass culture,' in
which personal preferences have become the object of manipulation. The Frankfurt School is also known for its refusal
to reduce cultural and aesthetic phenomena to an ideological
reflex of class interests. The theoreticians of this school have
produced major works on the subject of art and aesthetics, in
which the critical role of art in social transformation occupies
a central position. 'Art,' in the words of Horkheimer, 'since
it became autonomous, has preserved the utopia that evaporated
from religion.' It always yearns for an ideal society. The more
it realizes a perfect harmony between form and content, subjectivity and objectivity, function and expression, the more
art can be said to be genuine.[11]

The influence of Lukács on the Frankfurt School is beyond
doubt. For Lukács, art contains an everlasting, eternal value
when it grasps the essence of man's history, the highest form
of objectivity. By fusing subjectivity and objectivity, art can
be said to be the consciousness of humanity. Subjectivity is
the representation in the subject of the substance of the object
in its most general plane. Subjective appreciation of works of
art signifies the elevation of man to the category of totality,
identification of the receptor with the cause of mankind through

the suspension of everyday life. As Agnès Heller notes, artistic pleasure in the receiver is, for Lukács, a 'de-fetishized' experience, a cathartic experience through which the individual accedes to the 'generality' of humanity and experiences an identification with the cause of humanity.[12] In the same vein, the noted French sociologist Lucien Goldmann defined the greatness of works of art in terms of their objective representation of historical evolution.[13]

> The writer of genius seems to us to be the one who realizes a synthesis, whose work is at one and the same time the most immediate and the most philosophically aware, for his sensibility coincides with the ensemble of the process and of the historical evolution; the genius is he who, in order to speak about his own most concrete and immediate problems, implicitly raises the most general problems of his age and of his culture, and for whom, inversely, all the essential problems of his time are not mere intellectualizations or abstract convictions but realities, which are manifested in living and immediate fashion in his very feelings and intuitions.

The similarities between Gramsci and the Frankfurt School are striking. In his solitary reflections, Gramsci arrived at a non-deterministic conception of the relationship between structure and superstructure. Gramsci refused to conceive of art as a passive reflection of class interests. Art is autonomous and contains timeless values. Like the theoreticians of the Frankfurt School, Gramsci saw art as part of culture, one form through which the consciousness of an historical epoch can be expressed. He spoke of the necessity of creating an artistic 'order.' 'The absence of an artistic order... is related to the absence of an intellectual and moral order, that is to the absence of a historical organic development.'[14] In contrast to the Frankfurt School, however, while maintaining the principles of the historicity and autonomy of art and its independence from politics, he spoke of the necessity of 'popularizing art' in a sense much different from that of Soviet Marxism, as we shall see. Gramsci attempted to solve the antinomy of the historicity of art and its immortality, as Marx did, in a way closer to that of the Frankfurt School. He also attempted to solve another antinomy, the relation between artistic judgment and political judgment, artistic criticism and political criticism, in a word, the relationship between art and political praxis. Gramsci solved the antimony in such a way as to assure the immortality of art without compromising the integrity of his theory of 'absolute historicism.' But before we engage in a discussion of these concepts, we need also to review the most fundamental concepts of Croce's aesthetics which influenced Gramsci's views, but which also became the target of Gramsci's criticism.

Gramsci and Crocean aesthetics

Croce's general philosophical position is not completely Hegelian. It differs from it in many respects, one of which, and certainly the most important, is its application of Hegelian dialectics. Hegel's greatest contribution was his concept of the dialectics as a unity of opposites. Such dialectics applies only to concepts and phenomena that are opposites, that is true and false. There are phenomena that are not opposites but simply distinct, such as beauty and truth, useful and moral, Croce writes. Art and philosophy, for instance, are distinct and not opposites as Hegel claims. The conception of dialectics as a unity of opposites led Hegel to deny art. If, instead, dialectics is understood as a unity of 'distincts,' then art can be saved from the contingencies of history. Hegelian dialectics results in a synthesis in which art is identified with, and superseded by, philosophy. Crocean dialectics, in contrast, lead to a synthesis in which the two elements, qualitatively distinct, are not transcended but still retain their respective autonomy. Art, Croce writes, is independent of philosophy and exists independently of it. Croce distinguishes intuitive and conceptual knowledge. Intuitive knowledge is expressive knowledge, that is, knowledge obtained through the imagination. Conceptual knowledge is knowledge of the relations between things as established representationally by philosophy and science. Ultimately, all things are intuitions! 'Intuitive activity possesses intuitions to the extent that it expresses them.'[15] Artistic judgment is thus attained only through intuition and not philosophically or scientifically. 'Intuition gives us the world, the phenomenon; the concept gives the noumenon.'[16] Hence, the priority of art over science.

One of the first conclusions drawn by Croce concerns the long disputed problem of form and content in aesthetics. Hegelian aesthetics posits a unity of form and content as the manifestation of the absolute idea. For Croce, the reduction of the aesthetic fact to content alone, and the thesis of the unity of content and form, are incorrect (the first) or wrongly posited (second). In the aesthetic phenomenon expressions are not something added to impressions, but emanating from them. The essence of art is, for Croce, the form.[17] The reduction of content to form led Croce to assert the complete independence of art from the 'useful' and the 'moral' and the exclusion of the practical from aesthetics. He affirmed the 'practical innocence of art.'[18] Croce was not concerned with the purpose of art and its relation to history. Art is a subjective fruition, and creativity of the spirit. It is perfect and complete in the intellect of the artist. Artistic value thus resides in the spirit of those who create or re-create works of art. This explains his practical attitude toward the romanticist movement of his time. He defended the 'classics' and despised any form of aesthetic work that emphasized feelings and emotions.

Again, as in the treatment of all other subjects, Gramsci
found before him the old idealism vs materialism dichotomy.
The idealist, speculative and completely subjective conception
of art denied any dependence of the artistic phenomenon on
society, history and political praxis. Materialism had degenerated into a bureaucratic politization and formalization of art
typical of Russian Marxism. His task was then that of historicizing art against Croce, and liberating it from political
praxis against 'socialist realism.' In a word, Marxist aesthetics
had the complex task of solving Marx's antinomy of the historicity and autonomy of art.

From another point of view, the analysis of the artistic
phenomenon was a delicate problem. Gramsci had defined
Marxism as 'absolute historicism' and analyzed all socio-historical
phenomena, including science, objectivity, language, from
this standpoint. How then could the autonomy of art be asserted
without compromising the principles of his 'historicist' theory?
How could the a-temporal character of art be assured against
the involvement demanded by Marxist revolutionary praxis?
In other words, what is the role and function of art in socialist
transformation?

HISTORICITY AND AUTONOMY OF ART

Gramsci attempted to solve the complex problems of Marxist
aesthetics by introducing the notion of dialectics. Only by
accepting a dialectical perspective could the dangers of formalism, psychologism, sociologism or any other form of dogmatism
and determinism be avoided. Because human praxis is dialectical,
art necessarily reflects its contradictions and seizes, at the
same time, what is permanent in the historical process. Art is,
for Gramsci, an unfinished work. It is always ahead of the
times and looking imaginatively to the ideal society of the
future. Gramsci examines first the relationships between history
and art, and between content and form in the artistic phenomenon.

*The temporal and a-temporal dimensions of art and Gramscian
historicism*
Gramsci approaches the problem of art by asking two sociological questions: what is beauty in the works of art? And,
why art? To answer these questions it is necessary to establish
why a certain type of art is only enjoyed by the receivers,
and why poets write or painters paint. Croce answered
these questions by saying that works of art are produced in
order to be remembered. Artists, Gramsci counters, do not
exist in a vacuum. They live in a historically determined
society. Their images are not simply 'expressed' so that the
instant of their creation can be re-created. The artist is one
who objectivizes and historicizes his phantasms. The more

historical an artist is, the more objective and everlasting are his or her creations.[19]

The value of art is extrinsic to it. It resides in the relationship of the artist with his society, his time, and the general historical conditions. Art is not a product of itself, but of history. When a new art develops, in fact, new social relations are created, and with them a new culture, new feelings and images. Gramsci cited an important Crocean text: 'Poetry does not engender poetry; parthenogenesis does not take place; what is needed is the intervention of the masculin [sic!] element, that is, what is real, passional, practical and moral.... Once man is renewed and the spirit refreshed, a new affective life is created, than from it a new poetry will emerge.'[20] Gramsci accepts Croce's assertion but gives to it a Marxist interpretation.[21]

Literature does not engender literature, etc., that is ideologies do not create ideologies, superstructures do not engender superstructures... they are developed, not through parthenogenesis, but by the intervention of the 'masculin' [sic!] element, which is history, the revolutionary activity that creates a 'new man', that is new social relations.

Art is praxis, and as such depends on historical praxis. Such dependence, however, is not passive, static, unequivocal, as Gianni Scalia puts it, but dialectical and active. Art itself is a contradictory process tending toward an homogenization of meanings and expression of meanings.[22] It is not sufficient to demonstrate the historicity of art. It is necessary to know which art best expresses the same socio-historical phase. The way Gramsci posits the relationship between art and history is similar to that of Marx and Engels. Engels was an admirer of Balzac, in spite of his ideological, bourgeois beliefs, because he was able to depict the new men of the future society and predict the downfall of the aristocracy of his time. The art of Balzac is objective because it adheres to concrete reality. The same can be said of Pirandello's poetry, plays and short stories. His production is a contribution to the critique of the social and intellectual life of a phase of Italian history. As N. Stipcevic comments, Gramsci is interested in differentiating the ideological world of the artist and the 'beauty as such.' Beauty, however, is not a static element in a dynamic conception of the historical process. It changes with history. It changes even in the course of its permanence throughout history. The works of art acquire new meanings in the process of their re-creation. Thus, by transcending the intentions of their creators and the interests of their contemporaries, they transform themselves. This 'potentiality of art,' Stipcevic continues, explains its mysterious character and power in moving and attracting generations and generations of men.[23] The reasons for the permanence of art in history are for Gramsci not psychological, as in Marx (art as a remembrance of the social childhood of mankind!), but sociological and historical.

Gramsci, however, did not lay an emphasis on the problem of the aestheticity of art and its permanence across time. This concern was absent from all Italian aesthetics before the Second World War.[24]

He treats the problem of aesthetics in conjunction with the problem of hegemony and creation of a new culture. He asked himself the question: how is it possible that from the new socialist civilization already born, new artistic and literary forms had not yet sprung?[25] Art is an aspect of culture. There can be no movement or struggle for a new art apart from a struggle for a new culture.[26]

> To struggle for a new art would mean to struggle to create new individual artists, which is absurd, for artists cannot be created artificially. One has to speak of struggle for a new culture, that is for a new moral life, intimately connected with a new intuition of life, until it becomes a new way of experiencing and seeing reality...

We have seen how central the problem of the organization of culture is in Gramsci's theory of the revolution, to the extent that it became a primary element in the proletarian struggle to attain hegemony. Without doubt, the problem of art, literary criticism and role of the artist cannot be isolated from his general vision and socialist strategy to attain a new cultural hegemony.

The dialectical unity of content and form in art
Marxist aesthetics from its beginning has insisted on the unity of form and content in art, their interdependence, that is. It has also emphasized the priority of content over form. Any art form which attains a higher level of truth by necessity finds a higher form of expression. Russian aesthetics gradually eliminated from Marxism an important Hegelian acquisition, that is, the identification of the beautiful and the true, and came to regard art and reality, beauty and truth as irreconcilable opposites. It follows a total disregard for the 'form' in art under Stalin, and an outright opposition to 'formalism' prevailing in the years between 1921 and 1925 in Russia. Formalism reduced art to nothing but form and style, and remained indifferent to its 'content.'[27]

Hegelian idealism also insisted on the unity of content and form in order to determine what is beautiful and true in art. Such unity, however, was postulated a priori in the artist at the very moment of its creation. In the same vein, Croce made the principle of identity of form and content, the foundation of his aesthetic theory in opposition to the formalist school of aesthetics. In the aesthetic act, content and form cannot be separated, for no content can be imagined without form nor form without content. Intuition (content) and expression (form) cannot be separated. This dualism, for Croce, is resolved speculatively in an a priori synthesis in the spirit of the artist and not in the dynamics of history. Gramsci accepts the

principle of the identity of form and content, but transposes
it from the subject to history and gives it a new meaning. For
Croce, content is intuition and form is the expression; for
Gramsci, content is the 'mass of feelings and attitudes toward
life which circulate in the work of art.'[28] Understood in this
sense, content cannot be separated from the form (expression).
It follows that in art the artist's outlook on life cannot be
isolated from the manner in which he expresses its creation.
Croce's postulation of the unity of content and form was meant
to defend the idea of the complete independence of art from
philosophy and science and the superiority of intuitive knowledge over conceptual knowledge. Gramsci, in contrast, felt
the need to insert art in the dynamics of the historical process
and connect it to a concrete dialectics. To do this, Stipcevic
explains, Gramsci recurred to an intellectual operation also of
Crocean derivation. 'Identity of terms does not mean identity
of concepts.'[29] Thus, Gramsci concludes, it is legitimate to
distinguish (in their unity) content and form, and to affirm
the priority of one over the other.[30]

> To establish the principle that in the work of art one has to
> research solely the aesthetic character, one does not exclude
> the search for those feelings and attitude toward life which
> circulate in the work of art itself....What is excluded is that
> a work is beautiful for its moral and political content and
> not for its form.

Intervening in the polemics between those who insist on content
and those who insist on form in art, Gramsci, as Croce before
him, rejects the dualism. While Croce emphasizes the form,
Gramsci emphasizes the content. A passage is of great significance: 'content and form besides an "aesthetic" meaning, have
also an "historical" meaning.'[31] Art, in the ultimate analysis,
is form conditioned by the content, itself historically determined.
Continuing to uphold the principle that no priority of content
over form is given in the aesthetic act, one can only insist on
such priority historically, when there is a conflict for a new
culture. Thus, Gramsci, from a concept of absolute identity
of form and content, arrives at one of relative identity. This
new sense is necessitated by the notion of the historicity
of art and the revolutionary struggle for the creation of a new
culture.[32] Gramsci attempted to find a theoretical justification
for a relative autonomy of art within Marxist theory and
socialist political praxis. It can be said that this is Gramsci's
contribution to Marxist aesthetics. Obviously, he arrived at
the affirmation of the autonomy of art through Croce's concepts and intellectual operations.

Having examined the relationship between art and history,
Gramsci attempts to distinguish the aesthetic judgment and
historical judgment, aesthetic criticism and political criticism.

AESTHETIC PRAXIS AND POLITICAL PRAXIS: TENSIONS
BETWEEN AESTHETIC CRITICISM AND POLITICAL CRITICISM

There is no consensus among Gramscian scholars on how to
characterize his notes on literary criticism, or more generally,
aesthetic criticism. For some, the nature of Gramsci's aesthetic
reflections is sociological. Others find in his notes an important
nucleus of ideas and criteria sufficient to build a Marxist
aesthetics and aesthetic criticism.[33] To deal with these questions is merely an academic exercise.

Gramsci's interest in problems of aesthetics and aesthetic
criticism was not that of elaborating an aesthetic theory, rather
it was that of making clear to himself and other militant revolutionaries the nature and function of the critic in socialist
transformation. It is important to note that, despite the polemical tone of his aesthetic notes, he has been able to avoid
the error of politicizing art, aesthetic criticism and aesthetics,
tout court as in the case of 'socialist realism' in Russia. Gramsci
was aware of the tensions between artistic creation and politics,
aesthetic criticism and political criticism and attempted to
establish proper relations between them without compromising
the respective autonomy of art and aesthetic criticism.

Nature of Marxist aesthetic criticism
Again, a comparison with Croce is useful. Starting from the
premise that the work of art is complete and perfect in the
subject, Croce concluded that aesthetic criticism has no bear-
ing on the content of art but only on its form. It follows that
aesthetic criticism is formalist, technical and detached. In
literature, for instance, criticism aims at discriminating what
is poetry and non-poetry. As Stipcevic notes, criticism is,
for Croce, not a criticism of aesthetic values, but a pronouncement on the *existence* of the artistic phenomenon. This amounts
to saying that the value of a work of art is in its existence.
Aesthetic criticism discriminates between artistic and non-
artistic phenomena from the standpoint of the 'form.'[34] For
Gramsci, there are two series of facts: 'one of aesthetic
character, or pure art, the other of cultural politics (that is
mere politics).'[35] Hence, an aesthetic and political criticism.
He never defines the object and criteria of the first, but focuses
on the latter. And what is important to note is that he fuses
the two in a superior synthesis, that of cultural criticism.[36]
Aesthetic criticism is ultimately political.[37]

> The type of literary criticism proper to the philosophy of
> praxis... must fuse the struggle for a new culture, that is
> for a new humanism, the criticism of customs, feelings and
> conceptions of the world, with aesthetic criticism, or merely
> artistic in a passionate fervor, even in the form of sarcasm.

The best example of such criticism is provided by Francesço
De Sanctis. As Gramsci writes:[38]

> The criticism of De Sanctis is militant, not 'plainly' aesthetic;

it is the criticism of a period of cultural struggles, of contrasts between antagonistic conceptions of the world. The
analysis of the content, the criticism of the 'structure' of
works that is of the logical and historical-practical coherence
of the feelings represented artistically, are linked to this
cultural struggle.

To be sure, both Croce and De Sanctis are committed to an
ideology, but the latter offers a type of literary criticism far
superior to that of Croce precisely because he does not limit
himself to the criticism of the pure form, but of content and
form together. Here we recognize a familiar Marxist approach
best articulated by Lukács.[39] A given historical period is full
of contradictions. In it a fundamental activity and praxis predominates and represents a progressive moment in the development of history. This moment can be represented as progressive, reactionary, anachronistic, or in its general traits. The
latter is typically Marxist. Gramsci writes:[40]

> there are those who represent this predominant activity,
> this historical 'progressive point'; but how can one judge
> others who represent other activities or elements in the work
> of art? And these, are they also 'representative'? And,
> those who depict 'reactionary' and anachronistic elements,
> are they also the symbolizers of that aspect of the work of
> art? Must it be said that only those artists who seize all
> forces and elements in their essential conflict, that is those
> who seize the contradictions of the socio-historical totally,
> are truly representative artists?

This is why Marx and Engels admired Balzac and this why
Gramsci admires De Sanctis. Aesthetic criticism is eminently
historical in so far as it springs from the artist's relationship
to the history which is unfolding. As Scalia notes, Gramsci
insists that the artistic phenomenon be grounded within a
socio-cultural world, but that aesthetic criticism be distinct
from it.[41] In a letter from prison, Gramsci wrote:[42]

> Perhaps I made a distinction between aesthetic enjoyment and
> a positive value judgment of artistic beauty, i.e., between
> enthusiasm for a work of art in itself and moral enthusiasm,
> by which I mean a willing participation in the artist's ideo-
> logical world - a distinction which seems to me just and
> necessary. I can admire Tolstoy's *War and Peace* from an
> aesthetic point of view without agreeing with the ideological
> contents of the book. If both factors coincided, Tolstoy
> would be my vade mecum, my *livre de chevet*.

As to the general orientation of criticism, Gramsci distinguishes
a 'tendentious criticism' from a 'criticism of tendencies.' As
Guiducci has appropriately observed, Gramsci proposes the
latter. The characteristic features of such criticism are: the
capacity to comprehend and characterize all forces in conflict
among themselves and to encourage the development of the most
progressive ones.[43] 'Normal critical activity,' Gramsci writes,
'is mainly "cultural" in character and it is a criticism of

"tendencies", otherwise it would be a continuous massacre.[44]
If criticism is limited to the *form*, as in Croce, then it would be
a negative activity, or plainly dull criticism. Positive criticism,
instead, is directed to both, thus it is social and cultural
criticism. It is not a militant or neutral criticism that Gramsci
has in mind, but a criticism which is eminently historical.[45]

Aesthetic criticism and political criticism
Gramsci distinguishes aesthetic from political criticism. The
first bears on form, the latter on content. They are not, however, completely independent.[46]

> Two writers can represent (express) the same socio-historical
> moment, but one can be an artist, the other an hypocrite. To
> limit oneself to describe what the two represent or express
> socially, that is, by synthetizing more or less well the charac-
> teristics of a certain socio-historical period, means to barely
> touch the aesthetic problem. All this can be useful and
> necessary, and indeed it is, but in another sphere, that of
> political criticism, the criticism of customs, the struggle to
> destroy and transcend certain currents of feelings and
> beliefs, certain attitudes toward life and the world...

But how to decide who is truly an artist? 'This is the crux of
the polemics: X "wants" to express artificially a certain content but does not produce an artistic work... The political
critic claims that X is not an artist, but a "political opportunist".[47] The political critic does not intervene to express a value
judgment on the work of art, but to debunk its political pretensions. It does not demand a convergence and consonance
of artistic and political goals. It expresses a judgment on the
sincerity of artistic truths, not on the work of art per se, but
rather on the subject that creates it. Gramsci opposed the complete politicization of art as well as its complete autonomy.
Given the dependence of art on culture, and its practical importance in the organization of culture, tensions between art and
politics are inevitable.[48]

> The politician's pressures for the art of his times to express
> a specific cultural world is political activity and not artistic
> criticism: if the cultural world for which one fights is a liv-
> ing and necessary fact, its expansion will be inevitable, and
> it will produce its own artists. But, if despite the pressure,
> this inevitability is not perceived, this means that it was a
> question of a fictitious and artificial world...

Political criticism does not aim at educating authoritatively the
artist, but at clarifying his/her respective role in the process
of cultural reconstruction of society. The politician and the
artist are conscious of their limitations. But as art and political
praxis are both rooted in the same historical reality, the intervention of the latter in matters of aesthetics can be justified
only from an ethical standpoint. The politician tends to unmask
the hypocrisy of this or that artist, their non-adherence to
the objective development and direction of history. Gramsci

attempts to clarify further the functions of the two, in a text where the relationship between literature and politics is more seriously examined:[49]

> as far as the relation between literature and politics is con-
> cerned, one must take into account this criterion: the liter-
> ary man must have necessarily less precise and definite per-
> spectives than the politician, he should be less 'partisan' so
> to speak, but in a 'contradictory' way. For the politician any
> *a priori* 'fixed' image is reactionary: he conceives the whole
> movement in its becoming. The artist instead will have images
> 'fixed' and set in their definitive form. The politician ima-
> gines man as he is, and, at the same time, as he should be,
> in order to attain a certain end; his task is precisely that
> of pressing men to move, to come out from their present be-
> ing so that they could be able to reach collectively a set
> goal, that is to 'conform themselves' to an end. The artist
> represents necessarily 'what' he really finds of personal and
> non-conformist at a given time. Thus, from a political stand-
> point, the politician will never be satisfied with the artist,
> and he cannot be: he will find him always behind the times,
> always anachronistic, always outdone by the real movement.
> If history is a continuous process of liberation and self-
> consciousness, it is clear that each phase, *qua* history, in
> this case *qua* culture, will soon be transcended, and will no
> longer be of interest.

One is left with no doubt as to the ideological commitment of Gramsci to 'political criticism.' This is more progressive and more all-encompassing than aesthetic criticism. Yet, considering the fact that he was a militant revolutionary intellectual, he must be given credit for having recognized the value of aesthe-tic criticism and its relative independence from political criticism. In so doing, he avoided the dangers of the politicization of art, and its submission to party politics as happened in the Stalinist era and in Fascist Italy. One can disagree with Gramsci on this point. The disagreement, however, would be a matter of ethical choice. Gramsci chose to link art to society and cul-ture ethically and ideologically and not theoretically, Guiducci has written.[50] Certainly, Gramscian aesthetics is not open and flexible. And it cannot be, so long as the content of artistic production takes place within history. This does not prevent Marxist aesthetics from contributing to bringing about a better future.

The popular character of art forms

Gramsci's interest in aesthetics, as we have seen, is not philo-sophical nor theoretical, but sociological. Instead of asking what is beautiful in art, he is interested in knowing why a certain art is enjoyed by the public. Taking the example of literature, Gramsci notes that its popularity is not determined by 'beauty,' but rather by a specific content which is able to captivate the masses. 'Beauty is not sufficient. What is needed is a certain intellectual and moral content which is the elaborated and complete expression of the deepest aspirations of a certain public, that is the people-nation in a certain phase of its historical development.[51] The more literature adheres to culture and 'national feelings' in continuous development, the more it is popular in character. Gramsci pronounced a negative judgment on Italian literature. In its content and form it is cut off from the masses. This is the consequence of the separation of intellectuals from the masses. There is no common conception of the world: 'Popular feelings are not experienced by writers as their own.'[52] What makes art and literature popular is the adherence of its content to the feelings and experiences of the masses. 'The immediate contact between the reader and the writer takes place when the reader realizes the unity of content and form, the premise of which is a unity between the poetic and sentimental world. Otherwise the reader has to begin to translate the "language" of the content into his own language.'[53] As has been noted, when Gramsci speaks of the necessity of a popular literature, he does not refer to a class-related, proletarian literature. He is opposed to any tendency to create a proletarian art and literature, for they are phenomena which refer to the totality of the historical process, and not to a part of it. Some have attributed populist ideas to Gramsci. Populism is a form of neo-realism, according to which the people become the subject and object of artistic production. As a matter of fact, a populist art and literature would lead to common sense. We have seen how Gramsci has criticized common sense and how important the transformation of common sense into a superior conception of the world was for him. Artistic forms, for Gramsci, must aid the process of cultural elevation of the masses. The notion of 'popular' is in Gramsci always associated with that of 'national,' and is opposed to folklore and common sense. Folklore is a particularistic, provincial, anachronistic conception of the world, typical of a class lacking universal features. The notion of 'popular-national' refers to the most advanced, modern, cosmopolitan conception of the world.[54] It is true that at times he seems to advocate a populist form of literature.[55]

> The premise of the new literature cannot but be historical, political, popular. It must tend to develop what already exists, polemically or otherwise; what is important is that it is rooted in the *humus* of popular culture as is, with its tastes, its tendencies, etc., with its moral and intellectual world, be they backward or conventional.

Here is an example of going beyond single texts and grasping the general sense of Gramsci's thought. People's attitude toward art and the attraction exerted by artistic forms on the masses is always to be explained in terms of cultural and practical reasons. The masses are interested in the content of works of art more than the form. This explains why the masses are attracted to detective and adventure stories, thrillers and

romantic novels. Hence, the necessity for Marxist aesthetics
to focus on content to elevate the literary and artistic tastes
of the masses. As Stipcevic concludes, a 'popular literature'
which acts on the consciousness and knowledge and introduces
new revolutionary concepts in the common sense of the masses,
is for Gramsci of great hegemonic importance.[56]

Some general observations can be made at the conclusion of
this chapter. Gramsci has analyzed only some socio-historical
aspects of the aesthetic phenomenon. His intention was that
of grounding artistic creations in the dynamic and dialectical
reality of history. Art, thus, in the first place, must be linked
to the history of men and to concrete social relations. In this
respect, it is dependent, even if in a limited degree, on political
praxis. Second, art must be endowed with a certain autonomy
in regard to politics. Art emerges spontaneously and cannot
be imposed from above or the outside (as Stalin's art and
fascist art!). Third, art must facilitate the free development of
progressive revolutionary forces. Gramsci approached the
subject of artistic creation from a political perspective. Art is
social and historical, and as all other intellectual activities
diffuses itself and charms men because of practical and
external elements. What is of interest in art are always external
elements, those belonging to culture, which change according
to epochs, cultural climate and even personal moods. The
'barbaric metre' in Carducci's poems became an appealing
artistic innovation but only for the narrow circle of literary
men and those aspiring to become such, Gramsci wrote.[57] From
the standpoint of hegemony, Gramsci arrived at the affirmation
of the necessity of an active and conscious participation of the
artist to the process of its realization. This does not mean
politicization of art and submission to party politics, as in Lenin,
Stalin and Mao Tse-tung. When a social group comes to life
in history and aspires toward hegemony, from within it artists
will spontaneously emerge to express in a creative form the
exigencies of the new totality. Art is revolutionary, then,
when it springs from the interior of a renewed man.[58] When
Gramsci evokes the necessity of rendering art 'popular,' and
researching within it what is 'of interest' for the masses, he
is, in effect, subordinating the active role of the artist to the
consciousness of the needs of the masses. The artist's feeling
must harmonize subjective and objective elements. Lenin,
Mao and Gramsci all agree in condemning art for art's sake
and making the masses active and conscious participants in the
production of art. Mass participation in artistic production,
however, for Lenin and Mao can effectively take place only
through the creation of proletarian art and proletarian literature. Mao wrote:[59]

> Revolutionary literature and art are the products of the
> reflection on the life of the people in the brains of revolu-
> tionary writers and artists....The revolutionary struggle
> on the ideological and artistic fronts must be subordinate to

the political struggle because only through politics can the
needs of the class and the masses find expression in concentrated form.

The Marxism of Gramsci is profoundly humanist. He examines
both the intentions of the artist and his results. He speaks of
a rational conformism in art. Conformism is a concerted effort
to attain a practical end spontaneously and not by coercion.
Rational conformity does not deny individuality, originality
and creativity. There is a 'rational conformity,' for instance,
in architecture and this is, Gramsci writes, 'the expression
of the Beautiful according to the taste of a certain time,' that
is, the rational attainment of a set goal based on a certain taste
and technical knowledge.[60] If by originality one means doing
the opposite of what others do, then we have a mechanical,
artificial conformity imposed externally by narrow groups. An
architectural structure is the external manifestation of art,
the possibility given to the public to participate in the creation
of beauty. It is an interpretation of what is practical and useful, Gramsci notes. Is it possible to 'plan' art and the 'artist'
without eliminating his originality and individuality? Gramsci
answers, paradoxically, yes! Rational conformity, artistic
conformity and individualism can be dialectically fused. Individual originality implies, at its highest degree, maximum
sociality and historicity. The more the individual adheres to
the objective development of history, the more original he is.
While spontaneity per se leads to art for the artist's sake,
disciplined spontaneity leads to the most original artistic
creation.

EPILOGUE

Hobsbawm has written that Gramsci is probably the most
original Marxist theorist of the twentieth-century West.[1] Indeed,
his thought is predominant in contemporary Italian social
thought and is gradually rising to prominence within Western
social thought. We have analyzed and expounded in this study
on Gramsci's most original concepts within the context of a
macroscopic, historicist and dialectical conception of the historical development. It can be said that in the history of
Western sociological thought Gramsci represents and articulates
the Marxist response to the criticisms levelled by the most
prominent bourgeois classical social theorists, Durkheim, Pareto,
Weber, Michels and Mosca, to Marx's theory. Gramscian thought
is at the same time a critique and transcendence of bourgeois
sociologies still under the influence of Durkheimian and Weberian ideas. Gramsci took Marxism seriously, but maintained
toward it a critical stance and did not hesitate to incorporate
into it the most positive achievements of past philosophical
systems and conceptions. A critical frame of mind, he writes,
is the only fruitful stance in scientific research.[2]

In the formulation of historico-critical problems it is wrong
to conceive of scientific discussion as a process at law in
which there is an accused and a public prosecutor whose
professional duty it is to demonstrate that the accused is
guilty and has to be put out of circulation. In scientific
discussion, since it is assumed that the purpose of discussion is the pursuit of truth and the progress of science, the
person who shows himself most 'advanced' is the one who
takes up the point of view that his adversary may well be
expressing a need which should be incorporated, if only as
a subordinate aspect, in his own construction. To understand and to evaluate realistically one's adversary's position
and his reasons (and sometimes one's adversary is the whole
of past thought) means precisely to be liberated from the
prison of ideologies in the bad sense of the word – that of
blind ideological fanaticism. It means taking up a point of
view that is 'critical,' which for the purpose of scientific
research is the only fertile one.

Thus, it is not surprising to find in Gramsci's vision of
history, amalgamated in a perfect synthesis, Durkheim's idea
of the necessity of social consensus and collective beliefs to
stabilize society, the Weberian idea that economic behavior is
dependent upon men's general conception of their existence,

that is, the particular system of values prevailing in a given
society, and Marx's idea that it is political praxis which establishes in advance humanity's future. Gramsci shares with
Durkheim and Weber the need to analyze the qualitative aspects
of socio-cultural phenomena. In common with them, and Pareto
as well, Gramsci believes that collective beliefs are the basis
of an integrated society. Both objective and subjective factors
account for man's behavior. In this respèct they are all in
agreement in opposing any 'materialist' explanation of human
conduct. What sets Gramsci apart from all these theorists is
the acceptance of the notion of dialectic in the process of history.
For Durkheim socialism is an anomic phenomenon, the product
of lack of adjustment among various functions of the social
system, the enfeeblement of collective conscience. The restoration of consensus and higher organic solidarity could only be
accomplished through the 'division of labor,' social differentiation being the peaceful solution to social conflicts and social
crises. While Durkheim sacralizes society and all its components,
Gramsci humanizes it, historicizes and politicizes it. Society
is not a terminus a quo in the development of history, rather
the terminus ad quem, the culmination of the hegemonic expansion of a concrete 'social group.' Socialism, for Gramsci, is
the realization of a new social consensus, new social and moral
order. Such consensus is created not by 'society,' but by
political praxis within it.

   Weber, more than Durkheim, is closer to Gramsci's intellectual
vision. Both are descendants of the historical and idealist
school. This explains their common interests in history, philosophy, methodology, and problems of the relation between
science and human action, history and human subjectivity. They
both agree, against positivism, on the incomplete and superstructural character of science. Science is a rational action in
relation to a goal. Hence the subordination of scientific questions to the questions raised by individuals and meanings
assigned by them (Weber), and a given conception of the world
and political praxis (Gramsci). While Weber recurs to certain
procedures agreed upon by a collectivity to verify the subjective choices of individual scientists, Gramsci recurs to history and political praxis to verify scientific ideas. Weber and
Gramsci differ more sharply on their conception of 'political
sociology.' Social interaction is based on conflict, understood
by Weber in the Darwinian sense of peaceful competition and
subjected to rules agreed upon by all members of society.
Weber arrives at a theory of social integration not different
from that of Durkheim, according to which society is hierarchically and organically organized. As the process of rationalization of life continues there is a transition from *Gemeinschaft*
to *Gesellschaft*, a type of society in which all interests are
homogenized in an harmonious whole. In Weber's model of
society, one group is responsible for enforcing order and
administering rational action by means of power. The state

assures the perpetuation of a dominant group by demanding individuals' subservience to the common good. Weber's political sociology, R. Aron, writes, is an effort to understand contemporary history in the light of universal history, 'to make universal history intelligible in that it culminates in the present situation, - a culmination that is neutral and does not imply any value judgment.'[3] For Gramsci, the praxis of progressive groups changes both the present and past history and anticipates in the present a brighter future. Weber is the theorist of the automatism of bourgeois political economy, of a determined structure of the system of production guaranteed by an ethical and juridical superstructure. Hence derives the belief in the inevitability of the processes of rationalization and bureaucratization. The most efficient system of production is always a form of domination! Weber's view of historical development is thus metaphysical and fatalist. It remains a cry on behalf of the individual's freedoms in the face of the autonomous processes of rationalization and bureaucracy. Class conflict is a permanent feature of industrial societies. Socialism, Weber concludes, will not alter these processes but further enslave the individual.

Gramsci's starting point is the theory of historicity of bourgeois social order. Processes and institutions are all man's creations, thus susceptible to modification and change when man acquires the consciousness of their historicity. Revolutionary praxis, organized man's will, is capable of breaking up all laws of automatism. In this context Badaloni, a noted Gramsci scholar, observes that historicity leads to critical consciousness and critical consciousness leads to political will, the only force capable of modifying the structure itself. Both Weber and Gramsci agree that ideas become forces of change when translated into action. The ideas of Calvinism are concretized in the process of rationalization of economy. But while the will in Weber is an element sustaining the structure of capitalism, for Gramsci it is the force that can attack it.[4]

Lack of the notion of dialectic prevented both Durkheim and Weber from solving the problem of the crisis of modern societies. For both the source of antagonisms between social groups lies in their refusal to accept their essential functions in the world of production and administration of things. For Gramsci, the interests of a particular group are always those of a society 'in fieri.' And they are not only economic, but also political, cultural and ethical. As Gallino has put it, in order for a society 'in nuce' to become hegemonic, it needs to integrate the entire society. Social integration is not the harmonization of conflicting interests imposed by an abstract collective society or superordinate organism, as in Durkheim and Weber, rather the suppression of social, ethical and intellectual antagonisms.[5] Socialist integration is critical, voluntary and conscious, and demands the creation of a new culture, new structures and a new type of man, as we have seen in the course of this study.

As a sociologist, Gramsci analyzes the process of formation of collective wills, the manner in which they assert themselves in history and the type of integration they are able to realize.

Weber stresses individual praxis; Gramsci, collective praxis. The solution of social antagonisms is for Weber a matter of the individual's choice and commitment, for Gramsci it is of a collective will. Atomized individuals are not agents of historical transformation. Weber hopes that the emergence of charismatic leaders could save mankind from total rationalization and bureaucratization. Gramsci appeals instead to the masses to assert themselves and organize into a political force to take into their hands their own fate and destiny. Weber's position is that of a neutral intellectual whose interest is that of 'understanding' the development of history. Understanding is typical of those intellectuals (and sciences) who are over-whelmed by the complexity of modern life. Rationalization, over which individuals have no control, furthers the development of 'understanding' the sciences of history, culture and socio-logy. Against this orientation, which is fatalist and deter-minist, Gramsci asserts the primacy of will over intelligence. Revolutionary change can be expected not by a politicized human intelligence, but politicized human will. Intelligence, Gramsci writes, is pessimistic while will is optimistic. Intel-ligence cannot imagine what has not happened in history, that is, future history, as already happening. This will is optimistic in so far as it acts on the present, as it is, to transform it.[6]

Gramsci's work is sociological work in the same sense as that of Weber and all classical social theorists. He has knowledge of world history and a general vision of its development. He has developed a political and historicist conception of reality. As a 'sociologist of knowledge' he has insisted upon the social context of ideas; as a Marxist thinker he has consistently emphasized the conflictive nature of the social basis of thought, and as an historicist theoretician he has individuated in political praxis the main determinant of thought. Knowledge, for Gramsci, is always dependent upon a certain praxis. What distinguishes his theory of knowledge from that of classical sociologists is the notion of dialectics placed at its very core. But dialectics is not a fact, but an act. Thus, knowledge is objective to the extent that it adheres to the progressive forces of development in history. Hence, Gramsci's contention that dialectics is the realization of praxis. Gramsci's work represents an attempt to re-interpret all past history in the light of a praxis that is already hegemonic in the minds of those struggling for its realization. Gramsci's historicism is not Popper's historicism: a belief in the inevitability of laws of historical development. Rather, it is the belief of its rationality in the minds of those who struggle for the realization of a new hegemony. Any social group which asserts itself politically and culturally needs to develop an 'autonomous conception of the world,' a conception which includes a theory of history, knowledge and nature.

The philosophy of praxis is the conception of subaltern classes ascending toward political and cultural autonomy. Its truth resides in its historicity, that is, its capacity to engender a praxis in relation to a goal and to convert itself into a practical norm of conduct for the collectivity. The truth of the historicism of Marxism can ultimately be ascertained by a subjective and objective criterion. The first consists in the mass adhesion to an ideology, the latter in the capacity of an ideology to become an effective force of change in history.

We can list here the distinctive features of Gramsci's historicist conception of reality.

Historicism is the essential component of Marxism.

Historicism is a critique of any form of transcendence and metaphysics as well as an instrument for the comprehension of historical facts.

Historicism is a revolutionary perspective in so far as its practical function is the modification of social existence and existing social arrangements.

Marxism is the most 'integral' 'conception of the world,' a historical force of change and development. By offering a new vision of the world, it determines profound changes in the thinking and behavior of the masses.

The development of subaltern classes and their ascendant movement toward cultural, ideological and political hegemony is the most fundamental criterion for the analysis of sociohistorical phenomena.

The domination of a class over another is always the domination of a given Weltanschauung over another; consequently any revolutionary movement, if it is to be successful, has to be preceded by a profound intellectual and moral reform, by a radical transformation of human consciousness. Hegemony is a reform of human consciousness.

The realization of an ideological and political hegemony is the result of a dialectical relationship between the intellectuals and the masses. The establishment of such a relationship entails a necessary transformation of the role of the intellectual in society.

The political development of subaltern classes, in the last analysis, is a form of cultural development. That is to say, political activity aims at creating a new culture.

Cultural and ideological unification of society is the result of its structural unification.

One can understand Gramsci's growing appeal to the Western intelligentsia. His Marxism is open, disciplined, self-critical. It is a mature Marxism, solidly built on Marxist and Leninist principles, but profoundly humanistic, ethical and intellectual, for it is elaborated in opposition to the 'totalitarianism' of fascism and Stalinist Marxism and in a critical confrontation with the idealist philosophy prevailing at the time and the vulgar Marxism of Bukharin. In the words of George Lichtheim, Gramsci's Marxism represents an attempt to reconstruct the intellectual and cultural heritage of the Western world while preserving the most 'positive' achievements of past intellectual and political history.[7] The observation made by Stuart Hughes that Gramsci's thought is a 'totalitarian thought in liberal guise' is superficial at the best. For Gramsci, socialism brings to completion the task initiated by the bourgeoisie, that is the cultural and political emancipation of popular masses, the humanist and democratic movements of past history, and the structural and superstructural unification of all mankind.

NOTES

INTRODUCTION

1 E.J. Hobsbawm, The great Gramsci, 'The New York Review of Books,' vol.18, 1974, p.39.
2 The best biography of Gramsci in English is G. Fiori, 'Antonio Gramsci: Life of a Revolutionary,' New York, Dutton, 1971. For a more intellectual biography, see J.M. Cammett, 'Antonio Gramsci and the Origins of Italian Communism,' Stanford University Press, 1967; A. Davidson, 'Antonio Gramsci: Towards an Intellectual Biography,' Atlantic Highlands, N.J., Humanities Press, 1977.
3 This has been convincingly demonstrated by many Gramscian scholars. See, for instance, P. Piccone, Gramsci's Marxism: beyond Lenin and Togliatti, 'Theory and Society,' vol.3, no.4, 1976, pp.485-512 and A. Davidson, The varying seasons of Gramscian studies, 'Political Studies,' vol.20, no.4, 1972, pp.448-61.
4 See Fiori, op. cit., p.253 and p.289; Leonardo Paggi, Studi e interpretazioni recenti di Gramsci, 'Prassi Rivoluzionaria, Critica Marxista,' vol.3, 1966, pp.151-81; Maria A. Macciocchi, 'Pour Gramsci,' Paris, Editions du Seuil, 1974, pp.35-6 and M. Salvadori, 'Gramsci e il Problema Storico della Democrazia,' Turin, Piccola Biblioteca Einaudi, 1973, pp. 28-52.
5 Antonio Labriola was born in 1843 and died in 1904. He is called the first Italian Marxist philosopher and is known for his 'Essays on the Materialistic Conception of History,' which had a decisive influence on Gramsci. On this, see N. Badaloni, 'Il Marxismo di Gramsci,' Turin, Giulio Einaudi Editore, 1975. See also Leonardo Paggi, Gramsci's general theory of Marxism, in C. Mouffe, 'Gramsci and Marxist Theory,' London, Routledge & Kegan Paul, 1979, pp.113-67.
6 For a brief history of the evolution of Marxist thought see G. Lichtheim, 'A Short History of Socialism,' New York, Praeger Publishers, 1970.
7 Karl Marx and Frederick Engels, 'Selected Works,' Moscow, Foreign Languages Publishing House, 1958, vol.2, p.405.
8 Cited in A. Fried and R. Sanders, 'Socialist Thought,' Garden City, New York, Doubleday-Anchor Books, 1964, pp.436-7.
9 Cammett, op. cit., ch.2. See also M. Clark, 'Antonio Gramsci and the Revolution that Failed,' New Haven, Yale University Press, 1977, ch.3.
10 Antonio Gramsci, 'Selections from Political Writings 1910-1920,' trans. J. Mathews and ed. Q. Hoare, New York, International Publishers, 1977, p.12.
11 These early writings are now collected in five volumes published by Einaudi. See the annexed bibliography. A selection of these early political writings has been translated into English and published in 2 vols. by Lawrence & Wishart. See Antonio Gramsci, 'Selections from Political Writings 1910-1920,' and Antonio Gramsci, 'Selections from Political Writings 1921-1926,' New York, International Publishers, 1977 and 1978. A much smaller selection has been published by P. Cavalcanti and P. Piccone, 'History, Philosophy and Culture in the Young Gramsci,' St Louis, Telos Press, 1975. The 'New Edinburgh Review' in 1974 published three special editions on Gramsci (vols.23-4; 25-6; 27), translating a

selection of writings from the period 1919-1920.

12 See Antonio Gramsci, 'Notes on Journalism,' trans. G. Alkalay, 'Telos,' no.32, 1977, pp.139-51.

13 See Salvadori, op. cit., pp.5-71.

14 Many authoritative studies exist on the subject. See, for instance, Paolo Spriano, 'The Occupation of the Factories: Italy 1920,' trans. G.A. Williams, London, Pluto Press, 1975; M. Clark, op. cit.; Gwyn A. Williams, 'Proletarian Order: Antonio Gramsci, Factory Councils and the Origins of Communism in Italy, 1911-1921,' London, Pluto Press, 1975.

15 Badaloni, op. cit., p.104.

16 L. Paggi, 'Antonio Gramsci e il Moderno Principe,' Rome, Editori Riuniti, 1970.

17 Cammett, op. cit., p.87 and Badaloni, op. cit., p.102.

18 On this see Salvadori, op. cit.; F. De Felice, 'Serrati, Bordiga, Gramsci e il Problema della Rivoluzione in Italia 1919-1920,' Bari, De Donato Editore, 1971, pp.346-91.

19 On Gramsci and Bordiga much has been written. In English, see Cammett, op. cit., particularly ch.8; Clark, op. cit., and the general introduction to Antonio Gramsci, 'Selections from the Prison Notebooks,' New York, International Publishers, 1971, written by Quintin Hoare and Geoffrey Nowell Smith. A concise discussion and elucidation of the Gramsci-Bordiga split can be found in C. Boggs's review of the Spriano's and Williams's books, 'Telos,' 1977, vol.31, pp.202-20.

20 This is also the point of view articulated by Paggi, 'Antonio Gramsci e il Moderno Principe.'

21 Ibid., pp.430-1.

22 Throughout this study I use the most comprehensive selection of Gramsci's *Quaderni*, compiled and translated into English by Q. Hoare and G.N. Smith from the original Italian edition ('Quaderni del Carcere') published by Einaudi in six vols between 1948 and 1951. See Gramsci, 'Selections from the Prison Notebooks,' New York, International Publishers, 1971 (hereafter cited as PN). All Gramsci's texts are cited in their original. When texts are not available in translation, I use my own translations and refer to the original Italian publication, particularly, Antonio Gramsci, 'Quaderni del Carcere. Edizione Critica dell'Istituto Gramsci,' directed by Valentino Gerratana, Turin, Giulio Einaudi Editore, 1975. This four volume edition is hereafter cited as EC followed by the number of the notebook, the volume and the page.

23 For this summary I have utilized the excellent book by Giancarlo Jocteau, 'Leggere Gramsci,' Milan, Feltrinelli, 1975. For a discussion and analysis of the existing Italian literature on Gramsci, invaluable sources are Mouffe, op. cit., and Chantal Mouffe and Anne Sassoon-Showstack, Gramsci in France and Italy - A Review of the Literature, 'Economy and Society,' 1977, vol.6, no.1.

24 See P. Togliatti, Gramsci e il Leninismo, in 'Studi Gramsciani,' Rome, Editori Riuniti-Istituto Gramsciani, 1969, p.443. For a lengthy discussion on the evolution of the Leninist interpretation of Gramsci by Togliatti see Jocteau, op. cit., pp.27-58 and N. Auciello, 'Socialismo ed Egemonia in Gramsci e Togliatti,' Bari, De Donato, 1974, particularly the second part of the book. In English see A. Davidson, The Varying Seasons of Gramscian Studies.

25 Jocteau, op. cit., p.44.

26 F. Bellini and G. Galli, 'Storia del Partito Comunista Italiano,' Milan, Schwarz, 1953.

27 L. Maitan, 'Attualità di Gramsci e Politica Comunista,' Milan, Schwarz, 1955.

28 N. Matteucci, 'Antonio Gramsci e la Filosofia della Prassi,' Milan, Giuffrè Editore, 1951 and A. Garosci, Totalitarismo e storicismo nel pensiero di Antonio Gramsci, in his 'Pensiero Politico e Storiografia Moderna,' Pisa, Nistri-Lischi, 1954, pp.193-260.

29 The proceedings of this conference were published by the Istituto Gramsci.

See 'Studi Gramsciani. Atti del convegno tenuto a Roma nei gjorni 11-13 gennaio 1958,' Rome, Editori Riuniti-Istituto Gramsci, 1969, 2nd edn.
30 Jocteau, op. cit., p.88.
31 The proceedings of this conference are now published by the Istituto Gramsci in two volumes. See P. Rossi (ed.), 'Gramsci e la Cultura Contemporanea. Atti del convegno internazionale di studi Gramsciani tenuto a Cagliari on 23-7 April 1967,' Rome, Editori Riuniti-Istituto Gramsci, 1969 and 1970.
32 Salvadori, op. cit.
33 Paggi, 'Antonio Gramsci e il Moderno Principe,' introduction.
34 On this, see Badaloni, op. cit. For a comprehensive and critical view of Badaloni in English see G. Marramao, 'Telos,' 1977, no.31, pp.224-9.
35 See P. Spriano, 'Introduction to Gramsci, Scritti Politici,' Rome, Editori Riuniti, 1973.
36 G. Nardone, 'Il Pensiero di Gramsci,' Bari, De Donato, 1971.
37 J.-M. Piotte, 'La Pensée Politique de Gramsci,' Paris, Editions Anthropos, 1970.
38 H. Portelli, 'Gramsci et le Bloc Historique,' Paris, Presses Universitaires de France, 1972.
39 C. Riechers, 'Antonio Gramsci, Marxismus in Italien,' Frankfurt am Main, Europäische Verlaganstalt, 1970.
40 Among sociologists, Irving L. Horowitz has been one of the first to denounce the 'provincialism' of Anglo-Saxon scholars in dealing with the Italian philosophical and political thought of the twentieth century. Horowitz views Gramsci along with Gentile and Croce as the 'fundamental triumvirate of the Hegelian legacy in Italy.' See Horowitz, Discussion: on the social theories of Giovanni Gentile, 'Philosophy and Phenomenological Research,' 1960, p.264.
41 See C. Boggs, 'Gramsci's Marxism,' London, Pluto Press, 1976; J. Joll, 'Antonio Gramsci,' Harmondsworth, Penguin, 1977; A. Pozzolini, 'Antonio Gramsci: An Introduction to his Thought' (trans. A. Sassoon-Showstack), London, Pluto Press, 1970. Among articles we cite here the most significant contribution to Gramscian Studies: Alberto Martinelli, In defense of the dialectic: Antonio Gramsci's theory of revolution, 'Berkeley Journal of Sociology,' no.13, 1968, pp.1-27; J. Merrington, Theory and practice in Gramsci's Marxism, 'The Socialist Register,' ed. R. Miliband and J. Saville, New York, Monthly Review Press, 1968, pp.145-76; E. Genovese, On Antonio Gramsci, in 'For a New America,' eds J. Weinstein and D.W. Eakins, New York, Random House, 1970, pp.284-316; R. Giacchetti, Antonio Gramsci: the subjective revolution, in 'The Unknown Dimension,' eds D. Howard and K.E. Klare, New York, Basic Books, 1972, pp.147-68; J. Femia, Hegemony and consciousness in the thought of Antonio Gramsci, 'Political Studies,' vol.23, no.1, 1975, pp.29-48; T. Bates, Gramsci and the theory of hegemony, 'Journal of the History of Ideas,' vol.36, no.2, 1975, pp.351-66; P. Piccone, Gramsci's Hegelian Marxism, 'Political Theory,' vol.2, no.1, 1974, pp.32-45; J. Karabel, Revolutionary contradictions: Antonio Gramsci and the problem of intellectuals, 'Politics and Society,' vol.6, no.2, 1976, pp.123-72.
42 A. Sassoon-Showstack, 'Gramsci's Politics,' London, Croom Helm, 1980.
43 Mouffe, op. cit.,
44 C. Buci-Glucksmann, 'Gramsci and the State,' London, Lawrence & Wishart, 1979. See also 'State, transition and passive revolution,' in Mouffe, op. cit., pp.207-36.
45 Perry Anderson, The antinomies of Antonio Gramsci, 'New Left Review,' no.100, 1977, and 'Considerations on Western Marxism, 'London, Verso, 1979 (first published in 1976 by New Left Books).
46 B. De Giovanni, Lenin and Gramsci: state, politics and party, in Mouffe, op. cit., pp.259-88; A. Baldan, Gramsci as an historian of the 1930's, trans. G. Alkalay, 'Telos,' no.31, 1977, pp.100-11; P. Piccone, From Spaventa to Gramsci, 'Telos,' no.31, 1977, pp.35-65; N. Todd, Ideological superstructure in Gramsci and Mao Tse-Tung, 'Journal of the

History of Ideas,' vol.35, no.1, 1975, pp.148-56 and S. Hall, B. Lumley, and G. McLennan, Politics and ideology: Gramsci, in 'On Ideology,' Centre for Contemporary Cultural Studies, London, Hutchinson, 1977, pp.45-76.

1 MARXISM AS AN AUTONOMOUS AND INDEPENDENT WELTANSCHAUUNG

1 Benedetto Croce (1866-1952) is the most prominent intellectual figure in the Italian history of the twentieth century. He was a philosopher, historian and literary critic, whose voluminous writings on history, literature, aesthetics and history of philosophy exerted a profound influence on Gramsci. For a competent discussion of Croce's philosophy see Wildon Carr, 'The Philosophy of Benedetto Croce,' New York, Russell & Russell, 1969 and for an exhaustive analysis of Croce's influence on Gramsci see E. Garin, La formazione di Gramsci e Croce, 'Prassi Rivoluzionaria. Critica Marxista,' vol.3, 1967, pp.119-33; E. Agazzi, Filosofia della prassi e filosofia dello spirito, in A. Caracciolo and G. Scalia (eds), 'La Città Futura,' Milan, Feltrinelli, 1959, pp.187-269.
2 E. Garin, op. cit., p.122. See also E. Garin, Antonio Gramsci nella cultura italiana, in 'Studi Gramsciani. Atti del convegno tenuto a Roma nei giorni 11-13 gennaio 1958,' Rome, Editori Riuniti, 1969, 2nd edn, pp.3-14 and 395-418.
3 EC, Q.10, vol.II, p.1241.
4 L. Paggi, 'Antonio Gramsci e il Moderno Principe,' p.12.
5 N. Badaloni, Gramsci storicista di fronte al marxismo contemporaneo, in 'Prassi Rivoluzionaria. Critica Marxista,' vol.3, 1967, p.101.
6 EC, Q.10, vol.II, p.1320.
7 On the various meanings of 'dialectic' in Gramsci see, N. Bobbio, Nota sulla dialettica in Gramsci, in 'Studi Gramsciani,' op. cit., pp.73-86.
8 EC, Q.10, vol.II, pp.1241-2. We have drawn on many concepts discussed by Agazzi, op. cit., and M. Finocchiaro, Gramsci's Crocean Marxism, 'Telos,' no.41, 1979, pp.17-32.
9 N. Bukharin, 'Historical Materialism: A System of Sociology,' New York, Russell & Russell, 1965. For a more systematic analysis of Gramsci's critique of Bukharin, see A. Zanardo, Il 'Manuale' di Bukharin visto dai comunisti tedeschi e da Gramsci, in 'Studi Gramsciani,' op. cit., pp.337-68.
10 PN, p.420 and EC, Q.11, vol.II, p.1396.
11 The relation of structure and superstructure in Gramsci has been interpreted in various ways. N. Bobbio, one of the foremost Gramscian scholars, has presented Gramsci as the theoretician of the super-structure. We discuss this problem in chapter 5.
12 In our opinion, this is a fundamental criterion in Gramsci's analysis of socio-historical processes. It will be analyzed in chapters 3 and 4. See also, in this respect, G. Nardone, 'Il Pensiero di Gramsci,' Bari, De Donato Editore, 1971, pp.37-260.
13 PN, pp.57-8 and EC, Q.19, vol.III, p.2010.
14 For a more detailed examination of this idea see H. Portelli, 'Gramsci et le Bloc Historique,' Paris, Presses Universitaires de France, 1972, pp.145-50.
15 PN, p.346 and EC, Q.7, vol.II, pp.893-4.
16 PN, p.339 and EC, Q.11, vol.II, p.1391.
17 Portelli, op. cit.
18 PN, pp.365-6 and EC, Q.10, vol.II, pp.1250 and 1051.
19 See M.A. Macciocchi, 'Pour Gramsci,' Paris, Editions du Seuil, 1974, p.162.
20 G. Tamburrano, Gramsci e l'egemonia del proletariato, in 'Studi Gramsciani,' op. cit., pp.277-86.
21 PN, pp.392-3 and EC, Q.16, vol.III, p.1858.
22 PN, pp.388 and EC, Q.11, vol.II, p.1508.
23 PN, p.465 and EC, Q.11, vol.II, p.1437.

24 PN, p.399 and EC, Q.16, vol.III, p.1864.
25 PN, p.404 and EC, Q.11, vol.II, p.1487.
26 PN, pp.404-5 and EC, Q.11, vol.II, pp.1487-8.
27 N. Badaloni, Il fondamento teorico dello storicismo gramsciano, in P. Rossi (ed.), 'Gramsci e la Cultura Contemporanea,' Rome, Editori Riuniti-Istituto Gramsci, 1970,' vol.2, pp.73-80 and S. Graziano, Alcune considerazioni intorno all'umanesimo di Gramsci, in 'Studi Gramsciani,' op. cit., pp.149-64. A more systematic but concise treatment of Gramsci's historicist theory can also be found in J. Texier, 'Gramsci,' Paris, Editions Seghers, 1966, pp.63-88. In English, see L. Paggi, Gramsci's general theory of Marxism, 'Telos,' 1977, no.33, pp.27-70.
28 L. Althusser and E. Balibar, Marxism is not a historicism, in 'Reading Capital,' New York, Pantheon Books, 1970, p.140.
29 PN, p.352 and EC, Q.10, vol.II, p.1345.
30 PN, p.351 and EC, Q.10, vol.II, p.1344.
31 PN, p.352 and EC, Q.10, vol.II, p.1345.
32 A.R. Buzzi, 'La Teoria Politica de Antonio Gramsci,' Barcelona, Editorial Fontanella, 1969, p.128f.
33 P. Berger and T. Luckmann, 'The Social Construction of Reality: a Treatise in the Sociology of Knowledge,' Garden City, New York, Doubleday, 1966, p.2f.
34 G. Gurvitch, 'The Social Frameworks of Knowledge,' New York, Harper & Row, 1972, p.10.
35 K. Mannheim, 'Ideology and Utopia,' trans. L. Wirth and E. Shils, New York, Harcourt, Brace and World, 1936, and 'Essays on the Sociology of Knowledge,' London, Routledge & Kegan Paul, 1952, p.85.
36 Gurvitch, op. cit., pp.7-8.
37 W. Stark, 'The Sociology of Knowledge,' Chicago, Free Press, 1958, pp.46-172, and J. Gabel, Mannheim et le marxisme hongrois, 'L'homme et la société,' 1969, vol.11, pp.127-45.
38 Gabel, op. cit.
39 Few sociologists have examined the sociological aspects of Gramsci's theory. Among the few are L. Gallino, Gramsci e le scienze sociali, in Rossi, op. cit., vol.2, pp.81-108 and A. Pizzorno, Sul metodo di Gramsci: dalla storiografia alla scienza politica, in Rossi, op. cit., vol.2, pp.109-26.
40 On the problem of the 'historicization of science' and 'objectivity' see R. Guiducci, 'Filosofia della prassi e ricerca scientifica,' in Caracciolo and Scalia, op. cit., pp.273-97 and ch.6 of this study.
41 We have drawn some of these concepts from A. Schaff, 'Langage et Connaissance,' Paris, Editions Anthropos, 1969, p.289.
42 EC, Q.11, vol.II, p.1457. Gramsci's notes on science have been recently translated into English by M.A. Finocchiaro. See Science and 'scientific' ideologies, by Antonio Gramsci, 'Telos,' no.41, 1979, pp.131-55.
43 PN, p.368 and EC, Q.10, vol.II, pp.1290-1.
44 PN, p.445 and EC, Q.11, vol.II, pp.1415-16.
45 In the same perspective and certainly under Gramscian influence, Wiatr has characterized Marxist historicism as a 'form of consciousness,' whose practical function is the modification of human perception of social reality. See J. Wiatr, Sociology-Marxism-reality, in P. Berger (ed.), 'Marxism and Sociology: Views from Eastern Europe,' New York, Appleton-Century-Crofts, 1969, pp.18-36. On the problem of ideology and historicism in Gramsci, Lukács and Althusser see S. Hall et al., Politics and Ideology: Gramsci, in 'On Ideology,' Centre for Contemporary Cultural Studies, London, Hutchinson, 1977, pp.45-76.
46 PN, pp.332-30.

2 THE SPECIFICITY OF MARXIST SOCIOLOGY IN GRAMSCI'S THEORY

1 A. Gouldner, 'The Coming Crisis of Western Sociology,' New York, Basic Books, 1970, p.455f.
2 Ibid., For a critique see M. Kalab, The specificity of the Marxist conception of sociology, in Berger (ed.), 'Marxism and Sociology: Views from Eastern Europe,' New York, Appleton-Century-Crofts, 1969, p.72.
3 'Sociology...therefore became the philosophy of non-philosophers, an attempt to provide a schematic description and classification of historical and political facts, according to criteria built up on the model of natural science. It is therefore an attempt to derive "experimentally" the laws of evolution of human society in such a way as to "predict" that the oak tree will develop out of the acorn. Vulgar evolutionism is at the root of sociology, and sociology cannot know the dialectical principle with its passage from quantity to quality. But this passage disturbs any form of evolution and any law of uniformity understood in a vulgar evolutionist sense. In any case, any sociology presupposes a philosophy, a conception of the world, of which it is but a subordinate part.' PN, p.426 and EC, Q.11, vol.II, p.1432.
4 H. Marcuse, 'One-Dimensional Man,' Boston, Beacon Press, 1964, pp.145-99.
5 R. Aron, 'Main Currents in Sociological Thought,' Garden City, New York, Anchor Books, vol.1, 1968, p.7.
6 I.M. Zeitlin, 'Ideology and the Development of Sociological Theory,' Englewood Cliffs, N.J., Prentice-Hall, 1968.
7 See O. Mandic, The Marxist school of sociology: what is sociology in a Marxist sense? in Berger (ed.), op. cit., p.47f and L. Zivkovic, 'The Structure of Marxist Sociology,' in ibid., pp.98-127.
8 For a more comprehensive treatment of the status of Italian sociology in Gramsci's times see the article of G.J. Di Renzo, Sociology in Italy today,' International Review of Modern Sociology,' vol.1, 1972, pp.33-58.
9 PN, p.71 and EC, Q.19, vol.III, p.2022.
10 PN, p.403 and EC, Q.11, vol.II, p.1492.
11 PN, p.402 and EC, Q.7, vol.II, p.868.
12 See J. Texier, 'Gramsci,' Paris, Ed. Seghers, 1966, p.46 and L. Gallino, Gramsci e le scienze sociali, in P. Rossi (ed.), 'Gramsci e la Cultura Contemporanca,' Rome, Editori Riuniti-Istituto Gramsci, vol.2, 1970, p.84.
13 PN, p.411 and EC, Q.11, vol.II, p.1478 and Q.10, vol.II, p.1350.
14 PN, p.410 and EC, Q.11, vol.II, p.1477.
15 PN, p.411 and EC, Q.11, vol.II. p.1478.
16 PN, p.244 and EC, Q.15, vol.III, p.1766.
17 In order to understand the importance of Gramsci's criticism of Bukharin, it would have been necessary to describe the ideological situation of Marxism during the Second and Third Internationals. Since this discussion goes obviously beyor.d the limits imposed by the present study, the reader is referred to the excellent study of Zanardo, 'Il 'Manuale' di Bukharin visto dai comunisti tedeschi e da Gramsci, in 'Studi Gramsciani, Atti del convegno tenuto a Roma nei giorni 11-13 gennaio 1958,' Rome, Editori Riuniti, 1969, 2nd edn, pp.377-68.
18 This idea will be more seriously analyzed in chapter 3.
19 PN, p.429 and EC, Q.11, vol.II, p.1430.
20 See Gramsci's notes on science, PN, p.437f, and the analysis of this concept by Texier, op. cit., p.66f and by C. Luporini, La metodologia del marxismo nel pensiero di Gramsci, in 'Studi Gramsciani,' op. cit., pp.445-68.
21 PN, p.438 and EC, Q.11, vol.II, p.1403.
22 PN, p.430 and EC, Q.11, vol.II. p.1433.
23 N. Badaloni in P. Rossi, op. cit., pp.73-80.
24 Bukharin, for instance, writes: 'Some persons imagine that the theory of historical materialism should under no circumstances be considered a

Marxian sociology, and that it should not be expounded systematically; they believe that it is only a living *method* of historical knowledge....All such arguments are in error... for the theory of historical materialism has a definite place, it is not political economy, nor is it history; it is the general theory of society and the laws of its evolution, i.e., sociology.' N. Bukharin, 'Historical Materialism: A System of Sociology,' New York, Russell & Russell, 1965, pp.xiv-xv. He adds (p.30): 'Both in nature and society there exists objectively (i.e., regardless of whether we are conscious of it or not) a law that is causal in character.'

25 Bukharin, op. cit., p.xiv. On the theoretical problem of the relationship between Marxism and sociology it could be said that Gramsci's position does not differ from that of contemporary Marxist sociologists, such as Mandic, op. cit., pp.45-7. Marxism is a philosophical theory of society investigating the most general laws of historical development, but at the same time it is a methodological frame for the theoretical organization of concrete social phenomena. In its second aspect, it can be characterized as a sociology. Thus, Gramsci would argue that Marxism as a theory reaches a higher level of generalization or draws conclusions more general in scope than sociology, which in his Marxist conception limits itself to the investigation of how specific historical blocs emerge, function, and disintegrate. In such an effort sociology does not abstract from time and space as in the case of Marxist theory.

26 PN, p.446 and EC, Q.11, vol.II, p.1416.
27 PN, p.336 and EC, Q.11, vol.II, p.1338.
28 PN, p.332 and EC, Q.11, vol.II, p.1384.
29 See Gramsci's article on the Russian Revolution in 'Scritti Giovanili' (1914-18), Turin, Einaudi, 1958, p.149f. In English, see Antonio Gramsci, 'Selections from Political Writings, 1910-1920,' New York, International Publishers, 1977, pp.34-7.
30 L. Gallino, op. cit., pp.81-108 and A. Pizzorno, Sul metodo di Gramsci: dalla storiografia alla scienza politica, in P. Rossi, op. cit., pp.109-26.
31 PN, p.412 and EC, Q.11, vol.II, p.1479.
32 Pizzorno, op. cit. This is also the opinion of Buzzi and Piotte.
33 Some of these concepts will be analyzed in more detail in chapter 4.
34 The notion of 'social group' is commonly synonymous with that of class. When Gramsci speaks of 'essential' or 'fundamental' social groups, he means potentially hegemonic groups as in the case of the bourgeoisie during the French Revolution and the proletariat in socialist revolutions.
35 See Gramsci's notes on Italian History in PN, pp.55-90 and EC, Q.19, vol.III, pp.2010-34.
36 PN, pp.366-7 and EC, Q.10, vol.II, p.1244.
37 PN, pp.175-85 and EC, Q.13, vol.III, pp.1578-89.
38 PN, p.181 and EC, Q.13, vol.III, p.1584.
39 Ibid.
40 PN, p.182 and EC, Q.13, vol.III, p.1584.
41 PN, p.52 and EC, Q.25, vol.III, p.2288.
42 On this aspect see Boggs, Cammett and Tamburrano.
43 The concept of 'civil society' is one of the most original and controversial concepts in Gramsci's theory. It will be discussed in chapter 5. It suffices here to say that civil society is the 'ethical content' of the state.
44 PN, p.238 and EC, Q.7, vol.II, p.866.
45 Gramsci's theory of intellectuals is for some scholars the central theme of all his reflections. See J.-M. Piotte, 'La Pensée Politique de Gramsci,' Paris, Anthropos, 1970 and E. Garin, Politica e cultura in Gramsci (il problema degli intellettuali), in Rossi, op. cit., vol.1, pp.37-74.
46 PN, p.5 and EC, Q.12, vol.III, p.1513.
47 PN, p.10 and EC, Q.12, vol.III, p.1517.
48 G. Nardone, 'Il Pensiero di Gramsci,' Bari, De Donato Editore, 1971, p.69.
49 PN, p.151 and EC, Q.13, vol.III, p.1630.

50 PN, p.52 and EC, Q.15, vol.III, p.2289.
51 Nardone, op. cit., p.83.
52 PN, p.335 and EC, Q.11, vol.II, p.1387. 'Intellettualità totalitarie' has been translated as 'totalitarian intelligentsias.' In this context 'totalitarian' should be understood as all-encompassing and unifying intellectuals.
53 PN, pp.181-2 and EC, Q.13, vol.III, p.1584.
54 On the influence of Mosca, Pareto and Michels on Gramsci see G. Galli, Gramsci e le teorie delle 'élites,' in P. Rossi, op. cit., vol.2, pp.201-16.
55 R. Michels, 'Political Parties,' New York, Dover Publications, 1959, p.86.
56 PN, p.211 and EC, Q.13, vol.III, p.1604.
57 PN, p.129 and EC, Q.13, vol.III, p.1558.
58 EC, Q.6, vol.II, p.751.
59 PN, p.334 and EC, Q.11, vol.II, p.1386.
60 Piotte, op. cit., p.71.
61 V.I. Lenin, 'What is to Be Done?' Moscow, Progress Publishers, 1973, pp.31-2.
62 PN, p.418 and EC, Q.11, vol.II, p.1505.
63 Ibid.
64 PN, p.334 and EC, Q.11, vol.II, p.1386.
65 See A. Costa, Aspetti sociologici del pensiero gramsciano, in 'Studi Gramsciani,' op. cit., p.201.
66 PN, p.52 and EC, Q.25, vol.III, p.2288.

3 THE MASSES AND THE DYNAMICS OF HISTORY

1 See G. Lukács, 'History and Class Consciousness,' Cambridge, Mass., MIT Press, 1972, p.28.
2 G. Nardone, 'Il Pensiero di Gramsci,' Bari, De Donato Editore, 1971, p.18.
3 EC, Q.17, vol.III, p.1948,
4 PN, p.409 and EC, Q.7, vol.II, p.873.
5 EC, Q.16, vol.III, p.1878.
6 EC, Q.19, vol.III, pp.1983-4.
7 EC, Q.19, vol.III, p.1960 and Q.25, vol.III, pp.2284-5.
8 EC, Q.17, vol.III, p.1910.
9 EC, Q.17, vol.III, p.1913.
10 EC, Q.17, vol.III, p.1910.
11 EC, Q.19, vol.III, pp.2041-2. On this see Buzzi, op. cit., p.76.
12 PN, p.79 and EC, Q.19, vol.III, p.2029.
13 PN, p.77 and EC, Q.19, vol.III, p.2027.
14 A Gramsci, 'Scritti Giovanili,' Turin, Einaudi, 1958, p.150 and A. Gramsci, 'Selections from Political Writings, 1910-1920,' trans. J. Mathews and ed. Q. Hoare, New York, International Publishers, 1977, p.35.
15 A. Gramsci, 'L'Ordine Nuovo (1919-1920),' Turin, Einaudi, 1970, p.96 and Gramsci, 'Selections from Political Writings, 1910-1920,' p.173.
16 Gramsci, 'Scritti Giovanili,' p.78 and Gramsci, 'Selections from Political Writings,' p.17.
17 Ibid.
18 PN, p.180 and EC, Q.13, vol.III, p.1583.
19 PN, p.260 and EC, Q.8, vol.II, p.937.
20 PN, p.52 and EC, Q.25, vol.III, p.2288.
21 PN, p.53 and EC, Q.25, vol.III, p.2289.
22 EC, Q.19, vol.III, pp.1972-3.
23 PN, p.55 and EC, Q.19, vol.III, p.1973 and Q.25, vol.III, p.2283.
24 Nardone, op. cit., p.61.
25 PN, p.199 and EC, Q.3, vol.I, p.330.
26 PN, p.198 and EC, Q.3, vol.I, p.328-9.
27 Nardone, op. cit., p.75.
28 PN, p.381 and EC, Q.7, vol.II, pp.881-2.

29 PN, pp.57-8 and EC, Q.19, vol.III, pp.2010-1.
30 For a more detailed analysis of this particular interpretation of hegemony see C. Mouffe, Hegemony and ideology in Gramsci, in C. Mouffe (ed.), 'Gramsci and Marxist Theory,' London, Routledge & Kegan Paul, 1979, pp.168-204.
31 See Common Sense, in 'The Encyclopedia of Philosophy,' New York, Macmillan and the Free Press, 1967, vol.2. and in J. Grooten and G. Steenbergen, 'New Encyclopedia of Philosophy,' New York, Philosophy Library, 1972. For an analysis of 'common sense' and 'folklore' in Gramsci, see A. Cirese, Concezioni del mondo, filosofia spontanea, folclore, in P. Rossi (ed.), 'Gramsci e la Cultura Contemporanea,' Rome, Editori Riuniti-Istituto Gramsci, vol.2, 1970, pp.299-329; L.L. Satriani, Gramsci e il folclore: dal pittoresco alla contestazione, in ibid., pp.329-38 and C. Luporini, La metodologia del marxismo nel pensiero di Gramsci, in 'Studi Gramsciani, Atti del convegno tenuto a Roma nei giorni 11-13 gennaio 1958,' Rome, Editori Riuniti-Istituto Gramsci, 1969, pp.445-68.
32 P. Berger and T. Luckmann, 'The Social Construction of Reality,' New York, Doubleday, 1966, p.14.
33 PN, p.348 and EC, Q.10, vol.II, pp.1334-5.
34 PN, p.323 and EC, Q.11, vol.II, p.1375.
35 PN, p.326, note 5 and EC, Q.24, vol.III, p.2271.
36 PN, p.419 and EC, Q.11, vol.II, p.1396.
37 PN, p.422 and EC, Q.11, vol.II, pp.1398-9.
38 EC, Q.11, vol.II, p.1500.
39 PN, p.419 and EC, Q.11, vol.II, p.1506.
40 PN, p.420 and EC, Q.11, vol.II, p.1396.
41 PN, p.344 and EC, Q.10, vol.II, p.1255.
42 PN, pp.328 and 346 and EC, Q.11, vol.II, pp.1380 and 1486.
43 PN, p.328 and EC, Q.11, vol.II, p.1380.
44 EC, Q.27, vol.III, p.2314.
45 PN, p.323 and EC, Q.11, vol.II, p.1396.
46 EC, Q.27, vol.III, p.2312.
47 Ibid.
48 Ibid.
49 'There is a "popular religion" in catholic countries much different from the one systematized by the ecclesiastical hierarchy and the intellectuals.' Gramsci inserts here a penetrating remark: 'it must be seen if such an elaboration and systematization is needed to maintain the stratified and variegated character of folklore...' EC, Q.27, vol.III, p.2313.
50 PN, p.420 and EC, Q.11, vol.II, p.1397.
51 EC, Q.27, vol.III, p.2312.
52 EC, Q.9, vol.II, p.1105.
53 EC, Q.27, vol.III, p.2313.
54 EC, Q.5, vol.I, pp.679-80. The word 'collettività' has been translated here as 'collective feelings.'
55 EC, Q.14, vol.III, p.1660.
56 EC, Q.15, vol.III, p.1776.
57 See H. Portelli, 'Gramsci et le Bloc Historique,' Paris, Presses Universitaires de France, 1972, p.20.
58 PN, p.345 and EC, Q.10, vol.II, p.1255.
59 PN, p.337 and EC, Q.11, vol.II, p.1389.
60 PN, p.340 and EC, Q.11, vol.II, pp.1391-2.
61 PN, p.419 and EC, Q.11, vol.II, p.1396.
62 EC, Q.10, vol.II, pp.1383-4.
63 PN, p.332 and EC, Q.11, vol.II, p.1384.
64 PN, pp.331-2 and EC, Q.11, vol.II, pp.1383-4.
65 EC, Q.10, vol.II, p.1217.
66 PN, pp.54-5 and EC, Q.25, vol.III, p.2283.
67 EC, Q.10, vol.II, p.1242.
68 EC, Q.10, vol.II, p.1212.

69 EC, Q.10, vol.II, pp.1325-8.
70 PN, p.346 and EC, Q.11, vol.II, p.1486.
71 PN, p.348 and EC, p.1330.
72 PN, p.325 and EC, Q.11, vol.II, pp.1377-8.
73 PN, p.333 and EC, Q.11, vol.II, pp.1384-5.
74 PN, p.422 and EC, Q.11, vol.II, p.1399.
75 A. Zanardo, Il 'Manuale' di Bukharin visto dai comunisti tedeschi e da Gramsci, in 'Studi Gramsciani,' op. cit., p.340.
76 PN, p.334 and EC, Q.11, vol.II, p.1386.
77 PN, p.437 and EC, Q.11, vol.II, pp.1402-3.
78 PN, p.435 and EC, Q.11, vol.II, p.1425.
79 Ibid.
80 PN, p.442 and EC, Q.11, vol.II, p.1412.
81 PN, p.444 and EC, Q.11, vol.II, p.1415.
82 PN, p.421 and EC, Q.11, vol.II, p.1398.
83 EC, Q.11, vol.II, p.1398. On this idea see A. Broccoli, 'Antonio Gramsci e l'Educazione come Egemonia,' Firenze, La Nuova Italia Editrice, 1972.
84 PN, pp.330-1 and EC, Q.11, vol.II, p.1382.
85 PN, p.417 and EC, Q.15, vol.III, p.1826.
86 On the contrast between common sense and so-called absolutist sociologies see, for instance, J.D. Douglas, 'Understanding Everyday Life,' Chicago, Aldine, 1970, pp.3-44.
87 See H.R. Wagner's introduction to Alfred Schutz, 'On Phenomenology and Social Relations. Selected Writings,' University of Chicago Press, 1970, p.47.
88 Berger and Luckmann, op. cit., p.13.
89 Ibid., p.3.
90 Ibid., pp.13-14.
91 J.D. Douglas, op. cit., p.32.
92 H. Garfinkel, 'Studies in Ethnomethodology,' Englewood Cliffs, N.J., Prentice-Hall, 1967, p.11.
93 See S. Mennell, 'Sociological Theory: Uses and Unities,' New York, Praeger Publishers, 1974, p.52.
94 H. Marcuse, 'One-Dimensional Man,' Boston, Beacon Press, 1966, p.174.
95 Ibid., p.181.
96 N.K. Denzin, Symbolic interactionism and ethnomethodology, in J.D. Douglas, op. cit., p.262.
97 P. Berger, B. Berger and H. Kellner, 'The Homeless Mind,' New York, Vintage Books, 1974, p.196.

4 THE INTELLECTUALS AND THE DYNAMICS OF HISTORICAL BLOCS

1 H. Marcuse, 'One-Dimensional Man,' Boston, Beacon Press, 1964, p.xiii.
2 On this see also J.-M., Piotte, 'La pensée politique de Gramsci,' Paris, Editions Anthropos, 1970, chs 1 and 2, G. Nardone, 'Il Pensiero di Gramsci,' Bari, De Donato, 1971, pp.225-60, H. Portelli,'Gramsci et le Bloc Historique,' Paris, Presses Universitaires de France, 1972, ch.4, E. Garin, Politica e cultura in Gramsci (il problema degli intellettuali), in P. Rossi, 'Gramsci e la Cultura Contemporanea,' Rome, Editori Riuniti-Istituto Gramsci, vol.I, 1969, pp.37-74 and A.R. Buzzi, 'La Teoria Politica de Antonio Gramsci, 'Barcelona, Editorial Fontanella, 1969, pp.178-190. In English, see the informative article by J. Karabel, Revolutionary Contradictions: Antonio Gramsci and the Problem of Intellectuals, 'Politics and Society,' 1976, vol.6, no.2, pp.123-72.
3 R. Hofstadter, 'Anti-intellectualism in American Life,' New York, Harper & Row, 1966, pp.233-52.
4 Among others see P. Berger and T. Luckmann, 'The Social Construction of Reality,' New York, Doubleday, 1966, p.13f. and A. Schutz, 'Collected Papers,' The Hague, Nijhoff, vol.1, 1962, p.149.
5 R. Merton, 'Social Theory and Social Structure,' Chicago, Ill.,

Free Press, 1957, pp.219-22.
6 S.M. Lipset, 'Political Man: The Social Bases of Politics,' Garden City,
   New York, Anchor Books, 1963, pp.332-71; E. Shils, 'The Intellectual
   between Tradition and Modernity,' The Hague, Mouton, 1961 and L. Coser,
   'Men of Ideas,' New York, Free Press, 1965.
7 Coser, op. cit.; F. Znaniechi, 'The Social Role of the Man of Knowledge,'
   New York, Octagon Books, 1965; R. Dahrendorf, 'Society and Democracy
   in Germany,' Garden City, New York, Anchor Books, 1969 and K. von
   Beyme, Intellectuals, intelligentsia, in 'Marxism, Communism and Western
   Society: A Comparative Encyclopedia,' Herder & Herder, 1973, vol.IV,
   pp.301-12.
8 S.H. Hughes, 'Consciousness and Society,' New York, Knopf, 1958.
9 Coser, op. cit., Lipset, op. cit.
10 L.S. Feuer, 'Marx and the Intellectuals: a set of post-ideological essays,'
   New York, Anchor Books, 1969, pp.216-28 and 'The Scientific Intellectual,'
   New York, Vintage Books, 1963.
11 K. Marx and F. Engels, 'Selected Works,' Moscow, Foreign Languages
   Publishing House, vol.1, 1958, p.36. One finds in Marx and Engels the
   absence of a complete analysis of the intellectuals in socialist revolution
   with the exception of a statement in the 'Communist Manifesto': 'a
   portion of bourgeois ideologists who have raised themselves to the level
   of comprehending theoretically the historical movement as a "whole" have
   gone over to the proletariat.' For the reasons of such absence see Feuer,
   op. cit., pp.53-69. See also von Beyme, op. cit., which contains the
   most complete bibliography on the problem of intellectuals.
12 Mao Tse-tung, 'Selected Works,' Peking, Foreign Languages Press, 1971,
   p.457.
13 K. Mannheim, 'Ideology and Utopia,' trans. L. Wirth and E. Shils,
   New York, Harcourt, Brace World, Inc., 1936, p.102.
14 See E. Shils, The intellectuals and the powers, in P. Rieff, 'On
   Intellectuals,' Garden City, New York, Anchor Books, 1970, p.27f
   and Lipset, op. cit., p.333.
15 Gramsci did not produce a systematic work on intellectuals despite the
   title of one of his volumes, 'Gli Intellettuali e la organizzazione della
   cultura.' However, all his notes refer directly or indirectly to this theme.
16 PN, p.8 and EC, Q.12, vol.III, p.1516.
17 PN, p.9 and EC, Q.12, vol.III, pp.1550-1.
18 For numerous Gramsci scholars, the concept of historical blocs is the
   central theme of his thought. See A. Pizzorno, Sul metodo di Gramsci:
   dalla storiografia alla scienza politica, in Rossi, op. cit., vol.2, p.117
   and H. Portelli, op. cit., p.10.
19 A more systematic analysis of these ideas can be found in Nardone,
   op. cit., pp.39-361.
20 PN, p.331 and EC, Q.11, vol.II, pp.1383-4.
21 PN, pp.332-3 and EC, Q.11, vol.II, pp.1384-5.
22 PN, p.329 and EC, Q.11, vol.II, p.1381.
23 PN, p.5 and EC, Q.12, vol.III, p.1513.
24 PN, pp.452-3 and EC, Q.11, vol.II, pp.1406-7.
25 PN, p.5 and EC, Q.12, vol.III, p.1513.
26 PN, pp.6-7 and EC, Q.12, vol.III, p.1514.
27 Nardone, op. cit., p.236.
28 Gramsci's analysis of bourgeois revolutions has been discussed by
   G. Galasso, Gramsci e i problemi della storia italiana, in Rossi, op. cit.,
   vol.1, pp.305-54. For the specific cases of France, England and Germany,
   see Portelli, op. cit., pp.68-124 and Piotte, op. cit., pp.65-6.
29 PN, p.7 and EC, Q.12, vol.III, p.1515.
30 See Gramsci's notes on French politics in EC, Q.13, vol.III, pp.1635-50.
31 PN, p.10 and EC, Q.12, vol.III, p.1517.
32 EC, Q.6, vol.II, pp.695 and 719. See also EC, Q.5, vol.I, p.675.
33 Piotte, op. cit., p.15f.
34 PN, p.60 and EC, Q.19, vol.III, p.2012.

35 PN, p.105 and EC, Q.15, vol.III, pp.1822-3.
36 EC, Q.8, vol.II, pp.962-4.
37 See M. Salvadori, Gramsci e la questione meridionale, in Rossi, op. cit., vol.I, pp.391-438.
38 PN, p.83 and EC, Q.19, vol.III, p.2033.
39 PN, p.270 and EC, Q.15, vol.III, pp.1775-6.
40 PN, p.18 and EC, Q.12, vol.III, p.1526.
41 The case of capitalist development in the United States also illustrates Gramsci's thesis that the presence of a vast stratum of intellectuals tends to re-enforce the complex of the vast superstructure within a given historical bloc at the expense of the 'organicity' of its dependence upon the economic structure. Whereas in Europe the presence of a great number of traditional intellectuals provides a series of moral, intellectual, political, and economic checks generating 'opposition to speedy progress,' in the case of the United States one finds a surprising 'equilibrium,' among all intellectuals, Gramsci notes. Here, the 'lack of vast sedimentations of traditional intellectuals' has encouraged the development of a powerful superstructure organically linked to the industrial base. The United States is a case of firm equilibrium between the State and Civil Society. The capitalist system of production free from 'viscous parasitic sedimentations' of past history is able to develop a unified political, economic and cultural bloc. To be sure, critical intellectuals do exist, but their critical posture does not represent an inorganic element within the hegemonic structure of capitalism. Their critical outlook allows them to temporarily withdraw from the dominant ideology, so as to embrace it more intimately in the final analysis. See EC, Q.5, vol.I, pp.633-4.
   In the case of Central and South America, the 'industrial base is restricted and has not developed complicated superstructures' due to the presence of two categories of traditional intellectuals, the clergy and the military. Because of the rural origin of intellectuals, and predominance of latifundia, these intellectuals are tied organically to the clergy and landowning class. As a result, Gramsci writes, we have a situation in which 'the secular and bourgeois element has not reached the stage of being able to subordinate clerical and militaristic influence and interests to the secular politics of the modern state.' PN, p.22 and EC, Q.12, vol.III, p.1529.
42 PN, p.12 and EC, Q.12, vol.III, p.1518.
43 PN, p.12 and EC, Q.12, vol.III, p.1519.
44 PN, p.433 and EC, Q.11, vol.II, p.1423.
45 Ibid.
46 PN, p.15 and EC, Q.12, vol.III, p.1521.
47 Piotte, op. cit., p.62.
48 PN, p.20 and EC, Q.12, vol.III, pp.1525-6.
49 See M.A. Macciocchi, 'Pour Gramsci,' Paris, Editions du Seuil, 1974, ch.7.
50 For the concept of the party as a 'collective intellectual' see P. Togliatti, Il leninismo nel pensiero e nell'azione di A. Gramsci, in 'Studi Gramsciani. Atti del convegno tenuto a Roma nei giorni 11-13 gennaio, 1958,' Rome, Editori Riuniti-Istituto Gramsci, 1969, pp.15-35.
51 EC, Q.10, vol.II, p.1221.
52 PN, p.6 and EC, Q.12, vol.III, p.1513.
53 PN, p.333 and EC, Q.11, vol.II, p.1385.
54 PN, p.334 and EC, Q.11, vol.II, p.1386.
55 PN, p.10 and EC, Q.12, vol.III, p.1551.
56 Ibid.
57 PN, p.335 and EC, Q.11, vol.II, p.1387.
58 The role of the party is an important element in Gramsci's theory. A discussion of the Gramscian conception of the role of the party in socialist transformation can be found in A. Sassoon-Showstack, 'Gramsci's Politics,' London, Croom Helm, 1980.
59 PN, p.335 and EC, Q.11, vol.II, p.1387.

60 See ch.1 of this study and Boggs, 'Gramsci's Marxism,' London, Pluto Press, 1976, and the Hegelian interpretation of Gramsci by M.A. Finocchiaro, Gramsci's Crocean Marxism, 'Telos,' vol.41, 1979, pp.17–32. Very few have analyzed Gramsci's conception of Marxism as a religion, philosophy and science at the same time. See ibid., p.22.

61 PN, p.184 and EC, Q.13, vol.III, p.1587.

62 N. Bobbio, Gramsci e la concezione della società civile, in Rossi, op. cit., vol.1, pp.75–100; Portelli, op. cit., pp.47–67 and C. Boggs, Gramsci's 'Prison Notebooks,' 'Socialist Revolution,' vol.11, 1972, pp.79–118.

63 This is the theoretical position of many associated with the Journal 'Telos'. On this see, for instance, R. Giacchetti, Antonio Gramsci: the subjective revolution, in 'The Unknown Dimension,' ed. Dick Howard and K.E. Klare, New York, Basic Books, 1972, pp.147–68 and P. Piccone, Gramsci's Hegelian Marxism, 'Political Theory,' vol.2, 1974, pp.32–45.

64 See particularly PN, p.389.

65 See A. Broccoli, 'Antonio Gramsci e l'Educazione come Egemonia,' Firenza, La Nuova Italia Editrice, 1972, p.104. See also, in the same vein, H. Entwistle, 'Antonio Gramsci: Conservative Schooling for Radical Politics,' London, Routledge & Kegan Paul, 1979.

66 A. Gramsci, 'Scritti Giovanili,' Turin, Einaudi, 1958, p.24 and A. Gramsci, 'Selections from Political Writings, 1910–1920,' trans. J. Mathews and ed. Q. Hoare, New York, International Publishers, 1977, p.12.

67 L. Feuer, op. cit., 68.

68 Gramsci, 'Scritti Giovanili,' p.24 and Gramsci, 'Selections from Political Writings,' p.11.

69 A. Gramsci, 'L'Ordine Nuovo (1919–1920),' Turin, Einaudi, 1955, op. cit., p.157 and Gramsci, 'Selections from Political Writings,' p.333.

70 PN, p.418 and EC, Q.11, vol.II, p.1505.

71 Ibid.

72 Berger and Luckmann, op. cit., p.116.

73 See M. Weber, 'From Max Weber: Essays in Sociology,' trans. H.H. Gerth and C.W. Mills, New York, Oxford University Press, 1946, p.243.

74 I.M. Zeitlin, 'Ideology and the Development of Sociological Theory,' Englewood Cliffs, N.J., Prentice-Hall, 1968, pp.111–20.

75 Weber, op. cit., p.50.

76 E. Shils, Intellectuals, in 'International Encyclopedia of Social Sciences,' New York, Macmillan, vol.7, 1968, pp.399–414.

77 Berger and Luckmann, op. cit., p.110.

78 EC, Q.13, vol.III, p.1650.

79 EC, Q.15, vol.III, pp.1770–1.

80 PN, p.189 and EC, Q.13, vol.III, p.1634.

81 PN, p.188 and EC, Q.13, vol.III, p.1634.

82 Gramsci, 'Scritti Giovanili,' p.206. In English see P. Cavalcanti and P. Piccone, 'History, Philosophy and Culture in the Young Gramsci,' St Louis, Telos Press, 1975, p.81.

83 I.L. Horowitz, 'Foundations of Political Sociology,' New York, Harper & Row, 1972, p.xvif and F. Bon and M.-A. Burnier, 'Les Nouveaux Intellectuels,' Paris, Cujas, 1966, p.108.

84 Ibid., p.18.

85 Ibid., p.217f.

86 C. Anderson, 'The Political Economy of Social Class,' Englewood Cliffs, N.J., Prentice-Hall, 1974, pp.282–332.

87 Horowitz, op. cit., p.513.

88 Ibid., p.522f.

5 HEGEMONY IN MARXIST THEORY AND PRACTICE

1 Many have studied the notion of hegemony in Gramsci, but few have analyzed it in relation to the whole range of concepts of his theory. When the preoccupation is that of assessing the Marxist or Leninist

orthodoxy of Gramsci, the interpretations tend to be partial and misleading. This is the case, for instance, with P. Anderson, The Antinomies of Antonio Gramsci, 'New Left Review,' 1977, no.100 and A. Sassoon-Showstack, 'Gramsci's Politics,' London, Croom Helm, 1980. Hegemony is not viewed in the dynamic of the whole historical process, of which the phase of socialist transition is just a part. The philosophical aspects of Gramsci's notion of hegemony has been dealt only by some Italian and French commentators. In our opinion, Nardone has provided the most comprehensive treatment of such a notion.

2 E. Hobsbawm, Dall'Italia all'Europa, 'Il Contemporaneo' (Rinascita), 25 Jul 1975, p.16.
3 L. Gruppi, Il concetto di egemonia, 'Prassi Rivoluzionaria. Critica Marxista,' no.3, 1967, p.82.
4 A. Gramsci, 'L'Ordine Nuovo,' 15 March 1924.
5 PN, p.357 and EC, Q.7, vol.II, p.886.
6 PN, p.365 and EC, Q.10, vol.II, p.1250.
7 A. Gramsci, 'L'Ordine Nuovo,' Turin, Einaudi, 1955, p.137 and A. Gramsci, 'Selections from Political Writings, 1910-1920,' trans. J. Mathews and ed. Q. Hoare, New York, International Publishers, 1977, p.306.
8 See C. Boggs, Gramsci's 'Prison Notebooks,' 'Socialist Revolution,' vol.11, 1972, p.110.
9 J.-M. Piotte, 'La Pensée Politique de Gramsci,' Paris, Editions Anthropos, 1970, pp.170-5.
10 PN, p.240 and EC, Q.14, vol.III, pp.1728-9.
11 Piotte, op. cit., pp.174-5.
12 PN, pp.236-7 and EC, Q.7, vol.II, p.866.
13 Piotte, op. cit., p.169.
14 See V. Gerrantana's remarks at the Gramscian studies congress in Rome, in 'Studi Gramsciani. Atti del convegno tenuto a Roma, nei giorni 11-13 gennaio 1958,' Rome, Editori Riuniti-Istituto Gramsci, 1969, p.169.
15 N. Auciello, 'Socialismo ed Egemonia in Gramsci e Togliatti,' Bari, De Donato, 1974, p.58.
16 See H. Portelli, 'Gramsci et le Bloc Historique,' Paris, Presses Universitaires de France, 1972, 68; N. Bobbio, Gramsci e la concezione della società civile, in P. Rossi (ed.), 'Gramsci e la Cultura Contemporanea,' Editori Riuniti-Istituto Gramsci, vol.1, 1969, pp.90-4; A.R. Buzzi, 'La Teoria Politica di Antonio Gramsci,' Barcelona, Editorial Fontanella, 1969, p.226; Piotte, op. cit., p.250 and M.A. Macciocchi, 'Pour Gramsci,' Paris, Editions du Seuil, 1974, p.158.
17 A. Gramsci, Some aspects of the Southern Question, in A. Gramsci, 'Selections from Political Writings, 1921-26,' New York, International Publishers, 1978, pp.441-62.
18 A. Gramsci, 'The Modern Prince,' New York, International Publishers, 1967, p.30.
19 Ibid., p.36.
20 Bobbio, op. cit., p.95.
21 PN, pp.57-8 and EC, Q.19, vol.III, pp.2010-1.
22 Portelli, op. cit., p.68 and A. Davidson, The varying seasons of Gramscian studies, 'Political Studies,' vol.20, no.4, 1972, pp.448-61.
23 P. Togliatti, Gramsci e il leninismo, in 'Studi Gramsciani,' op. cit., p.443.
24 P. Togliatti, Il leninismo nel pensiero e nell'azione di A. Gramsci, in 'Studi Gramsciani,' op. cit., p.24.
25 Gruppi, op. cit., pp.80-1 and 'Il concetto di Egemonia in Gramsci,' Rome, Editori Riuniti, 1972, pp.88-9 and 99f.
26 PN, p.106 and EC, Q.15, vol.III, p.1823.
27 S. Cambareri, Il concetto di egemonia del proletariato, in 'Studi Gramsciani,' op. cit., p.90f.
28 Portelli, op. cit., pp.70-2.
29 Piotte, op. cit., pp.126-7.
30 G. Tamburrano, Gramsci e l'egemonia del proletariato, in 'Studi

Gramsciani,' op. cit., p.280f.
31 Bobbio, op. cit., pp.93-7. A translation of this article in English is now available. See Gramsci and the conception of civil society, in C. Mouffe (ed.), 'Gramsci and Marxist Theory,' London, Routledge & Kegan Paul, 1979, pp.21-47.
32 N. Auciello, op. cit., p.91, note 101.
33 PN, p.264 and EC, Q.6, vol.II, p.800.
34 PN, p.260 and EC, Q.8, vol.II, p.937.
35 PN, p.60 and EC, Q.19, vol.III, pp.2012-3.
36 EC, Q.10, vol.II, p.1249.
37 G. Nardone, 'Il Pensiero di Gramsci,' Bari, De Donato, 1971, p.127.
38 Ibid., p.130f.
39 PN, p.182 and EC, Q.13, vol.III, p.1584.
40 Nardone, op. cit., p.135.
41 G.A. Williams, The concept of 'egemonia' in the thought of Antonio Gramsci: some notes on interpretation, 'Journal of the History of Ideas,' no.4, 1960, p.587.
42 See J. Cammett, 'Antonio Gramsci and the Origins of Italian Communism,' Stanford University Press, 1967, p.205.
43 On this, see N. Badaloni, Il fondamento teorico dello storicismo gramsciano, in Rossi, op. cit., vol.1, pp.166-7.
44 PN, p.365 and EC, Q.10, vol.II, p.1250.
45 'Hegel's Philosophy of Right,' trans. T.M. Knox, Oxford, Clarendon Press, 1965, p.10.
46 Ibid., p.160.
47 Ibid., p.189.
48 Engels, Feuerbach and the End of Classical German Philosophy, in Marx and Engels, 'Selected Works,' Moscow, Foreign Languages Publishing House, 1958, vol.2, pp.394-5. See also K. Marx's 'Preface to the Critique of Political Economy,' in ibid., p.362.
49 See Marx and Engels, 'The German Ideology,' ed. C.J. Arthur, New York, International Publishers, 1972, p.57.
50 See S. Avineri, 'The Social and Political Thought of Karl Marx,' London, Cambridge University Press, 1969, p.35.
51 N. Bobbio, op. cit., p.85 and Portelli, op. cit., p.14.
52 PN, p.12 and EC, Q.12, vol.III, p.1518.
53 Portelli, op. cit., p.29.
54 Ibid., p.30.
55 PN, pp.264-5 and EC, Q.6, vol.II, p.800.
56 Nardone, op. cit., pp.148-58.
57 PN, p.244 and EC, Q.15, vol.III, p.1765.
58 PN, p.261 and EC, Q.6, vol.II, p.801.
59 PN, p.160 and EC, Q.13, vol.III, p.1590.
60 PN, p.262 and EC, Q.6, vol.II, pp.763-4.
61 Bobbio, op. cit., p.84.
62 Portelli, op. cit., p.38.
63 PN, p.268 and EC, Q.8, vol.II, p.1020.
64 Ibid.
65 PN, pp.258-9 and EC, Q.8, vol.II, p.1049.
66 Bobbio, op. cit., p.98.
67 K. Marx and F. Engels, op. cit., vol.1, p.363.
68 Ibid., vol.2, pp.488-9.
69 Bobbio, op. cit., p.88f.
70 PN, pp.366-7 and EC, Q.10, vol.II, p.1244.
71 J. Texier, Gramsci, théoricien des superstructures, sur le concept de la société civile, 'La Pensée,' 1968, no.139, p.47. This important article is now available in English. See Gramsci, theoretician of the super-structures, in C. Mouffe (ed.), op. cit., pp.48-79.
72 PN, p.377 and EC, Q.7, vol.II, p.869. On this see also Portelli, op. cit., p.63.
73 EC, Q.10, vol.II, p.1321.

74 PN, p.366 and EC, Q.8, vol.II, p.1051.
75 PN, pp.407-8 and EC, Q.7, vol.II, p.871.
76 Portelli, op. cit., p.67.
77 PN, p.466 and EC, Q.11, vol.II, p.1443.
78 PN, p.408 and EC, Q.7, vol.II, p.872.
79 See E. Agazzi, Filosofia della prassi e filosofia dello spirito, in
   A. Caracciolo and G. Scalia, 'La Città Futura,' Milan, Feltrinelli, 1959,
   p.223.
80 EC, Q.10, vol.II, p.1300.
81 EC, Q.10, vol.II, pp.1224 and 1319.
82 EC, Q.10, vol.II, p.1319.
83 Nardone, op. cit., p.332.
84 Ibid., p.448.
85 PN, p.466 and EC, Q.11, vol.II, p.1443.
86 Nardone, op. cit., p.357.
87 PN, p.367 and EC, Q.10, vol.II, p.1244.
88 Marx and Engels, op. cit., vol.1, p.363.
89 Nardone, op. cit., p.443.
90 Buzzi, op. cit., p.184.
91 PN, p.350 and EC, Q.10, vol.II, p.1331.
92 PN, p.360 and EC, Q.10, vol.II, p.1338.
93 Antonio Gramsci, 'Lettres de Prison,' Paris, Gallimard, 1971, p.444.
94 For a discussion of Gramsci's pedagogy see L. Borghi, Educazione e
   scuola in Gramsci, in Rossi, op. cit., vol.1, pp.207-38 and A. Broccoli,
   'Antonio Gramsci e l'Educazione come Egemonia,' Firenze, La Nuova
   Italia Editrice, 1972.
95 L. Gallino, Gramsci e le scienze sociali, in Rossi, op. cit., p.106.
96 L. Borghi, Educazione e scuola in Gramsci, in Rossi, op. cit., pp.224-5.
97 PN, p.324 and EC, Q.11, vol.II, p.1376.
98 EC, Q.12, vol.III, pp.1540-1.
99 PN, p.286 and EC, Q.22, vol.III, p.2146.
100 M. Salvadori, 'Gramsci e il problema storico della democrazia,' Turin,
   Piccola Biblioteca Einaudi, 1973, pp.154-61.
101 PN, p.280 and EC, Q.22, vol.III, p.2140.
102 See Introduction by translators, PN, p.277.
103 PN, p.285 and EC, Q.22, vol.III, p.2146.
104 PN, p.293 and EC, Q.22, vol.III, p.2157.
105 Buzzi, op. cit., pp.185-6 and M.A. Manacorda, 'Il principio educativo in
   Gramsci,' Rome, Armando Armando Editore, 1970, p.220.
106 PN, p.302 and EC, Q.22, vol.III, p.2165.
107 Ibid.
108 PN, p.298 and EC, Q.22, vol.III, p.2160.
109 PN, p.281 and EC, Q.22, vol.III, p.2141.
110 Antonio Gramsci, 'Letters from Prison,' trans. Lynne Lawner, New York,
   Harper Colophon Books, 1973, p.183.
111 PN, p.281 and EC, Q.22, vol.III, p.2141.
112 PN, p.317 and EC, Q.22, vol.III, p.2179.
113 EC, Q.9, vol.II, p.1138.
114 PN, p.303 and EC, Q.22, vol.III, p.2166.
115 EC, Q.7, vol.II, p.862.
116 PN, p.259 and EC, Q.8, vol.II, p.1050.

6 SCIENCE, POLITICAL PRAXIS AND HISTORICISM

1 R.G. Collingwood, 'The Idea of History,' New York, Oxford University
   Press, 1956, p.84.
2 Ibid., p.165.
3 L. Colletti, 'From Rousseau to Lenin: Studies in Ideology and Society,'
   New York, Monthly Review Press, 1972, p.30.
4 H. Fleischer, 'Marxism and History,' New York, Harper & Row, 1973, p.13.

5 We have been referring for this brief survey to Collingwood, op. cit., pp.190-204.
6 PN, p.426 and EC, Q.11, vol.II, p.1432.
7 See the excellent treatment of this problem by I. Fetscher, 'Marx and Marxism,' New York, Herder & Herder, 1971, pp.148-81.
8 PN, p.390 and EC, Q.16, vol.III, p.1855.
9 J. Texier, 'Gramsci,' Paris, Editions Seghers, 1966, p.36.
10 PN, p.462 and EC, Q.11, vol.II, p.1435.
11 Ibid.
12 Cited in Z.A. Jordon, The dialectical materialism of Lenin, in J.V. Downton and D.K. Hart (ed.), 'Perspectives on Political Philosophy,' Hinsdale, Ill., Dryden Press, 1973, vol.3, p.37.
13 PN, p.465 and EC, Q.11, vol.II, p.1442.
14 PN, p.466 and EC, Q.11, vol.II, p.1443.
15 PN, p.467 and EC, Q.11, vol.II, p.1443.
16 G. Nardone, 'Il Pensiero di Gramsci,' Bari, De Donato, 1971, p.464.
17 PN, p.446 and EC, Q.11, vol.II, p.1416.
18 PN, p.442 and EC, Q.11, vol.II, p.1413.
19 M. Tronti, Alcune questioni intorno al marxismo di Gramsci, in 'Studi Gramsciani. Atti del convegno tenuto a Roma nei giorni 11-13 gennaio 1958,' Rome, Editori Riuniti-Istituto Gramsci, 1969, p.314.
20 PN, p.446 and EC, Q.11, vol.II, p.1448.
21 PN, p.368 and EC, Q.10, vol.II. p.1290.
22 PN, p.448 and EC, Q.11, vol.II, p.1449.
23 PN, pp.445-6 and EC, Q.11, vol.II, p.1416.
24 PN, p.396 and EC, Q.16, vol.III, p.1861.
25 PN, p.442 and EC, Q.11, vol.II, p.1413.
26 PN, p.444 and EC, Q.11, vol.II, p.1415.
27 On the meanings of the notion of dialectic in Gramsci, see N. Bobbio, Nota sulla dialettica in Gramsci, in 'Studi Gramsciani,' op. cit., pp.73-86 and Texier, op. cit., p.94f.
28 PN, p.372 and EC, Q.11, vol.II, p.1492.
29 See Fetscher, op. cit., p.68.
30 Jordon, op. cit., p.68.
31 Ibid., p.55.
32 See A. Sabetti, Il rapporto uomo-natura nel pensiero del Gramsci e la fondazione della scienza, in 'Studi Gramsciani,' op. cit., p.247.
33 K. Marx, 'The Economic and Philosophical Manuscripts of 1844,' ed. D.J. Struik, New York, International Publishers, 1972, p.143.
34 PN, p.442 and EC, Q.11, vol.II, p.1413.
35 PN, p.431 and EC, vol.II, pp.1447-8.
36 EC, Q.11, vol.II, p.1457. I am citing the English translation of Gramsci's notes on 'Science and "scientific" ideologies,' published in 'Telos,' 1979, no.41, p.154.
37 EC, Q.11, vol.II, p.1456 and 'Telos,' no.41, p.154.
38 EC, Q.11, vol.II, p.1458 and 'Telos,' no.41, pp.154-5.
39 PN, pp.457-8 and EC, Q.11, vol.II, p.1421.
40 PN, p.461 and EC, Q.17, vol.III, p.1926.
41 EC, Q.11, vol.II, p.1456 and 'Telos,' no.41, p.154.
42 Ibid., p.1457 and 'Telos,' no.41, p.155.
43 PN, p.352 and EC, Q.10, vol.II, p.1345.
44 EC, Q.6, vol.II, p.826.
45 Ibid., p.817.
46 PN, p.446 and EC, Q.11, vol.II, p.1449. Of the same opinion are the authors S. Hall, B. Lumley and G. McLennan, Politics and ideology: Gramsci, in 'On Ideology,' Centre for Contemporary Cultural Studies, London, Hutchinson, 1977, p.55.
47 PN, p.446 and EC, Q.11, vol.II, p.1416.
48 EC, Q.11, vol.II, pp.1455-6.
49 Ibid., p.1457 and 'Telos,' no.41, p.154.
50 See Nardone, op. cit., p.472.

51 Ibid., p.475.
52 See R. Guiducci, Filosofia della prassi e ricerca scientifica, in A. Caracciolo and G. Scalia, 'La Città Futura,' Milan, Feltrinelli, 1959, pp.290-1.
53 A. Schaff, 'Langage et Connaissance,' Paris, Editions Anthropos, 1969, p.305. See also the excellent article by S. Hall, The hinterland of science: ideology and the 'sociology of knowledge,' in Hall et al., op. cit., pp.9-32.
54 K. Marx and F. Engels, 'Selected Works,' Moscow, Foreign Languages Publishing House, 1958, vol.2, p.403.
55 PN, p.346 and EC, Q.11, vol.II, p.1486.
56 A. Gramsci, 'Scritti Giovanili,' Turin, Einaudi, 1958, p.85.
57 PN, p.346 and EC, Q.11, vol.II, p.1486.
58 Gramsci, 'Scritti Giovanili,' p.154.
59 PN, p.445 and EC, vol.II, p.1416.
60 Ibid.
61 PN, p.446 and EC, Q.11, vol.II, p.1416.
62 Ibid.
63 Nardone, op. cit., p.471.
64 EC, Q.10, vol.II, p.1226.
65 PN, p.445 and EC, Q.11, vol.II, pp.1415-16.
66 Guiducci, op. cit., p.279.
67 N. Badaloni, Gramsci storicista di fronte al marxismo contemporaneo, 'Prassi Rivoluzionaria Critica Marxista,' vol.3, 1967, p.100, note 2.
68 L. Althusser and E. Balibar, Marxism is not a historicism, in 'Reading Capital,' New York, Pantheon Books, 1970, p.119. For a discussion of ideology and historicism in Gramsci and the structuralist appropriation of Gramsci by Althusser and Poulantzas, see S. Hall et al., op. cit.
69 Ibid., p.136.
70 Ibid., p.137.
71 Ibid., pp.139-40.
72 L. Althusser, 'For Marx,' New York, Pantheon Books, 1969, p.223.
73 Ibid., p.231.
74 Ibid., pp.235-6.
75 PN, p.377 and EC, Q.11, vol.II, p.869.
76 Althusser, op. cit., p.168.
77 PN, p.339 and EC, Q.11, vol.II, p.1393.
78 Althusser and Balibar, op. cit., p.59.
79 PN, p.365 and EC, Q.15, vol.III, p.1780.
80 PN, p.334 and EC, Q.11, vol.II, p.1386.
81 PN, p.369 and EC, Q.10, vol.II, p.1267.
82 Ibid.
83 PN, p.335 and EC, Q.11, vol.II, pp.1386-7.
84 Nardone, op. cit., pp.481-98.
85 PN, p.438 and EC, Q.11, vol.II, p.1403.

7 LANGUAGE, POLITICAL PRAXIS AND HISTORICISM

1 See B. Anglani, La critica letteraria in Gramsci, in 'Prassi Rivoluzionaria Critica Marxista,' vol.3, 1967, pp.208-30 and G. Petronio, Gramsci e la critica letteraria, in 'Studi Gramsciani.' Atti del convegno tenuto a Roma nei giorni 11-13 gennaio 1958,' Rome, Editori Riuniti-Istituto Gramsci, 1969, pp.223-41.
2 A. Schaff, 'Langage et connaissance,' Paris, Editions Anthropos, 1967, p.199.
3 K. Marx, and F. Engels, 'The German Ideology,' ed. C.J. Arthur, New York, International Publishers, 1972, p.51.
4 Letter of Engels to J. Bloc in K. Marx and F. Engels, 'Selected Works,' Moscow, Foreign Languages Publishing House, 1958, vol.2, p.489.
5 For the best exposition of Marr's linguistic theories, see L.L. Thomas,

'The Linguistic Theories of N.J. Marr,' Berkeley, University of California Press, 1967.
6 J. Stalin, Marxism in linguistics, in B. Lang and F. Williams (eds), 'Marxism and Art,' New York, David McKay, 1972, pp.80-7.
7 See W.R. Schmalstieg, Structural linguistics in the Soviet Union, in A. Simirenko, 'Social Thought in the Soviet Union,' Chicago, Quadrangle Books, 1969, p.361.
8 So writes L. Rosiello, Problemi linguistici negli scritti di Gramsci, in P. Rossi, 'Gramsci e la Cultura Contemporanea,' Rome, Editori Riuniti-Istituto Gramsci, 1970, vol.2, p.354.
9 A. Gramsci, 'Letters from Prison,' trans. and ed. Lynne Lawner, New York, Harper Colophon Books, 1975, p.80. In this same letter Gramsci reveals his plan to write a work für ewig on 4 major subjects, one of which is a study of comparative linguistics from a theoretical and methodological standpoint.
10 Schaff, op. cit., pp.3-27.
11 E. Sapir, 'Language,' New York, Harvest, 1949, pp.224-5.
12 EC, Q.6, vol.II, p.738.
13 Ibid.
14 See Rosiello, op. cit., p.362.
15 See J.O. Hertzler, 'A Sociology of Language,' New York, Random House, 1965, pp.10-13.
16 EC, Q.3, vol.I, p.352.
17 EC, Q.6, vol.II, p.700.
18 Ibid.
19 Gramsci severely criticized Bartoli for co-operating with Bertoni in the compilation of a 'Manual of Linguistics,' whose theoretical part was written by Bertoni. For a more detailed analysis of the relationship between Bartoli, Bertoni and Croce on the problem of linguistics, see Rosiello, op. cit., pp.363-6.
20 EC, Q.29, vol.III, p.2342.
21 PN, p.451 and EC, Q.11, vol.II, p.1427.
22 PN, p.453 and EC, Q.11, vol.II, p.1407.
23 PN, pp.451-2 and EC, Q.11, vol.II, p.1428.
24 PN, p.349 and EC, Q.10, vol.II, p.1331.
25 PN, p.349 and EC, Q.10, vol.II, p.1330.
26 EC, Q.29, vol.III, p.2346.
27 EC, Q.6, vol.II, p.739.
28 PN, p.450 and EC, Q.11, vol.II, p.1438.
29 EC, Q.29, vol.III, p.2341.
30 Ibid., pp.2341-2.
31 Ibid.
32 Rosiello, op. cit., p.358.
33 EC, Q.29, vol.III, p.2343.
34 Ibid.
35 Ibid.
36 See Gramsci's note on Grammar and technique, in EC, Q.29, vol.III, p.2348f.
37 L. Paggi, 'Antonio Gramsci e il Moderno Principe,' Rome, Editori Riuniti, 1970, p.76.
38 EC, Q.3, vol.I, p.353.
39 A. Gramsci, 'Scritti Giovanili,' Turin, Einaudi, 1958, p.176 and P. Cavalcanti and P. Piccone (eds), 'History, Philosophy and Culture in the Young Gramsci,' St Louis, Telos Press, 1975, pp.29-33.
40 Ibid.
41 Paggi, op. cit., p.77.
42 A. Gramsci, 'Scritti Giovanili,' p.178 and 'History, Philosophy and Culture in the Young Gramsci,' p.33.
43 EC, Q.3, vol.I, pp.353-4.
44 Ibid.
45 EC, Q.5, vol.I, p.640.

46 Ibid., p.645.

8 AESTHETICS, POLITICAL PRAXIS AND HISTORICISM

1 G. Della Volpe, Intervention at the Gramsci Congress in 'Studi Gramsciani. Atti del convegno tenuto a Roma nei giorni 11-13 gennaio 1958,' Rome, Editori Riuniti-Istituto Gramsci, 1969, pp.543-52.

2 The most salient studies on Gramsci's aesthetics are those of Gianni Scalia, Metodologia e sociologia della letteratura in Gramsci, in A. Caracciolo and G. Scalia, 'La Città Futura,' Milan, Feltrinelli, 1959, pp.331-68; B. Anglani, La critica lettararia in Gramsci, in 'Prassi Rivoluzionaria. Crticia Marxista,' vol.3, 1967; G. Petronio, Gramsci e la critica letteraria, in 'Studi Gramsciani,' op. cit.; N. Sapegno, Gramsci e i problemi della letteratura, in P. Rossi,'Gramsci e la Cultura Contemporanea,' Rome, Editori Riuniti-Istituto Gramsci, 1969, vol.1, pp.265-77; N. Stipcevic, 'Gramsci e i problemi letterari,' Milano, Mursia, 1968. See also R. Williams, 'Marxism and Literature,' London, Oxford University Press, 1977.

3 K. Marx, 'Introduction to the Critique of Political Economy,' in B. Lang and F. Williams, 'Marxism and Art,' New York, David McKay, 1972, p.37.

4 Ibid., p.38.

5 Ibid.

6 H. Arvon, 'Marxist Esthetics,' trans. H. Lane, Ithaca, Cornell University Press, 1973, p.12.

7 G. Plekhanov, On art for art's sake, in D. Craig, 'Marxists on Literature, An Anthology,' Harmondsworth, Penguin Books, 1975, pp.272-81.

8 V.I. Lenin, Party organization and party literature, in Lang and Williams, op. cit., p.56.

9 See L. Trotsky, Proletarian culture and proletarian art, in Lang and Williams, op. cit., p.73.

10 See the Introduction in Craig, op. cit., for a brief summary of socialist realism.

11 See M. Jay, 'The Dialectical Imagination: A History of the Frankfurt School and the Institute of Social Research, 1923-1950', Boston, Little, Brown, 1973, p.173ff.

12 A. Heller, L'esthétique de Gyorgy Lukács, 'L'Homme et la Société,' no.9, 1968, pp.221-31.

13 Cited in Arvon, op. cit., p.xix.

14 EC, Q.23, vol.III, p.2242.

15 B. Croce, 'Aesthetic as Science of Expression and General Linguistic,' trans. D. Ainslie, London, Macmillan, 1922, p.8.

16 Ibid., p.31.

17 For a more systematic analysis see Stipcevic, op. cit., p.25ff.

18 Croce, op. cit., p.51.

19 EC, Q.14, vol.III. p.1686.

20 EC, Q.6, vol.II, p.732.

21 Ibid.

22 Scalia, op. cit., pp.338-9.

23 Stipcevic, op. cit., p.50f.

24 Ibid.

25 A. Giordano, 'Gramsci,' Milano, Sansoni Editori, 1971, p.122.

26 EC, Q.23, vol.II, p.2192.

27 Arvon, op. cit., p.43ff.

28 EC, Q.15, vol.III, p.1793.

29 PN, p.456 and EC, Q.11, vol.II, p.1410. See also Stipcevic, op. cit., p.28.

30 EC, Q.15, vol.III, p.1793.

31 EC, Q.14, vol.III, p.1738.

32 Petronio, op. cit., p.228.

33 On the first position, see Scalia, A. Guiducci, Sapegno, Anglani; on the second, see Petronio.
34 Stipcevic, op. cit., pp.40-1.
35 EC, Q.15, vol.III, p.1793.
36 Anglani, op. cit., p.219.
37 EC, Q.23, vol.III, p.2188.
38 Ibid.
39 Petronio, op. cit., p.229.
40 EC, Q.23, vol.III, p.2187.
41 Scalia, op. cit., p.342.
42 A. Gramsci, 'Letters from Prison,' trans. Lynne Lawner, New York, Harper Colophon Books, 1975, p.245f.
43 Guiducci, op. cit., p.375.
44 EC, Q.23, vol.III, p.2231.
45 Scalia, op. cit., p.351.
46 EC, Q.23, vol.III, p.2187.
47 EC, Q.15, vol.III, pp.1793-4.
48 Ibid.
49 Ibid., pp.1820-1.
50 Guiducci, op. cit., pp.378-9.
51 EC, Q.21, vol.III, p.2113.
52 Ibid., p.2114.
53 EC, Q.6, vol.II, p.732.
54 EC, Q.14, vol.III, p.1660.
55 EC, Q.15, vol.III, p.1822.
56 Stipcevic, op. cit., p.70.
57 EC, Q.5, vol.I, p.586.
58 EC, Q.21, vol.III, p.2109.
59 Mao Tse-tung, 'On Literature and Art,' Peking, Foreign Languages Press, 1967, p.18 and p.26.
60 EC, Q.14, vol.III, p.1656.

EPILOGUE

1 E.J. Hobsbawm, The great Gramsci, 'The New York Review of Books,' vol.21, 4 April 1974, p.39.
2 PN, pp.343-4 and EC, Q.10, vol.II, p.1263.
3 R. Aron, 'Main Currents in Sociological Thought,' trans. B. Brewster, New York, Anchor, vol.II, 1969, p.282.
4 N. Badaloni, Il fondamento teorico dello storicismo gramsciano, in P. Rossi (ed.), 'Gramsci e la Cultura Contemporanea,' Rome, Editori Riuniti-Istituto Gramsci, vol.2, 1970, p.76.
5 L. Gallino, Gramsci e le scienze sociali, in P. Rossi, op. cit., vol.2, p.103.
6 EC, Q.9, vol.II, p.1131.
7 G. Lichtheim, 'A Short History of Socialism,' New York, Praeger Publishers, 1970, p.302f.

BIBLIOGRAPHY

This bibliography consists of three parts. The first part lists Gramsci's works and other collections in Italian and English (when translated). The second part includes the major critical studies on Gramsci. The third part lists all the works consulted in the preparation of the present study.

GRAMSCI'S WORKS

1 *Works published in Italian*
'Scritti Giovanili,' 1914-1918, Turin, Einaudi, 1958.
'Sotto la Mole,' 1916-1920, Turin, Einaudi, 1960.
'L'Ordine Nuovo (1919-1920),' Turin, Einaudi, 1955.
'Socialismo e Fascismo. L'Ordine Nuovo, 1921-1922,' Turin, Einaudi, 1967.
'La Costruzione del Partito Comunista, 1923-1926,' Turin, Einaudi, 1971.
All the above works contain the bulk of articles published in 'L'Avanti,' 'Il Grido del Popolo' and 'L'Ordine Nuovo,' between 1914 and 1926, before Gramsci's incarceration.
'Lettere del Carcere.' Edition prepared by Elsa Fubini and Sergio Caprioglio, Turin, Einaudi, 1965. This contains 428 letters written by Gramsci to members of his family.
'Quaderni del Carcere,' Turin, Einaudi, 1966, 6th edn. They consist of thirty-two prison notebooks published by Einaudi under these titles: vol.I, 'Il Materialismo storico e la filosofia di Benedetto Croce;' vol.II, 'Gli Intellettuali e l'organizazzione della cultura;' vol.III, 'Il Risorgimento;' vol.IV, 'Note sul Machiavelli, sulla politica e sullo Stato moderno;' vol.V, 'Letteratura e vita nazionale;' vol.VI, 'Passato e Presente.'
Antonio Gramsci, 'Quaderni del Carcere, Edizione Critica dell'Istituto Gramsci,' prepared under the direction of Valentino Gerratana, Turin, Einaudi, 1975. This critical edition presents Gramsci's notes in their original version and chronological order. The editor has distinguished texts A, B and C. The first include texts of first composition, the third those of second composition, and the second those texts of unique composition in their final form. The critical edition consists of 4 volumes: vol.I, Quaderni 1-5 (1929-1932), pp.lxviii-682; vol.II, Quaderni 6-11 (1930-1933), pp.685-1509; vol.III, Quaderni 12-29 (1932-1935), pp.1513-2362; vol.IV, Apparato critico, pp.2365-3369.

2 *Other publications and anthologies*
'Scritti 1915-1921,' Milan, Quaderni de 'Il Corpo,' 1968. It contains 125 articles not included in the Einaudi publications.
'Scritti Politici,' Rome, Editori Riuniti, 1967. A compilation of important political writings of Gramsci edited and annotated by Paolo Spriano, the noted historian of the Italian Communist Party.
'La Questione Meridionale,' Rome, Editori Riuniti, 1966. This work contains a selection of Gramsci's texts on the problem of Southern Italy and an important introduction by Franco De Felice and Valentino Parlato. It contains also the important unfinished essay, 'Alcuni temi della quistione meridionale,' written by Gramsci immediately before his arrest.

'Duemila Pagine di Gramsci,' Milan, Il Saggiatore, 1964. This anthology in two volumes contains a selection of Gramsci's texts, a great number of unpublished Gramsci's letters and an excellent introduction by G. Ferrata and N. Gallo.

3 *English translations of Gramsci's works*
'The Modern Prince and Other Writings,' trans. with an introduction by L. Marks, New York, International Publishers, 1967. A very limited selection of Gramsci's texts taken from vol.1, 2, and 4 of Einaudi's publications.
'The Open Marxism of Antonio Gramsci,' trans. and annotated by C. Marzani, New York, Cameron Associates, 1957. A very brief selection of texts from vol.1 of the Einaudi edition.
'Selections from the Prison Notebooks of Antonio Gramsci,' ed., trans. and annotated Q. Hoare and G.N. Smith, New York, International Publishers, 1971. A more comprehensive but still incomplete selection of texts from the 'Quaderni del Carcere' published by Einaudi.
Antonio Gramsci, 'Selections from Political Writings, 1910-1920,' trans. J. Mathews and ed. Q. Hoare, New York, International Publishers, 1977.
— 'Selections from Political Writings, 1921-1926,' trans. and ed. Q. Hoare, New York, International Publishers, 1978.
The last two volumes contain the most comprehensive selection of Gramsci's pre-prison years writings.
'History, Philosophy and Culture in the Young Gramsci,' ed. P. Cavalcanti and P. Piccone, St Louis, Telos Press, 1975. There is a selection of articles from the period 1914-18.
'New Edinburgh Review,' ed. by C.K. Maisels, 1974. Three special numbers on Gramsci. They contain a wide selection of Gramsci's writings and letters from prison.
A. Davidson, 'Antonio Gramsci: The Man, His Ideas,' Sydney, Australian Left Review, 1969. This book contains the translation of Gramsci's notes on 'Folklore' in vol.4 of the 'Quaderni,' published by Einaudi.
Antonio Gramsci, 'Letters from Prison,' selected and trans. Lynne Lawner, New York, Harper Colophon Books, 1973.
— Notes on Journalism, trans. G.R. Alkalay, 'Telos,' no.32, 1977, pp.139-51.
— Science and 'scientific' ideologies, trans. M.A. Finocchiaro, 'Telos,' no.41, 1979, pp.151-5.

CRITICAL STUDIES

Adamson, W.L., 'Hegemony and Revolution: Antonio Gramsci's Political and Cultural Theory,' Berkeley, University of California Press, 1980.
Adler, F., Factory Councils, Gramsci and the industrialist, 'Telos,' no.31, 1977, pp.67-99.
Agazzi, E., Filosofia della prassi e filosofia dello spirito, in 'La Città Futura,' ed. A. Caracciolo and G. Scalia, Milan, Feltrinelli, 1959, pp. 187-269.
Althusser, L. and Balibar, E., Marxism is not a historicism, in 'Reading Capital,' New York, Pantheon Books, 1970.
Amendola, G., Rileggendo Gramsci, in 'Prassi Rivoluzionaria. Critica Marxista,' vol.3, 1967, pp.3-45.
Anderson, Perry, 'Considerations on Western Marxism,' London, Verso Editions, 1979.
—The antinomies of Antonio Gramsci, 'New Left Review,' no.100, November 1976-January 1977, pp.5-78.
Anglani, B., La critica letteraria in Gramsci, in 'Prassi Rivoluzionaria. Critica Marxista,' vol.3, 1967, pp.208-30.
Auciello, N., 'Socialismo ed Egemonia in Gramsci e Togliatti,' Bari, De Donato, 1974.
Badaloni, N., Gramsci storicista di fronte al marxismo contemporaneo, in 'Prassi Rivoluzionaria. Critica Marxista,' vol.3, 1967, pp.96-118.

Badaloni, N., Il fondamento teorico dello storicismo gramsciano, in P. Rossi, 'Gramsci e la Cultura Contemporanea,' vol.II, 1970, pp.73-80.
—'Marxismo come storicismo,' Milan, Feltrinelli, 1962.
—'Il Marxismo italiano degli anni sessanta,' Rome, Editori Riuniti, 1971.
—'Il Marxismo di Gramsci,' Turin, Giulio Einaudi Editore, 1975.
Badia, G., Gramsci et R. Luxemburg, 'Nouvelle Critique,' no.30, 1970, pp.71-3.
Baldan, A., Gramsci as an historian of the 1930s, 'Telos,' no.31, 1977, pp.100-11.
Bates, T.R., Gramsci and the theory of hegemony, 'Journal of the History of Ideas,' vol.36, no.2, 1975, pp.351-66.
Bellini, F., and Galli, G., 'Storia del Partito Comunista Italiano,' Milan, Schwarz, 1953.
Bobbio, N., Gramsci e la concezione della società civile, in P. Rossi, 'Gramsci e la Cultura Contemporanea,' vol.1, 1969, pp.75-100.
—Gramsci and the conception of civil society, in C. Mouffe (ed.), 'Gramsci and Marxist Theory,' 1979.
—Nota sulla dialettica in Gramsci, in 'Studi Gramsciani,' pp.73-86.
Boggs, C., Gramsci's 'Prison Notebooks,' 'Socialist Revolution,' vol.11, 1972, pp.79-118.
—Gramsci's 'Prison Notebooks,' Part II, 'Socialist Revolution,' vol.12, 1972, pp.29-56.
—'Gramsci's Marxism,' London, Pluto Press, 1976.
Bon, F. and Burnier, M.-A., 'Les Nouveaux Intellectuels,' Paris, Cujas, 1966.
Borghi, I., Educazione e scuola in Gramsci, in P. Rossi (ed.), 'Gramsci e la Cultura Contemporanea,' vol.1, 1969, pp.207-38.
Broccoli, A., 'Antonio Gramsci e l'Educazione come Egemonia,' Firenza, La Nuova Italia Editrice, 1972.
Buci-Glucksmann, C., 'Gramsci and the State,' London, Lawrence & Wishart, 1980.
—State, transition and passive revolution, in C. Mouffe, 'Gramsci and Marxist Theory,' 1979, pp.207-36.
Buzzi, A.R., 'La Teoria Politica de Antonio Gramsci,' Barcelona, Editorial Fontanella, 1969.
Cambareri, S., Il concetto di egemonia nel pensiero di A. Gramsci, in 'Studi Gramsciani,' pp.87-94.
Cammett, J.M., 'Antonio Gramsci and the Origins of Italian Communism,' California, Stanford University Press, 1967.
—Socialism and participatory democracy, in G. Fischer, 'The Revival of American Socialism,' selected papers of the Socialist Scholars Conference, New York, Oxford University Press, 1971, pp.41-60.
Caracciolo, A. and Scalia, G., 'La Città Futura,' Milan, Feltrinelli, 1959.
Centre for Contemporary Cultural Studies, 'On Ideology,' London, Hutchinson, 1977.
Cerroni, U., Gramsci e il superamento della separazione tra società e stato, in 'Studi Gramsciani,' 1969, pp.105-14.
Cessi, R., Problemi della storia d'Italia nell'opera di Gramsci, in 'Studi Gramsciani,' 1969, pp.47-52.
Cirese, A., Concezione del mondo, filosofia spontanea, folclore, in P. Rossi, 'Gramsci e la Cultura Contemporanea,' vol.2, pp.299-328.
Clark, M., 'Antonio Gramsci and the Revolution that Failed,' New Haven, Yale University Press, 1977.
Davidson, A., 'Antonio Gramsci: Towards an Intellectual Biography,' Atlantic Highlands, N.J., Humanities Press, 1977.
—The varying seasons of Gramscian studies, 'Political Studies,' vol.20, no.4, 1972, pp.448-61.
De Felice, F., 'Serrati, Bordiga, Gramsci,' Bari, De Donato Editore, 1971.
De Giovanni, B., Lenin and Gramsci: state, politics and party, in C. Mouffe, 'Gramsci and Marxist Theory,' 1979, pp.259-88.
Entwistle, H., 'Antonio Gramsci: Conservative Schooling for Radical Politics,' London, Routledge & Kegan Paul, 1979.

Femia, J., Hegemony and consciousness in the thought of Antonio Gramsci, 'Political Studies,' vol.23, no.1, 1975, pp.29-48.

Finocchiaro, M.A., Gramsci's Crocean Marxism, 'Telos,' vol.41, 1979, pp.17-32.

Fiori, G., 'Antonio Gramsci: Life of a Revolutionary,' New York, 1971.

—Gramsci e il mondo sardo, in P. Rossi, 'Gramsci e la Cultura Contemporanea,' vol.1, 1969, pp.439-85.

Fubini, E., Bibliografia gramsciana, in P. Rossi, 'Gramsci e la Cultura Contemporanea,' vol.1, 1969, pp.477-544.

Galli, G., Gramsci e le teorie delle 'élites,' in P. Rossi, 'Gramsci e la Cultura Contemporanea,' vol.1, 1969, pp.305-54.

Gallino, L., Gramsci e le scienze sociali, in P. Rossi, 'Gramsci e la Cultura Contemporanea,' vol.2, 1970, pp.81-108.

Garin, E., Antonio Gramsci nella cultura italiana, in 'Studi Gramsciani,' 1969, pp.3-14.

—Politica e cultura in Gramsci (il problema degli intellettuali), in P. Rossi, 'Gramsci e la Cultura Contemporanea,' vol.1, 1969, pp.37-74.

—La Formazione di Gramsci e Croce, 'Prassi Rivoluzionaria. Critica Marxista,' vol.3, 1967, pp.119-33.

Genovese, E., On Antonio Gramsci, in J. Weinstein and D.W. Eakins (eds), 'For a New America,' New York, Random House, 1970, pp.284-316.

Giacchetti, R., Antonio Gramsci: the subjective revolution, in D. Howard and K.E. Klare (eds), 'The Unknown Dimension,' New York, Basic Books, 1972, pp.147-68.

Giordano, A., 'Gramsci, la vita, il pensiero,' Milan, Accademia Sansoni Editori, 1971.

Graziano, S., Alcune considerazioni intorno all'umanesimo di Gramsci, in 'Studi Gramsciani,' 1969, pp.149-64.

Gruppi, L., I rapporti tra pensiero ed essere nella concezione di A. Gramsci, in 'Studi Gramsciani,' 1969, pp.165-81.

—Il concetto di egemonia, 'Prassi Rivoluzionaria. Critica Marxista,' no.3, 1967, pp.78-95.

—'Il concetto di Egemonia in Gramsci,' Rome, Editori Riuniti, 1972.

Guiducci, A., A proposito di estetica in Gramsci, in A. Caracciolo and G. Scalia (eds), 'La Città Futura,' Milan, Feltrinelli, 1959, pp.369-89.

Guiducci, R., Filosofia della prassi e ricerca scientifica, in A. Caracciolo and G. Scalia (eds), 'La Città Futura,' 1959, pp.271-97.

Hall, S., Lumley, B., and McLennan, G., Politics and Ideology: Gramsci in Centre for Contemporary Cultural Studies, 'On Ideology,' London, Hutchinson, 1977, pp.45-76.

Hobsbawm, E., The great Gramsci, 'The New York Review of Books,' vol.21, 4 April 1974, pp.39-44.

Hughes, S.H., 'Consciousness and Society,' New York, Knopf, 1958.

Jocteau, G., 'Leggere Gramsci. Una guida alle interpretazioni,' Milan, Feltrinelli, 1975.

Joll, J., 'Antonio Gramsci,' Harmondsworth, Penguin Books, 1977.

Karabel, J., Revolutionary contradictions: Antonio Gramsci and the problem of intellectuals, 'Politics and Society,' vol.6, no.2, 1976, pp.123-72.

Luporini, C., La metodologia filosofica del marxismo nel pensiero di Gramsci, in 'Studi Gramsciani,' 1969, pp.37-46.

—La metodologia del marxismo nel pensiero di Gramsci, in 'Studi Gramsciani,' 1969, pp.445-68.

Macciocchi, M.A., 'Pour Gramsci,' Paris, Editions du Seuil, 1974.

Maitan, L., 'Attualità di Gramsci e Politica Comunista,' Milan, Schwarz, 1955.

Manacorda, M.A., 'Il Principio Educativo in Gramsci,' Rome, Armando, 1970.

Markovic, Mihailo, Gramsci on the unity of philosophy and politics, 'Praxis,' no.3, 1967, pp.333-9.

Martano, G., Il problema della autonomia della filosofia della prassi nel pensiero di A. Gramsci, in 'Studi Gramsciani,' 1969, pp.190-8.

Martinelli, A., In defense of the dialectic: Antonio Gramsci's theory of revolution, 'Berkeley Journal of Sociology,' no.13, 1968, pp.1-27.

Massucco, C.A., Aspetti sociologici del pensiero gramsciano, in 'Studi Gramsciani,' 1969, pp.199-211.

Matteucci, N., 'Antonio Gramsci e le Filosofia della Prassi,' Milan, Giuffre Editore, 1951.

Merrington, J., Theory and practice in Gramsci's Marxism, 'The Socialist Register,' ed. R. Miliband and J. Saville, New York, Monthly Review Press, 1968, pp.145-76.

Mouffe, C. (ed.), 'Gramsci and Marxist Theory,' London, Routledge & Kegan Paul, 1979.

Mouffe, C., and Sassoon-Showstack, A., Gramsci in France and Italy - a review of the literature, 'Economy and Society,' 1977, vol.6, no.1.

Nardone, G., 'Il Pensiero di Gramsci,' Bari, De Donato, 1971.

Ormea, F., 'Gramsci e il Futuro dell'Uomo,' Rome, Coines Edizioni, 1975.

Paggi, L., 'Antonio Gramsci e il Moderno Principe,' Rome, Editori Riuniti, 1970.

—Studi e interpretazioni recenti di Gramsci, 'Prassi Rivoluzionaria. Critica Marxista,' vol.3, 1966, pp.151-81.

—La redazione 'culturale' del 'Grido del Popolo,' 'Prassi Rivoluzionaria. Critica Critica Marxista,' vol.3, 1967, pp.134-74.

—Gramsci's general theory of Marxism, in C. Mouffe, 'Gramsci and Marxist Theory,' 1979, pp.113-67.

Papi, F., La concezione della storicità nel pensiero di Gramsci, in 'Studi Gramsciani,' 1969, pp.213-22.

Petronio, G., Gramsci e la critica letteraria, in 'Studi Gramsciani,' 1969, pp.223-41.

Piccone, P., Gramsci's Hegelian Marxism, 'Political Theory,' vol.2, no.1, 1974, pp.32-45.

—Gramsci's Marxism: beyond Lenin and Togliatti, 'Theory and Society,' vol.3, no.4, 1976, pp.485-512.

—From Spaventa to Gramsci, 'Telos,' no.31, 1977, pp.35-65.

Piotte, J.-M., 'La pensée politique de Gramsci,' Paris, Editions Anthropos, 1970.

Pizzorno, A., Sul metodo di Gramsci: dalla storiografia alla scienza politica, in P. Rossi, 'Gramsci e la Cultura Contemporanea,' vol.2, 1970, pp.109-26.

Portelli, H., 'Gramsci et le Bloc Historique,' Paris, Presses Universitaires de France, 1972.

—'Gramsci e la Questione Religiosa,' Milan, G. Mazzotta Editore, 1976.

Pozzolini, A., 'Che cosa ha 'veramente' detto Gramsci,' Rome, Ubaldini Editore, 1968.

Ragionieri, E., Gramsci e il dibattito teorico nel movimento operaio internazionale, in P. Rossi, 'Gramsci e la Cultura Contemporanea,' vol.1, 1969, pp.101-47.

Romano, S., 'Antonio Gramsci,' Turin, Utet, 1965.

Rosiello, L., La componente linguistica dello storicismo gramsciano, in A. Caracciolo and G. Scalia (eds), 'La Città Futura,' 1959, pp.299-327.

Rossi, P. (ed.), 'Gramsci e la Cultura Contemporanea,' Rome, Editori Riuniti-Istituto Gramsci, 2 vols, 1969 and 1970.

Rutigliano, E., The ideology of labor and capitalist rationality in Gramsci, 'Telos,' 1977, no.31, pp.91-9.

Sabetti, A., Il rapporto uomo-natura nel pensiero di Gramsci e la fondazione della scienza, in 'Studi Gramsciani,' 1969, pp.242-52.

Salvadori, M., Gramsci e la questione meridionale, in P. Rossi, 'Gramsci e la Cultura Contemporanea,' vol.1, 1969, pp.487-533.

—'Gramsci e il Problema Storico della Democrazia,' Turin, Piccola Biblioteca Einaudi, 1973.

—Gramsci and the P.C.I.: two conceptions of hegemony, in C. Mouffe, 'Gramsci and Marxist Theory,' 1979, pp.237-58.

Sapegno, N., Gramsci e i problemi della letteratura, in P. Rossi, 'Gramsci e la Cultura Contemporanea,' vol.1, 1969, pp.265-77.

Sassoon-Showstack, A., 'Gramsci's Politics,' London, Croom Helm, 1980.

Sassoon-Showstack, A., 'A Gramsci Reader,' London, Writers and Readers Publishing Co-operative, 1981.
Satriani, L., Gramsci e il folclore: dal pittoresco alla contestazione, in P. Rossi, 'Gramsci e la Cultura Contemporanea,' vol.2, 1970, pp.329-38.
Scalia, G., Metodologia e sociologia della letteratura in Gramsci, in A. Caracciolo and G. Scalia (eds), 'La Città Futura,' 1959, pp.329-68.
Seroni, A., La distinzione fra' 'critica d'arte' (estetica) e 'critica politica' in Gramsci, in 'Studi Gramsciani,' 1969, pp.259-67.
Sichirollo, Hegel, Gramsci e il Marxismo, in 'Studi Gramsciani,' 1969, pp.270-6.
Spriano, P., 'Storia del Partito Comunista Italiano,' Turin, Einaudi, 1968.
—'Antonio Gramsci and the Party: The Prison Years,' London, Lawrence & Wishart, 1979.
—'The Occupation of the Factories: Italy 1920,' trans. G.A. Williams, London, Pluto Press, 1975.
Stipcevic, N., 'Gramsci e i problemi letterari,' Milan, Mursia, 1968.
'Studi Gramsciani. Atti del convegno tenuto a Roma nei giorni 11-13 gennaio 1958,' Rome, Editori Riuniti-Istituto Gramsci, 1969.
Tamburrano, G., Gramsci e l'egemonia del proletariato, in 'Studi Gramsciani,' 1969, pp.277-86.
—'Antonio Gramsci, La vita, il pensiero, l'azione,' Manduria, Lacaita, 1963.
Texier, J., 'Gramsci,' Paris, Editions Seghers, 1966.
—Gramsci, théoricien des superstructures, 'La Pensée,' no.139, 1968, pp.37-60.
—Gramsci in France, in P. Rossi, 'Gramsci e la Cultura Contemporanea,' vol.2, pp.371-9.
Todd, N., Ideological superstructure in Gramsci and Mao Tse-Tung, 'Journal of the History of Ideas,' vol.35, no.1, 1975, pp.148-56.
Togliatti, P., 'Gramsci and Other Essays,' London, Lawrence & Wishart, 1979.
—'Gramsci,' Rome, Editori Riuniti, 1967.
—Tra materialismo dialettico e filosofia della prassi: Gramsci e Labriola, in A. Caracciolo and G. Scalia (eds), 'La Città Futura,' 1959, pp.138-86.
Tronti, M., Alcune questioni intorno al marxismo di Gramsci, in 'Studi Gramsciani,' 1969, pp.305-21.
Urbani, G., Cultura e scuola unitaria, 'Prassi Rivoluzionaria. Critica Marxista,' no.3, 1967, pp.231-9.
Williams, Gwyn A., The concept of 'egemonia' in the thought of Antonio Gramsci: some notes on interpretation, 'Journal of the History of Ideas,' no.4, 1960, pp.586-99.
—'Proletarian Order: Antonio Gramsci, Factory Councils and the Origins of Communism in Italy, 1911-1921,' London, Pluto Press, 1975.
Zanardo, A., Il 'Manuale' di Bukharin visto dai comunisti tedeschi e da Gramsci, in 'Studi Gramsciani,' 1969, pp.337-68.

GENERAL BIBLIOGRAPHY

Anderson, C., 'The Political Economy of Social Class,' Englewood Cliffs, N.J., Prentice-Hall, 1974.
Althusser, L., 'For Marx,' New York, Pantheon Books, 1969.
—'Essays in Self-Criticism,' London, New Left Books, 1976.
Althusser, L. and Balibar, E., 'Reading Capital,' New York, Pantheon Books, 1970.
Aron, R., 'Main Currents in Sociological Thought,' trans. B. Brewster, New York, Anchor Books, 1969, 2 vols.
Arvon, H., 'Marxist Esthetics,' trans. H. Lane, Ithaca, Cornell University Press, 1973.
Avineri, S., 'The Social and Political Thought of Karl Marx,' London, Cambridge University Press, 1969.
Berger, P. (ed.), 'Marxism and Sociology: Views from Eastern Europe,' New York, Appleton-Century-Crofts, 1969.

Berger, P. and Luckmann, T., 'The Social Construction of Reality. A
  Treatise in the Sociology of Knowledge,' New York, Doubleday, 1966.
Bukharin, N., 'Historical Materialism: A System of Sociology,' New York,
  Russell & Russell, 1965.
Carr, W., 'The Philosophy of Benedetto Croce,' New York, Russell &
  Russell, 1969.
Colletti, L., 'From Rousseau to Lenin: Studies in Ideology and Society,'
  trans. by J. Merrington and J. White, New York, Monthly Review
  Press, 1972.
Collingwood, R.G., 'The Idea of History,' New York, Oxford University
  Press, 1956.
Coser, L., 'Men of Ideas,' New York, Free Press, 1965.
Craig, D., 'Marxists on Literature, An Anthology,' Harmondsworth,
  Penguin Books, 1975.
Croce, B., 'Aesthetic as Science of Expression and General Linguistic,'
  trans. D. Ainslie, London, Macmillan, 1922.
Dahrendorf, R., 'Society and Democracy in Germany,' Garden City,
  New York, Anchor Books, 1969.
Di Renzo, G.J., Sociology in Italy today, 'International Review of Modern
  Sociology,' vol.1, 1972, pp.35-58.
Douglas, J.D., 'Understanding Everyday Life: Toward the Reconstruction
  of Sociological Knowledge,' Chicago, Aldine, 1970.
Fetscher, I., 'Marx and Marxism,' New York, Herder & Herder, 1971.
Feuer, L., 'Marx and the Intellectuals: A Set of Post-Ideological Essays,'
  Garden City, New York, Anchor Books, 1969.
Fleischer, H., 'Marxism and History,' trans. E. Mobsbacher, New York,
  Harper Torchbooks, 1973.
Fried, A., and Sanders, R., 'Socialist Thought,' Garden City, New York,
  Doubleday-Anchor Books, 1964.
Garaudy, R., 'The Crisis of Communism. The turning point of socialism,'
  New York, Grove Press, 1970.
Garfinkel, H., 'Studies in Ethnomethodology,' Englewood Cliffs, N.J.,
  Prentice-Hall, 1967.
Goldmann, L., 'Recherches dialectiques,' Paris, Editions Gallimard, 1959.
Gouldner, A., 'The Coming Crisis of Western Sociology,' New York,
  Basic Books, 1970.
Gurvitch, G., 'The Social Frameworks of Knowledge,' New York, Harper
  & Row, 1972.
Hegel, G.W.F. 'Hegel's Philosophy of Right,' trans. T.M. Knox, Oxford,
  Clarendon Press, 1965.
Heller, A., L'ésthétique de Gyorgy Lukács, 'L'Homme et la Société,' no.9,
  1968, pp.221-31.
Hertzler, J. O., 'A Sociology of Language,' New York, Random House, 1965.
Hofstadter, R., 'Anti-intellectualism in American Life,' New York,
  Harper & Row, 1966.
Horowitz, I.L., 'Foundations of Political Sociology,' New York, Harper
  & Row, 1972.
Jay, M., 'The Dialectical Imagination: A History of the Frankfurt School
  and the Institute of Social Research, 1923-1950,' Boston, Little, Brown,
  1973.
Jordon, Z.A., The dialectical materialism of Lenin, in J.V. Downton and D.K.
  Hart, 'Perspectives on Political Philosophy,' vol.3, Hinsdale, The Dryden
  Press, 1973.
Kalab, M., The specificity of the Marxist conception of sociology, in P. Berger,
  'Marxism and Sociology,' 1969, pp.58-76.
Karp-Zanotti, A., Elite theory and ideology, 'Social Research,' vol.2,
  1970, pp.275-95.
Lang, B. and Williams, F., 'Marxism and Art. Writings in Aesthetics and
  Criticism,' New York, David McKay, 1972.
Lenin, V.I., 'What is to be done?' Moscow, Progress Publishers, 1973.
Lichtheim, G., 'A Short History of Socialism,' New York,

Praeger Publishers, 1970.
Lipset, S.M., 'Political Man: The Social Bases of Politics,' Garden City, New York, Anchor Books, 1963.
Lukács, G., 'History and Class Consciousness,' Cambridge, Mass., MIT Press, 1972.
Mandic, O., The Marxist School of Sociology: What is Sociology in a Marxist sense? in P. Berger (ed.), 'Marxism and Sociology,' 1969, pp.37-57.
Mannheim, K., 'Ideology and Utopia,' trans. L. Wirth and E. Shils, New York, Harcourt, Brace & World, Inc., 1936.
—'Essays on the Sociology of Knowledge,' London, Routledge & Kegan Paul, 1952.
Mao Tse-Tung, 'On Literature and Art,' Peking, Foreign Languages Press, 1967.
Marcuse, H., 'One-Dimensional Man,' Boston, Beacon Press, 1964.
Marx, K., 'The Economic and Philosophical Manuscripts of 1844,' ed. D.J. Struik, New York, International Publishers, 1972.
Marx, K., and Engels, F., 'Selected Works,' Moscow, Foreign Languages Publishing House, 1958, 2 vols.
Marx, K., and Engels, F., 'The German Ideology,' ed. C.J. Arthur, New York, International Publishers, 1972.
Merton, R., 'Social Theory and Social Structure,' Chicago, Ill., Free Press, 1957.
Natanson, M., 'Philosophy of the Social Sciences: A Reader,' New York, Random House, 1963.
Rieff, P., 'On Intellectuals,' Garden City, New York, Anchor Books, 1970.
Sapir, E., 'Language,' New York, Harvest, 1949.
Schaff, A., 'Langage et Connaissance,' Paris, Editions Anthropos, 1969.
Schmalstieg, W.R., Structural linguistics in the Soviet Union, in A. Simirenko, 'Social Thought in the Soviet Union,' Chicago, Quadrangle Books, 1969.
Schutz, A., 'Collected Papers,' The Hague, Nijhoff, 1962.
Shils, E., 'The Intellectual between Tradition and Modernity,' The Hague, Mouton, 1961.
Simirenko, A., 'Social Thought in the Soviet Union,' Chicago, Quadrangle Books, 1969.
Stark, W., 'The Sociology of Knowledge: An Essay in Aid of a Deeper Understanding of the History of Ideas,' Chicago, Free Press, 1958.
Thomas, L.L., 'The Linguistic Theories of N.J. Marr,' Berkeley, University of California Press, 1967.
Wagner, H., (ed.), 'Alfred Schutz. On Phenomenology and Social Relations,' University of Chicago Press, 1970.
Weber, M., 'The Methodology of the Social Sciences,' Chicago, Ill., Free Press, 1949.
Williams, R., 'Marxism and Literature,' London, Oxford Univerity Press, 1977.
Zeitlin, I.M., 'Ideology and the Development of Sociological Theory,' Englewood Cliffs, N.J., Prentice-Hall, 1968.

INDEX

action, see praxis
activity, human, 34
Adorno, Theodor, 201
aesthetic praxis, 208-14
aesthetics, 22-3, 183, 190, 197-214;
  art for art's sake, 213, 214; conformism and, 214; Croce's, 30;
  Hegelian, 198-9; Marxist theory of,
  197-204; philosophy and, 203; politics and, 208, 201-11; popularity and,
  211-14; value and, 203
Agazzi, E., 175
alienation, 124
Althusser, L., 16, 20, 39, 175-80
Americanism, 147-52
Anderson, C., 124
Anderson, Perry, 19, 20-1
Anglani, B., 181, 198
anti-intellectualism, 121
Aron, Raymond, 47, 217
art, see aesthetics
artistic freedom, 200
Arvon, Henry, 199
Auciello, N., 131, 134, 135
Aufhebung, 30
automatism, 38-9
autonomy, 86; of art, 204-7, 210, 213;
  intellectual, 120; of language, 182,
  187; of Marxism, 160
'Avanti', 7

Badaloni, Nicola, 17, 175, 217
Balzac, H. de, 205, 209
Bartoli, M., 182-3, 184, 185, 239n
beauty, 205, 211
Belinski, V.G., 201
Bellini, Fulvio, 14
Benjamin, Walter, 201
Berger, P.L., 41, 83, 99, 121, 122
Bernstein, Eduard, 3, 5, 161, 166
Bertoni, G., 185-6, 239n
Bobbio, Norberto, 16, 29, 134-5, 139,
  140, 142, 143
Boggs, C., 19
bohemianism, 150-1
Bolshevik Party, 4
Bon, F., 123, 124
Bordiga, Amadeo, 2, 8, 10, 11, 14
bourgeois domination, 36, 56-7, 86,

137; civil society, and, 141; in
  England, 112; in France, 109-10; in
  Germany, 112; in Italy, 110-12, 114
bourgeoisie: ideology of, 33-4, 36, 60;
  legitimated by positivism, 47
Buci-Glucksmann, Christine, 19-20
Bukharin, Nikolai, 3, 4, 31-2, 46, 50,
  53-5, 161, 166, 197, 219; historical
  materialism theory, 94-6, 159-60; on
  science, 169, 171
bureaucracy, 121-2
Buzzi, A.R., 13, 40, 149

Calvinism, 217
Cambareri, S., 134
Cammett, J.M., 6, 13, 19
capitalism: American, 232n; class
  conflict under, 5; containment of
  crises by, 12, 22; hegemony eroded,
  118; integration of masses under,
  129; revolution and, 55, 129
Carli, F., 48
catharsis, 17, 143
Catholicism, 87, 91, 105, 109-10
causation, laws of, 52-3
charismatic leaders, 64, 218
Chernyshevski, N.G., 201
Chomsky, Noam, 190
Christianity, 160
'Città Futura, La', 7
civil society: groups in, 139, political
  society and, 16, 61, 126, 134-5,
  137-42, 152-3; state and, 1, 61
class: economistic to hegemonic, 17;
  types of, 80
class alliances, 131-2
class conflict, 30, 40, 217; eliminated
  under capitalism, 5; in Italy, 59
class consciousness, 64, 129-30
classless societies, 30, 43
coercion, 135, 145
cognitive process and cognition,
  45-7; praxis and, 52; subjective
  factors in, 44
collective beliefs, 216
collective intellectual, 116; the party
  as, 133
collective man, 147-52
collective will, 63, 218; common

251